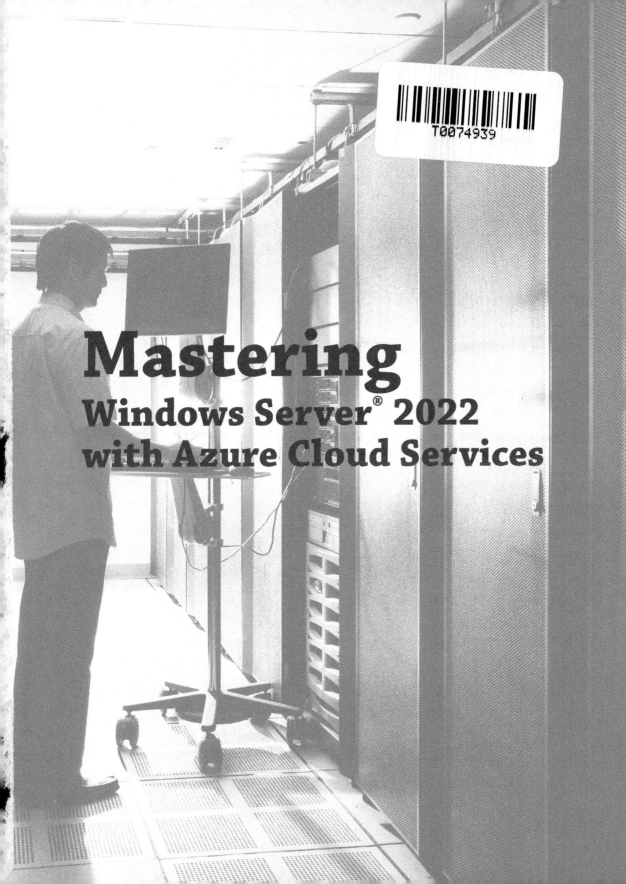

Mastering
Windows Server® 2022
with Azure Cloud Services

Mastering

Windows Server® 2022 with Azure Cloud Services IaaS, PaaS, and SaaS

William Panek, Microsoft MVP

SYBEX®

A Wiley Brand

Published by John Wiley & Sons, Inc., Hoboken, New Jersey.
Published simultaneously in Canada and the United Kingdom.

ISBN: 978-1-119-79892-7
ISBN: 978-1-119-79909-2 (ebk.)
ISBN: 978-1-119-79893-4 (ebk.)

This book is dedicated to the three ladies of my life: Crystal, Alexandria, and Paige.

This book is also dedicated to a great man and friend, Doug Bassett. Doug has been a coworker and Technical Editor on many of my books. Unfortunately, my friend, passed away before this book was released. He was an incredible person and one of the best IT Trainers that I have ever worked with. His friendship will be missed greatly.

About the Author

 William Panek holds the following certifications: MCP, MCP+I, MCSA, MCSA+ Security and Messaging, MCSE-NT (3.51 & 4.0), MCSE 2000, 2003, 2012/2012 R2, MCSE+Security and Messaging, MCDBA, MCT, MCTS, MCITP, CCNA, CCDA, and CHFI. Will is also a five-time Microsoft MVP winner.

After many successful years in the computer industry, Will decided that he could better use his talents and his personality as an instructor. He began teaching for schools such as Boston University and the University of Maryland, just to name a few. He has done consulting and training for some of the biggest government and corporate companies in the world including the United States Secret Service, Cisco, United States Air Force, and US Army.

Will currently lives in New Hampshire with his wife and two daughters. Will was also a Representative in the New Hampshire House of Representatives from 2010 to 2012. In his spare time, he likes to do blacksmithing, golfing, and riding his Harley. Will is also a commercially rated helicopter pilot.

Acknowledgments

I would like to thank my wife and best friend, Crystal. She is always the light at the end of my tunnel. I want to thank my two daughters, Alexandria, and Paige, for all of their love and support during the writing of all my books. The three of them are my support system and I couldn't do any of this without them.

I want to thank all of my family and friends who always help me when I'm writing my books. I want to thank my brothers Rick, Gary, and Rob. I want to thank my father for all of his love and support.

I want to thank everyone on my Sybex team, especially my development editor Kim Wimpsett, who helped me make this the best book possible.

I want to also thank Doug Bassett, who has been the technical editor of many of my books. Doug has been a really great friend and he always inspired me to be the best I could be.

Finally, I want to thank everyone else behind the scenes at Sybex that helped make this book possible. It's truly an amazing thing to have so many people work on my books to help make them the very best. I can't thank you all enough for your hard work.

Contents at a Glance

Contents

Introduction

This book is drawn from more than 30 years of IT experience. I have taken that experience and translated it into a Windows Server 2022 book that will help you install and configure Windows Server 2022 while avoiding all of the possible configuration pitfalls.

Many Microsoft books just explain the Windows operating system, but I go a step further by providing many in-depth, step-by-step procedures to support my explanations of how the operating system performs at its best.

Microsoft Windows Server 2022 is the newest version of Microsoft's server operating system software. Microsoft has taken the best of their previous Windows Server versions and combined them into the latest creation, Windows Server 2022.

Windows Server 2022 eliminates many of the problems that plagued the previous versions of Windows Server, and it includes a much faster boot time and shutdown. It is also easier to install and configure, and it barely stops to ask the user any questions during installation. In this book, I will show you what features are installed during the automated installation and where you can make changes if you need to be more in charge of your operating system and its features.

This book takes you through all the ins and outs of Windows Server 2022, including installation, configuration, Group Policy objects, auditing, backups, the cloud, and so much more.

Windows Server 2022 has improved on Microsoft's desktop environment, made networking easier, enhanced searching capability, and improved performance—and that's only scratching the surface.

When all is said and done, this is a technical book for IT professionals who want to take Windows Server 2022 to the next step. With this book, you will not only learn Windows Server 2022, but you will also become a Windows Server 2022 expert.

Who Should Read This Book?

This book is intended for individuals who want to learn about Windows Server 2022 and connecting that network to the cloud.

This book will not only help anyone who is looking to learn the real ins and outs of the Windows Server 2022 operating system but it will also show you how to connect the Windows Server 2022 network to the cloud.

What's Inside?

Here is a glance at what's in each chapter:

Chapter 1: Understanding Windows Server 2022   In the first chapter, I explain the requirements and steps required to install and configure Windows Server 2022.

Chapter 2: Understanding Virtualization   This chapter will introduce you to virtual networking, virtual hard disks, migration types, and Integration Services.

Chapter 3: Installing and Configuring Hyper-V   This chapter will show you the virtualization requirements, understand how to build virtual machines, and know the different ways to build virtual machines.

Chapter 4: Installing Windows Server 2022   This chapter will show you how to implement and configure Windows Server 2022. You will learn about the different ways and different versions of Windows Server 2022.

Chapter 5: Understanding IP   In the chapter, I show you how TCP/IP gets configured on a server and within a network. I also show you how to subnet an IPv4 network. I also show you how to work with IPv6.

Chapter 6: Implementing DNS   This chapter shows you how to install Windows Server 2022 DNS in an enterprise environment.

Chapter 7: Understanding Active Directory   In this chapter I will explain the benefits of using Active Directory. I will explain how Forests, Trees, and Domains work and I will also show you how to install Active Directory.

Chapter 8: Administering Active Directory   This chapter shows you how to create accounts in Active Directory. I will show you how to do bulk imports into Active Directory and also how to create and manage groups. I will also show you how to create and manage service accounts.

Chapter 9: Configuring DHCP   I take you through the advantages and benefits of using Windows Server 2022 Dynamic Host Configuration Protocol (DHCP).

Chapter 10: Building Group Policies   This chapter will show you how to implement and configure Group Policy Objects (GPOs).

Chapter 11: Advanced Group Policy Options   This chapter shows you how to use GPOs to deploy and manage software applications. I will also show you how to lock applications down by using GPOs.

Chapter 12: Understanding Cloud Concepts   I take you through the advantages and benefits of using and understanding cloud concepts.

Chapter 13: Configuring Azure   This chapter will show you the benefits of understanding and using Azure. I will show you how to use the Azure portal and dashboard to configure Azure options.

Chapter 14: Understanding Azure Active Directory   In this chapter, I will dive into the world of Azure Active Directory. Azure Active Directory is Azure's database for controlling the Azure environment.

Chapter 15: Creating a Hybrid Network   In this chapter, I will show you how to connect your on-site domain to Azure using Azure AD Connect. I will also show you how to set up and manage this connection.

Chapter 16: Understanding Microsoft Endpoint   In this chapter, I will talk about the benefits of using Microsoft Endpoint and the tools and applications that will help IT administrators manage their software and applications.

Chapter 17: Configuring Security   In this chapter, I am also going to talk about defending your Windows systems by using the built-in security features called Windows Defender Security Center. I will show you the different ways that you can protect your system using the Defender Security Center options.

Chapter 18: Creating Azure Policies   In this chapter, I will discuss how to set up and configure Azure policies. Setting up Azure policies will allow administrators to set rules on how users and devices connect to your Azure network.

Recommended Home Lab Setup

To get the most out of this book, you will want to make sure you complete the exercises through-out the chapters. To complete the exercises, you will need one of two setups. First, you can set up a machine with Windows Server 2022 and complete the labs using a regular Windows Server 2022 machine.

The second way to set up Windows Server 2022 (the way I set up Server 2022) is by using virtualization. I set up Windows Server 2022 as a virtual hard disk (VHD), and I did all the labs this way. The advantages of using virtualization are that you can always just wipe out the system and start over without losing a real server. Plus, you can set up multiple virtual servers and create a full lab environment on one machine.

How to Contact Sybex or the Author

Sybex strives to keep you supplied with the latest tools and information you need for your work. Please check the website at www.wiley.com, where I'll post additional content and updates that supplement this book should the need arise.

You can contact me by going to my website at www.willpanek.com. You can also watch free videos on Microsoft networking at www.youtube.com/c/williampanek.

How to Contact the Publisher

If you believe you have found a mistake in this book, please bring it to our attention. At John Wiley & Sons, we understand how important it is to provide our customers with accurate content, but even with our best efforts an error may occur.

In order to submit your possible errata, please email it to our Customer Service Team at wileysupport@wiley.com with the subject line "Possible Book Errata Submission."

Chapter 1

Understanding Windows Server 2022

So, you have decided to start down the track of Windows Server 2022. The first question we must ask ourselves is what's the first step? Well, the first step is to learn about what's new about the Windows Server 2022 features and benefits that are available and how these features can help improve your organization's network.

So that's where I am going to start. I will talk about the different Windows Server 2022 versions and what version may be best for you. So, let's dive right into the server by talking about some of the features and advantages of Windows Server 2022.

IN THIS CHAPTER YOU'LL LEARN

◆ Understand the roles and features in Windows Server 2022

◆ Understand the different versions of Windows Server 2022

◆ Know the features and roles that have been removed

Features and Advantages of Windows Server 2022

Before deciding to install and configure Windows Server 2022, it's first important to learn about some of the features and the advantages it offers. Windows Server 2022 is built off of the solid foundation of Windows Server 2016, but Microsoft has stated that Windows Server 2022 is "The cloud-ready operating system." This means that many of the features of Windows Server 2022 are built and evolve around cloud-based software and networking.

I will talk about all of these features in greater detail throughout this book. What follows are merely brief descriptions of some of the features of Windows Server 2022.

Built-in Security   Microsoft has always tried to make sure that their operating systems are as secure as possible but with Windows Server 2022, Microsoft has included Windows Defender Advanced Threat Protection (ATP). This feature helps stop attackers on your system and allows a company to meet any compliance requirements.

Active Directory Certificate Services   *Active Directory Certificate Services (AD CS)* provides a customizable set of services that allow you to issue and manage *public key infrastructure (PKI) certificates*. These certificates can be used in software security systems that employ public key technologies.

Active Directory Domain Services   *Active Directory Domain Services (AD DS)* includes new features that make deploying domain controllers simpler and that let you implement them faster. AD DS also makes the domain controllers more flexible, both to audit and to authorize for access to files. Moreover, AD DS has been designed to make performing administrative tasks easier through consistent graphical and scripted management experiences.

Active Directory Federation Services   *Active Directory Federation Services (AD FS)* provides Internet-based clients with a secure identity access solution that works on both Windows and non-Windows operating systems. AD FS gives users the ability to do a *single sign-on (SSO)* and access applications on other networks without needing a secondary password. Federation Services is one of the ways that you can connect your on-site domain with the cloud.

Active Directory Lightweight Directory Services   *Active Directory Lightweight Directory Services (AD LDS)* is a *Lightweight Directory Access Protocol (LDAP)* directory service that provides flexible support for directory-enabled applications, without the dependencies and domain-related restrictions of AD DS.

Active Directory Rights Management Services   *Active Directory Rights Management Services (AD RMS)* provides management and development tools that let you work with industry security technologies, including encryption, certificates, and authentication. Using these technologies allows organizations to create reliable information protection solutions.

Application Server   *Application Server* provides an integrated environment for deploying and running custom, server-based business applications.

BitLocker   *BitLocker* is a tool that allows you to encrypt the hard drives of your computer. By encrypting the hard drives, you can provide enhanced protection against data theft or unauthorized exposure of your computers or removable drives that are lost or stolen.

BranchCache   *BranchCache* allows data from files and web servers on a wide area network (WAN) to be cached on computers at a local branch office. By using BranchCache, you can improve application response times while also reducing WAN traffic. Cached data can be either distributed across peer client computers (distributed cache mode) or centrally hosted on a server (hosted cache mode). BranchCache is included with Windows Server 2022 and Windows 10 / Windows 11.

Containers   Windows Server 2022 has started focusing on an isolated operating system environment called Dockers. Dockers allow applications to run in isolated environments called containers. Containers are separate locations where applications can operate without affecting other applications or other operating system resources. To understand Dockers and containers, think of virtualization.

Virtual machines are operating systems that run in their own space on top of another operating system. Dockers and containers allow an application to run in its own space and because of this, it doesn't affect other applications. There are two different types of containers to focus on:

> **Windows Server Containers**   Windows Server 2022 allows for an isolated application to run by using a technology called process and namespace isolation. Windows Server 2022 containers allow applications to share the system's kernel with their container and all other containers running on the same host.

Hyper-V Containers   Windows Server 2022 Hyper-V containers add another virtual layer by isolating applications in their own optimized virtual machine. Hyper-V containers work differently than Windows Server containers in the fact that the Hyper-V containers do not share the system's kernel with other Hyper-V containers.

Credential Guard   Credential Guard helps protect a system's credentials and this helps avoid pass the hash attacks. Credential Guard offers better protection against advanced persistent threats by protecting credentials on the system from being stolen by a compromised administrator or malware.

Credential Guard can also be enabled on Remote Desktop Services servers and Virtual Desktop Infrastructure so that the credentials for users connecting to their sessions are protected.

DHCP   *Dynamic Host Configuration Protocol (DHCP)* is an Internet standard that allows organizations to reduce the administrative overhead of configuring hosts on a TCP/IP-based network. Some of the features are DHCP failover, policy-based assignment, and the ability to use Windows PowerShell for DHCP Server.

DNS   *Domain Name System (DNS)* services are used in TCP/IP networks. DNS will convert a computer name or fully qualified domain name (FQDN) to an IP address. DNS also has the ability to do a reverse lookup and convert an IP address to a computer name. DNS allows you to locate computers and services through user-friendly names.

Failover Clustering   *Failover Clustering* gives an organization the ability to provide high availability and scalability to networked servers. Failover clusters can include file share storage for server applications, such as Hyper-V and Microsoft SQL Server, and for applications that run on physical servers or virtual machines.

File Server Resource Manager   *File Server Resource Manager* is a set of tools that allows administrators to manage and control the amount and type of data stored on the organization's servers. By using File Server Resource Manager, administrators have the ability to set up file management tasks, use quota management, get detailed reports, set up a file classification infrastructure, and configure file-screening management.

File and Storage Services   *File and Storage Services* allows an administrator to set up and manage one or more file servers. These servers can provide a central location on your network where you can store files and then share those files with network users. If users require access to the same files and applications or if centralized backup and file management are important issues for an organization, administrators should set up network servers as a file server.

Group Policy   *Group policies* are a set of rules and management configuration options that you can control through the Group Policy settings. These policy settings can be placed on users' computers throughout the organization.

Hyper-V   *Hyper-V* is one of the most changed features in Windows Server 2022. Hyper-V allows an organization to consolidate servers by creating and managing a virtualized computing environment. It does this by using virtualization technology that is built into Windows Server 2022.

Hyper-V allows you to run multiple operating systems simultaneously on one physical computer. Each virtual operating system runs in its own virtual machine environment.

Windows Server 2022 Hyper-V now allows an administrator to protect their corporate virtual machines using the feature called Shielded Virtual Machine. Shielded Virtual Machines are encrypted using BitLocker and the VMs can only run-on approved Hyper-V host systems.

Hyper-V also now includes a feature called containers. Containers add a new unique additional layer of isolation for and containerized applications.

IPAM   *IP Address Management (IPAM)* is one of the features first introduced with Windows Server. IPAM allows an administrator to customize and monitor the IP address infrastructure on a corporate network.

Kerberos Authentication   Windows Server 2022 uses the *Kerberos authentication* protocol and extensions for password-based and public key authentication. The Kerberos client is installed as a *security support provider (SSP)*, and it can be accessed through the *Security Support Provider Interface (SSPI)*.

Managed Service Accounts   Stand-alone *managed service accounts*, originally created for Windows Server 2008 R2 and Windows 7, are configured domain accounts that allow automatic password management and *service principal names* (SPNs) management, including the ability to delegate management to other administrators.

Nested Virtualization   Windows Server 2016 introduced a new Hyper-V feature called Nested Virtualization. Nested Virtualization allows administrators to create virtual machines within virtual machines. As an instructor, this was an awesome new feature. Now I can build a Windows Server 2022 Hyper-V Server with a training virtual machine. Then when I get to the part when I need to teach Hyper-V, I can just do that right in the classroom virtual machine. There are numerous possibilities and we will talk more about them throughout this book.

Nano Server   Windows Server 2016 introduced a brand new type of server installation called Nano Server. Nano Server requires an administrator to remotely administer the server operating system. It was primarily designed and optimized for private clouds and datacenters. Nano Server is very similar to Server Core, but the Nano Server operating system uses significantly smaller hard drive space, has no local logon capability, and only supports 64-bit applications and tools.

Networking   There are many networking technologies and features in Windows Server 2022, including BranchCache, Data Center Bridging (DCB), NIC Teaming, and many more.

Network Load Balancing   The *Network Load Balancing (NLB)* feature dispenses traffic across multiple servers by using the TCP/IP networking protocol. By combining two or more computers that are running applications in Windows Server 2022 into a single virtual cluster, NLB provides reliability and performance for mission-critical servers.

Network Policy and Access Services   Use the *Network Policy Server (NPS) and Access Services* server role to install and configure *Network Access Protection (NAP)*, secure wired and wireless access points, and RADIUS servers and proxies.

Print and Document Services   *Print and Document Services* allows an administrator to centralize print server and network printer tasks. This role also allows you to receive scanned documents from network scanners and route the documents to a shared network resource, Windows SharePoint Services site, or email addresses. Print and Document Services also provides fax servers with the ability to send and receive faxes while also giving the administrator the ability to manage fax resources such as jobs, settings, reports, and fax devices on the fax server.

PowerShell Direct   Windows Server 2016 included a new simple way to manage Hyper-V virtual machines called PowerShell Direct. PowerShell Direct is a powerful set of parameters for the PSSession cmdlet called VMName. This will be discussed in greater detail in the Hyper-V chapters and it is included with Windows Server 2022.

Remote Desktop Services   Before Windows Server 2008, we used to refer to this as Terminal Services. *Remote Desktop Services* allows users to connect to virtual desktops, RemoteApp programs, and session-based desktops. Using Remote Desktop Services allows users to access remote connections from within a corporate network or from the Internet.

Security Auditing   *Security auditing* gives an organization the ability to help maintain the security of an enterprise. By using security audits, you can verify authorized or unauthorized access to machines, resources, applications, and services. One of the best advantages of security audits is to verify regulatory compliance.

Smart Cards   Using *smart cards* (referred to as *two-factor authentication*) and their associated *personal identification numbers (PINs)* is a popular, reliable, and cost-effective way to provide authentication. When using smart cards, the user not only must have the physical card but also must know the PIN to be able to gain access to network resources. This is effective because even if the smart card is stolen, thieves can't access the network unless they know the PIN.

Software Defined Networking   Software Defined Networking (SDN) allows an administrator to centrally configure and manage their physical and virtual network devices. These devices include items such as routers, switches, and gateways in your datacenter.

Telemetry   The *Telemetry* service allows the Windows Feedback Forwarder to send feedback to Microsoft automatically by deploying a Group Policy setting to one or more organizational units. Windows Feedback Forwarder is available on all editions of Windows Server 2022, including Server Core.

TLS/SSL (Schannel SSP)   *Schannel* is a security support provider (SSP) that uses the *Secure Sockets Layer (SSL)* and *Transport Layer Security (TLS)* Internet standard authentication protocols together. The Security Support Provider Interface is an API used by Windows systems to allow security-related functionality, including authentication.

Volume Activation   Windows Server 2022 *Volume Activation* will help your organization benefit from using this service to deploy and manage volume licenses for a medium to large number of computers.

Web Server (IIS)   The *Web Server (IIS)* role in Windows Server 2022 allows an administrator to set up a secure, easy-to-manage, modular, and extensible platform for reliably hosting websites, services, and applications.

Windows Deployment Services *Windows Deployment Services* allows an administrator to install Windows operating systems remotely. Administrators can use Windows Deployment Services to set up new computers by using a network-based installation.

Windows PowerShell Desired State Configuration Windows Server 2016 created a new PowerShell management platform called Windows PowerShell Desired State Configuration (DSC). DSC enables the deployment and management of configuration data for software services and it also helps manage the environment in which these services run.

DSC allows administrators to use Windows PowerShell language extensions along with new Windows PowerShell cmdlets and resources. DSC allows you to declaratively specify how a corporation wants their software environment to be configured and maintained.

DSC allows you to automate tasks like enabling or disabling server roles and features, manage registry settings, manage files and directories, manage groups and users, deploy software, and run PowerShell scripts to just name a few.

Windows Server Backup Feature The *Windows Server Backup* feature gives an organization a way to back up and restore Windows servers. You can use Windows Server Backup to back up the entire server (all volumes), selected volumes, the system state, or specific files or folders.

Windows Server Update Services *Windows Server Update Services (WSUS)* allows administrators to deploy application and operating system updates. By deploying WSUS, administrators have the ability to manage updates that are released through Microsoft Windows Update to computers in their network. This feature is integrated with the operating system as a server role on a Windows Server 2022 system.

Deciding Which Windows Server 2022 Version to Use

You may be wondering which version of Windows Server 2022 is best for your organization. After all, Microsoft offers the following four versions of Windows Server 2022.

Windows Server 2022 Datacenter This version is designed for organizations that are looking to migrate to a highly virtualized, private cloud environment. Windows Server 2022 Datacenter has full Windows Server functionality with unlimited virtual instances.

Windows Server 2022 Standard This version is designed for organizations with physical or minimally virtualized environments. Windows Server 2022 Standard has full Windows Server functionality with two virtual instances.

Windows Server 2022 Datacenter: Azure Edition Windows Server Azure Edition is a Windows Server version designed specifically to operate either as an Azure IaaS VM or as a VM on an Azure Stack HCI cluster.

Windows Server 2022 Essentials This version is ideal for small businesses that have as many as 25 users and 50 devices. Windows Server 2022 Essentials has a simpler interface and preconfigured connectivity to cloud-based services but no virtualization rights.

Table 1.1 will show you the locks and limitations of Windows Server 2022 Standard and Windows Server 2022 Datacenter. This chart was taken directly from Microsoft's website.

TABLE 1.1: Windows Server 2022 Locks and Limits

LOCKS AND LIMITS	WINDOWS SERVER 2022 STANDARD	WINDOWS SERVER 2022 DATACENTER
Maximum number of users	Based on CALs	Based on CALs
Maximum SMB connections	16,777,216	16,777,216
Maximum RRAS connections	unlimited	unlimited
Maximum IAS connections	2,147,483,647	2,147,483,647
Maximum RDS connections	65,535	65,535
Maximum number of 64-bit sockets	64	64
Maximum number of cores	unlimited	unlimited
Maximum RAM	24 TB	24 TB
Can be used as virtualization guest	Yes, 2 virtual machines, plus one Hyper-V host per license	Yes, unlimited virtual machines, plus one Hyper-V host per license
Server can join a domain	yes	yes
Edge network protection/firewall	no	no
DirectAccess	yes	yes
DLNA codecs and web media streaming	Yes, if installed as Server with Desktop Experience	Yes, if installed as Server with Desktop Experience

Table 1.2 shows you the difference between Windows Server 2022 Standard vs. Windows Server 2022 Datacenter. This chart was taken directly from Microsoft's website.

TABLE 1.2: Windows Server 2022 Standard vs. Datacenter

WINDOWS SERVER ROLES AVAILABLE	WINDOWS SERVER 2022 STANDARD	WINDOWS SERVER 2022 DATACENTER
Active Directory Certificate Services	Yes	Yes
Active Directory Domain Services	Yes	Yes

TABLE 1.2: Windows Server 2022 Standard vs. Datacenter *(CONTINUED)*

WINDOWS SERVER ROLES AVAILABLE	WINDOWS SERVER 2022 STANDARD	WINDOWS SERVER 2022 DATACENTER
Active Directory Federation Services	Yes	Yes
AD Lightweight Directory Services	Yes	Yes
AD Rights Management Services	Yes	Yes
Device Health Attestation	Yes	Yes
DHCP Server	Yes	Yes
DNS Server	Yes	Yes
Fax Server	Yes	Yes
File and Storage Services	Yes	Yes
Host Guardian Service	Yes	Yes
Hyper-V	Yes	Yes, including Shielded Virtual Machines
Network Controller	No	Yes
Network Policy and Access Services	Yes, when installed as Server with Desktop Experience	Yes, when installed as Server with Desktop Experience
Print and Document Services	Yes	Yes
Remote Access	Yes	Yes
Remote Desktop Services	Yes	Yes
Volume Activation Services	Yes	Yes
Web Services (IIS)	Yes	Yes
Windows Deployment Services	Yes	Yes
Windows Server Essentials Experience	No	No
Windows Server Update Services	Yes	Yes

Table 1.3 will show you the features of Windows Server 2022 Standard and Windows Server 2022 Datacenter. This chart was taken directly from Microsoft's website.

TABLE 1.3:   Windows Server 2022 Standard vs. Datacenter

WINDOWS SERVER FEATURES INSTALLABLE WITH SERVER MANAGER (OR POWERSHELL)	WINDOWS SERVER 2022 STANDARD	WINDOWS SERVER 2022 DATACENTER
.NET Framework 3.5	Yes	Yes
.NET Framework 4.7	Yes	Yes
Background Intelligent Transfer Service (BITS)	Yes	Yes
BitLocker Drive Encryption	Yes	Yes
BitLocker Network Unlock	Yes, when installed as Server with Desktop Experience	Yes, when installed as Server with Desktop Experience
BranchCache	Yes	Yes
Client for NFS	Yes	Yes
Containers	Yes (unlimited Windows containers; up to two Hyper-V containers)	Yes (unlimited Windows and Hyper-V containers)
Data Center Bridging	Yes	Yes
Direct Play	Yes, when installed as Server with Desktop Experience	Yes, when installed as Server with Desktop Experience
Enhanced Storage	Yes	Yes
Failover Clustering	Yes	Yes
Group Policy Management	Yes	Yes
Host Guardian Hyper-V Support	No	Yes
I/O Quality of Service	Yes	Yes
IIS Hostable Web Core	Yes	Yes
Internet Printing Client	Yes, when installed as Server with Desktop Experience	Yes, when installed as Server with Desktop Experience
IPAM Server	Yes	Yes
iSNS Server service	Yes	Yes

TABLE 1.3:   Windows Server 2022 Standard vs. Datacenter   *(CONTINUED)*

WINDOWS SERVER FEATURES INSTALLABLE WITH SERVER MANAGER (OR POWERSHELL)	WINDOWS SERVER 2022 STANDARD	WINDOWS SERVER 2022 DATACENTER
LPR Port Monitor	Yes, when installed as Server with Desktop Experience	Yes, when installed as Server with Desktop Experience
Management OData IIS Extension	Yes	Yes
Media Foundation	Yes	Yes
Message Queueing	Yes	Yes
Multipath I/O	Yes	Yes
MultiPoint Connector	Yes	Yes
Network Load Balancing	Yes	Yes
Peer Name Resolution Protocol	Yes	Yes
Quality Windows Audio Video Experience	Yes	Yes
RAS Connection Manager Administration Kit	Yes, when installed as Server with Desktop Experience	Yes, when installed as Server with Desktop Experience
Remote Assistance	Yes, when installed as Server with Desktop Experience	Yes, when installed as Server with Desktop Experience
Remote Differential Compression	Yes	Yes
RSAT	Yes	Yes
RPC over HTTP Proxy	Yes	Yes
Setup and Boot Event Collection	Yes	Yes
Simple TCP/IP Services	Yes, when installed as Server with Desktop Experience	Yes, when installed as Server with Desktop Experience
SMB 1.0/CIFS File Sharing Support	Installed	Installed
SMB Bandwidth Limit	Yes	Yes
SMTP Server	Yes	Yes
SNMP Service	Yes	Yes
Software Load Balancer	Yes	Yes
Storage Replica	Yes	Yes

WINDOWS SERVER FEATURES INSTALLABLE WITH SERVER MANAGER (OR POWERSHELL)	**WINDOWS SERVER 2022 STANDARD**	**WINDOWS SERVER 2022 DATACENTER**
Telnet Client	Yes	Yes
TFTP Client	Yes, when installed as Server with Desktop Experience	Yes, when installed as Server with Desktop Experience
VM Shielding Tools for Fabric Management	Yes	Yes
WebDAV Redirector	Yes	Yes
Windows Biometric Framework	Yes, when installed as Server with Desktop Experience	Yes, when installed as Server with Desktop Experience
Windows Defender features	Installed	Installed
Windows Identity Foundation 3.5	Yes, when installed as Server with Desktop Experience	Yes, when installed as Server with Desktop Experience
Windows Internal Database	Yes	Yes
Windows PowerShell	Installed	Installed
Windows Process Activation Service	Yes	Yes
Windows Search Service	Yes, when installed as Server with Desktop Experience	Yes, when installed as Server with Desktop Experience
Windows Server Backup	Yes	Yes
Windows Server Migration Tools	Yes	Yes
Windows Standards-Based Storage Management	Yes	Yes
Windows TIFF IFilter	Yes, when installed as Server with Desktop Experience	Yes, when installed as Server with Desktop Experience
WinRM IIS Extension	Yes	Yes
WINS Server	Yes	Yes
Wireless LAN Service	Yes	Yes
WoW64 support	Installed	Installed
XPS Viewer	Yes, when installed as Server with Desktop Experience	Yes, when installed as Server with Desktop Experience

TABLE 1.3: Windows Server 2022 Standard vs. Datacenter *(CONTINUED)*

WINDOWS SERVER FEATURES INSTALLABLE WITH SERVER MANAGER (OR POWERSHELL)	WINDOWS SERVER 2022 STANDARD	WINDOWS SERVER 2022 DATACENTER
Best Practices Analyzer	Yes	Yes
Direct Access	Yes	Yes
Dynamic Memory (in virtualization)	Yes	Yes
Hot Add/Replace RAM	Yes	Yes
Microsoft Management Console	Yes	Yes
Minimal Server Interface	Yes	Yes
Network Load Balancing	Yes	Yes
Windows PowerShell	Yes	Yes
Server Core installation option	Yes	Yes
Server Manager	Yes	Yes
SMB Direct and SMB over RDMA	Yes	Yes
Software-defined Networking	No	Yes
Storage Migration Service	Yes	Yes
Storage Replica	Yes, 1 partnership and 1 resource group with a single 2TB volume	Yes, unlimited
Storage Spaces	Yes	Yes
Storage Spaces Direct	No	Yes
Volume Activation Services	Yes	Yes
VSS (Volume Shadow Copy Service) integration	Yes	Yes
Windows Server Update Services	Yes	Yes
Windows System Resource Manager	Yes	Yes
Server license logging	Yes	Yes
Inherited activation	As guest if hosted on Datacenter	Can be a host or a guest
Work Folders	Yes	Yes

Once you choose what roles are going on your server, you must then decide how you're going to install Windows Server 2022. There are two ways to install Windows Server 2022. You can upgrade a Windows Server 2012 R2 (or above) machine to Windows Server 2022, or you can do a clean install of Windows Server 2022. If you are running any version of Server before 2012 R2, you must first upgrade to Windows Server 2012 R2 or 2016 before upgrading to Windows Server 2022. If you decide that you are going to upgrade, there are specific upgrade paths you must follow.

NOTE Microsoft's best practice recommendation for installing servers is to always do a clean install and not an upgrade. Upgrading from Windows Server 2012 R2 and higher is possible. But, Microsoft recommends that you always do a clean install of a server.

Your choice of Windows Server 2022 version is dictated by how your current network is designed. If you are building a network from scratch, then it's pretty straightforward. Just choose the Windows Server 2022 version based on your server's tasks. However, if you already have a version of Windows Server 2012 installed, you should follow the recommendations in Table 1.4, which briefly summarize the supported upgrade paths to Windows Server 2022.

TABLE 1.4:   Supported Windows Server 2022 Upgrade Path Recommendations

CURRENT SYSTEM	UPGRADED SYSTEM
Windows Server 2012 Standard	Windows Server 2016 Standard or Datacenter
Windows Server 2012 Datacenter	Windows Server 2016 Datacenter
Windows Server 2012 R2 Standard	Windows Server 2022 Standard or Datacenter
Windows Server 2012 R2 Datacenter	Windows Server 2022 Datacenter
Windows Server 2012 R2 Essentials	Windows Server 2022 Essentials
Hyper-V Server 2012 R2	Hyper-V Server 2019
Windows Storage Server 2016 Standard	Windows Storage Server 2022 Standard
Windows Storage Server 2016 Datacenter	Windows Storage Server 2022 Datacenter
Hyper-V Server 2016	Hyper-V Server 2019

Deciding on the Type of Installation

One of the final choices you must make before installing Windows Server 2022 is what type of installation you want. There are three ways to install Windows Server 2022.

WINDOWS SERVER 2022 (DESKTOP EXPERIENCE)

This is the version with which most administrators are familiar. This is the version that uses *Microsoft Management Console (MMC)* windows, and it is the version that allows the use of a mouse to navigate through the installation.

WINDOWS SERVER 2022 SERVER CORE

This is a bare-bones installation of Windows Server 2022. You can think of it this way: If Windows Server 2022 (Desktop Experience) is a top-of-the-line luxury car, then Windows Server 2022 Server Core is the stripped-down model with manual windows, cloth seats, and no air conditioning. It might not be pretty to look at, but it gets the job done.

> ### Real World Scenario
>
> #### SERVER CORE
>
> Here is an explanation of Server Core that I have used ever since it was introduced in Windows Server 2008.
>
> I am a *huge* sports fan. I love watching sports on TV, and I enjoy going to games. If you have ever been to a hockey game, you know what a hockey goal looks like. Between hockey periods, the stadium workers often bring out a huge piece of Plexiglas onto the ice. There is a tiny square cut out of the bottom of the glass. The square is just a bit bigger than a hockey puck itself.
>
> Now they pick some lucky fan out of the stands, give them a puck at center ice, and then ask them to shoot the puck into the net with the Plexiglas in front of it. If they get it through that tiny little square at the bottom of the Plexiglas, they win a car or some such great prize.
>
> Well, Windows Server 2022 (Desktop Experience) is like regular hockey with an open net, and Windows Server 2022 Server Core is the Plexiglas version. Because Windows Server 2022 Server Core has the plexiglass, Microsoft refers to this is a smaller attack surface.

Server Core supports a limited number of roles.

- Active Directory Certificate Services (AD CS)
- Active Directory Domain Services (AD DS)
- Active Directory Federation Services (AD FS)
- Active Directory Lightweight Directory Services (AD LDS)
- Active Directory Rights Management Services (AD RMS)
- Application Server
- DHCP Server
- DNS Server
- Fax Server
- File and Storage Services
- BITS Server
- BranchCache

- Hyper-V
- Network Policy and Access Services
- Print and Document Services
- Remote Access
- Remote Desktop Services
- Volume Activation Services
- Web Server (IIS)
- Windows Deployment Services
- Windows Server Update Services
- .NET Framework 3.5 Features
- .NET Framework 4.5 Features
- Streaming Media Services
- Failover Clustering
- iSCSI
- Network Load Balancing
- MPIO
- qWave
- Telnet Server/Client
- Windows Server Migration Tools
- Windows PowerShell 5.0

Server Core does not have the normal Windows interface or GUI. Almost everything has to be configured via the command line or, in some cases, using the Remote Server Administration Tools from a full version of Windows Server 2022. While this might scare off some administrators, it has the following benefits:

Reduced Management   Because Server Core has a minimum number of applications installed, it reduces management effort.

Minimal Maintenance   Only basic systems can be installed on Server Core, so it reduces the upkeep you would need to perform in a normal server installation.

Smaller Footprint   Server Core requires only 1 GB of disk space to install and 2 GB of free space for operations.

Tighter Security   With only a few applications running on a server, it is less vulnerable to attacks.

Server Core App Compatibility Feature on Demand   Windows Server 2022 now includes the Server Core App Compatibility feature on demand (FOD). This feature drastically improves the application compatibility of the Windows Server Core installation. It does this by containing a subset of components from Windows Server 2022 with the Desktop Experience but without adding the Windows Server Desktop Experience graphical environment. The advantage is that this helps increase the functionality and compatibility of Windows Server 2022 Server Core while keeping it as lean as possible.

The prerequisites for Server Core are basic. It requires the Windows Server 2022 installation media, a product key, and the hardware on which to install it.

After you install the base operating system, you use PowerShell or the remote administrative tools to configure the network settings, add the machine to the domain, create and format disks, and install roles and features. It takes only a few minutes to install Server Core, depending on the hardware.

🌐 Real World Scenario

BETTER SECURITY

When I started in this industry more than 20 years ago, I was a programmer. I used to program computer hospital systems. When I switched to the networking world, I continued to work under contract with hospitals and with doctors' offices.

One problem I ran into is that many doctors are affiliated with hospitals, but they don't actually have offices within the hospital. Generally, they have offices either near the hospital or, in some cases, right across the street.

Here is the issue: Do we put servers in the doctors' offices, or do we make the doctor log into the hospital network through a remote connection? Doctors' offices normally don't have computer rooms, and we don't want to place a domain controller or server on someone's desk. It's just unsafe!

This is where Windows Server 2022 Server Core can come into play. Since it is a slimmed-down version of Windows and there is no GUI, it makes it harder for anyone in the office to hack into the system. Also, Microsoft introduced a new domain controller in Windows Server 2008 called a *read-only domain controller (RODC)*. As its name suggests, it is a read-only version of a domain controller (explained in detail later in this book).

With Server Core and an RODC, you can feel safer placing a server on someone's desk or in any office. Server Core systems allow you to place servers in areas where you would never have placed them before. This can be a great advantage to businesses that have small, remote locations without full server rooms.

WINDOWS SERVER 2022 NANO SERVER

Windows Server 2016 introduced a new type of server installation called Nano Server. Nano Server allows an administrator to remotely administer the server operating system. It was primarily designed and optimized for private clouds and datacenters. Nano Server is very similar to Server Core, but the Nano Server operating system uses significantly smaller hard drive space, has no local logon capability, and only supports 64-bit applications and tools.

Removed Features

As of with all new versions of Windows Servers, Microsoft always decides to remove or retire features or services that are no longer needed. The following are Features and Services were replaced starting with Windows Server 2022.

IIS 6 Management Compatibility   The following Features were removed in the first release of Windows Server 2022: IIS 6 Metabase Compatibility (Web-Metabase), IIS 6 Management Console (Web-Lgcy-Mgmt-Console), IIS 6 Scripting Tools (Web-Lgcy-Scripting), and IIS 6 WMI Compatibility (Web-WMI).

IIS Digest Authentication   Microsoft plans to replace the IIS Digest Authentication method. Administrators should use other authentication methods. These methods include Client Certificate Mapping and Windows Authentication.

Internet Storage Name Service (iSNS)   iSNS is being replaced for the Server Message Block (SMB) feature. This feature offers basically the same functionality with additional features.

RSA/AES Encryption for IIS   The RSA/AES Encryption for IIS method is being replaced due to the improved Cryptography API: Next Generation (CNG) method.

Windows PowerShell 2.0   The Windows PowerShell 2.0 version has been surpassed by multiple more recent versions. Administrators can get the superior features and performance if they use Windows PowerShell 5.0 or later.

The following are Features and Services are being replaced starting with Windows Server 2022 version 1803.

File Replication Service   File Replication Services were first introduced in Windows Server 2003 R2. They have now been replaced with DFS Replication.

Hyper-V Network Virtualization (HNV)   Hyper-V Network Virtualization (HNV) has been replaced because Network Virtualization is now included in Windows Server 2022 as part of the Software Defined Networking (SDN) solution. Software Defined Networking (SDN) also includes items such as the Network Controller, Software Load Balancing, User-Defined Routing, and Access Control Lists.

Table 1.5 shows all of the Features and Roles that are no longer being developed. The next two tables were taken directly from Microsoft's website.

TABLE 1.5:   Features and Roles No Longer Being Developed

FEATURE OR ROLES	ADMINISTRATORS CAN USE. . .
Business Scanning, also called Distributed Scan Management (DSM)	The Scan Management functionality was introduced in Windows Server 2008 R2 and enabled secure scanning and the management of scanners in an enterprise. We're no longer investing in this feature, and there are no devices available that support it.

TABLE 1.5:   Features and Roles No Longer Being Developed   *(CONTINUED)*

FEATURE OR ROLES	ADMINISTRATORS CAN USE. . .
IPv4/6 Transition Technologies (6to4, ISATAP, and Direct Tunnels)	6to4 has been disabled by default since Windows 10 / Windows 11, version 1607 (the Anniversary Update), ISATAP has been disabled by default since Windows 10 / Windows 11, version 1703 (the Creators Update), and Direct Tunnels has always been disabled by default. Please use native IPv6 support instead.
MultiPoint Services	We're no longer developing the MultiPoint Services role as part of Windows Server. MultiPoint Connector services are available through Feature on Demand for both Windows Server and Windows 10 / Windows 11. You can use Remote Desktop Services, in particular the Remote Desktop Services Session Host, to provide RDP connectivity.
Offline symbol packages (Debug symbol MSIs)	We're no longer making the symbol packages available as a downloadable MSI. Instead, the Microsoft Symbol Server is moving to be an Azure-based symbol store. If you need the Windows symbols, connect to the Microsoft Symbol Server to cache your symbols locally or use a manifest file with SymChk.exe on a computer with internet access.
Remote Desktop Connection Broker and Remote Desktop Virtualization Host in a Server Core installation	Most Remote Desktop Services deployments have these roles co-located with the Remote Desktop Session Host (RDSH), which requires Server with Desktop Experience; to be consistent with RDSH we're changing these roles to also require Server with Desktop Experience. We're no longer developing these RDS roles for use in a Server Core installation. If you need to deploy these roles as part of your Remote Desktop infrastructure, you can install them on Windows Server 2016 with Desktop Experience.

These roles are also included in the Desktop Experience installation option of Windows Server 2022. You can test them in the Windows Insider build of Windows Server 2022—just be sure to choose the LTSC image.

RemoteFX 3D Video Adapter (vGPU)	We're developing new graphics acceleration options for virtualized environments. You can also use Discrete Device Assignment (DDA) as an alternative.
Software Restriction Policies in Group Policy	Instead of using the Software Restriction Policies through Group Policy, you can use AppLocker or Windows Defender Application Control to control which apps users can access and what code can run in the kernel.

FEATURE OR ROLES	ADMINISTRATORS CAN USE...
Storage Spaces in a Shared configuration using a SAS fabric	Deploy Storage Spaces Direct instead. Storage Spaces Direct supports the use of HLK-certified SAS enclosures, but in a non-shared configuration, as described in the Storage Spaces Direct hardware requirements.
Windows Server Essentials Experience	We're no longer developing the Essentials Experience role for the Windows Server Standard or Windows Server Datacenter SKUs. If you need an easy-to-use server solution for small-to-medium businesses, check out our new Microsoft 365 for business solution, or use Windows Server 2016 Essentials.

Table 1.6 shows the Features that are no longer being developed starting with Windows Server 2022.

TABLE 1.6:   Features No Longer Being Developed in Windows Server 2022

FEATURE	INSTEAD YOU CAN USE
Hyper-V vSwitch on LBFO	In a future release, the Hyper-V vSwitch will no longer have the capability to be bound to an LBFO team. Instead, it must be bound via Switch Embedded Teaming (SET).
XDDM-based remote display driver (new)	Starting with this release the Remote Desktop Services uses a Windows Display Driver Model (WDDM) based Indirect Display Driver (IDD) for a single session remote desktop. The support for Windows 2000 Display Driver Model (XDDM) based remote display drivers will be removed in a future release. Independent Software Vendors that use XDDM-based remote display driver should plan a migration to the WDDM driver model. For more information on implementing remote display indirect display driver ISVs can reach out to rdsdev@ microsoft.com.
UCS log collection tool (new)	The UCS log collection tool, while not explicitly intended for use with Windows Server, is nonetheless being replaced by the Feedback hub on Windows 10 / Windows 11.
Key Storage Drive in Hyper-V	We're no longer working on the Key Storage Drive feature in Hyper-V. If you're using generation 1 VMs, check out Generation 1 VM Virtualization Security for information about options going forward. If you're creating new VMs, use Generation 2 virtual machines with TPM devices for a more secure solution.
Trusted Platform Module (TPM) management console	The information previously available in the TPM management console is now available on the Device security page in the Windows Defender Security Center.

TABLE 1.6: Features No Longer Being Developed in Server 2022 *(CONTINUED)*

FEATURE	INSTEAD YOU CAN USE
Host Guardian Service Active Directory attestation mode	We're no longer developing Host Guardian Service Active Directory attestation mode—instead we've added a new attestation mode, host key attestation, that's far simpler and equally as compatible as Active Directory based attestation. This new mode provides equivalent functionality with a setup experience, simpler management and fewer infrastructure dependencies than the Active Directory attestation. Host key attestation has no additional hardware requirements beyond what Active Directory attestation required, so all existing systems will remain compatible with the new mode.
OneSync service	The OneSync service synchronizes data for the Mail, Calendar, and People apps. We've added a sync engine to the Outlook app that provides the same synchronization.
Remote Differential Compression API support	Remote Differential Compression API support enabled synchronizing data with a remote source using compression technologies, which minimized the amount of data sent across the network.
WFP lightweight filter switch extension	The WFP lightweight filter switch extension enables developers to build simple network packet filtering extensions for the Hyper-V virtual switch. You can achieve the same functionality by creating a full filtering extension. As such, we'll be removing this extension in the future.

The Bottom Line

Understand the roles and features in Windows Server 2022.   Choosing the right server operating system depends on the roles and features that you need for your organizational needs. The proper operating system depends on the job functions and requirements that are needed to set your network up properly.

Master It   You are an administrator that needs to set up a Windows Server that needs easy access for connecting to the cloud. You are not worried about physical security since the server will be locked in a secure server room.

Understand the different versions of Windows Server 2022.   When choosing how to set up Windows Server 2022, there are different ways that you can set up how the system functions. You can choose between using the GUI version of Windows Server 2022 or a non-GUI version.

Master It   One of the important things that you need to know is how the server needs to be set up. You are an administrator that needs to set up Windows Server 2022. The server will not be in a secure server room. You need to choose a version of Windows Server 2022 installation that addresses these security concerns.

Know the features and roles that have been removed.   Understanding what features and roles have been removed or are no longer being developed is an important task.

Master It   You are the administrator for your organization and you need to choose a server version that allows for Active Directory, DNS, DHCP, and other features.

Chapter 2

Understanding Virtualization

One of the greatest advancements in servers over the last decade has been the ability to have one physical server but run multiple servers on top of that one physical box. This is known as *virtualization*.

In this chapter, I will talk about virtualization and how it works. Since this is a Mastering Microsoft Server 2022 book, we will focus most of our attention on Microsoft's version of virtualization called Hyper-V.

Hyper-V is a server role in Windows Server 2022 that allows you to virtualize your environment and therefore run multiple virtual operating system instances simultaneously on a physical server. This not only helps you to improve server utilization but also helps you to create a more cost-effective and dynamic system.

Hyper-V allows an organization of any size to act and compete with other organizations of any size. A small company can buy a single server and then virtualize that server into multiple servers. Hyper-V gives a small company the ability to run multiple servers on a single box and compete with a company of any size.

For large organizations, an administrator can consolidate multiple servers onto Hyper-V servers thus saving an organization time and money by using fewer physical boxes but still having all the servers needed to run the business.

In this chapter, you will also get a solid understanding of what is important in virtualization and in what areas of your work life you can use it. In Chapter 3, "Installing and Configuring Hyper-V," I will show you how to actually install and configure Hyper-V on a Windows Server 2022 system.

IN THIS CHAPTER YOU'LL LEARN

- ◆ Understand server virtualization
- ◆ Understand the Hyper-V features

Introduction to Virtualization

Virtualization is a method for abstracting physical resources from the way that they interact with other resources. For example, if you abstract the physical hardware from the operating system, you get the benefit of being able to move the operating system between different physical systems.

This is called *server virtualization*. But there are also other forms of virtualization available, such as presentation virtualization, desktop virtualization, and application virtualization. I will now briefly explain the differences between these forms of virtualization:

Server Virtualization   This basically enables multiple servers to run on the same physical host server. Hyper-V is Microsoft's server virtualization tool that allows you to turn physical machines into virtual machines and manage them on fewer physical servers. Thus, you will be able to consolidate physical servers. So, you can have less physical hardware but just as many individual servers that are needed to run your entire network. The individual machines that run on the host server are called virtual machines. Virtual machines are just guest servers that run on top of the Hyper-V host server system.

Presentation Virtualization   When you use *presentation virtualization*, your applications run on a different computer, and only the screen information is transferred to your computer. An example of presentation virtualization is Microsoft Remote Desktop Services in Windows Server 2022.

Desktop Virtualization   *Desktop virtualization* provides you with a virtual machine on your desktop, comparable to server virtualization. You run your complete operating system and applications in a virtual machine so that your local physical machine just needs to run a very basic operating system. An example of this form of virtualization is Microsoft Virtual PC.

Application Virtualization   *Application virtualization* helps prevent conflicts between applications on the same PC. Thus, it helps you to isolate the application running environment from the operating system installation requirements by creating application-specific copies of all shared resources. It also helps reduce application-to-application incompatibility and testing needs. An example of an application virtualization tool is Microsoft Application Virtualization (App-V).

When it comes to server virtualization, there are many different players in the game. The original king of virtualization is VMware. VMware was the first company to really take server virtualization to the next level.

At the same time, Microsoft had smaller versions of virtualization such as Virtual Server. In 2008 Microsoft released its first version of Hyper-V. To say that Windows Server 2008 Hyper-V had flaws would be a kind way of putting it.

But as Microsoft continued to release versions of Windows Server, it kept improving Hyper-V. When Microsoft released Windows Server 2012 and 2012 R2, it made huge leaps and bounds. Then Windows Server 2016 took Hyper-V to another level. A level now where they could actually compete with VMware and other virtual vendors. The big advantage of Hyper-V is that it comes included with Windows Server.

So how do we get a Windows Server to allow multiple servers to all run on the same machine? Well, the great thing about virtualization is that it is all done for us using the Microsoft Windows Hypervisor.

The Windows *hypervisor* is a thin layer of software that sits between the hardware and the Windows Server 2022 operating system. This thin layer allows one physical machine to run multiple operating systems in different virtual machines at the same time. The hypervisor is the mechanism that is responsible for maintaining isolation between the different Hyper-V partitions.

The hypervisor allows the Hyper-V host server to have multiple virtual machines running on the same machine at one time. So now you may be wondering how many virtual machines you can run at the same time. This is all going to depend on your machine's hardware and the licensing you own. For example, physical memory and processor are just two examples of hardware that would need to be increased depending on how many virtual machines you want to run. Also, other features loaded into the virtual environment may require even higher hardware demands, like clustering. We will talk more about the hypervisor later in the chapter.

So since we are going to be focusing on Microsoft's version of virtualization, let's take a look at some of the Hyper-V features that you get.

Hyper-V Features

As a lead-in to the virtualization topic and Hyper-V, I will start with a list of key features, followed by a list of supported guest operating systems. This should provide you with a quick, high-level view of this feature before you dig deeper into the technology.

KEY FEATURES OF HYPER-V

The following are the key features of Hyper-V:

Architecture   The hypervisor-based architecture, which has a 64-bit microkernel, provides a new array of device support as well as performance and security improvements.

Automatic Virtual Machine Activation (AVMA)   *Automatic Virtual Machine Activation (AVMA)* is a feature that allows administrators to install virtual machines on a properly activated Windows Server 2022 system without the need to manage individual product keys for each virtual machine. When AVMA is used, virtual machines get bound to the licensed Hyper-V server as soon as the virtual machine starts. The virtual machines can move the AVMA-licensed VM to other hosts, but the VM can only run one instance and it can only be on a host set up for AVMA. It is bound to the host it is running on, but it can move from host to host as long as the hosts are AVMA.

Discrete Device Assignment   One feature of Windows Server 2022 is the ability to use Discrete Device Assignment (DDA). DDA allows an administrator to take full advantage of performance and application compatibility improvements in the user experience by allowing the system's graphics cards to be directly assigned to a virtual machine. This allows the graphics card processor to be fully available to the virtual desktops that are utilizing the native driver of the graphics card processor as well as the network card's storage features.

Dynamic Memory   *Dynamic Memory* is a feature of Hyper-V that allows it to balance memory automatically among running virtual machines. Dynamic Memory allows Hyper-V to adjust the amount of memory available to the virtual machines in response to the needs of the virtual machines. So, for example, if you set the max RAM to 16GB but it only needs 8GB while running, it will only use the 8GB. So it can use the entire 16GB in the previous example if needed, but it will only use what it needs if Dynamic Memory is enabled. Dynamic Memory is currently available for Hyper-V in Windows Server 2022.

Enhanced Session Mode   *Enhanced Session Mode* enhances the interactive session of the Virtual Machine Connection for Hyper-V administrators who want to connect to their virtual machines. It gives administrators the same functionality as a remote desktop connection when the administrator is interacting with a virtual machine.

In previous versions of Hyper-V, the virtual machine connection gave you limited functionality while you connected to the virtual machine screen, keyboard, and mouse. An administrator could use an RDP connection to get full redirection abilities, but that would require a network connection to the virtual machine host.

Enhanced Session Mode gives administrators the following benefits for local resource redirection:

- Display configuration
- Audio
- Printers
- Clipboard
- Smart cards
- Drives
- USB devices
- Supported Plug and Play devices

Fibre Channel   The virtual Fibre Channel feature allows you to connect to the Fibre Channel storage unit from within the virtual machine. *Virtual Fibre Channel* allows an administrator to use their existing Fibre Channel to support virtualized workloads. Hyper-V users have the ability to use Fibre Channel storage area networks (SANs) to virtualize the workloads that require direct access to SAN logical unit numbers (LUNs).

Hardware Architecture   Hyper-V's architecture provides improved utilization of resources such as networking, memory, and disks.

Hyper-V Nesting   Windows Server 2022 has a feature of Hyper-V called Hyper-V nesting. Hyper-V nesting allows you to run a virtual machine in a virtual machine. So, let's say that you build a new 2016 Hyper-V server. You install Windows Server 2022 into a virtual machine. Then in that virtual machine, you can install Hyper-V and build other virtual machines within the first virtual machine. This is new to Windows Server 2022 and can be very useful in training situations. You can install a Windows Server 2022 virtual machine and still show others how to install and create virtual machines in the original virtual machine. To enable Hyper-V nesting, you would run the following PowerShell command on the Hyper-V Host. The virtual machines must be in the OFF State when this command is run (this means the virtual machines must be turned off).

```
Set-VMProcessor -VMName <VMName> -ExposeVirtualizationExtensions $true
```

Network Isolation   One nice feature of using Microsoft Hyper-V network virtualization is the ability of Hyper-V to keep virtual networks isolated from the physical network infrastructure of the hosted system. Because administrators can set up Hyper-V software–defined virtualization policies, you are no longer limited by the IP address assignment or VLAN isolation requirements of the physical network. Hyper-V allows for built-in network isolation to keep the virtual network separated from the physical network.

Network Load Balancing   Hyper-V provides support for *Windows Network Load Balancing (NLB)* to balance the network load across virtual machines on different servers.

Non-Uniform Memory Access   Non-Uniform Memory Access (NUMA) is a multiprocessor memory architecture that allows a processor to access its local memory quicker than memory located on another processor. NUMA allows a system to access memory quickly by providing separate memory on each processor. Processors can access their local assigned memory thus speeding the system performance. Normally a multi-processor system runs into performance issues when multiple processors access the same memory at the same time. NUMA helps prevent this by allowing processors to access their own memory. Memory that is dedicated to a processor is referred to as a NUMA node.

Operating System Support   Both 32-bit and 64-bit operating systems can run simultaneously in Hyper-V. Also, different platforms like Windows, Linux, and others are supported.

Quick Migration   Hyper-V's *quick migration* feature provides you with the functionality to run virtual machines in a clustered environment with switchover capabilities when there is a failure. Thus, you can reduce downtime and achieve higher availability of your virtual machines.

Resource Metering   Hyper-V *resource metering* allows an organization to track usage within the business's departments. It allows an organization to create a usage-based billing solution that adjusts to the provider's business model and strategy.

RemoteFX   Windows Server 2022 Hyper-V RemoteFX allows for an enhanced user experience for RemoteFX desktops by providing a 3D virtual adapter, intelligent codecs, and the ability to redirect USB devices in virtual machines.

Scripting   Using the Windows Management Instrumentation (WMI) interfaces and APIs, you can easily build custom scripts to automate processes in your virtual machines.

Shared Virtual Hard Disk   Windows Server 2022 Hyper-V has a feature called Shared Virtual Hard Disk. *Shared Virtual Hard Disk* allows an administrator to cluster virtual machines by using shared virtual hard disk (VHDX) files.

Shared virtual hard disks allow an administrator to build a high availability infrastructure, which is important if you are setting up either a private cloud deployment or a cloud-hosted environment for managing large workloads. Shared virtual hard disks allow two or more virtual machines to access the same virtual hard disk (VHDX) file.

Shielded Virtual Machines   Shielded Virtual Machines are a generation 2 Virtual Machine that uses a virtual Trusted Platform Module chip and it's encrypted using Windows BitLocker. Shielded Virtual Machines allow enterprise administrators to provide a more secure environment for their tenant Virtual Machines.

Support for Symmetric Multiprocessors   Support for up to 64 processors in a virtual machine environment provides you with the ability to run applications as well as multiple virtual machines faster.

Virtual Machines   Virtual machines are the operating systems that run on the virtual server. They can be full operating systems or smaller versions of operating systems. The virtual machines are the actual virtual environment that these operating systems run in. They can communicate and operate on a network the same way a physical server can.

Virtual Machine Snapshot   You can take snapshots of running virtual machines, which provides you with the capability to recover to any previous virtual machine snapshot state quickly and easily.

Virtual Machine Queue   Windows Server 2022 Hyper-V includes a feature called Virtual machine queue (VMQ) as long as the hardware is VMQ compatible network hardware. VMQ uses packet filtering to provide data from an external virtual machine network directly to virtual machines. This helps reduce the overhead of routing packets from the management operating system to the virtual machine.

Once VMQ is enabled on Hyper-V, a dedicated queue is created on the physical network adapter for each virtual network adapter to use. When data arrives for the virtual network adapter, the physical network adapter places that data in a queue and once the system is available, all of the data in the queue is delivered to the virtual network adapter.

To enable the virtual machine queue on a specific virtual machine, enter the settings for the virtual machine and expand Network Adapter. Click on Hardware Acceleration and on the right-hand window; check the box for Enable virtual machine queue.

SUPPORTED GUEST OPERATING SYSTEMS

Guest operating systems are the operating systems that run in the virtual environment. Depending on your version of Windows Server 2022, depends on how many virtual machines can be loaded based on licensing. Windows Server 2022 Standard allows you to have the Host system and two virtual machines. You can purchase additional licensing to allow more virtual machines, but the default is 2 virtual machines.

Windows Server 2022 Datacenter can have unlimited virtual machines along with the Hyper-V Host system. The maximum number of VMs that can run at once is 1024.

Once you purchase the appropriate version of Windows Server and licensing, an administrator can start creating virtual machines with guest operating systems.

The following guest operating systems have been successfully tested on Hyper-V and are hypervisor aware. Table 2.1 shows all of the guest server operating systems and the maximum number of virtual processors. Table 2.2 shows all of the guest client operating systems and the maximum number of virtual processors.

TABLE 2.1:   Hyper-V Guest Server Operating Systems

GUEST OPERATING SYSTEM (SERVER)	MAXIMUM NUMBER OF VIRTUAL PROCESSORS
Windows Server 2022	64 for Generation 1 VMs and 240 for Generation 2 VMs
Windows Server 2019	64 for Generation 1 VMs and 240 for Generation 2 VMs
Windows Server 2016	64 for Generation 1 VMs and 240 for Generation 2 VMs
Windows Server 2012 and Server 2012 R2	64

GUEST OPERATING SYSTEM (SERVER)	MAXIMUM NUMBER OF VIRTUAL PROCESSORS
Windows Server 2008 R2 with Service Pack 1 (SP1)	64
Windows Server 2008 R2	64
Windows Server 2008 with Service Pack 2 (SP2)	8
Red Hat Enterprise Linux 5.7 and 5.8	64
Red Hat Enterprise Linux 6.0–6.3	64
SUSE Linux Enterprise Server 11 SP2	64
Open SUSE 12.1	64

TABLE 2.2   Hyper-V Guest Client Operating Systems

GUEST OPERATING SYSTEM (CLIENT)	MAXIMUM NUMBER OF VIRTUAL PROCESSORS
Windows 11	32
Windows 10	32
Windows 8.1	32
CentOS 5.7 and 5.8	64
CentOS 6.0–6.3	64
Red Hat Enterprise Linux 5.7 and 5.8	64
Red Hat Enterprise Linux 6.0–6.3	64
SUSE Linux Enterprise Server 11 SP2	64
Open SUSE 12.1	64

NOTE   The list of supported guest operating systems may always be extended. Please check the official Microsoft Hyper-V site to obtain a current list of supported operating systems: https://docs.microsoft.com/en-us/windows-server/virtualization/hyper-v/ hyper-v-on-windows-server.

Hyper-V Architecture

This section will provide you with an overview of the Hyper-V architecture (see Figure 2.1). I'll explain the differences between a hypervisor-aware and a non-hypervisor-aware child partition.

FIGURE 2.1

Hyper-V architecture

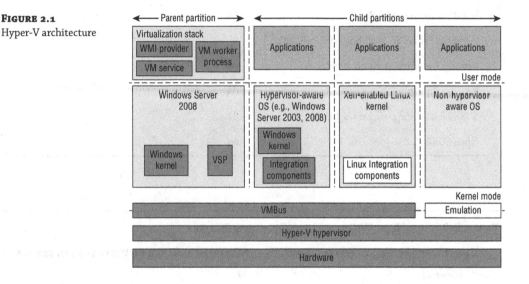

As you can see, Hyper-V is based on the microkernel architecture. As I stated earlier in the chapter, Hyper-V provides a virtualization layer called a hypervisor that runs directly on the system hardware. You can see that the hypervisor is similar to what the kernel is to Windows. It is a software layer responsible for the interaction with the core hardware and works in conjunction with an optimized instance of Windows Server 2022 that allows running multiple operating systems on a physical server simultaneously. The Hyper-V architecture consists of the hypervisor and parent and child partitions.

The Windows Server 2022 operating system runs in the parent partition, and it delivers the WMI provider for scripting as well as the VM service.

Virtual machines each run in their own child partitions. Child partitions do not have direct access to hardware resources; instead, they have a virtual view of the resources, which are called *virtual devices*.

If you're running a hypervisor-aware operating system like Windows Server 2008, Windows Server 2008 R2, Windows Server 2012, Windows Server 2016, or Windows Server 2022 in your virtual machine, any request to the virtual devices is redirected via the high-speed bus to the devices in the parent partition, which will manage the requests.

By default, only Windows Server 2008 R2 and newer are hypervisor-aware operating systems. Once you install Hyper-V Integration Components on an operating system other than Windows Server 2008 R2 and newer, it will be hypervisor aware. Microsoft provides a hypervisor adapter to make Linux hypervisor aware.

Non-hypervisor-aware operating systems (for example, Windows Server 2003) use an emulator to communicate with the Windows hypervisor, which is slower than molasses in the winter.

Hyper-V Operating Systems

To use virtualization in Windows Server 2022, you need to consider the basic software requirements for Hyper-V. Hyper-V runs only on the following editions of the Windows Server 2022 operating system:

◆ Windows Server 2022 Standard edition

◆ Windows Server 2022 Datacenter edition

Hyper-V was first introduced by Microsoft in 2008 and with every version of Windows Server, Hyper-V has gotten better and better. The following Windows Server 2019 servers will also run Hyper-V. I understand that this is a Mastering Windows Server 2022 book, but I know many administrators may run both Windows Server 2016 and Windows Server 2022 together.

◆ Windows Server 2016 Standard edition

◆ Windows Server 2016 Datacenter edition

◆ Microsoft Hyper-V Server 2016 edition

Linux and FreeBSD Image Deployments

One of the features of Windows Server 2022 is the ability for Hyper-V to support Linux and FreeBSD virtual machines. Hyper-V now can support these new virtual machines because Hyper-V has the ability to emulate Linux and FreeBSD devices. Because Hyper-V now has the ability to emulate these two devices, no additional software needs to be installed on Hyper-V.

Unfortunately, because Hyper-V has to emulate these devices, you lose some of the Hyper-V functionality like high performance and full management of the virtual machines. So, it's a tradeoff. You get to run Linux and FreeBSD type Hyper-V virtual machines, but you lose some of the benefits of Hyper-V.

But wait; there is a way to get your Hyper-V functionality back. This issue can be resolved as long as you install Hyper-V on machines that can support Linux and FreeBSD operating systems. The drivers that are needed on Hyper-V are called Linux Integration Services (LIS) and FreeBSD Integrated Services (FIS). By putting these drivers on a device that can handle Linux and FreeBSD, you can then have Hyper-V with all of the features Microsoft offers.

To get these drivers and make Hyper-V work will all of its functionality, you must make sure that you install a newer release of Linux that includes LIS. To get the most out of FreeBSD you must get a version after 10.0. For FreeBSD versions that are older than 10.0, Microsoft offers ports that work with BIS drivers that need to be installed. Hyper-V will work with Linux and FreeBSD without the need of any additional drivers or equipment. By having drivers and equipment that supports Linux and FreeBSD, you just get all of the Hyper-V features that your organization may need.

Virtualization in Azure

Another way to set up virtualization is to do it in Microsoft Azure. When using virtualization in Azure, it works basically the same way as it does on Windows Server 2022. The one main difference is the way you create virtual machines.

In Chapter 3, "Installing and Configuring Hyper-V," I will show you how to actually install and configure Hyper-V on a Windows Server 2022 system. In Microsoft Azure, you need to do configuration on your virtual machines, but Azure actually creates the virtual machines for you. You need to just choose which operating system you want to use and the settings and Azure does the rest.

Then an administrator just needs to fine-tune the virtual machine and that's it. In Chapter 15 "Creating a Hybrid Network," I will show you how to build and configure virtualization in the Azure environment.

The Bottom Line

Understand server virtualization.   Choosing the right type of virtualization can help an organization access the applications that you need to run properly on your network.

Master It   You are an administrator that needs to set up a network that will need multiple servers running. Your organization can't afford to buy servers for each server that is needed.

Understand the Hyper-V features.   Knowing the advantages of Hyper-V is important so that you can create and configure Hyper-V virtualization properly. There are different virtualization vendors. By knowing the features of Hyper-V, you can determine if it's the right virtual server for your organization.

Master It   You are an IT admin for a mid-size company. Your company is thinking about using Hyper-V for both Windows and Linux operating systems.

## Chapter 3

Installing and Configuring Hyper-V

As I stated in Chapter 2 "Understanding Virtualization," virtual servers have been one of the fastest-growing technologies in IT. Microsoft's version of virtualization is called Hyper-V.

In this chapter, I will explain how to install and configure Microsoft Hyper-V. As an IT Administrator, it is very important to understand how Hyper-V virtual machines are installed and configured properly.

Hyper-V gives you the ability to run multiple servers on a single physical box. But making sure that the virtual machines are configured properly is one of the most important tasks that an IT Administrator can perform. Properly set-up virtual machines can make or break a network.

These virtual machines can run your entire network and if these machines have issues, your entire network can cause errors throughout the network. Virtual machines can also be set up on Azure, but we will cover setting up Azure virtual machines later in this book when we dive into the Azure environment. So, let's start building and configuring virtual machines on Windows Server 2022.

IN THIS CHAPTER YOU'LL LEARN

- ◆ Know the virtualization requirements
- ◆ Know how to build virtual machines
- ◆ Know the different ways to build virtual machines

Hyper-V Installation and Configuration

The following sections explain how to install the Hyper-V role using Server Manager in Windows Server 2022 Full installation mode or the command line mode in Windows Server 2022 Server Core. We will then take a look at Hyper-V as part of Server Manager before discussing how to use the Hyper-V Manager. Finally, we will look at the Hyper-V server settings and then cover two important areas for Hyper-V: virtual networks and virtual hard disks.

Hyper-V Requirements

The following sections will describe the hardware and software requirements for installing the Hyper-V server role. It is important to understand these requirements for obtaining your software license as well as for planning for server hardware. When you understand the requirements, you can design and configure a Hyper-V solution that will meet the needs of your applications.

HARDWARE REQUIREMENTS

In addition to the basic hardware requirements for Windows Server 2022, there are requirements for running the Hyper-V server role on your Windows server. They are listed in Table 3.1.

TABLE 3.1: Hardware Requirements for Hyper-V

REQUIREMENT AREA	DEFINITION
CPU	x64-compatible processor with Intel VT or AMD-V technology enabled. Hardware Data Execution Prevention (DEP), specifically Intel XD bit (execute disable bit) or AMD NX bit (no execute bit), must be available and enabled. Minimum: 1.4GHz. Recommended: 2GHz or faster.
Memory	Minimum: 1GB RAM. Recommended: 4GB RAM or greater. (Additional RAM is required for each running guest operating system.) Maximum: 1TB.
Hard disk	Minimum: 8GB. Recommended: 20GB or greater. (Additional disk space needed for each guest operating system.)

The Add Roles Wizard in Server Manager additionally verifies the hardware requirements. A good starting point is to check your hardware against the Microsoft hardware list to make sure that Windows Server 2022 supports your hardware. If you try to install the Hyper-V server role on a computer that does not meet the CPU requirements, you'll get a warning window that looks like Figure 3.1.

FIGURE 3.1
Warning window that
Hyper-V cannot
be installed

Install the Hyper-V Role

Now it's time to see how to install the Hyper-V server role on the two installation options of Windows Server 2022, namely, a Full installation and a Server Core installation.

INSTALLING HYPER-V IN FULL INSTALLATION MODE

You can install the Hyper-V server role on any Windows Server 2022 installation for which the Full option was chosen. In addition, the server must meet both the hardware and software requirements. The installation process is simple, as exercise 3.1 demonstrates.

EXERCISE 3.1:   Installing Hyper-V in Full Installation Mode

1. Open Server Manager.

2. In Server Manager, choose option 2, Add Roles And Features.

3. At the Select Installation Type page, choose the role-based or feature-based installation. Click Next.

4. On the Select Destination Server screen, choose Select A Server From The Server Pool and choose the server to which you want to add this role. Click Next.

5. On the Select Server Roles screen, click the check box next to Hyper-V (see Figure 3.2). When the Add Features dialog box appears, click the Add Features button. Then click Next.

FIGURE 3.2
Server Manager
Add Features

6. At the Select Features screen, click Next.

7. At the Hyper-V introduction screen, click Next.

8. At the Create Virtual Switches screen (see Figure 3.3), choose your adapter and click Next.

FIGURE 3.3
Virtual Switch Screen

9. At the Virtual Machine Migration screen, click Next. You want to use migration only if you have multiple Hyper-V servers. Since we will have only one for this exercise, just skip this screen.

10. At the Default Stores screen, accept the defaults and click Next.

11. At the Confirmation screen, click the Install button.

12. After the installation is complete, click the Close button.

13. Restart your server.

INSTALLING HYPER-V IN SERVER CORE

The Server Core installation option is included in Windows Server 2022. It creates an operating system installation without a GUI shell. You can either manage the server remotely from another system or use the Server Core's command-line interface.

This installation option provides the following benefits:

- Reduces attack surface (because fewer applications are running on the server)

- Reduces maintenance and management (because only the required options are installed)

- Requires less disk space and produces less processor utilization

- Provides a minimal parent partition

- Reduces system resources required by the operating system as well as the attack surface

By using Hyper-V on a Server Core installation, you can fundamentally improve availability because the attack surface is reduced and the downtime required for installing patches is optimized. It will thus be more secure and reliable with less management.

To install Hyper-V for a Windows Server 2022 installation, you must execute the following command in the command-line interface:

```
Dism /online /enable-feature /featurename:Microsoft-Hyper-V
```

Hyper-V in Server Manager

As with all of the other Windows Server 2022 roles, the Hyper-V role neatly integrates into Server Manager. Server Manager filters the information just for the specific role and thus displays only the required information. As you can see in Figure 3.4, the Hyper-V Summary page shows related event log entries, the state of the system services for Hyper-V, and useful resources and support.

FIGURE 3.4
Hyper-V in
Server Manager

Using Hyper-V Manager

Hyper-V Manager is the central management console to configure your server and create and manage your virtual machines, virtual networks, and virtual hard disks. Unlike Virtual Server 2005, where you managed all virtual machines through a web interface, Hyper-V Manager is managed through a Microsoft Management Console (MMC) snap-in. You can access it either in Server Manager or by using Administrative Tools ➤ Hyper-V Manager. Figure 3.5 shows how Hyper-V Manager looks once you start it.

Hyper-V Manager is available for the following current operating systems:

◆ Windows Server 2022

◆ Windows Server 2016

◆ Windows Server 2012 R2

◆ Windows Server 2012

◆ Windows 10 / Windows 11

◆ Windows Server 2019

FIGURE 3.5
Hyper-V Manager

You can use Hyper-V Manager to connect to any Full or Server Core installation remotely. Besides Hyper-V Manager, you can use the WMI interface for scripting Hyper-V.

Configure Hyper-V Settings

In this section, you will get an overview of the available Hyper-V settings for the server. You configure all server-side default configuration settings like default locations of your configuration files or the release key. You can open the Hyper-V Settings page (see Figure 3.6) in Hyper-V Manager by clicking Hyper-V Settings in the Actions pane.

The Hyper-V Settings page includes the following settings:

Virtual Hard Disks   Specifies the default location of your virtual hard disk files (.vhd and .vdhx).

Virtual Machines   Specifies the default location of your virtual machine configuration files. It includes the Virtual Machine XML configuration files (part of the Virtual Machines folder) as well as related snapshots (part of the Snapshot folder).

Physical GPUs   This feature allows for graphical processing unit (GPU) accelerated video within a virtual machine. The GPU will allow you to support 3D GPU accelerated graphics.

NUMA Spanning   An administrator can configure Hyper-V to allow virtual machines to span nonuniform memory architecture (NUMA) nodes. When the physical computer has NUMA nodes, this setting provides virtual machines with additional computing resources. Spanning NUMA nodes can help you run more virtual machines at the same time. However, using NUMA can decrease overall performance.

Live Migrations   *Live migration* allows a Hyper-V administrator to relocate running virtual machines easily from one node of the failover cluster to another node in the same cluster.

FIGURE 3.6
Hyper-V Settings

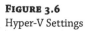

Storage Migrations *Storage Migration* allows an administrator to move their virtual machine storage from one location to another. This setting allows you to specify how many storage migrations can be performed at the same time on this system.

Replication Configuration This setting allows you to configure this computer as a Replica Server to another Hyper-V server. Hyper-V Replica allows administrators to replicate their Hyper-V virtual machines from one Hyper-V host at a primary site to another Hyper-V host at the Replica site. Each node of the failover cluster that is involved in Replica must have the Hyper-V server role installed. One of the servers in the Hyper-V replication needs to be set up as a Replica Broker to allow the replication to work properly.

Keyboard Defines how to use Windows key combinations. Options are Physical Computer, Virtual Machine, and Virtual Machine Only When Running Full Screen.

Mouse Release Key Specifies the key combination to release the mouse in your virtual machine. Options are Ctrl+Alt+left arrow, Ctrl+Alt+right arrow, Ctrl+Alt+space, and Ctrl+Alt+Shift.

Reset Check Boxes Resets any check boxes that hide pages and messages when checked. This will bring any window up again on which you checked the Do Not Show This Window Again check box.

Manage Virtual Switches

A *virtual network* provides the virtual links between nodes in either a virtual or physical network. Virtual networking in Hyper-V is provided in a secure and dynamic way because you can granularly define virtual network switches for their required usage. For example, you can define a private or internal virtual network if you don't want to allow your virtual machines to send packages to the physical network.

To allow your virtual machines to communicate with each other, you need virtual networks. Just like normal networks, virtual networks exist only on the host computer and allow you to configure how virtual machines communicate with each other, with the host, and with the network or the Internet. You manage virtual networks in Hyper-V using Virtual Switch Manager, as shown in Figure 3.7.

FIGURE 3.7
Virtual Switch Manager

Using *Virtual Switch Manager*, you can create, manage, and delete virtual switches. You can define the network type as external, internal only, or private.

External   Any virtual machine connected to this virtual switch can access the physical network. You would use this option if you want to allow your virtual machines to access, for example, other servers on the network or the Internet. This option is used in production environments where your clients connect directly to the virtual machines.

Internal   This option allows virtual machines to communicate with each other as well as the host system but not with the physical network. When you create an internal network, it also creates a local area connection in Network Connections that allows the host machine to communicate with the virtual machines. You can use this if you want to separate your host's network from your virtual networks.

Private   When you use this option, virtual machines can communicate with each other but not with the host system or the physical network; thus, no network packets are hitting the wire. You can use this to define internal virtual networks for test environments or labs, for example.

On the external and internal-only virtual networks, you also can enable virtual LAN (VLAN) identification. You can use VLANs to partition your network into multiple subnets using a VLAN ID. When you enable virtual LAN identification, the NIC that is connected to the switch will never see packets tagged with VLAN IDs. Instead, all packets traveling from the NIC to the switch will be tagged with the access mode VLAN ID as they leave the switch port. All packets traveling from the switch port to the NIC will have their VLAN tags removed. You can use this if you are already logically segmenting your physical machines and also use it for your virtual ones.

Exercise 3.2 explains how to create an internal-only virtual switch.

EXERCISE 3.2:   Creating an Internal Virtual Network

1. Click the Windows Key ➤ Administrative Tools ➤ Hyper-V Manager.
2. In Hyper-V Manager, in the Actions pane, choose Virtual Switch Manager.
3. On the Virtual Switch page, select Private and click the Create Virtual Switch button.
4. On the New Virtual Switch page, enter **Private Virtual Network** in the Name field.
5. Click OK.

When you create the internal virtual switch, a network device is created in Network Connections, as shown in Figure 3.8.

This is also the case when you create an external virtual network because it will replace the physical network card of the host machine to give the parent partition a virtual network card that is also used in the child partitions.

Unlike with Virtual Server 2005, Hyper-V binds the virtual network service to a physical network adapter only when an external virtual network is created. The benefit of this is that the performance is better if you do not use the external virtual network option. The downside, however, is that there will be a network disruption when you create or delete an external virtual network.

NOTE   Communication between the virtual machine and the local host computer is not configured automatically. Once you install a virtual machine, you need to make sure that the TCP/IP settings are in agreement with the set things you define in the virtual network card. Start with a ping from your host machine to the virtual machines to verify that communication is working.

Managing Virtual Hard Disks

In addition to virtual networks, you need to manage virtual hard disks that you attach to your virtual machines. A virtual hard disk in Hyper-V, apart from a pass-through disk, is a VHD or VHDX file that basically simulates a hard drive on your virtual machine.

The following sections will first show you what types of virtual hard disks are available and then show you how to create them. You will also learn about what options are available to manage virtual hard disks.

TYPES OF HARD DISKS

Depending on how you want to use the disk, Hyper-V offers various types, as described in Table 3.2.

TABLE 3.2:   Virtual Hard Disks in Hyper-V

TYPE OF DISK	DESCRIPTION	WHEN TO USE IT
Dynamically expanding	This disk starts with a small VHD file and expands it on demand once an installation takes place. It can grow to the maximum size you defined during creation. You can use this type of disk to clone a local hard drive during creation.	This option is effective when you don't know the exact space needed on the disk and when you want to preserve hard disk space on the host machine. Unfortunately, it is the slowest disk type.
Fixed size	The size of the VHD file is fixed to the size specified when the disk is created. This option is faster than a dynamically expanding disk. However, a fixed-size disk uses up the maximum defined space immediately. This type is ideal for cloning a local hard drive.	A fixed-size disk provides faster access than dynamically expanding or differencing disks, but it is slower than a physical disk.
Differencing	This type of disk is associated in a parent-child relationship with another disk. The differencing disk is the child, and the associated virtual disk is the parent. Differencing disks include only the differences to the parent disk. By using this type, you can save a lot of disk space in similar virtual machines. This option is suitable if you have multiple virtual machines with similar operating systems.	Differencing disks are most commonly found in test environments and should not be used in production environments.
Physical (or pass-through disk)	The virtual machine receives direct pass-through access to the physical disk for exclusive use. This type provides the highest performance of all disk types and thus should be used for production servers where performance is the top priority. The drive is not available for other guest systems.	This type is used in high-end datacenters to provide optimum performance for VMs. It's also used in failover cluster environments.

CREATING VIRTUAL HARD DISKS

To help you gain practice in creating virtual hard disks, the following three exercises will teach you how to create a differencing hard disk, how to clone an existing disk by creating a new disk, and how to configure a physical or pass-through disk to your virtual machine. First, in Exercise 3.3, you will learn how to create a differencing virtual hard disk.

EXERCISE 3.3: Creating a Differencing Hard Disk

1. Open Hyper-V Manager.

2. In Hyper-V Manager, on the Actions pane, choose New ➤ Hard Disk.

3. In the New Virtual Hard Disk Wizard, click Next on the Before You Begin page.

4. At the Choose Disk Format screen, choose VHDX and click Next. The size of your VHDs depends on which format you choose. If you're going to have a VHD larger than 2,040GB, use VHDX. If your VHD is less than 2,040GB, then you should use VHD.

5. On the Choose Disk Type page, select Fixed Size and click Next.

6. On the Specify Name And Location page, enter the new name of the child disk (for example, newvirtualharddisk.vhd). You can also modify the default location of the new VHD file if you want. Click Next to continue.

7. Next, on the Configure Disk page, you need to specify the size of the VHD file. Choose a size based on your hard disk and then click Next to continue. I used 60GB as our test size.

8. On the Completing The New Virtual Hard Disk Wizard page, verify that all settings are correct and click Finish to create the hard disk.

The process to add a physical or pass-through disk to a virtual machine is quite different. For this, first you need to create the virtual machine, and then you open the virtual machine settings to configure the physical disk. If you want to add a physical disk to a virtual machine, the physical disk must be set as Offline in Disk Management, as shown in Figure 3.9.

FIGURE 3.9
In Disk Management, you can set disks as Offline.

To access Disk Management, click the Windows key, choose Administrative Tools ➤ Computer Management, expand Storage in the left pane, and click Disk Management.

NOTE You cannot share a physical disk among multiple virtual machines or with the host system.

Physical or pass-through disks might not be that important if your use of virtualization is based on test environments, but they become crucial when you need to plan for highly available virtual datacenters. This is especially true if you consider using failover clusters to provide the Quick Migration feature, which is when you should consider matching one logical unit number (LUN) from your enterprise storage system or storage area network (SAN) as one physical disk. This provides you with the optimum performance you need in such an environment.

MANAGING VIRTUAL HARD DISKS

Hyper-V also provides two tools to manage virtual hard disks: Inspect Disk and Edit Disk. These tools are available on the Actions pane in Hyper-V Manager.

Inspect Disk   This provides you with information about the virtual hard disk. It shows you not only the type of the disk but also information such as the maximum size for dynamically expanding disks and the parent VHD for differencing disks.

Edit Disk   This provides you with the Edit Virtual Hard Disk Wizard, which you can use to compact, convert, expand, merge, or reconnect hard disks. Figure 3.10 shows you the wizard's options when you select a dynamically expanding disk.

FIGURE 3.10
The Edit Virtual Hard
Disk Wizard

Table 3.3 provides you with an overview of what you can do with the wizard.

TABLE 3.3:   Edit Disk Overview

ACTION	DESCRIPTION
Compact	Reduces the size of a dynamically expanding or differencing disk by removing blank space from deleted files.
Convert	Converts a dynamically expanding disk to a fixed disk or vice versa.
Expand	Increases the storage capacity of a dynamically expanding disk or a fixed virtual hard disk.
Merge	Merges the changes from a differencing disk into either the parent disk or another disk (applies to differencing disks only!).
Reconnect	If a differencing disk no longer finds its referring parent disk, this option can reconnect the parent to the disk.

GENERATION 1 VS. GENERATION 2 VHDs

Previous versions of Hyper-V had some pretty major drawbacks. One big drawback was that Hyper-V could not boot a virtual machine from a virtual hard drive that was SCSI. Believe it or not, SCSI controllers were not even recognized by Hyper-V unless you installed the Integration Services component.

Another issue that the previous versions of Hyper-V had was the inability to copy files from the Hyper-V host to the virtual machines without the use of a network connection in the virtual machine. The older versions of Hyper-V, prior to Windows Server 2016, are now considered generation 1 versions. Why is it so important to know which generations of Hyper-V you should use or need to use?

Hyper-V generations help determine what functionality and what virtual hardware you can use in your virtual machine. Windows Server 2022 Hyper-V supports both virtual machine generations: generation 1 and generation 2.

As already explained, previous versions of Hyper-V are considered generation 1, and this provides the same virtual hardware to the virtual machine as in previous versions of Hyper-V.

Generation 2 is included with Windows Server 2022, and it provides better functionality on the virtual machines, including Secure Boot (which is enabled by default), the ability to boot from a SCSI virtual hard disk or boot from a SCSI virtual DVD, the ability to use a standard network adapter to PXE boot, and Unified Extensible Firmware Interface (UEFI) firmware support. Generation 2 now gives you the ability to support UEFI firmware instead of BIOS-based firmware. On a virtual machine that is Generation 2, you can configure Secure Boot, Enable TPM, and set security policies by clicking on the Security section of the virtual machines properties.

So, when you create VHDs in Windows Server 2022, one of your choices will be the ability to create the VHDs as a generation 1 or generation 2 VHDs. If you need the ability to have your VHDs run on older versions of Hyper-V, make them generation 1 VHDs. If they are going to run only on Windows Server 2012 R2 and above, make your VHDs generation 2 and take advantage of all the new features and functionality.

Configuring Virtual Machines

The following sections cover the topics of creating and managing virtual machines as well as how to back up and restore virtual machines using features such as Import and Export and Snapshot.

Creating and Managing Virtual Machines

It is important to learn how to create a virtual machine, how to change its configuration, and how to delete it. You will take a look at the Virtual Machine Connection tool and install the Hyper-V Integration Components onto a virtual machine.

VIRTUAL MACHINES

Virtual machines define the child partitions in which you run operating system instances. Each virtual machine is separate and can communicate with the others only by using a virtual network. You can assign hard drives, virtual networks, DVD drives, and other system components to it. A virtual machine is similar to an existing physical server, but it no longer runs on dedicated hardware—it shares the hardware of the host system with the other virtual machines that run on the host.

Exercise 3.4 shows you how to create a new virtual machine. Before completing this exercise, download an eval copy of Windows Server from Microsoft's website (`www.microsoft.com/downloads`). Make sure the file downloaded is an image file (`.iso`). You will use this image to install the operating system into the virtual machine.

EXERCISE 3.4:   Creating a New Virtual Machine

1. Open Hyper-V Manager (see Figure 3.11).

FIGURE 3.11
Hyper-V Manager

2. In Hyper-V Manager, on the Actions pane, choose New ➤ Virtual Machine.

3. In the New Virtual Machine Wizard, click Next on the Before You Begin page.

4. On the Specify Name And Location page, give your virtual machine a name and change the default location of the virtual machine configuration files. Click Next to continue.

5. The Specify Generation screen is next. Choose Generation 2 (see Figure 3.12) and click Next.

FIGURE 3.12
Specify Generation
Screen

6. On the Assign Memory page (see Figure 3.13), define how much of your host computer's memory you want to assign to this virtual machine. Remember that once your virtual machine uses up all of your physical memory, it will start swapping to disk, thus reducing the performance of all virtual machines. Click Next to continue.

7. On the Configure Networking page (see Figure 3.14), select the virtual network that you previously configured using Virtual Network Manager. Click Next to continue.

8. On the next page, you configure your virtual hard disk (see Figure 3.15). You can create a new virtual hard disk, select an existing disk, or choose to attach the hard disk later. Be aware that you can create only a dynamically expanding virtual disk on this page; you cannot create a differencing, physical, or fixed virtual hard disk there. However, if you created the virtual hard disk already, you can, of course, select it. Click Next to continue.

FIGURE 3.13
VM RAM

FIGURE 3.14
Configure
Networking Page

FIGURE 3.15
Virtual Hard
Disk Page

9. On the Installation Options page (see Figure 3.16), you can select how you want to install your operating system. You have the option to install an operating system later, install the operating system from a boot CD/DVD-ROM where you can select a physical device or an image file (ISO file), install an operating system from a floppy disk image (VFD file, or a virtual boot floppy disk), or install an operating system from a network-based installation server. The last option will install a legacy network adapter to your virtual machine so that you can boot from the network adapter. Select Install An Operating System from a bootable CD/DVD-ROM and choose Image File (.iso). Then click Next.

FIGURE 3.16
Installing OS screen

10. On the Completing The New Virtual Machine Wizard summary page (see Figure 3.17), verify that all settings are correct. You also have the option to start the virtual machine immediately after creation. Click Next to create the virtual machine.

FIGURE 3.17
Completing the New
Virtual Machine
Wizard screen

11. Repeat this process and create a few more virtual machines.

After completing Exercise 3.4, you will have a virtual machine available in Hyper-V Manager. Initially, the state of the virtual machine will be Off. Virtual machines can have the following states: Off, Starting, Running, Paused, and Saved. You can change the state of a virtual machine in the Virtual Machines pane by right clicking the virtual machine's name, as shown in Figure 3.18, or by using the Virtual Machine Connection window.

FIGURE 3.18
Options available when
right clicking a
virtual machine

Here is a list of some of the state options (when the VM is running) available for a virtual machine:

Start   Turn on the virtual machine. This is similar to pressing the power button when the machine is turned off. This option is available when your virtual machine is Off or in Saved state.

Turn Off   Turn off the virtual machine. This is similar to pressing the power-off button on the computer. This option is available when your virtual machine is in Running, Saved, or Paused state.

Shut Down   This option shuts down your operating system. You need to have the Hyper-V Integration Components installed on the operating system; otherwise, Hyper-V will not be able to shut down the system.

Save   The virtual machine is saved to disk in its current state. This option is available when your virtual machine is in Running or Paused state.

Pause   Pause the current virtual machine, but do not save the state to disk. You can use this option to release processor utilization quickly from this virtual machine to the host system.

Reset   Reset the virtual machine. This is like pressing the reset button on your computer. You will lose the current state and any unsaved data in the virtual machine. This option is available when your virtual machine is in Running or Paused state.

Resume   When your virtual machine is paused, you can resume it and bring it online again.

CHANGING CONFIGURATION ON AN EXISTING VIRTUAL MACHINE

To change the configuration settings on an existing virtual machine, you right-click your virtual machine's name in the Virtual Machines pane in Hyper-V Manager and choose Settings. You can change settings such as memory allocation and hard drive configuration. All items that you can configure are described in the following list:

Add Hardware   Add devices to your virtual machine, namely, a SCSI controller, a network adapter, or a legacy network adapter. A legacy network adapter is required if you want to perform a network-based installation of an operating system.

BIOS   This is the replacement of the virtual machine's BIOS. Because you can no longer enter the BIOS during startup, you need to configure it with this setting. You can turn Num Lock on or off and change the basic startup order of the devices.

Memory   Change the amount of random access memory (RAM) allocated to the virtual machine.

Processor   Change the number of logical processors this virtual machine can use and define resource control to balance resources among virtual machines by using a relative weight.

IDE Controller   Add/change and remove devices from the IDE controller. You can have hard drives or DVD drives as devices. Every IDE controller can have up to two devices attached, and by default, you have two IDE controllers available.

Hard Drive   Select a controller to attach to this device as well as to specify the media to use with your virtual hard disk. The available options are Virtual Hard Disk File (with additional buttons labeled New, Edit, Inspect, and Browse that are explained in the virtual hard disk section) and Physical Hard Disk. You can also remove the device here.

DVD Drive   Select a controller to attach to this device and specify the media to use with your virtual CD/DVD drive. The available options are None, Image File (ISO Image), and Physical CD/DVD Drive Connected To The Host Computer. You also can remove the device here.

SCSI Controller   Configure all hard drives that are connected to the SCSI controller. You can add up to 63 hard drives to each SCSI controller, and you can have multiple SCSI controllers available.

Network Adapter   Specify the configuration of the network adapter or remove it. You can also configure the virtual network and MAC address for each adapter and enable virtual LAN identification. The network adapter section also allows you to control Bandwidth Management.

Bandwidth Management allows an administrator to specify how the network adapter will utilize network bandwidth. Administrators have the ability to set a minimum network bandwidth that a network adapter can use and a maximum bandwidth. This gives administrators greater control over how much bandwidth a virtual network adapter can use.

COM1 and COM2   Configure the virtual COM port to communicate with the physical computer through a named pipe. You have COM1 and COM2 available.

Diskette   Specify a virtual floppy disk file to use.

Name   Edit the name of the virtual machine and provide some notes about it.

Integration Services   Define what integration services are available to your virtual machine. Options are Operating System Shutdown, Time Synchronization, Data Exchange, Heartbeat, and Backup (Volume Snapshot).

Snapshot File Location   Define the default file location of your snapshot files.

Smart Paging File Location   This area allows you to set up a paging file for your virtual machine. Windows Server 2022 has a Hyper-V feature called *Smart Paging*. If you have a virtual machine that has a smaller amount of memory than what it needs for startup memory, when the virtual machine gets restarted, Hyper-V then needs additional memory to restart the virtual machine. Smart Paging is used to bridge the memory gap between minimum memory and startup memory. This allows your virtual machines to restart properly.

Automatic Start   Define what this virtual machine will do when the physical computer starts. Options are Nothing, Automatically Start If The Service Was Running, and Always Start This Virtual Machine. You also can define a start delay here.

Automatic Stop   Define what this virtual machine will do when the physical computer shuts down. Options are Save State, Turn Off, and Shut Down.

NOTE Please be aware that only some settings can be changed when the virtual machine's state is Running. It is best practice to shut down the virtual machine before you modify any setting.

DELETING VIRTUAL MACHINES

You can also delete virtual machines using Hyper-V Manager. This deletes all of the configuration files, as shown in Figure 3.19.

FIGURE 3.19
Delete Virtual Machine
warning window

Make sure you manually delete any virtual disks that were part of the virtual machines to free up disk space. Virtual disks are *not* deleted when you delete a virtual machine.

VIRTUAL MACHINE CONNECTION

Similar to the Virtual Machine Remote Control (VMRC) client that was available with Virtual Server 2005 R2 and previous versions, Hyper-V comes with Virtual Machine Connection to connect to virtual machines that run on a local or remote server.

You can use it to log onto the virtual machine and use your computer's mouse and keyboard to interact with the virtual machine. You can open Virtual Machine Connection in Hyper-V Manager by double-clicking a virtual machine or by right-clicking a virtual machine and selecting Connect. If your virtual machine is turned off, you might see a window similar to the one in Figure 3.20.

Virtual Machine Connection not only provides you with functionality similar to that of Hyper-V Manager, such as being able to change the state of a virtual machine, but it also provides you with additional features that are especially useful when you want to work with a virtual machine.

File Access Settings or Exit Virtual Machine Connection Change the state of a virtual machine and create or revert a snapshot. Additionally, you have the options to send Ctrl+Alt+Delete to your virtual machine and Insert Integration Services Setup Disk.

Context-Sensitive Buttons Provide Quick Access to Key Features These buttons are available under the menu bar to provide you with fast access to the most important features. It will show an administrator the connection of a running VM.

FIGURE 3.20
Virtual Machine
Connection window
when the machine is
turned off

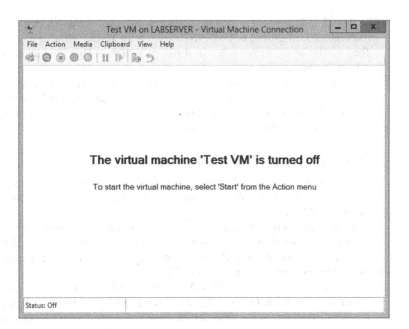

NIC TEAMING

NIC Teaming, also known as load balancing and failover (LBFO), gives an administrator the ability to allow multiple network adapters on a system to be placed into a team. Independent hardware vendors (IHVs) have required NIC Teaming, but until Windows Server 2012, NIC Teaming was *not* part of the Windows Server operating system.

To be able to use NIC Teaming, the computer system must have at least one Ethernet adapter. If you want to provide fault protection, an administrator must have a minimum of two Ethernet adapters. One advantage of Windows Server 2022 is that an administrator can set up 32 network adapters in a NIC team.

NIC Teaming is a common practice when setting up virtualization. This is one way that you can have load balancing with Hyper-V.

NIC Teaming gives an administrator the ability to allow a virtual machine to use virtual network adapters in Hyper-V. The advantage of using NIC Teaming in Hyper-V is that the administrator can use NIC Teaming to connect to more than one Hyper-V switch. This allows Hyper-V still to have connectivity even if the network adapter under the Hyper-V switch gets disconnected.

An administrator can configure NIC Teaming in either Server Manager or PowerShell. NIC teaming can be configured in different configuration models including Switch Independent or Switch Dependent.

Switch Independent means the switch is unaware of the NIC team and the NIC team is responsible for figuring out how to distribute the traffic without the switch's help or knowledge. They can be on the same switch or different switches. They do have to be in the same vlan/subnet/broadcast domain.

Switch Dependent means that the switch determines how to distribute traffic. They can be on the same switch or in a multi-chassis switch with a shared ID between the various chassis.

If you use Switch Independent NIC Teaming, your NICs can be on different switches but both switch ports must be on the same subnet.

REMOTE DIRECT MEMORY ACCESS

When most of us think of Hyper-V, we think of a group of virtual machines sharing access to a systems resource. With Windows Server 2022, Hyper-V includes Remote Direct Memory Access (RDMA).

RDMA allows one computer to directly access memory from the memory of another computer without the need of interfacing with either one's operating system. This gives systems the ability to have high throughput and low-latency networking. This is very useful when it comes to clustering systems (including Hyper-V).

Windows Server 2012 R2 RDMA services couldn't be bound to a Hyper-V Virtual Switch and because of this, Remote Direct Memory Access and Hyper-V had to be on the same computer as the network adapters. Because of this, there was a need for a higher number of physical network adapters that were required to be installed on the Hyper-V host.

Because of the improvements of RDMA on Windows Server 2022, administrators can use less network adapters while using RDMA.

SWITCH EMBEDDED TEAMING

Earlier we discussed NIC Teaming but we also have the ability to do Switch Embedded Teaming (SET). SET can be an alternative to using NIC Teaming in environments that include Hyper-V and the Software Defined Networking (SDN) stack in Windows Server 2022. SET is available in all versions of Windows Server 2022 that include Hyper-V and SDN stack.

SET does use some of the functionality of NIC Teaming into the Hyper-V Virtual Switch, but SET allows an administrator to combine a group of physical adapters (minimum of 1 adapter and a maximum of 8 adapters) into software based virtual adapters.

By using virtual adapters, you get better performance and greater fault tolerance in the event of a network adapter going bad. For SET to be enabled, all of the physical network adapters must be installed on the same physical Hyper-V host.

One of the requirements of SET is that all network adapters that are members of the SET group be identical adapters. This means that they need to be the same adapter types from the same manufacturers.

One main difference between NIC Teaming and Set is that SET only supports Switch Independent mode setups. Again, this means that Switch Independent mode means the NICs control the teaming. They could be on the same or different switches.

Administrators need to create a SET team at the same time that they create the Hyper-V Virtual Switch. Administrators can do this by using the Windows PowerShell command `New-VMSwitch`.

At the time an administrator creates a Hyper-V Virtual Switch, the administrator needs to include the EnableEmbeddedTeaming parameter in their command syntax. The following example shows a Hyper-V switch named StormSwitch:

```
New-VMSwitch -Name StormSwitch -NetAdapterName "NIC 1","NIC 2" -
EnableEmbeddedTeaming $true
```

Administrators also have the ability to remove a SET team by using the following PowerShell command. This example removes a Virtual Switch named StormSwitch.

```
Remove-VMSwitch "StormSwitch"
```

STORAGE QUALITY OF SERVICE

Windows Server 2022 Hyper-V includes a feature called *Storage Quality of Service (QoS)*. Storage QoS allows a Hyper-V administrator to manage how virtual machines access storage throughput for virtual hard disks.

Storage QoS gives an administrator the ability to guarantee that the storage throughput of a single VHD cannot adversely affect the performance of another VHD on the same host. It does this by giving administrators the ability to specify the maximum and minimum I/O loads based on I/O operations per second (IOPS) for each virtual disk in your virtual machines.

To configure Storage QoS, you would set the maximum IOPS values (or limits) and set the minimum values (or reserves) on virtual hard disks for virtual machines.

NOTE   If you are using shared virtual hard disks, Storage QoS will not be available.

INSTALLING HYPER-V INTEGRATION COMPONENTS

Hyper-V *Integration Components*, also called *Integration Services*, are required to make your guest operating system hypervisor-aware. Similar to the VM Additions that were part of Microsoft Virtual Server 2005, these components improve the performance of the guest operating system once they are installed. From an architectural perspective, virtual devices are redirected directly via the VMBus; thus, quicker access to resources and devices is provided.

If you do not install the Hyper-V Integration Components, the guest operating system uses emulation to communicate with the host's devices, which of course makes the guest operating system slower.

Exercise 3.5 shows you how to install Hyper-V Integration Components on one of your virtual machines running Windows Server 2022.

EXERCISE 3.5: Installing Hyper-V Integration Components

1. Open Hyper-V Manager.

2. In Hyper-V Manager, in the Virtual Machines pane, right-click the virtual machine on which you want to install Hyper-V Integration Components and click Start.

3. Right-click the virtual machine again and click Connect. Meanwhile, your virtual machine should already be booting.

4. If you need to log into the operating system of your virtual machine, you should do so.

5. Starting with Windows Server 2016, integration services aren't installed via an emulated floppy like it was prior to Windows Server 2016. Instead, they are installed as a windows update. So now that the virtual machine is set up, do your updates on the Hyper-V host along with the updates for the Hyper-V guest. After you reboot, integration components should now be installed and ready to go.

Linux and FreeBSD Image Deployments

As explained in Chapter 2, one of the features of Windows 2022 is the ability for Hyper-V to support Linux and FreeBSD virtual machines. Hyper-V now can support these new virtual machines because Hyper-V has the ability to emulate Linux and FreeBSD devices. Because Hyper-V now has the ability to emulate these two devices, no additional software needs to be installed on Hyper-V.

Unfortunately, because Hyper-V has to emulate these devices, you lose some of the Hyper-V functionality like high performance and full management of the virtual machines. So it's a trade-off. You get to run Linux and FreeBSD type Hyper-V virtual machines but you lose some of the benefits of Hyper-V.

But wait; there is a way to get your Hyper-V functionality back. This issue can be resolved as long as you install Hyper-V on machines that can support Linux and FreeBSD operating systems. The drivers that are needed on Hyper-V are called Linux Integration Services (LIS) and FreeBSD Integrated Services (FIS). By putting these drivers on a device that can handle Linux and FreeBSD, you can then have Hyper-V with all of the features Microsoft offers.

To get these drivers and make Hyper-V work will all of its functionality, you must make sure that you install a newer release of Linux that includes LIS. To get the most out of FreeBSD you must get a version after 10.0. For FreeBSD versions that are older than 10.0, Microsoft offers ports that work with BIS drivers that need to be installed. Hyper-V will work with Linux and FreeBSD without the need of any additional drivers or equipment. By having drivers and equipment that supports Linux and FreeBSD, you just get all of the Hyper-V features that your organization may need.

NOTE I have personally installed Kali Linux and Parrot Linux on Windows Server 2022 Hyper-V. So, you have many different options when installing Linux. The installation screens will be different but the installation of these versions of Linux can be easily done. The only issue that I have encountered when installing Kali and Parrot is that I need to choose Generation 1 when installing these versions.

In Exercise 3.6, I will show you how to install Linux into a virtual machine. I will then walk you through a full installation of a Linux Server. Before you complete this lab, you must download a copy of Linux. For this exercise, I downloaded a free copy of Linux Ubuntu as an image file (.iso). If you choose a different version of Linux, the installation screens during the exercise may be different.

EXERCISE 3.6:   Creating a Linux Virtual Machine

1. Open Hyper-V Manager.

2. In the right hand window under Actions, click New ➤ Virtual Machine.

3. At the Before You Begin screen, just choose Next.

4. At the Specify Name And Location screen, Enter in the name of the Linux virtual machine and the location you would like to store the virtual machine files. Then click Next.

5. At the Generation screen, choose Generation 2 and click Next.

6. At the Assign Memory screen, enter the amount of memory you want to allocate to this virtual machine. I am using 12GB (12000MB). Click Next.

7. Choose which network connection you want to use and click Next.

8. At the Connect Virtual Hard Disk screen, choose Create a virtual hard disk. Set the location of where you want the files to reside and also how much space you want to use (I chose 127GB). Click Next.

9. At the Installation Options screen, choose Install an Operating system from a bootable image file and point to your Linux .iso download. Click Next.

10. At the Completing the New Virtual Machine Wizard screen, make sure all of the settings are correct and choose Finish.

11. After the virtual machine was created, click on the virtual machine and on the right side under Linux, click Start.

12. When the Linux install starts, click your Language.

13. At the Ubuntu menu, choose Install Ubuntu Server.

14. Again, you will need to choose your language for the install.

15. Choose your country.

16. On the detect keyboard layout, choose No. Choose your keyboard (ours is US Normal). The installation will Continue.

17. Next you will choose a hostname. I am keeping the default of Ubuntu. Click Continue.

18. Enter your user account (full name) and click Continue.

19. Enter your username. First name is fine and click Continue.

20. Type in your password and click Continue. Do not choose to show your password in clear. You will then be asked to re-enter your password and click Continue.

21. When it asks you to encrypt your home directory, choose No.

22. The install will try to figure out your time zone. If it picks correct, chose Yes. If it doesn't, choose No and enter your time zone.

23. The next screen will ask you about setting up a Partition disk. I am going to allow Linux to configure the disk (Guided) and I will allow it to use the entire drive with a Logical Volume Manager (LVM). So I am choosing Guided - Use Entire Disk And Set Up LVM.

24. It will then ask about partition type. I am choosing SCSI3.

25. The next screen will verify your choices for partitioning. Choose Yes.

26. It will then verify your disk size and then if you want to continue. Choose the disk size and then choose Yes to continue.

27. The next screen will ask you if you use a Proxy server for internet access. If you use a Proxy, put it in and if you don't, just click Continue.

28. You will be asked about updates for Linux. Choose how you want to do your updates. Since this is a test virtual machine, I am choosing No automatic updates.

29. At the Software selection screen, choose what software you want installed during this process. I chose DNS, Samba File Server, and standard system utilities. Click Continue.

30. At the GRUB boot screen, click Yes to install the GRUB boot loader. This is OK since we have no other operating system on this virtual machine.

31. Once the installation is complete, choose Continue. At this point, Linux will restart and ask you for your login and password. After you enter them, you will be at a Linux prompt.

32. Type shutdown at the prompt to shut down the virtual machine.

Now that we have installed Linux (or FreeBSD), the next step is to help improve the Hyper-V performance. As I stated earlier, this issue will be resolved as long as we install the drivers that are needed on Hyper-V called Linux Integration Services (LIS) and FreeBSD Integrated Services (FIS). By putting these drivers on a device that can handle Linux and FreeBSD, you can then have Hyper-V with all of the features Microsoft offers.

NOTE Depending on what version of Linux or FreeBSD that you installed, you will need to download some additional updates to get the best performance out of Hyper-V. The following Microsoft website has a list of links for the different versions of Linux and FreeBSD updates. https://docs .microsoft.com/en-us/windows-server/virtualization/hyper-v/ Supported-Linux-and-FreeBSD-virtual-machines-for-Hyper-V-on-Windows.

In Exercise 3.7, I will show you how to install the additional updates needed for the Linux Ubuntu version (20.10) that I installed in Exercise 3.6.

EXERCISE 3.7: Updating Linux Ubuntu 20.10

1. Open Hyper-V Manager.

2. Start the Linux virtual machine by clicking on the Linux virtual machine and clicking Start on the right-hand menu.

3. At the Ubuntu login, enter the login and password that you created in Exercise 3.6.

4. Since we are using Ubuntu 20.10, we need to install the latest virtual kernel to have up-to-date Hyper-V capabilities. To install the virtual HWE kernel, run the following commands as root (or sudo):

```
sudo apt-get update
```

5. You will be asked for your password. Enter your password.

6. Next type in the following command:

```
sudo apt-get install linux-image-virtual
```

7. You will be asked to confirm your choice by typing Y and hit enter.

8. Type in the following command;

```
sudo apt-get install linux-tools-virtual linux-cloud-tools-virtual
```

9. You will be asked to confirm your choice by typing Y and hit enter.

10. After everything is installed, you are ready to go. You can clear the screen by typing Clear and hit enter. To shut down the system, type shutdown.

Finally, if you want to setup the Linux or FreeBSD virtual machines to use the advantages of secure boot, you would need to run the following PowerShell command on the Hyper-V server:

```
Set-VMFirmware -VMName "VMname" -EnableSecureBoot Off
```

PowerShell Commands

One of the things that Microsoft has stated is that the exams are going to be more PowerShell intensive. So, I wanted to add a PowerShell section showing the different PowerShell commands that you can use for Hyper-V. This table has been taken directly from Microsoft's website. Table 3.4 explains just some of the PowerShell commands that you can use with Hyper-V.

NOTE This table shows you just some of the PowerShell commands for Hyper-V. To see a more comprehensive list, please visit Microsoft's website at https://docs.microsoft.com/en-us/powershell/module/hyper-v/?view=win10-ps.

TABLE 3.4: Hyper-V PowerShell commands

COMMAND	EXPLANATION
Add-VMDvdDrive	Adds a DVD drive to a virtual machine.
Add-VMHardDiskDrive	Adds a hard disk drive to a virtual machine.
Add-VMMigrationNetwork	Adds a network for virtual machine migration on one or more virtual machine hosts.
Add-VMNetworkAdapter	Adds a virtual network adapter to a virtual machine.

TABLE 3.4:   Hyper-V PowerShell commands (CONTINUED)

COMMAND	EXPLANATION
Add-VMSwitch	Adds a virtual switch to an Ethernet resource pool.
Checkpoint-VM	Creates a checkpoint of a virtual machine.
Convert-VHD	Converts the format, version type, and block size of a virtual hard disk file.
Copy-VMFile	Copies a file to a virtual machine.
Debug-VM	Debugs a virtual machine.
Disable-VMConsoleSupport	Disables keyboard, video, and mouse for virtual machines.
Disable-VMMigration	Disables migration on one or more virtual machine hosts.
Dismount-VHD	Dismounts a virtual hard disk.
Enable-VMConsoleSupport	Enables keyboard, video, and mouse for virtual machines.
Enable-VMMigration	Enables migration on one or more virtual machine hosts.
Enable-VMReplication	Enables replication of a virtual machine.
Enable-VMResourceMetering	Collects resource utilization data for a virtual machine or resource pool.
Export-VM	Exports a virtual machine to disk.
Export-VMSnapshot	Exports a virtual machine checkpoint to disk.
Get-VHD	Gets the virtual hard disk object associated with a virtual hard disk.
Get-VHDSet	Gets information about a VHD set.
Get-VHDSnapshot	Gets information about a checkpoint in a VHD set.
Get-VM	Gets the virtual machines from one or more Hyper-V hosts.
Get-VMDvdDrive	Gets the DVD drives attached to a virtual machine or snapshot.
Get-VMHardDiskDrive	Gets the virtual hard disk drives attached to one or more virtual machines.
Get-VMMemory	Gets the memory of a virtual machine or snapshot.
Get-VMNetworkAdapter	Gets the virtual network adapters of a virtual machine, snapshot, management operating system, or of a virtual machine and management operating system.
Get-VMProcessor	Gets the processor of a virtual machine or snapshot.

TABLE 3.4:   Hyper-V PowerShell commands *(CONTINUED)*

COMMAND	EXPLANATION
Get-VMReplication	Gets the replication settings for a virtual machine.
Get-VMSwitch	Gets virtual switches from one or more virtual Hyper-V hosts.
Merge-VHD	Merges virtual hard disks.
Mount-VHD	Mounts one or more virtual hard disks.
Move-VM	Moves a virtual machine to a new Hyper-V host.
New-VHD	Creates one or more new virtual hard disks.
New-VM	Creates a new virtual machine.
New-VMGroup	Creates a virtual machine group.
New-VMSwitch	Creates a new virtual switch on one or more virtual machine hosts.
Remove-VHDSnapshot	Removes a snapshot from a VHD set file.
Remove-VM	Deletes a virtual machine.
Remove-VMHardDiskDrive	Deletes one or more virtual hard disks (VHDs) from a virtual machine (VM).
Remove-VMNetworkAdapter	Removes one or more virtual network adapters from a virtual machine.
Remove-VMReplication	Removes the replication relationship of a virtual machine.
Remove-VMSan	Removes a virtual storage area network (SAN) from a Hyper-V host.
Remove-VMSwitch	Deletes a virtual switch.
Rename-VM	Renames a virtual machine.
Rename-VMGroup	Renames virtual machine groups.
Resize-VHD	Resizes a virtual hard disk.
Restart-VM	Restarts a virtual machine.
Save-VM	Saves a virtual machine.
Set-VHD	Sets properties associated with a virtual hard disk.
Set-VM	Configures a virtual machine.
Set-VMBios	Configures the BIOS of a Generation 1 virtual machine.
Set-VMMemory	Configures the memory of a virtual machine.

TABLE 3.4: Hyper-V PowerShell commands *(CONTINUED)*

COMMAND	EXPLANATION
Set-VMNetworkAdapter	Configures features of the virtual network adapter in a virtual machine or the management operating system.
Set-VMProcessor	Configures one or more processors of a virtual machine.
Set-VMReplicationServer	Configures a host as a Replica server.
Set-VMSan	Configures a virtual storage area network (SAN) on one or more Hyper-V hosts.
Set-VMSwitch	Configures a virtual switch.
Stop-VM	Shuts down, turns off, or saves a virtual machine.
Suspend-VM	Suspends, or pauses, a virtual machine.

The Bottom Line

Know the virtualization requirements.   Understanding server requirements that are needed to install and configure Hyper-V.

Master It   You are an administrator that needs to set up Hyper-V virtualization. You are not sure what features of Hyper-V will need to be configured based on the system's requirements.

Know how to build virtual machines.   Understanding how to build and configure virtual machines is one of the most important tasks when building a virtual network. Understanding how the Hyper-V role works on Windows Server 2022 is important so that when you set up and configure Hyper-V, you understand what is happening within the virtual machines.

Master It   You are an administrator for a mid-size company. Your company has asked you to build and configure new virtual machines using Hyper-V.

Chapter 4

Installing Windows Server 2022

So, now it is to install Windows Server 2022. In this chapter, I will show you how to install Windows Server 2022. I will show you how to install the Desktop (GUI) version of Server 2022 and I will also show you how to install the Server Core version of Server 2022.

I will also show you how to get updates for the Windows Server and then I will show you how to set up a Windows Server Update Services (WSUS). Finally, I will talk about using Features on Demand.

In Chapter 1, "Understanding Windows Server 2022," I showed you the benefits of using Windows Server 2022 along with its features. Now it's time for us to do that installation.

IN THIS CHAPTER YOU'LL LEARN

- ◆ Learn which Server 2022 version to install

- ◆ Understand how to deploy updates

NOTE   The Windows Server 2022 installation can be done on a virtual server. You can use any virtualization software as long as its supports Windows Server 2022 and 64-bit processors. This is the reason I explained virtualization in the previous chapters. I will be installing Windows Server 2022 on Windows Hyper-V. The installation is exactly the same as installing Windows Server 2022 on a physical machine.

Installing the Windows Server 2022 OS

In the following sections, I am going to walk you through two different types of installs. I will show you how to do a full install of Windows Server 2022 Datacenter (Desktop Experience), and then I will show you how to install the Server Core version of the same software.

NOTE   For these labs, I am using the full release of Windows Server 2022 Datacenter, but you can use Windows Server 2022 Standard.

Installing with the Desktop Experience

In Exercise 4.1, I will show you how to install Windows Server 2022 Datacenter (Desktop Experience). This installation will have a Graphical User Interface (GUI) and this means that an administrator will be able to control the applications on the Desktop and the operating system functions with a mouse.

WINDOWS INSTALLATION

At the time of this writing, I used a full release of Windows Server 2022 Datacenter that I down-loaded from my MSDN account. Microsoft is constantly releasing new versions of Windows Server 2022. For this reason, there may be some screens that have changed somewhat since this book was published. But the installation should be very close from what I will do here.

EXERCISE 4.1   Installing Windows Server 2022 Datacenter (Desktop Experience)

1. Insert the Windows Server 2022 installation media and restart the machine. You may be asked to press any key to start the installation.

2. At the first screen, Windows Server 2022 (see Figure 4.1) will ask you to configure your language, time and currency, and keyboard. Make your selections and click Next.

FIGURE 4.1
Windows Server
2022 Setup

3. At the next screen (see Figure 4.2), click the Install now button.

FIGURE 4.2
Install Now Screen

4. Depending on what version of Windows Server 2022 you have (MSDN, TechNet, and so on), you may be asked to enter a product key. If this screen appears, enter your product key and click Next. If this screen does not appear, just go to step 5.

5. The Select The Operating System That You Want To Install screen then appears. Choose the Windows Server 2022 Datacenter (Desktop Experience) selection (see Figure 4.3) and click Next.

FIGURE 4.3
Windows Server Edition

6. The license terms screen appears. After reading the Windows Server 2022 license agreement, check the I Accept The License Terms check box and click Next.

7. On the Which Type Of Installation Do You Want? screen (see Figure 4.4), choose Custom: Install Windows Only (Advanced).

FIGURE 4.4
Windows Server Installation

8. The next screen will ask you where you want to install Windows. If your hard disk is already formatted as NTFS, click the drive and then click Next. If the hard disk is not yet set up or formatted, choose the New link and create a partition. After creating the partition, choose the Primary partition and click the Format link. Once the format is done, make sure you choose the new partition and click Next.

9. The Installing Windows screen will appear next. This is where the files from your media will be installed onto the system (see Figure 4.5). The machine will reboot during this installation.

FIGURE 4.5
Installing Windows screen

10. After the machine is finished rebooting, a screen requesting the administrator password will appear (see Figure 4.6). Type in your password. (P@ssword is used in this exercise. Do NOT use this password in a live environment.) Your password must meet the password complexity requirements (three of the following four are needed for complexity: one capitalized, one lowercase letter, one lower case, one number, and/or one special character). Click Finish.

FIGURE 4.6
Customize
Settings screen

11. Next, log into the system. Press Ctrl+Alt+Del, and type in the administrator password. The machine will set up the properties of the administrator account.

12. Notice that the Server Manager dashboard automatically appears (see Figure 4.7). You may receive a message about using the Windows Admin Center. Just close that message. We will use the Windows Admin Center later in this book. Your Windows Server 2022 installation is now complete.

FIGURE 4.7
Windows Server
Manager Dashboard

13. Close Server Manager.

After you have logged into the Windows Server 2022 Datacenter system, you will notice some features right away. The first is that there is a Start button in the lower-left corner of the screen. We will be using the Start Menu a lot throughout this book.

NOTE Administrators can also access the Start button by clicking the Windows key on a standard keyboard.

So now that we have installed the Windows Server 2022 Datacenter (Desktop version), we are going to install Windows Server 2022 Datacenter Server Core.

Installing Windows Server 2022 Server Core

In Chapter 1, I talked about the difference between the Desktop version and the Server Core version of Windows Server 2022. The Server Core version of server does not have a GUI interface. This means that there are no wizards, Start Menus, or user Desktops. Once the system boots up, you need to use Command Prompt or PowerShell commands to configure the system.

In Exercise 4.2, you will learn how to install Windows Server 2022 Server Core. You'll notice that the steps are similar to the ones in Exercise 4.1, with a couple of exceptions. As mentioned earlier, Server Core is a command-line configuration of Windows Server 2022.

EXERCISE 4.2   Installing Windows Server 2022 Using Server Core

1. Insert the Windows Server 2022 installation media and restart the machine. You may be asked to press any key to start the installation.

2. At the first screen, Windows Server 2022 will prompt you to configure your language, time and currency, and keyboard. Make your selections and click Next.

3. At the next screen, click the Install Now button.

4. Depending on what version of Windows Server 2022 you have (MSDN, TechNet, and so on), you may be asked to enter a product key. If this screen appears, enter your product key and click Next. If this screen does not appear, just go to step 5.

5. The Select The Operating System That You Want To Install screen then appears. Choose the Windows Server 2022 Datacenter selection (see Figure 4.8) and click Next.

6. The license terms screen appears. After reading the Windows Server 2022 license agreement, check the I Accept The License Terms check box and click Next.

7. At the Which Type Of Installation Do You Want? screen, choose Custom: Install Windows Only (Advanced).

8. The next screen will ask you where you want to install Windows. If your hard disk is already formatted as NTFS, click the drive and then click Next. If the hard disk is not set up or formatted, choose the New link and create a partition. After creating the partition, choose the Primary partition and click the Format link. Once the partition is formatted, make sure you choose the new partition and click Next.

9. The Installing Windows screen will appear next. This is where the files from your media will be installed onto the system. The machine will reboot during this installation.

FIGURE 4.8
Windows Server Edition

10. After the machine is finished rebooting, a screen requesting the administrator password will appear. Click on OK (see Figure 4.9) and then type in your password. (P@ssword is used in this exercise. Do NOT use this password in a live environment.) You will be asked to put your password in a second time. Your password must meet the password complexity requirements (one capitalized letter, one lower case, one number, and/or one special character).

FIGURE 4.9
Change Password Screen

11. After the password is changed, a screen will appear telling you that the password has changed (see Figure 4.10). Press the Enter key.

FIGURE 4.10
Password
Changed Screen

12. You will be automatically logged in. You will notice that the command prompt will appear (see Figure 4.11). Your Windows Server 2022 Server Core installation is now complete.

FIGURE 4.11
Server Core
Command Prompt

13. If you want to do a quick configuration of Server Core, type **PowerShell** and press Enter. This will put you into a PowerShell prompt. Type **sconfig** and press Enter. You will now be able to do some basic configuration of the Server Core system (see Figure 4.12). You can run Sconfig in the Command Prompt, but I recommend that you start using PowerShell for all of your configuration. PowerShell is a much more powerful tool and you should use it every time you can to get used to it.

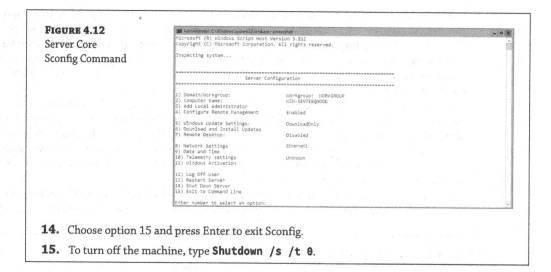

FIGURE 4.12
Server Core
Sconfig Command

14. Choose option 15 and press Enter to exit Sconfig.

15. To turn off the machine, type **Shutdown /s /t 0**.

NOTE   I will be showing many PowerShell commands throughout this book. I will show you the PowerShell commands needed to configure and maintain Windows Server 2022 Server Core throughout this entire book.

Activating and Servicing Windows

After you complete the installation of Windows Server 2022, the next step is activating the operating system. Windows Server 2022 gives you a few different options when it comes to activation.

In the past, many administrators would use the Volume Activation Management Tool (VMAT) to activate both Microsoft operating systems and Microsoft products like Office. Administrators can still use VMAT to activate Microsoft products like Office, but with the release of Windows Server 2022, there are some new ways to help administrators activate the operating systems.

So let's take a look at some of the different activation options that you have with Windows Server 2022 operating system.

Key Management Service

Windows Server 2022 Key Management Service (KMS) gives your Windows computers an easy and automated way for them to get activated. KMS allows your computers to get activated right on your local network without the need of contacting Microsoft. For this to happen, you must set up a KMS client-server network. KMS clients are able to contact KMS servers as long as either your network uses either a static TCP/IP configuration or you have a Domain Name System (DNS) server set up.

To configure KMS hosts systems; you must configure and retrieve Volume Activation information. This is done by using a Software License Manager (referred to as SL Manager) script (Slmgr.vbs). This script can be run on a local system or a remote system but it needs to be run from a user's account that uses an elevated command prompt. KMS host systems can be any Windows client operating system running Windows Vista or higher and any Server above Windows Server 2003.

To create or modify the Slmgr.vbs script, an administrator can use either the Wscript.exe or Cscript.exe application. Slmgr.vbs uses the Wscript.exe scripting engine by default. After an administrator makes any changes to the Slmgr.vbs script, the Software Licensing Service must be restarted. This can be done by using the Services Microsoft Management Console (MMC) or by running the net stop and net start commands at an elevated command prompt (net stop sppsvc and net start sppsvc).

The Slmgr.vbs script has different command-line switches that you can use (shown in Table 4.1) shows you some of the different switches that you can use with the Slmgr.vbs script.

TABLE 4.1:   Slmgr.vbs Switches

PARAMETER	DESCRIPTION
/ato	This switch is used for retail and volume system editions with a KMS host key or a Multiple Activation Key (MAK) installed. The /ato command prompts Windows to try to do an online activation. For any systems that are using a Generic Volume License Key (GVLK), this will make the system attempt to do a KMS activation.
/cdns	This switch allows an administrator to disable KMS host automatic DNS publishing.
/cpri	Administrators can use this switch to lower the priority of KMS host processes.
/dli	Administrators can use this switch on the KMS host to view the current KMS activation count.
/dlv	When an administrator uses this switch, the license information for the installed operating system is displayed.
/ipk	This command will try to install a 5x5 product key.
/sai activationInterval	This switch allows an administrator to change how often a KMS client attempts to activate itself when it cannot find a KMS host. The default setting is 120 minutes, but you can change the interval by replacing ActivationInterval with the number of minutes you want to set.
/sdns	This switch allows an administrator to enable KMS host automatic DNS publishing.
/spri	This allows an administrator to set the CPU priority of the KMS host processes to Normal.

PARAMETER	DESCRIPTION
/sprt PortNumber	Using this switch allows an administrator to change the default TCP communications port on a KMS host from 1688 to whichever port the admin wants to use. To change the default port number, replace the PortNumber switch with the TCP port number to use.
/sri RenewalInterval	This switch allows an administrator to change how often a KMS client attempts to renew its activation by contacting a KMS host. If you need to change the default of 10080 (7 days), just replace RenewalInterval with a number of minutes you want to use.

To run Slmgr.vbs remotely, administrators must supply additional parameters. They must include the computer name of the target computer as well as a username and password of a user account that has local administrator rights on the target computer. If run remotely without a specified username and password, the script uses the credentials of the user running the script.

```
slmgr.vbs TargetComputerName [username] [password] /parameter [options]
```

Automatic Virtual Machine Activation

Another Windows Server 2022 activation method is called Automatic Virtual Machine Activation (AVMA). The main advantage of AVMA is that it works the same way a proof-of-purchase works. Once there is proof that the Windows Server 2022 operating system is used in accordance with Microsoft Software License terms, AVMA allows you to install virtual machines on that Windows Server operating system without the need of using or managing product keys for each virtual machine.

AVMA attaches the virtual machine activation to the properly activated Hyper-V machine during the startup process. One of the nice advantages to using AVMA is that AVMA will provide administrators with real-time reporting data. When your virtual servers are properly activated using volume or OEM licensing, AVMA gives an organization many benefits like activating virtual machines in remote areas and also activating virtual machines even if no Internet connection is present.

Another advantage of AVMA activations is that virtual machines are activated as long as the Hyper-V server is legally licensed. This helps consulting companies in the fact that they do not need to access client virtual machines to activate the machines as long as the Hyper-V server is properly licensed. Also, hosting companies can use the server logs to help keep the virtual machines running properly.

AVMA requires Windows Server 2022 with the Hyper-V role installed. AVMA can also run on Windows Server 2012, Windows Server 2012 R2, and Windows Server 2016 if needed. Table 4.2 shows the Windows Server 2022 AVMA (5x5) Keys that are available from Microsoft's website (https://docs.microsoft.com/en-us/windows-server/get-started-19/vm-activation-19).

TABLE 4.2:   Windows Server 2022 AVMA Keys

EDITION	AVMA KEY
Datacenter	H3RNG-8C32Q-Q8FRX-6TDXV-WMBMW
Standard	TNK62-RXVTB-4P47B-2D623-4GF74
Essentials	2CTP7-NHT64-BP62M-FV6GG-HFV28
Edition	**AVMA Key (Server 2022 versions 1909, 1903, and 1809)**
Datacenter	H3RNG-8C32Q-Q8FRX-6TDXV-WMBMW
Standard	TNK62-RXVTB-4P47B-2D623-4GF74
Edition	**AVMA Key (Server 2022 versions 1803 and 1709)**
Datacenter	TMJ3Y-NTRTM-FJYXT-T22BY-CWG3J
Standard	C3RCX-M6NRP-6CXC9-TW2F2-4RHYD

Active Directory-Based Activation

One of the best advantages of using Windows Servers is the ability to install Active Directory onto your corporate network. Active Directory is just a centralized database of objects for a corporation; that centralized database is called a domain.

For companies running Active Directory, administrators can use this to their advantage when it comes to activation. Active Directory–Based Activation (ADBA) allows administrators to activate computers right through the domain connection.

Many organizations have remote locations and at these locations there is company owned software that needs to be registered. Normally administrators would use a retail key or a Multiple Activation Key (MAK) to get these products activated. The nice thing about ADBA is that as long as the computers are connected to the domain, the software and products can be activated through the domain.

When an Administrator joins a Windows computer to the domain, the ADBA will automatically activate the computers version of Windows either online with Microsoft or through the use of an activation proxy.

Servicing Windows Server 2022

Now that we have looked at some of the ways to activate your Windows Server 2022 systems, let's take a look at how you can service your Windows Server systems. Table 4.3 will shows the different versions for Windows Server 2022 and which servicing model each version uses.

TABLE 4.3:   Servicing Models for Windows Server 2022

INSTALLATION OPTION	LTSB SERVICING	SEMI-ANNUAL SERVICING
Desktop Experience	Yes	No
Server Core	Yes	Yes
Nano Server	No	Yes

LONG TERM SERVICING BRANCH

Before the release of Windows Server 2022, Windows operating systems used the 5+5 servicing models. What this meant was there were five years of mainstream support and five years of extended support for the different versions of the Windows operating systems. This model will continue to be used in Windows Server 2022 (Desktop Support and Server Core), but it will be known as Long Term Servicing Branch (LTSB).

SEMI-ANNUAL CHANNEL

The Semi-Annual Channel is an excellent option for administrators who want to take advantage of the new operating system capabilities in Server Core or Nano Server containers. Windows Server 2022 products in the Semi-Annual Channel will have new releases of the server available twice a year. One will get released in the spring and one will get released in the fall. Each release will be supported for 18 months from the initial release date.

Many of the features included with the Semi-Annual Channel will be rolled into the following Long-Term Servicing Channel release of Windows Server. The editions, functionality, and supporting content may vary from each release depending on customer feedback.

The Semi-Annual Channel will be available to volume-licensed customers that have Software Assurance, as well as customers using the Azure Marketplace or other cloud-based service providers and loyalty programs like organizations having Visual Studio Subscriptions.

Configuring Windows Server Updates

When Microsoft releases a new operating system, users will encounter issues and security deficiencies. Both of these can cause your network to have many problems. So to help fix these issues, Microsoft will release updates and security fixes on a weekly basis. It is important for an IT department to keep their network systems up to date with these fixes.

Well there are two main ways to do this. You can let your users all connect to Microsoft's website one at a time and grab updates or you can set up a Windows Server Update Services (WSUS) server to get these updates. Then that WSUS server can release the updates to your users. This helps a company because when all your users connect to Microsoft to get the same updates, it's a waste of bandwidth and time. Also, as an IT person, we may not want all of the Microsoft updates to be deployed to our clients without viewing and testing them first.

I can tell you from first-hand experience that there have been times when I deployed an update from Microsoft and it caused more issues than it fixed. So having the ability to view and test updates on a test system ensures that the updates that we are deploying work the way that they are supposed to. So let's take a look at some of the tools that you need to understand when dealing with updates.

Windows Update   This utility attaches to the Microsoft website through a user-initiated process, and it allows Windows users to update their operating systems by downloading updated files (critical and noncritical software updates).

Windows Server Update Services (WSUS)   This utility is used to deploy a limited version of Windows Update to a corporate server, which in turn provides the Windows updates to client computers within the corporate network. This allows clients that are limited to what they can access through a firewall to be able to keep their Windows operating systems up-to-date.

Windows Update

Windows Update is available for most Windows operating systems and it allows the system to receive updates from Microsoft. Examples of updates include security fixes, critical updates, updated help files, and updated drivers.

If you (as an administrator) want to use Windows Update, click Start ➤ Settings ➤ Update and Security. You would then see the following options:

When The Last Updates Were Done   When you enter into the Windows Update settings, the first thing you will see is when the last updates were done (if any).

Check For Updates Button   This allows you to manually check to see if any updates are available for the operating system. When an administrator clicks this button (shown in Figure 4.13), the system will check for updates. If any updates are found, they will be downloaded and installed.

FIGURE 4.13
Windows Update
control panel

Update History   This allows you to track all of the updates that you have applied to your server.

Change Active Hours   This setting allows you to set your active hours on the system. So, for example, if you worked on this system or the server was most active from 8:00 a.m. to 6:00 p.m., you can set those hours so that Windows Update knows when to download and install updates.

Restart Options   This setting allows you to customize when the system will restart after the machine receives its updates.

Advanced Options   You can use this option to customize what updates you receive when you use Windows Update.

NOTE   The information that is collected by Windows Update includes the operating system and version number, the Edge version, the version information for any software that can be updated through Windows Update, the Plug and Play ID numbers for installed hardware, and the region and language settings. Windows Update will also collect the product ID and product key to confirm that you are running a licensed copy of Windows, but this information is retained only during the Windows Update session and it is not stored. No personal information that can be used to identify users of the Windows Update service is collected.

Windows Server 2022 updates will recognize when you have a network connection and will automatically search for any updates for your computer from the Windows Update website (as long as an Internet connection is available) or from a WSUS server (explained in the next section).

If any updates are identified, they will be downloaded using *Background Intelligent Transfer Services (BITS)*. BITS is a bandwidth-throttling technology that allows downloads to occur using idle bandwidth only. This means that downloading automatic updates will not interfere with any other Internet traffic.

If Windows Update detects any updates for your computer, you will see an update icon in the notification area of the Taskbar.

As stated before, an administrator can configure Windows Update by selecting Start ➪ Settings ➪ Update and Security. You can manually check for updates by clicking the Check For Updates button.

After the updates get downloaded to the server, you will see a status window showing you the update status of the updates being downloaded and installed (see Figure 4.14).

After some updates are downloaded and installed, you may be required to reboot the server. As seen in Figure 4.15, you can choose to reboot the server now or you can click the Schedule The Restart link and choose when you want the server to reboot. Scheduling the server to reboot after hours can be a good option for organizations that can't have the server taken down during the day. I would recommend that an administrator is nearby in the event that an update causes the server from restarting properly. This is very rare, but it does happen.

Once updates have been installed, you can click the Update History link to see all of the previous updates. When you click this link, you will be shown the updates that have been installed and also have the ability to uninstall any updates (see Figure 4.16).

FIGURE 4.14
Seeing the Update Status

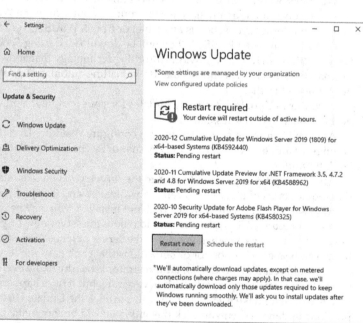

FIGURE 4.15
The Restart Now button

FIGURE 4.16
Viewing your
Update History

You also have the ability to set advanced options in the Updates section. One of the advanced options is to download other Microsoft updates for other Microsoft products (for example, you get Office updates at the same time you get operating system updates). Administrators also have the ability to defer upgrades (see Figure 4.17).

FIGURE 4.17
Viewing
Advanced Options

When you decide to defer upgrades, new Windows features will not be downloaded or installed during the upgrade process. Deferring upgrades will not affect the Windows Server 2022 system from getting security updates. Deferring upgrades will only prevent you from getting the newest Windows features as soon as they are released.

Using Windows Server Update Services

Windows Server Update Services (WSUS), formerly known as Software Update Services (SUS), is used to leverage the features of Windows Update within a corporate environment. WSUS downloads Windows updates to a corporate server, which in turn provides the updates to the internal corporate clients. This allows administrators to test and have full control over what updates are deployed within the corporate environment. WSUS is designed to work in medium-sized corporate networks that are not using System Center.

ADVANTAGES OF USING WSUS

Using WSUS has many advantages:

♦ It allows an internal server within a private intranet to act as a virtual Windows Update server.

♦ Administrators have selective control over what updates are posted and deployed from the public Windows Update site. No updates are deployed to client computers unless an administrator first approves them.

♦ Administrators can control the synchronization of updates from the public Windows Update site to the WSUS server either manually or automatically.

♦ Administrators can configure Automatic Updates on client computers to access the local WSUS server as opposed to the public Windows Update site.

♦ WSUS checks each update to verify that Microsoft has digitally signed it. Any updates that are not digitally signed are discarded.

♦ Administrators can selectively specify whether clients can access updated files from the intranet or from Microsoft's public Windows Update site, which is used to support remote clients.

♦ Administrators can deploy updates to clients in multiple languages.

♦ Administrators can configure client-side targeting to help client machines get updates. Client-side targeting allows your organization's computers to automatically add themselves to the computer groups that were created in the WSUS console.

♦ Administrators can configure a WSUS statistics server to log update access, which allows them to track which clients have installed updates. The WSUS server and the WSUS statistics server can coexist on the same computer.

♦ Administrators can manage WSUS servers remotely using HTTP or HTTPS.

WSUS Server Requirements

To act as a WSUS server, the server must meet the following requirements:

- ◆ It must be running Windows Server 2008, Windows Server 2008 R2, Windows Server 2012, Windows Server 2012 R2, Windows Server 2016, Windows Server 2019, or Windows Server 2022.

- ◆ It must have all of the most current security patches applied.

- ◆ It must be running Internet Information Services (IIS) 6.0 or newer.

- ◆ It must be connected to the network.

- ◆ It must have an NTFS partition with 100 MB free disk space to install the WSUS server software, and it must have 6 GB of free space to store all of the update files.

- ◆ It must use BITS version 2.0.

- ◆ It must use Microsoft Management Console 3.0.

- ◆ It must use Microsoft Report Viewer Redistributable 2008 or higher.

- ◆ Windows Defender should be enabled on the WSUS server.

If your WSUS server meets the following system requirements, it can support up to 15,000 WSUS clients:

- ◆ Pentium III 700 MHz processor

- ◆ 512 MB of RAM

Installing the WSUS Server

WSUS should run on a dedicated server, meaning that the server will not run any other applications except IIS, which is required. Microsoft recommends that you install a clean or new version of Windows Server 2008, Windows Server 2008 R2, Windows Server 2012, Windows Server 2012 R2, Windows Server 2016, Windows Server 2019, or Windows Server 2022 and apply any service packs or security-related patches.

Exercise 4.3 walks you through the installation process for WSUS.

EXERCISE 4.3   Installing a WSUS Server

1. Choose Server Manager by clicking the Server Manager icon on the Taskbar.

2. Click option number 2, Add Roles And Features. If a Before You Begin screen appears, just click Next.

3. Choose Role-based or featured-based installation and click Next.

4. Choose your server and click Next.

5. Choose Windows Server Update Services (see Figure 4.18). Click the Add Features button when the dialog box appears. Then click Next.

FIGURE 4.18
Choosing to
Install WSUS

6. At the Select Features screen, just click Next.

7. At the Windows Server Update Services screen, click Next.

8. At the Select Role Services screen, make sure that WID Connectivity and WSUS Services are both checked (see Figure 4.19). Click Next.

FIGURE 4.19
Select Role Screen

9. At the Content Location Selection screen, make sure the check box Store Updates In The Following Location is checked and enter the path of where you want your updates stored. After you do this, click Next (see Figure 4.20). If you uncheck this box, updates are not stored locally. They are downloaded from Microsoft only once they are approved. This will help save hard drive space. But we are going to store our updates locally.

FIGURE 4.20
Content Location
Selection screen

10. At the Web Server Role screen, click Next.

11. At the Role Services screen, just accept the defaults and click Next.

12. At the Confirmation screen, shown in Figure 4.21, check the box to Restart the destination server automatically if required. Then click the Install button.

FIGURE 4.21
Confirmation Screen

13. The installation will begin (shown in Figure 4.22), and you will see the progress. Once the installation is complete, click Close.

FIGURE 4.22
Status Screen

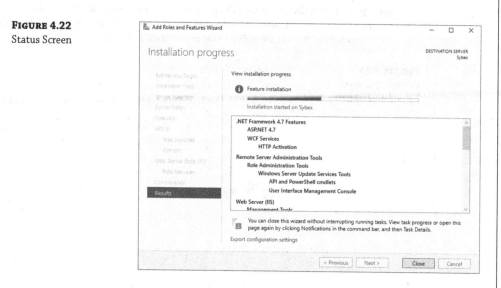

14. In Server Manager, click the WSUS link on the left side. Then click the More link (see Figure 4.23) next to Configuration Required For Windows Server Update Services.

FIGURE 4.23
Status Screen

15. At the All Servers Task Details And Notifications screen, click the Launch Post-Installation Tasks link.

16. The installation process will automatically continue. Once it is finished, you will see Complete under Stage. Close the All Servers Task Details And Notifications screen.

17. Close Server Manager.

18. If a WSUS Configure Options box appears, just close it. You will set options in the next exercise.

CONFIGURING A WSUS SERVER

Configuring a WSUS machine is a straightforward process. The easiest way to do it is to use the WSUS Server Configuration Wizard. This wizard walks you through the WSUS setup process, and it makes it easy to configure WSUS. When in the WSUS snap-in, you can configure different options.

Update Source And Proxy Server   This option allows you to configure whether this WSUS server synchronizes either from Microsoft Update or from another WSUS server on your network.

Products And Classifications   This option allows you to select the products for which you want to get updates and the type of updates that you want to receive.

Update Files And Languages   This option allows you to choose whether to download update files and where to store these update files. This option also allows you to choose which update languages you want downloaded.

Synchronization Schedule   This option allows you to configure how and when you synchronize your updates. Administrators can choose to synchronize manually or to set up a schedule for daily automatic synchronization.

Automatic Approvals   This option allows you to specify how to approve installation of updates automatically for selected groups and how to approve revisions to existing updates.

Computers   This option allows you to set computers to groups or use Group Policy or Registry settings on the computer to receive updates.

Server Cleanup Wizard   This option allows you to clean out old computers, updates, and update files from your server.

Reporting Rollup   This option allows you to choose whether to have replica downstream servers roll up computer and update status to this WSUS server.

Email Notifications   This option allows you to set up email notifications for WSUS. You can be notified when new updates are synchronized, or you can get email status reports. This option also allows you to set up the email server's information on your WSUS server.

Microsoft Update Improvement Program This option allows you to choose whether you want to participate in the Microsoft Update Improvement Program. When you choose to participate in this program, your WSUS server will automatically send information to Microsoft about the quality of your updates. This following information is included:

◆ How many computers are in the organization

◆ How many computers successfully installed each update

◆ How many computers failed to install each update

Personalization This option allows you to personalize the way information is displayed for this server. This option also allows you to set up a to-do list for WSUS.

WSUS Server Configuration Wizard This option allows you to set up many of the preceding options by just using this one setup wizard.

In Exercise 4.4, you will learn how to set up some of the WSUS server options. To complete this exercise, you need to have an Internet connection that can communicate with Microsoft.

EXERCISE 4.4 Setting WSUS Server Options

1. Open the Windows Server Update Services snap-in from Administrative Tools by pressing the Start key and then choosing Administrative Tools (see Figure 4.24). The Windows Server Update Services snap-in will be at the bottom of the list alphabetically. Double-click on the Windows Server Update Services snap-in.

FIGURE 4.24
Administrative Tools

---

2. The WSUS Server Configuration Wizard appears. Click Next at the Before You Begin screen.

3. At the Join Microsoft Update Improvement Program screen, uncheck the Yes box and click Next. If you want to participate in the Microsoft Update Improvement Program, keep the check box checked.

4. At the Choose Upstream Server screen, choose Synchronize From Microsoft Update and click Next.

5. Fill in the information at the Specify Proxy Server screen if you need to use a proxy server. If you do not need a proxy server, just click Next.

6. At the Connect To Upstream Server screen, click the Start Connecting button (see Figure 4.25). This step can take a while depending on your connection speed. Once it's finished connecting, click Next.

FIGURE 4.25
Connect to Upstream
Server screen

7. At the Language screen, choose which languages that you need updates for and click the Next button.

8. At the Choose Products screen (Figure 4.26), scroll down and choose the products for which you want to receive updates. Then click Next. You should only choose the products that you have in your organization. The more items you choose, the more space your network will need.

FIGURE 4.26
Choose Products screen

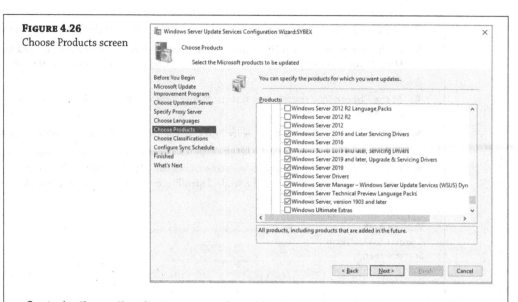

9. At the Choose Classifications screen, choose the classifications of updates you would like and click Next.

10. The Set Sync Schedule screen will appear next. At this screen, you can choose whether you want manual or automatic synchronizations. For this exercise, choose Synchronize Manually and click Next.

11. At the Finish screen, you can click Begin Initial Synchronization and click Finish. Be advised, this initial sync can take some time to finish. So if you don't have time to complete it now, you can always synchronize later.

12. Close WSUS.

Testing and Approving Updates

The administrator should test and approve updates before they are deployed to WSUS clients. The testing should be done on a test machine that is not used for daily tasks.

You also want to make sure that the WSUS test client has Windows Defender or a third-party antivirus type software on it. This ensures that when the updates are loaded onto this test system, the updates will be checked against possible viruses, antimalware, spyware, or any other type of malicious software.

There are many reasons why you should pre-test the updates. There has been times in the past (and it doesn't happen a lot) when Microsoft has released an update that has caused issues on a network. Microsoft does its very best job to ensure that all updates are tested before deploying them but depending on how your network is set up; the update may not perform the same way as it was intended. So by testing updates before deploying them, you ensure that the updates will not cause your network any unseen issues.

To approve updates, from the welcome screen, click Updates on the site's toolbar. Make your settings on the Updates page that appears.

Viewing the Synchronization Log

To view the synchronization log, click the Reports button on the site's toolbar from the welcome screen. The Reports page will appear. Click Synchronization Results to view the results.

Configuring a Disconnected Network

You have the ability to use WSUS on a disconnected network. To do so, you download the updates to the Internet-connected WSUS server. After the download is complete, you can export the updates and then import the updates to the disconnected network.

CHOOSING PRODUCTS TO UPDATE

One of the toughest decisions that you will have to make when setting up a network and a WSUS server is which products are we (the IT department) going to allow in my network environment. The more Microsoft products that we choose, the more updates we will need.

But you have to make sure you choose the products that are needed and make sure those updates get done. As IT professionals, some of the products we need to look at may not be things we think of right away. For example, we want to make sure that when we choose our products, we include Windows Defender.

As stated in the section "Testing and Approving Updates" earlier in this chapter, Windows Defender protects your systems against viruses, spyware, antimalware, and other malicious software. As new viruses get released, we need to make sure we protect our network systems against those viruses. By making sure we always have the up-to-date protection ensures that we can battle against these attacks.

Also, as new operating systems come out (for example, Windows Server 2022), we as IT members want to make sure we have the latest security updates and improvements. This will not only ensure that our networks run at peak performance but it will also ensure that we fix any security loopholes that hackers may have figured out in the operating system.

WSUS CLIENT REQUIREMENTS

WSUS clients run a special version of Automatic Updates that is designed to support WSUS. The following enhancements to Automatic Updates are included:

◆ Clients can receive updates from a WSUS server as opposed to the public Microsoft Windows Update site.

◆ The administrator can schedule when the downloading of updated files will occur.

◆ Clients can be configured via Group Policy or through editing the Registry.

◆ Updates can occur when an administrative account or nonadministrative account is logged on.

The following client platforms are the only ones that WSUS currently supports:

◆ Windows 7

◆ Windows 8

◆ Windows 10

- Windows 11

- Windows Server 2008 and 2008 R2

- Windows Server 2012 and 2012 R2

- Windows Server 2016

- Windows Server 2019

- Windows Server 2022

CONFIGURING THE WSUS CLIENTS

You can configure WSUS clients in two ways. The method you use depends on whether you use Active Directory in your network.

In a nonenterprise network (not running Active Directory), you would configure Automatic Updates through the Control Panel. Each client's Registry would then be edited to reflect the location of the server providing the automatic updates.

Within an enterprise network, using Active Directory, you would typically see Automatic Updates configured through Group Policy. Group Policy is used to manage configuration and security settings via Active Directory. Group Policy is also used to specify what server a client will use for Automatic Updates. If Automatic Updates is configured through Group Policy, the user will not be able to change Automatic Updates settings by choosing Control Panel ⇨ System (for XP) or Windows Update (for Windows 8, Windows 7, Windows Vista, Windows Server 2008, Windows Server 2008 R2, Windows Server 2012, Windows Server 2012 R2, and Windows Server 2022).

Configuring a Client in a Non–Active Directory Network

The easiest way to configure the client to use Automatic Updates is through the Control Panel. However, you can also configure Automatic Updates through the Registry. The Registry is a database of all your server settings. You can access it by choosing Start ⇨ Run and typing **regedit** in the Run dialog box. Automatic Updates settings are defined through HKEY_LOCAL_ MACHINE\Software\Policies\Microsoft\Windows\WindowsUpdate\AU.

Table 4.4 lists some of the Registry options that you can configure for Automatic Updates.

TABLE 4.4: Selected Registry keys and values for Automatic Updates

REGISTRY KEY	OPTIONS FOR VALUES
NoAutoUpdate	0: Automatic Updates are enabled (default).
	1: Automatic Updates are disabled.
	2: Notify of download and installation.
	3: Autodownload and notify of installation.
	4: Autodownload and schedule installation.

REGISTRY KEY	OPTIONS FOR VALUES
	5: Automatic Updates is required, but end users can configure.
ScheduledInstallDay	1: Sunday.
	2: Monday.
	3: Tuesday.
	4: Wednesday.
	5: Thursday.
	6: Friday.
	7: Saturday.
UseWUServer	0: Use public Microsoft Windows Update site.
	1: Use server specified in WUServer entry.

To specify what server will be used as the Windows Update server, you edit two Registry keys, which are found here:

```
HKEY_LOCAL_MACHINE\Software\Policies\Microsoft\Windows\WindowsUpdate
```

◆ The WUServer key sets the Windows Update server using the server's HTTP name—for example, http://intranetSUS.

◆ The WUStatusServer key sets the Windows Update intranet WSUS statistics server by using the server's HTTP name—for example, http://intranetSUS.

Configuring a Client in an Active Directory Network

If the WSUS client is part of an enterprise network using Active Directory, you would configure the client via Group Policy. In Exercise 4.5, we will walk you through the steps needed to configure the Group Policy object (GPO) for WSUS clients. The *Group Policy Management Console (GPMC)* needs to be installed to complete this exercise. If you don't have the GPMC installed, you can install it using the Server Manager utility.

EXERCISE 4.5   Configuring a GPO for WSUS

1. Open the GPMC by pressing the Windows key and selecting Administrative Tools ➢ Group Policy Management.

2. Expand the forest, domains, and your domain name. Under your domain name, click Default Domain Policy. Right-click and choose Edit.

3. Under the Computer Configuration section, expand Policies ➢ Administrative Templates ➢ Windows Components ➢ Windows Update.

4. In the right pane, double-click the Configure Automatic Updates option. The Configure Automatic Updates Properties dialog box appears. Click the Enabled button. Then, in the drop-down list, choose Auto Download And Notify For Install. Click OK.

5. Double-click Specify Intranet Microsoft Update Service Location Properties. This setting allows you to specify the server from which the clients will get the updates. Click Enabled. In the two server name boxes, enter **//servername** (the name of the server on which you installed WSUS in Exercise 4.3). Click OK.

6. To configure the rescheduling of automatic updates, double-click Reschedule Automatic Updates Scheduled Installations. You can enable and schedule the amount of time that Automatic Updates waits after system startup before it attempts to proceed with a scheduled installation that was previously missed. Click Enabled. Enter **10** in the Startup (Minutes) box. Click OK.

7. To configure auto-restart for scheduled Automatic Updates installations, double-click No Auto-Restart For Scheduled Automatic Updates Installations. When you enable this option, the computer is not required to restart after an update. Enable this option and click OK.

8. Close the GPMC.

Configuring Client-Side Targeting

Administrators can use a GPO to enable client-side targeting. Client machines can be automatically added into the proper computer group once the client computer connects to the WSUS server. Client-side targeting can be a very useful tool when an administrator has multiple client computers and the administrator needs to automate the process of assigning those computers to computer groups.

Administrators can enable client-side targeting on the WSUS server by clicking the Use Group Policy Or Registry Settings On Client Computers option on the Computers Options page.

1. On the WSUS console toolbar, click Options and then click Computer Options.

2. In Computer Options, choose one of the following options:

   ◆ If an administrator wants to create groups and assign computers through the WSUS console (server-side targeting), click Use The Move Computers Task In Windows Server Update Services.

   ◆ If an administrator wants to create groups and assign computers by using Group Policy settings on the client computer (client-side targeting), click Use Group Policy Or Registry Settings On Computers.

3. Under Tasks, click the Save Settings button and then click OK.

Microsoft has announced that many of their configuration options will eventually be moving to be PowerShell. So I will show you some of the available PowerShell commands for Updates.

So Table 4.5 will show you some of the different PowerShell commands that are available for WSUS administration.

NOTE Table 4.5 is just a partial list of PowerShell commands for WSUS. To see a complete list, visit Microsoft's website at https://docs.microsoft.com/en-us/powershell/module/updateservices/?view=win10-ps.

TABLE 4.5:   WSUS administration commands

POWERSHELL COMMAND	DESCRIPTION
Add-WsusComputer	This command allows an administrator to add a client computer to a WSUS target group.
Approve-WsusUpdate	This allows an administrator to approve an update that can then be applied to clients.
Deny-WsusUpdate	This allows an administrator to deny an update.
Get-WsusClassification	Administrators can use this command to get the list of all WSUS classifications available on the server.
Get-WsusComputer	This command allows administrators to view the WSUS computer object that represents the client computer.
Get-WsusProduct	Administrators can use this command to get the list of all WSUS products available on the server.
Get-WsusUpdate	This command shows you the WSUS update object and the details about that update.
Get-WsusServer	This command allows administrators to view the WSUS update server object.
Invoke-WsusServerCleanup	Allows an administrator to initiate the cleanup process on the WSUS server.
Set-WsusClassification	Sets whether the classifications of updates are enabled on the WSUS server.

Understanding Features On Demand

One of the problems in previous versions (prior to Windows Server 2012) of Windows Server was how roles and features were stored on the hard disk. Before the introduction of Windows Server 2012, even if a server role or feature was disabled on a server, the binary files for that role or feature were still present on the disk. The problem with this approach is that, even if you disable the role, it still consumes space on your hard drive.

Features On Demand in Windows Server 2012 solves this issue because not only can administrators disable a role or feature, they can also completely remove the role or feature's files. Windows Server 2022 has continued with Features on Demand and administrators can choose what Roles and Features they want to use, when they want to use them.

Once this is done, a state of Removed is shown in Server Manager, or the state of Disabled With Payload Removed is shown in the Deployment Image Servicing and Management (Dism.exe) utility. To reinstall a role or feature that has been completely removed, you must have access to the installation files.

NOTE   The Deployment Image Servicing and Management (Dism.exe) utility is talked about throughout this entire book. DISM will be discussed in great detail when we discuss Windows imaging.

If you want to remove a role or feature completely from the system, use -Remove with the Uninstall-WindowsFeature cmdlet of Windows PowerShell.

If you want to reinstall a role or feature that has been removed completely, use the Windows PowerShell -Source option of the Install-WindowsFeature Server Manager cmdlet. Using the -Source option states the path where the WIM image files and the index number of the image will be located. If an administrator decides not to use the -Source option, Windows will use Windows Update by default.

When you're using the Features On Demand configuration, if feature files are not available on the server computer and the installation requires those feature files, Windows Server 2022 can be directed to get those files from a side-by-side feature store, which is a shared folder that contains feature files. It is available to the server on the network, from Windows Update, or from installation media. This can be overwritten using the -Source option in the Windows PowerShell utility.

SOURCE FILES FOR ROLES OR FEATURES

Offline virtual hard disks (VHDs) cannot be used as a source for installing roles or features that have been completely removed. Only sources for the same version of Windows Server 2022 are supported.

To install a removed role or feature using a WIM image, follow these steps:

1. Run the following command:

   ```
   Get-windowsimage -imagepath \install.wim
   ```

   In step 1, *imagepath* is the path where the WIM files are located.

2. Run the following command:

   ```
   Install-WindowsFeature featurename -Source wim: path:index
   ```

   In step 2, *featurename* is the name of the role or feature from Get-WindowsFeature. *path* is the path to the WIM mount point, and *index* is the index of the server image from step 1.

To add or remove a role or feature, you must have administrative rights to the Windows Server 2022 machine.

The Bottom Line

Know which Server 2022 version to install   Understanding which version of Windows Server 2022 that is proper for your organization.

> **Master It**   You are an administrator that needs to set up a server in a secure locked environment. You want to have a server desktop for easy management of the server.

Master It   You are an administrator that needs to set up a server in a non-secure environment. You are worried about security and want to make sure that it is more difficult for any to make changes on the server.

Understand how to deploy updates   It is important to understand the different ways that you can deploy updates to your servers and client operating systems. You can allow your servers and users to connect to Microsoft and all get the same updates or you can control the updates using WSUS.

Master It   You are an administrator that needs to set up a server that allows all of your servers and end-users to get company approved updates for their operating systems and Microsoft applications.

Chapter 5

Understanding IP

In this chapter, I will discuss the most important protocol used in a Microsoft Windows Server 2022 network: Transmission Control Protocol/Internet Protocol (TCP/IP).

TCP/IP is actually multiple protocols bundled together: Transmission Control Protocol (TCP) and the Internet Protocol (IP). TCP/IP is a suite of protocols developed by the US Department of Defense's Advanced Research Projects Agency in 1969.

This chapter is divided into two main topics: First I'll talk about TCP/IP version 4 (IPv4), and then I'll discuss TCP/IP version 6 (IPv6). IPv4 is still used in Windows Server 2022, and it was the primary version of TCP/IP in all previous versions of Windows. However, IPv6 is the most recent version of TCP/IP. IPv6 has been out for many years and it has become more popular with every new release of Windows.

IN THIS CHAPTER YOU'LL LEARN

- ◆ Understand subnetting and when to use it
- ◆ Understand subnet masks

Understanding TCP/IP

The easiest way to understand how IP works is to think about telephone numbers. IP addresses are just telephone numbers assigned to a computer. When one computer wants to talk to another computer, you can connect to it by using its telephone number (IP address).

I mentioned that TCP/IP is actually two protocols bundled together: TCP and IP. These protocols sit on a four-layer TCP/IP model.

Details of the TCP/IP Model

The four layers of the TCP/IP model are as follows (see Figure 5.1):

Application Layer   The *Application layer* is where the applications that use the protocol stack reside. These applications include File Transfer Protocol (FTP), Trivial File Transfer Protocol (TFTP), Simple Mail Transfer Protocol (SMTP), and Hypertext Transfer Protocol (HTTP).

Transport Layer   The *Transport layer* is where the two Transport layer protocols reside. These are TCP and the User Datagram Protocol (UDP). TCP is a connection-oriented protocol, and delivery is guaranteed. UDP is a connectionless protocol. This means that UDP does its best job to deliver the message, but there is no guarantee.

Internet Layer The *Internet layer* is where IP resides. *IP* is a connectionless protocol that relies on the upper layer (Transport layer) for guaranteeing delivery. *Address Resolution Protocol (ARP)* also resides on this layer. ARP turns an IP address into a Media Access Control (MAC) address. All upper and lower layers travel through the IP protocol.

Link Layer The data link protocols like Ethernet and Token Ring reside in the *Link layer*. This layer is also referred to as the *Network Access layer*.

FIGURE 5.1
TCP/IP model

How TCP/IP Layers Communicate

When an application like FTP is called upon, the application moves down the layers and TCP is retrieved. TCP then connects itself to the IP protocol and gets released onto the network through the Link layer (see Figure 5.2). This is a connection-oriented protocol because TCP is the protocol that guarantees delivery.

When an application like TFTP gets called, the application moves down the layers and UDP is retrieved. UDP then connects itself to the IP protocol and gets released onto the network through the Link layer. This is a connectionless protocol because UDP does not have guaranteed delivery.

Understanding Port Numbers

TCP and UDP rely on port numbers assigned by the *Internet Assigned Numbers Authority (IANA)* to forward packets to the appropriate application process. Port numbers are 16-bit integers that are part of a message header. They identify the application software process with which the packet should be associated. For example, let's say that a client has a copy of Internet Explorer and a copy of Mail open at the same time. Both applications are sending TCP requests across the Internet to retrieve web pages and email, respectively. How does the computer know which return packets to forward to Internet Explorer and which packets to forward to Mail?

FIGURE 5.2
TCP/IP process

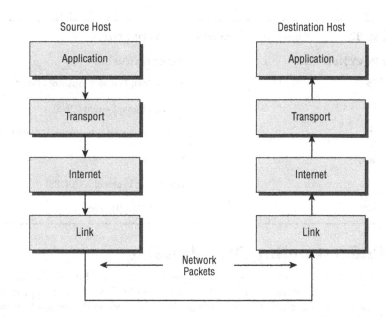

When making a connection, the client chooses a source port for the communication that is usually in the range 1024–65535 (or sometimes in the range 1–65535). This source port then communicates with a destination port of 80 or 110 on the server side. Every packet destined for Internet Explorer has a source port number of 80 in the header, and every packet destined for Mail has a source port number of 110 in the header.

Table 5.1 describes the most common port numbers (you might need to know these for the exam). You can visit www.iana.org to get the most current and complete list of port numbers. It's good to become familiar with specific port numbers because it's a benefit to be able to determine from memory the ports that, for example, allow or block specific protocols in a firewall. Allowing only port 80, for instance, does not ensure that all web traffic will be allowed. You must also allow port 443 for certain secure web traffic.

NOTE   Simply because a port is "well known" doesn't mean that a given service must run on it. It's technically valid to run any service on any port, but doing so is usually a bad idea. For example, if you chose to run your web server on TCP port 25, clients would need to type www.example.com:25 to reach your website from most browsers.

TABLE 5.1:   Common port numbers

PORT NUMBER	DESCRIPTION
20	FTP data
21	FTP control
23	Telnet

TABLE 5.1:   Common port numbers   *(CONTINUED)*

PORT NUMBER	DESCRIPTION
25	Simple Mail Transfer Protocol (SMTP)
53	Domain Name System (DNS)
80	Hypertext Transfer Protocol (HTTP), Web
88	Kerberos
110	Post Office Protocol v3 (POP3)
443	Secure HTTP (HTTPS)

Understanding IP Addressing

Understanding IP addressing is critical to understanding how IP works. An IP address is a numeric identifier assigned to each device on an IP network. This type of address is a logical software address that designates the device's location on the network. It isn't the physical hardware address hard coded in the device's network interface card.

In the following sections, you will see how IP addresses are used to identify uniquely every machine on the network (MAC address).

The Hierarchical IP Addressing Scheme

An IP address consists of 32 bits of information. These bits are divided into four sections (some-times called *octets* or *quads*) containing 1 byte (8 bits) each. There are three common methods for specifying an IP address:

◆   Dotted decimal, as in 130.57.30.56

◆   Binary, as in 10000010.00111001.00011110.00111000

◆   Hexadecimal, as in 82 39 1E 38

All of these examples represent the same IP address.

The 32-bit IP address is a structured, or hierarchical, address as opposed to a flat, or nonhier-archical, address. Although IP could have used either *flat addressing* or *hierarchical addressing*, its designers elected to use the latter for a very good reason, as you will now see.

IP ADDRESS STRUCTURE

IP addressing works the same way. Instead of the entire 32 bits being treated as a unique identi-fier, one part of the IP address is designated as the network address (or network ID) and the other part as a node address (or host ID), giving it a layered, hierarchical structure. Together, the IP address, the network address, and the node address uniquely identify a device within an IP network.

The network address—the first two sets of numbers in an IP address—uniquely identifies each network. Every machine on the same network shares that network address as part of its IP address, just as the address of every house on a street shares the same street name. In the IP address 130.57.30.56, for example, 130.57 is the network address.

The node address—the second two sets of numbers—is assigned to, and uniquely identifies, each machine in a network, just as each house on the same street has a different house number. This part of the address must be unique because it identifies a particular machine—an individual, as opposed to a network. This number can also be referred to as a *host address*. In the sample IP address 130.57.30.56, the node address is .30.56.

Understanding Network Classes

The designers of the Internet decided to create classes of networks based on network size. For the small number of networks possessing a very large number of nodes, they created the Class A network. At the other extreme is the Class C network, reserved for the numerous networks with small numbers of nodes. The class of networks in between the very large and very small ones is predictably called the Class B network.

The default subdivision of an IP address into a network and node address is determined by the class designation of your network. Table 5.2 summarizes the three classes of networks, which will be described in more detail in the following sections.

TABLE 5.2: Network address classes

CLASS	MASK BITS	LEADING BIT PATTERN	DECIMAL RANGE OF FIRST OCTET OF IP ADDRESS	ASSIGNABLE NETWORKS	MAXIMUM NODES PER NETWORK
A	8	0	1–126	126	16,777,214
B	16	10	128–191	16,384	65,534
C	24	110	192–223	2,097,152	254

TIP Classless Inter-Domain Routing (CIDR), explained in detail later in this chapter, has effectively done away with these class designations. You will still hear about and should still know the meaning behind the class designations of addresses because they are important to understanding IP addressing. However, when you're working with IP addressing in practice, CIDR is more important to know.

To ensure efficient routing, Internet designers defined a mandate for the leading bits section of the address for each different network class. For example, because a router knows that a Class A network address always starts with a number between 1-126, it can quickly apply the default mask, if necessary, after reading only the first bit of the address. Table 5.2 illustrates how the leading bits of a network address are defined. When considering the subnet masking between network and host addresses, the number of bits to mask is important. For example, in a Class A network, 8 bits are masked, making the default subnet mask 255.0.0.0; in a Class C, 24 bits are masked, making the default subnet mask 255.255.255.0.

Some IP addresses are reserved for special purposes and shouldn't be assigned to nodes. Table 5.3 describes some of the reserved IP addresses. See RFC 3330 for others.

TABLE 5.3: Special network addresses

ADDRESS	FUNCTION
Entire IP address set to all 0s	Depending on the mask, this network (that is, the network or subnet of which you are currently a part) or this host on this network.
A routing table entry of all 0s with a mask of all 0s	Used as the default gateway entry. Any destination address masked by all 0s produces a match for the all 0s reference address. Because the mask has no 1s, this is the least desirable entry, but it will be used when no other match exists.
Network address 127	Reserved for loopback tests. Designates the local node, and it allows that node to send a test packet to itself without generating network traffic.
Node address of all 0s	Used when referencing a network without referring to any specific nodes on that network. Usually used in routing tables.
Node address of all 1s	Broadcast address for all nodes on the specified network, also known as a *directed broadcast*. For example, 128.2.255.255 means all nodes on the Class B network 128.2. Routing this broadcast is configurable on certain routers.
169.254.0.0 with a mask of 255.255.0.0	The "link-local" block used for autoconfiguration and communication between devices on a single link. Communication cannot occur across routers. Microsoft uses this block for Automatic Private IP Addressing (APIPA).
Entire IP address set to all 1s (same as 255.255.255.255)	Broadcast to all nodes on the current network; sometimes called a limited broadcast or an all-1s broadcast. *This broadcast is not routable.*
10.0.0.0/8 172.16.0.0 to 172.31.255.255 192.168.0.0/16	The private-use blocks for Classes A, B, and C. As noted in RFC 1918, the addresses in these blocks must never be allowed into the Internet, making them acceptable for simultaneous use behind NAT servers and non-Internet-connected IP networks.

In the following sections, you will look at the three network types.

CLASS A NETWORKS

In a Class A network, the first byte is the network address, and the three remaining bytes are used for the node addresses. The Class A format is Network.Node.Node.Node.

For example, in the IP address 49.22.102.70, 49 is the network address, and 22.102.70 is the node address. Every machine on this particular network would have the distinctive network address of 49. Within that network, however, you could have a large number of machines.

There are 126 possible Class A network addresses. Why? The length of a Class A network address is 1 byte, and the first bit of that byte is reserved, so 7 bits in the first byte remain available for manipulation. This means that the maximum number of Class A networks is 128. (Each of the 7 bit positions that can be manipulated can be either a 0 or a 1, and this gives you a total of 2^7 positions, or 128.) But to complicate things further, it was also decided that the network address of all 0s (0000 0000) would be reserved. This means that the actual number of usable Class A network addresses is 128 minus 1, or 127. Also, 127 is a reserved number (a network address of 0 followed by all 1s [0111 1111], so you actually start with 128 addresses minus the 2 reserved, and you're left with 126 possible Class A network addresses.

Each Class A network has 3 bytes (24 bit positions) for the node address of a machine, which means that there are 2^{24}, or 16,777,216, unique combinations. Because addresses with the two patterns of all 0s and all 1s in the node bits are reserved, the actual maximum usable number of nodes for a Class A network is 2^{24} minus 2, which equals 16,777,214.

CLASS B NETWORKS

In a Class B network, the first 2 bytes are assigned to the network address, and the remaining 2 bytes are used for node addresses. The format is Network.Network.Node.Node.

For example, in the IP address 130.57.30.56, the network address is 130.57, and the node address is 30.56.

The network address is 2 bytes, so there would be 2^{16} unique combinations. But the Internet designers decided that all Class B networks should start with the binary digits 10. This leaves 14 bit positions to manipulate; therefore, there are 16,384 (or 2^{14}) unique Class B networks.

This gives you an easy way to recognize Class B addresses. If the first 2 bits of the first byte can be only 10, that gives you a decimal range from 128 up to 191 in the first octet of the IP address. Remember that you can always easily recognize a Class B network by looking at its first byte, even though there are 16,384 different Class B networks. If the first octet in the address falls between 128 and 191, it is a Class B network, regardless of the value of the second octet.

A Class B network has 2 bytes to use for node addresses. This is 2^{16} minus the two patterns in the reserved-exclusive club (all 0s and all 1s in the node bits) for a total of 65,534 possible node addresses for each Class B network.

CLASS C NETWORKS

The first 3 bytes of a Class C network are dedicated to the network portion of the address, with only 1 byte remaining for the node address. The format is Network.Network.Network.Node.

In the example IP address 198.21.74.102, the network address is 198.21.74, and the node address is 102.

In a Class C network, the first three bit positions are always binary 110. Three bytes, or 24 bits, minus 3 reserved positions leaves 21 positions. There are therefore 2^{21} (or 2,097,152) possible Class C networks.

The lead bit pattern of 110 equates to decimal 192 and runs through 223. Remembering our handy easy-recognition method, this means you can always spot a Class C address if the first byte is in the range 192–223, regardless of the values of the second and third bytes of the IP address.

Each unique Class C network has 1 byte to use for node addresses. This leads to 2^8, or 256, minus the two special patterns of all 0s and all 1s, for a total of 254 node addresses for each Class C network.

NOTE   Class D networks, used for multicasting only, use the address range 224.0.0.0 to 239.255.255.255 and are used, as in broadcasting, as destination addresses only. Class E networks (reserved for future use at this point) cover 240.0.0.0 to 255.255.255.255. Addresses in the Class E range are considered within the experimental range.

Subnetting a Network

If an organization is large and has lots of computers or if its computers are geographically dispersed, it makes good sense to divide its colossal network into smaller ones connected by routers. These smaller networks are called *subnets*. The benefits of using subnets are as follows:

Reduced Network Traffic   We all appreciate less traffic of any kind, and so do networks. Without routers, packet traffic could choke the entire network. Most traffic will stay on the local network—only packets destined for other networks will pass through the router and to another subnet. This traffic reduction also improves overall performance.

Simplified Management   It's easier to identify and isolate network problems in a group of smaller networks connected together than within one gigantic one.

UNDERSTANDING THE BENEFITS OF SUBNETTING

To understand one benefit of subnetting, consider a hotel or office building. Say that a hotel has 1,000 rooms with 75 rooms to a floor. You could start at the first room on the first floor and number it 1; then when you get to the first room on the second floor, you could number it 76 and keep going until you reach room 1,000. But someone looking for room 521 would have to guess on which floor that room is located. If you were to "subnet" the hotel, you would identify the first room on the first floor with the number 101 (1 = Floor 1 and 01 = Room 1), the first room on the second floor with 201, and so on. The guest looking for room 521 would go to the fifth floor and look for room 21.

An organization with a single network address (comparable to the hotel building mentioned in the sidebar "Understanding the Benefits of Subnetting") can have a subnet address for each individual physical network (comparable to a floor in the hotel building). Each subnet is still part of the shared network address, but it also has an additional identifier denoting its individual subnetwork number. This identifier is called a *subnet address*.

Subnetting solves several addressing problems:

◆   If an organization has several physical networks but only one IP network address, it can handle the situation by creating subnets.

◆ Because subnetting allows many physical networks to be grouped together, fewer entries in a routing table are required, notably reducing network overhead.

◆ These things combine collectively to yield greatly enhanced network efficiency.

The original designers of the Internet Protocol envisioned a small Internet with only tens of networks and hundreds of hosts. Their addressing scheme used a network address for each physical network. As you can imagine, this scheme and the unforeseen growth of the Internet created a few problems. The following are two examples:

Not Enough Addresses   A single network address can be used to refer to multiple physical networks, but an organization can request individual network addresses for each one of its physical networks. If all of these requests were granted, there wouldn't be enough addresses to go around.

Gigantic Routing Tables   If each router on the Internet needed to know about every physical network, routing tables would be impossibly huge. There would be an overwhelming amount of administrative overhead to maintain those tables, and the resulting physical overhead on the routers would be massive (CPU cycles, memory, disk space, and so on). Because routers exchange routing information with each other, an additional, related consequence is that a terrific overabundance of network traffic would result.

Although there's more than one way to approach these problems, the principal solution is the one that I'll cover in this book—subnetting. As you might guess, *subnetting* is the process of carving a single IP network into smaller logical subnetworks. This trick is achieved by subdividing the host portion of an IP address to create a subnet address. The actual subdivision is accomplished through the use of a subnet mask (covered later in the chapter).

In the following sections, you will see exactly how to calculate and apply subnetting.

Implementing Subnetting

Before you can implement subnetting, you need to determine your current requirements and plan on how best to implement your subnet scheme.

HOW TO DETERMINE YOUR SUBNETTING REQUIREMENTS

Follow these guidelines to calculate the requirements of your subnet:

1. Determine the number of required network IDs: one for each subnet and one for each wide area network (WAN) connection.

2. Determine the number of required host IDs per subnet: one for each TCP/IP device, including, for example, computers, network printers, and router interfaces.

3. Based on these two data points, create the following:

   ◆ One subnet mask for your entire network

   ◆ A unique subnet ID for each physical segment

   ◆ A range of host IDs for each unique subnet

HOW TO IMPLEMENT SUBNETTING

Subnetting is implemented by assigning a subnet address to each machine on a given physical network. For example, in Figure 5.3, each machine on subnet 1 has a subnet address of 1.

The default network portion of an IP address can't be altered without encroaching on another administrative domain's address space, unless you are assigned multiple consecutive classful addresses. To maximize the efficient use of the assigned address space, machines on a particular network share the same network address. In Figure 5.3, you can see that all of the Widget Inc. machines have a network address of 130.57. That principle is constant. In subnetting, it's the host address that's manipulated—the network address doesn't change. The subnet address scheme takes a part of the host address and recycles it as a subnet address. Bit positions are stolen from the host address to be used for the subnet identifier. Figure 5.4 shows how an IP address can be given a subnet address.

FIGURE 5.3
A sample subnet

Because the Widget Inc. network is a Class B network, the first two bytes specify the network address and are shared by all machines on the network, regardless of their particular subnet. Here every machine's address on the subnet must have its third byte read 0000 0001. The fourth byte, the host address, is the unique number that identifies the actual host within that subnet. Figure 5.5 illustrates how a network address and a subnet address can be used together.

When implementing subnetting, you need some type of hardware installed onto the network. Most of us will just use a router. But if you do not want to purchase an expensive router, there is another way.

FIGURE 5.4
Network vs. host
addresses

Class B address

Network address	Host address
130.57.	1.56
1000 0010. 0011 1001.	0000 0001. 0011 1000

Class B address with a subnet address

Network address	Subnet	Host address
1000 0010. 0011 1001.	0000 0001. 0011 1000	

FIGURE 5.5
The network address
and its subnet

The Internet

Router D

130.57.1.56 ----- 130.57.1.70
Subnet 1

130.57.1.22

Router A

Router B

Router C

One way that you can implement subnetting is by using a Windows Server 2022 machine with multiple NIC adapters configured with routing enabled on the server. This type of router is called a *multihomed router*. This is an inexpensive way to set up a router using a Microsoft server, but it may not be the best way. Many companies specialize in routers, and these routers offer many more features and more flexibility than a multihomed router.

How to Use Subnet Masks

For the subnet address scheme to work, every machine on the network must know which part of the host address will be used as the network address. This is accomplished by assigning each machine a subnet mask.

The network administrator creates a 32-bit subnet mask comprising 1s and 0s. The 1s in the subnet mask represent the positions in the IP address that refer to the network and subnet addresses. The 0s represent the positions that refer to the host part of the address. Figure 5.6 illustrates this combination.

FIGURE 5.6
The subnet mask revealed

Subnet mask code

1s = Positions representing network or subnet addresses
0s = Positions representing the host address

Subnet mask for Widget, Inc.

1111 1111. 1111 1111. 1111 1111. 0000 0000

| Network address positions | Subnet positions | Host positions |

In the Widget Inc. example, the first two bytes of the subnet mask are 1s because Widget's network address is a Class B address, formatted as Network.Network.Node.Node. The third byte, normally assigned as part of the host address, is now used to represent the subnet address. Hence, those bit positions are represented with 1s in the subnet mask. The fourth byte is the only part of the example that represents the host address.

The subnet mask can also be expressed using the decimal equivalents of the binary patterns. The binary pattern of 1111 1111 is the same as decimal 255. Consequently, the subnet mask in the example can be denoted in two ways, as shown in Figure 5.7.

FIGURE 5.7
Different ways to represent the same mask

Subnet mask in binary: 1111 1111. 1111 1111. 1111 1111. 0000 0000
Subnet mask in decimal: 255   .   255   .   255   .   0

(The spaces in the above example are only for illustrative purposes.
The subnet mask in decimal would actually appear as 255.255.255.0.)

Not all networks need to have subnets, and therefore they don't need to use custom subnet masks. In this case, they are said to have a *default* subnet mask. This is basically the same as saying that they don't have any subnets except for the one main subnet on which the network is running. Table 5.4 shows the default subnet masks for the different classes of networks.

TABLE 5.4: Default subnet masks

CLASS	FORMAT	DEFAULT SUBNET MASK
A	Network.Node.Node.Node	255.0.0.0
B	Network.Network.Node.Node	255.255.0.0
C	Network.Network.Network.Node	255.255.255.0

Once the network administrator has created the subnet mask and has assigned it to each machine, the IP software applies the subnet mask to the IP address to determine its subnet address. The word *mask* carries the implied meaning of "lens" in this case; that is, the IP software looks at its IP address through the lens of its subnet mask to see its subnet address. Figure 5.8 illustrates an IP address being viewed through a subnet mask.

FIGURE 5.8
Applying the
subnet mask

Subnet mask code

1s = Positions representing network or subnet addresses
0s = Positions representing the host address

Positions relating to the subnet address

Subnet mask: 1111 1111. 1111 1111. 1111 1111. 0000 0000

IP address of a machine on subnet 1: 1000 0010. 0011 1001. 0000 0001. 0011 1000
(Decimal: 130.57.1.56)

Bits relating to the subnet address

In this example, the IP software learns through the subnet mask that, instead of being part of the host address, the third byte of its IP address is now going to be used as a subnet address. The IP software then looks in its IP address at the bit positions that correspond to the mask, which are 0000 0001.

The final step is for the subnet bit values to be matched up with the binary numbering convention and converted to decimal. In the Widget Inc. example, the binary-to-decimal conversion is simple, as illustrated in Figure 5.9.

FIGURE 5.9
Converting the subnet
mask to decimal

Binary numbering convention

Position/value: ←—— (continued)   128 64 32 16 8 4 2 1

Widget third byte: 0 0 0 0 0 0 0 1

Decimal equivalent: 0 + 1 = 1

Subnet address: 1

By using the entire third byte of a Class B address as the subnet address, it is easy to set and determine the subnet address. For example, if Widget Inc. wants to have a subnet 6, the third byte of all machines on that subnet will be 0000 0110 (decimal 6 in binary).

Using the entire third byte of a Class B network address for the subnet allows for a fair number of available subnet addresses. One byte dedicated to the subnet provides eight bit positions. Each position can be either a 1 or a 0, so the calculation is 2^8, or 256. Thus, Widget Inc. can have up to 256 total subnetworks, each with up to 254 hosts.

Although RFC 950 prohibits the use of binary all 0s and all 1s as subnet addresses, today almost all products actually permit this usage. Microsoft's TCP/IP stack allows it, as does the software in most routers (provided you enable this feature, which sometimes is not the case by default). This gives you two additional subnets. However, you should not use a subnet of 0 (all 0s) unless all the software on your network recognizes this convention.

How to Calculate the Number of Subnets

The formulas for calculating the maximum number of subnets and the maximum number of hosts per subnet are as follows:

2^x number of masked bits in subnet mask = maximum number of subnets

$2 \times$ number of unmasked bits in subnet mask − 2 = maximum number of hosts per subnet

In the formulas, *masked* refers to bit positions of 1, and *unmasked* refers to bit positions of 0. The downside to using an entire byte of a node address as your subnet address is that you reduce the possible number of node addresses on each subnet. As explained earlier, without a subnet, a Class B address has 65,534 unique combinations of 1s and 0s that can be used for node addresses. The question then is why would you ever want 65,534 hosts on a single physical network?

The trade-off is acceptable to most who ask themselves this question. If you use an entire byte of the node address for a subnet, you then have only 1 byte for the host addresses, leaving only 254 possible host addresses. If any of your subnets are populated with more than 254 machines, you'll have a problem. To solve it, you would then need to shorten the subnet mask, thereby lengthening the number of host bits and increasing the number of host addresses. This gives you more available host addresses on each subnet. A side effect of this solution is that it shrinks the number of possible subnets.

Figure 5.10 shows an example of using a smaller subnet address. A company called Acme Inc. expects to need a maximum of 14 subnets. In this case, Acme does not need to take an entire byte from the host address for the subnet address. To get its 14 different subnet addresses, it needs to snatch only 4 bits from the host address ($2^4 = 16$). The host portion of the address has 12 usable bits remaining ($2^{12} - 2 = 4,094$). Each of Acme's 16 subnets could then potentially have a total of 4,094 host addresses, and 4,094 machines on each subnet should be plenty.

An Easier Way to Apply Subnetting

Now that you have the basics of how to subnet down, you'll learn an easier way. If you have learned a different way and it works for you, stick with it. It does not matter how you get to the finish line, just as long as you get there. But if you are new to subnetting, Figure 5.11 will make it easier for you.

FIGURE 5.10

An example of a smaller subnet address

Acme, Inc.

Network address: 132.8 (Class B; net.net.host.host)

Example IP address: 1000 0100. 0000 1000. 0001 0010. 0011 1100

Decimal: 132 . 8 . 18 . 60

Subnet Mask Code

1s = Positions representing network or subnet addresses
0s = Positions representing the host address

Subnet mask:

Binary: 1111 1111. 1111 1111. 1111 0000. 0000 0000

Decimal: 255 . 255 . 240 . 0

(The decimal 240 is equal to the binary 1111 0000.)

Positions relating to the subnet address

Subnet mask: 1111 1111. 1111 1111. 1111 0000. 0000 0000

IP address of a Acme machine: 1000 0100. 0000 1000. 0001 0010. 0011 1100
(Decimal: 132.8.18.60)

Bits relating to the subnet address

Binary-to-Decimal Conversions for Subnet Address

Subnet mask positions:	1	1	1	1	0	0	0	0
Position/value: ← (continue)	128	64	32	16	8	4	2	1
Third byte of IP address:	0	0	0	1	0	0	1	0
Decimal equivalent:					0 + 16 = 16			
Subnet address for this IP address:					16			

This chart may look intimidating, but it's really simple to use once you have done it a few times.

TIP Remember that, on this chart, 1s equal subnets and 0s equal hosts. If you get this confused, you will get wrong answers in the following exercises.

Watch the Hosts column on the lower end of the chart. This represents the number of addresses available to you after the two reserved addresses have been removed. The following exercises provide some examples.

FIGURE 5.11
Will Panek's IPv4
subnetting chart

Subnet Mask	128	64	32	16	8	4	2	1
255	1	1	1	1	1	1	1	1
254	1	1	1	1	1	1	1	0
252	1	1	1	1	1	1	0	0
248	1	1	1	1	1	0	0	0
240	1	1	1	1	0	0	0	0
224	1	1	1	0	0	0	0	0
192	1	1	0	0	0	0	0	0
128	1	0	0	0	0	0	0	0
0	0	0	0	0	0	0	0	0

0 = HOSTS   1 = SUBNETS   **Will Panek's Chart**

	Power		Subnets		Hosts
2 x	2	=	4	-2	2
2 x	3	=	8	-2	6
2 x	4	=	16	-2	14
2 x	5	=	32	-2	30
2 x	6	=	64	-2	62
2 x	7	=	128	-2	126
2 x	8	=	256	-2	254
2 x	9	=	512	-2	510
2 x	10	=	1024	-2	1022
2 x	11	=	2048	-2	2046
2 x	12	=	4096	-2	4094
2 x	13	=	8192	-2	8190
2 x	14	=	16384	-2	16382
2 x	15	=	32768	-2	32766

Subnet Mask Exercise 5.1   Class C, 10 Hosts per Subnet

You have a Class C address, and you require 10 hosts per subnet.

1. Write down the following:

   255.255.255.____

   The blank is the number you need to fill in.

2. Look under the Hosts column and choose the first number that is larger than 10 (the number of hosts per subnet you need). You should have come up with 14.

3. Move across the page and look at number in the Power column. The power number is 4.

4. Go to the top of the chart and look for the row with exactly four 0s (hosts). Find the number at the beginning of the row.

The number at the beginning of the row is 240. That's your answer. The subnet mask should be 255.255.255.240.

Subnet Mask Exercise 5.2   Class C, 20 Hosts per Subnet

You have a Class C address, and you need 20 hosts per subnet.

1. Write down the following:

   255.255.255.___

2. Look under the Hosts column and find the first number that covers 20. (This should be 30.)

3. Go across to the power number (5).

4. Go to the top part of the chart and find the row with exactly five 0s from right to left.

The number at the beginning of the row is 224. Your answer should be 255.255.255.224.

Subnet Mask Exercise 5.3   Class C, Five Subnets

Now you have a Class C address, and you need five subnets. Remember that subnets are represented by 1s in the chart.

1. Write down the following:

   255.255.255.___

2. Look under the Subnets column and find the first number that covers 5. (This should be 8.)

3. Go across to the power number. (This should be 3.)

4. Go to the top part of the chart and find out which row has exactly three 1s (remember, 1s are for subnets) from left to right.

Your answer should be 255.255.255.224.

Subnet Mask Exercise 5.4   Class B, 1,500 Hosts per Subnet

This one is a bit harder. You have a Class B address, and you need 1,500 hosts per subnet. Because you have a Class B address, you need to fill in the third octet of numbers. The fourth octet contains eight 0s.

1. Write down the following:

   255.255.___.0

2. Look at the Hosts column and find the first number that covers 1,500. (This should be 2,046.)

3. Go across and find the power number. (This should be 11.)

4. Remember, you already have eight 0s in the last octet. So, you need only three more. Find the row with three 0s.

You should come up with an answer of 255.255.248.0. This actually breaks down to 11111111.11111111.11111000.00000000, and that's how you got the 11 zeros.

Subnet Mask Exercise 5.5   Class B, 3,500 Hosts per Subnet

You have a Class B address, and you need 3,500 hosts per subnet.

1. Write down the following:

   255.255.___.0

> **2.** Look at the Hosts column and find the first number that covers 3,500. (This should be 4,094.)
>
> **3.** Go across and find the power number. (This should be 12.)
>
> **4.** Remember, you already have eight 0s in the last octet, so you need only four more. Count for four zeros from right to left.
>
> You should come up with an answer of 255.255.240.0. Again, this actually breaks down to 1111111 1.11111111.11110000.00000000, and that's how you got the 12 zeros.

TIP   If you get a question that gives you both the hosts and the subnets, always figure out the larger number first. Then, depending on the mask you have decided to use, make sure that the lower number is also correct with that mask.

Now try some more subnet mask exercises using the data that follows:

Class B address

1,000 hosts per subnet

Class C address

45 hosts per subnet

192.168.0.0

10 subnets

Class B address

25 subnets

Class B address

4,000 hosts per subnet

Class B address

2,000 hosts per subnet

25 subnets

Here are the answers. If any of your answers are wrong, follow the previous examples and try to work through them again.

Class B address

1,000 hosts per subnet 255.255.252.0

Class C address

45 hosts per subnet 255.255.255.192

192.168.0.0

10 subnets 255.255.255.240

Class B address

25 subnets 255.255.248.0

Class B address

4,000 hosts per subnet 255.255.240.0

Class B address

2,000 hosts per subnet

25 subnets 255.255.248.0

Applying Subnetting the Traditional Way

Sometimes subnetting can be confusing. After all, it can be quite difficult to remember all of those numbers. You can step back a minute and take a look at the primary classes of networks and how to subnet each one. Let's start with Class C because it uses only 8 bits for the node address, so it's the easiest to calculate. In the following sections, I will explain how to subnet the various types of networks.

SUBNETTING CLASS C

If you recall, a Class C network uses the first 3 bytes (24 bits) to define the network address. This leaves you 1 byte (8 bits) with which to address hosts. So if you want to create subnets, your options are limited because of the small number of bits available.

If you break down your subnets into chunks smaller than the default Class C, then figuring out the subnet mask, network number, broadcast address, and router address can be confusing. To build a sturdy base for subnetting, study the following techniques for determining these special values for each subnet, but also learn and use the more efficient technique presented in the later section "Quickly Identifying Subnet Characteristics Using CIDR" and the earlier section "An Easier Way to Apply Subnetting." Table 5.5 summarizes how you can break down a Class C network into one, two, four, or eight smaller subnets, and it gives you the subnet masks, network numbers, broadcast addresses, and router addresses. The first three bytes have simply been designated x.y.z. (Note that the table assumes you can use the all-0s and all-1s subnets too.)

TABLE 5.5:   Setting up Class C subnets

NUMBER OF DESIRED SUBNETS	SUBNET MASK	NETWORK NUMBER	ROUTER ADDRESS	BROADCAST ADDRESS	REMAINING NUMBER OF IP ADDRESSES
1	255.255.255.0	x.y.z.0	x.y.z.1	x.y.z.255	253
2	255.255.255.128	x.y.z.0	x.y.z.1	x.y.z.127	125
	255.255.255.128	x.y.z.128	x.y.z.129	x.y.z.255	125
4	255.255.255.192	x.y.z.0	x.y.z.1	x.y.z.63	61
	255.255.255.192	x.y.z.64	x.y.z.65	x.y.z.127	61
	255.255.255.192	x.y.z.128	x.y.z.129	x.y.z.191	61
	255.255.255.192	x.y.z.192	x.y.z.193	x.y.z.255	61
8	255.255.255.224	x.y.z.0	x.y.z.1	x.y.z.31	29
	255.255.255.224	x.y.z.32	x.y.z.33	x.y.z.63	29
	255.255.255.224	x.y.z.64	x.y.z.65	x.y.z.95	29
	255.255.255.224	x.y.z.96	x.y.z.97	x.y.z.127	29
	255.255.255.224	x.y.z.128	x.y.z.129	x.y.z.159	29
	255.255.255.224	x.y.z.160	x.y.z.161	x.y.z.191	29
	255.255.255.224	x.y.z.192	x.y.z.193	x.y.z.223	29
	255.255.255.224	x.y.z.224	x.y.z.225	x.y.z.255	29

For example, suppose you want to chop up a Class C network, 200.211.192.x, into two subnets. As you can see in the table, you'd use a subnet mask of 255.255.255.128 for each subnet. The first subnet would have the network number 200.211.192.0, router address could be the first available host address of 200.211.192.1, and broadcast address 200.211.192.127. You could assign IP addresses 200.211.192.2 through 200.211.192.126—that's 125 additional different IP addresses.

TIP   Heavily subnetting a network results in the loss of a progressively greater percentage of addresses to the network number, broadcast address, and router address.

The second subnet would have the network number 200.211.192.128, router address 200.211.192.129, and broadcast address 200.211.192.255.

Determining the Subnet Numbers for a Class C Subnet

The first subnet always has a 0 in the interesting octet. In the example, it would be 200.211.192.0, the same as the original nonsubnetted network address. To determine the subnet numbers for the additional subnets, first you have to determine the incremental value:

1. Begin with the octet that has an interesting value (other than 0 or 255) in the subnet mask. Then subtract the interesting value from 256. The result is the incremental value.

   If again you use the network 200.211.192.x and a mask of 255.255.255.192, the example yields the following equation: 256 − 192 = 64. Thus, 64 is your incremental value in the interesting octet—the fourth octet in this case. Why the fourth octet? That's the octet with the interesting value, 192, in the mask.

2. To determine the second subnet number, add the incremental value to the 0 in the fourth octet of the first subnet.

   In the example, it would be 200.211.192.64.

3. To determine the third subnet number, add the incremental value to the interesting octet of the second subnet number.

   In the example, it would be 200.211.192.128.

4. Keep adding the incremental value in this fashion until you reach the actual subnet mask number.

   For example, 0 + 64 = 64, so your second subnet is 64. And 64 + 64 is 128, so your third subnet is 128. And 128 + 64 is 192, so your fourth subnet is 192. Because 192 is the subnet mask, this is your last subnet. If you tried to add 64 again, you'd come up with 256, an unusable octet value, which is always where you end up when you've gone too far. This means your valid subnets are 0, 64, 128, and 192 (total of 4 subnets on your network).

The numbers between the subnets are your valid host and broadcast addresses. For example, the following are valid hosts for two of the subnets in a Class C network with a subnet mask of 192:

◆   The valid hosts for subnet 64 are in the range 65–126, which gives you 62 hosts per subnet.

   (You can't use 127 as a host because that would mean your host bits would be all 1s. The all-1s format is reserved as the broadcast address for that subnet.)

◆   The valid hosts for subnet 128 are in the range 129–190, with a broadcast address of 191.

As you can see, this solution wastes a few addresses—six more than not subnetting at all, to be exact. In a Class C network, this should not be hard to justify. The 255.255.255.128 subnet mask is an even better solution if you need only two subnets and expect to need close to 126 host addresses per subnet.

Calculating Values for an Eight-Subnet Class C Network

What happens if you need eight subnets in your Class C network?

By using the calculation of 2^x, where x is the number of subnet bits, you would need 3 subnet bits to get eight subnets ($2^3 = 8$). What are the valid subnets, and what are the valid hosts of each subnet? Let's figure it out.

11100000 is 224 in binary, and it would be the interesting value in the fourth octet of the subnet mask. This must be the same on all workstations.

To figure out the valid subnets, subtract the interesting octet value from 256 (256 – 224 = 32), so 32 is your incremental value for the fourth octet. Of course, the 0 subnet is your first subnet, as always. The other subnets would be 32, 64, 96, 128, 160, 192, and 224. The valid hosts are the numbers between the subnet numbers, except the numbers that equal all 1s in the host bits. These numbers would be 31, 63, 95, 127, 159, 191, 223, and 255. Remember that using all 1s in the host bits is reserved for the broadcast address of each subnet.

The valid subnets, hosts, and broadcasts are as follows:

Subnet	Hosts	Broadcast
0	1–30	31
32	33–62	63
64	65–94	95
96	97–126	127
128	129–158	159
160	161–190	191
192	193–222	223
224	225–254	255

You can add one more bit to the subnet mask just for fun. You were using 3 bits, which gave you 224. By adding the next bit, the mask now becomes 240 (11110000).

By using 4 bits for the subnet mask, you get 16 subnets because $2^4 = 16$. This subnet mask also gives you only 4 bits for the host addresses, or $2^4 - 2 = 14$ hosts per subnet. As you can see, the number of hosts per subnet gets reduced rather quickly for each host bit that gets reallocated for subnet use.

The first valid subnet for subnet 240 is 0, as always. Because 256 – 240 = 16, your remaining subnets are then 16, 32, 48, 64, 80, 96, 112, 128, 144, 160, 176, 192, 208, 224, and 240. Remember that the actual interesting octet value also represents the last valid subnet, so 240 is the last valid subnet number. The valid hosts are the numbers between the subnets, except for the numbers that are all 1s—the broadcast address for the subnet.

Table 5.6 shows the numbers in the interesting (fourth) octet for a Class C network with eight subnets.

TABLE 5.6: Fourth octet addresses for a Class C network with eight subnets

SUBNET	HOSTS	BROADCAST
0	1–14	15
16	17–30	31
32	33–46	47
48	49–62	63
64	65–78	79
80	81–94	95
96	97–110	111
112	113–126	127
128	129–142	143
144	145–158	159
160	161–174	175
176	177–190	191
192	193–206	207
208	209–222	223
224	225–238	239
240	241–254	255

SUBNETTING CLASS B

Because a Class B network has 16 bits for host addresses, you have plenty of available bits to play with when figuring out a subnet mask. Remember that you have to start with the leftmost bit and work toward the right. For example, a Class B network would look like x.y.0.0, with the default mask of 255.255.0.0. Using the default mask would give you one network with 65,534 hosts.

The default mask in binary is 11111111.11111111.00000000.00000000. The 1s represent the corresponding network bits in the IP address, and the 0s represent the host bits. When you're creating a subnet mask, the leftmost bit(s) will be borrowed from the host bits (0s will be turned into 1s) to become the subnet mask. You then use the remaining bits that are still set to 0 for host addresses.

If you use only 1 bit to create a subnet mask, you have a mask of 255.255.128.0. If you use 2 bits, you have a mask of 255.255.192.0, or 11111111.11111111.11000000.00000000.

As with subnetting a Class C address, you now have three parts of the IP address: the network address, the subnet address, and the host address. You figure out the subnet mask numbers the same way as you did with a Class C network (see the previous section, "Calculating Values for an Eight-Subnet Class C Network"), but you'll end up with a lot more hosts per subnet.

There are four subnets, because $2^2 = 4$. The valid third-octet values for the subnets are 0, 64, 128, and 192 (256 − 192 = 64, so the incremental value of the third octet is 64). However, there are 14 bits (0s) left over for host addressing. This gives you 16,382 hosts per subnet ($2^{14} − 2 = 16,382$).

The valid subnets and hosts are as follows:

Subnet	Hosts	Broadcast
x.y.0.0	x.y.0.1 through x.y. 63.254	x.y.63.255
x.y.64.0	x.y.64.1 through x.y.127.254	x.y.127.255
x.y.128.0	x.y.128.1 through x.y.191.254	x.y.191.255
x.y.192.0	x.y.192.1 through x.y.255.254	x.y.255.255

You can add another bit to the subnet mask, making it 11111111.11111111.11100000.00000000, or 255.255.224.0. This gives you eight subnets ($2^3 = 8$) and 8,190 hosts. The valid subnets are 0, 32, 64, 96, 128, 160, 192, and 224 (256 − 224 = 32). The subnets, valid hosts, and broadcasts are listed here:

Subnet	Hosts	Broadcast
x.y.0.0	x.y.0.1 through x.y.31.254	x.y.31.255
x.y.32.0	x.y.32.1 through x.y.63.254	x.y.63.255
x.y.64.0	x.y.64.1 through x.y.95.254	x.y.95.255
x.y.96.0	x.y.96.1 through x.y.127.254	x.y.127.255
x.y.128.0	x.y.128.1 through x.y.159.254	x.y.159.255
x.y.160.0	x.y.160.1 through x.y.191.254	x.y.191.255
x.y.192.0	x.y.192.1 through x.y.223.254	x.y.223.255
x.y.224.0	x.y.224.1 through x.y.255.254	x.y.255.255

The following are the breakdowns for a 9-bit mask and a 14-bit mask:

◆ If you use 9 bits for the mask, it gives you 512 subnets (2^9). With only 7 bits for hosts, you still have 126 hosts per subnet ($2^7 − 2 = 126$). The mask looks like this:

11111111.11111111.11111111.10000000, or 255.255.255.128

◆ If you use 14 bits for the subnet mask, you get 16,384 subnets (2^{14}) but only two hosts per subnet ($2^2 − 2 = 2$). The subnet mask would look like this:

11111111.11111111.11111111.11111100, or 255.255.255.252

SUBNET MASK USE IN AN ISP

You may be wondering why you would use a 14-bit subnet mask with a Class B address. This approach is actually very common. Let's say you have a Class B network and use a subnet mask of 255.255.255.0. You'd have 256 subnets and 254 hosts per subnet. Imagine also that you are an Internet service provider (ISP) and have a network with many WAN links, a different one between you and each customer. Typically, you'd have a direct connection between each site. Each of these links must be on its own subnet or network. There will be two hosts on these subnets—one address for each router port. If you used the mask described earlier (255.255.255.0), you would waste 252 host addresses per subnet. But by using the 255.255.255.252 subnet mask, you have more subnets available, which means more customers—each subnet with only two hosts, which is the maximum allowed on a point-to-point circuit.

You can use the 255.255.255.252 subnet mask only if you are running a routing algorithm such as Enhanced Interior Gateway Routing Protocol (EIGRP) or Open Shortest Path First (OSPF). These routing protocols allow what is called *Variable Length Subnet Masking (VLSM)*. VLSM allows you to run the 255.255.255.252 subnet mask on your interfaces to the WANs and run 255.255.255.0 on your router interfaces in your local area network (LAN) using the same classful network address for all subnets. It works because these routing protocols transmit the subnet mask information in the update packets that they send to the other routers. Classful routing protocols, such as RIP version 1, don't transmit the subnet mask and therefore cannot employ VLSM.

SUBNETTING CLASS A

Class A networks have even more bits available than Class B and Class C networks. A default Class A network subnet mask is only 8 bits, or 255.0.0.0, giving you a whopping 24 bits for hosts to play with. Knowing which hosts and subnets are valid is a lot more complicated than it was for either Class B or Class C networks.

If you use a mask of 11111111.1111111.00000000.00000000, or 255.255.0.0, you'll have 8 bits for subnets, or 256 subnets (2^8). This leaves 16 bits for hosts, or 65,534 hosts per subnet ($2^{16} - 2 = 65534$).

If you split the 24 bits evenly between subnets and hosts, you would give each one 12 bits. The mask would look like this: 11111111.11111111.11110000.00000000, or 255.255.240.0. How many valid subnets and hosts would you have? The answer is 4,096 subnets each with 4,094 hosts ($2^{12} - 2 = 4,094$).

The second octet will be somewhere between 0 and 255. However, you will need to figure out the third octet. Because the third octet has a 240 mask, you get 16 (256 − 240 = 16) as your incremental value in the third octet. The third octet must start with 0 for the first subnet, the second subnet will have 16 in the third octet, and so on. This means that some of your valid subnets are as follows (not in order):

Subnet	Hosts	Broadcast
x.0-255.0.0	x.0-255.0.1 through x.0-255.15.254	x.0-255.15.255
x.0-255.16.0	x.0-255.16.1 through x.0-255.31.254	x.0-255.31.255

Subnet	Hosts	Broadcast
x.0-255.32.0	x.0-255.32.1 through x.0-255.47.254	x.0-255.47.255
x.0-255.48.0	x.0-255.48.1 through x.0-255.63.254	x.0-255.63.255

They go on in this way for the remaining third-octet values through 224 in the subnet column.

Working with Classless Inter-Domain Routing

Microsoft uses an alternate way to write address ranges, called *Classless Inter-Domain Routing* (*CIDR*; pronounced "cider"). CIDR is a shorthand version of the subnet mask. For example, an address of 131.107.2.0 with a subnet mask of 255.255.255.0 is listed in CIDR as 131.107.2.0/24 because the subnet mask contains 24 1s. An address listed as 141.10.32.0/19 would have a subnet mask of 255.255.224.0, or 19 1s (the default subnet mask for Class B plus 3 bits). This is the nomenclature used in all Microsoft exams (see Figure 5.12).

FIGURE 5.12
Subnet mask represented by 1s

Subnet mask in binary: 1111 1111. 1111 1111. 1111 1111. 0000 0000

Subnet mask in decimal: 255 . 255 . 255 . 0

(The spaces in the above example are only for illustrative purposes.
The subnet mask in decimal would actually appear as 255.255.255.0.)

Let's say an Internet company has assigned you the following Class C address and CIDR number: 192.168.10.0/24. This represents the Class C address of 192.168.10.0 and a subnet mask of 255.255.255.0.

Again, CIDR represents the number of 1s turned on in a subnet mask. For example, a CIDR number of /16 stands for 255.255.0.0 (11111111.11111111.00000000.00000000).

The following is a list of all of the CIDR numbers (starting with a Class A default subnet mask) and their corresponding subnet masks:

CIDR	Mask	CIDR	Mask	CIDR	Mask
/8	255.0.0.0	/17	255.255.128.0	/25	255.255.255.128
/9	255.128.0.0	/18	255.255.192.0	/26	255.255.255.192
/10	255.192.0.0	/19	255.255.224.0	/27	255.255.255.224
/11	255.224.0.0	/20	255.255.240.0	/28	255.255.255.240
/12	255.240.0.0	/21	255.255.248.0	/29	255.255.255.248
/13	255.248.0.0	/22	255.255.252.0	/30	255.255.255.252
/14	255.252.0.0	/23	255.255.254.0	/31	255.255.255.254
/15	255.254.0.0	/24	255.255.255.0	/32	255.255.255.255
/16	255.255.0.0				

QUICKLY IDENTIFYING SUBNET CHARACTERISTICS USING CIDR

Given the limited time you have to dispatch questions in the structured environment of a Microsoft certification exam, every shortcut to coming up with the correct answer is a plus. The following method, using CIDR notation, can shave minutes off the time it takes you to complete a single question. Since you already understand the underlying binary technology at the heart of subnetting, you can use the following shortcuts, one for each address class, to come up with the correct answer without working in binary.

Identifying Class C Subnet Characteristics

Consider the host address 192.168.10.50/27. The following steps flesh out the details of the subnet of which this address is a member:

1. Obtain the CIDR-notation prefix length for the address by converting the dotted-decimal mask to CIDR notation.

   In this case, /27 corresponds to a mask of 255.255.255.224. Practice converting between these notations until it becomes second nature.

2. Using the closest multiple of 8 that is greater than or equal to the prefix length, compute the interesting octet (the octet that increases from one subnet to the next in increments other than 1 or 0). Divide this multiple by 8. The result is a number corresponding to the octet that is interesting.

   In this case, the next multiple of 8 greater than 27 is 32. Dividing 32 by 8 produces the number 4, pointing to the fourth octet as the interesting one.

3. To compute the incremental value in the interesting octet, subtract the prefix length from the next higher multiple of 8, which in this case is 32. The result (32 − 27) is 5. Raise 2 to the computed value ($2^5 = 32$). The result is the incremental value of the interesting octet.

4. Recall the value of the interesting octet from the original address (50 in this case). Starting with 0, increment by the incremental value until the value is exceeded. The values then are 0, 32, 64, and so on.

5. The subnet in question extends from the increment that is immediately less than or equal to the address's interesting octet value to the address immediately before the next increment. In this example, 192.168.10.50/27 belongs to the subnet 192.168.10.32, and this subnet extends to the address immediately preceding 192.168.10.64, which is its broadcast address, 192.168.10.63.

   Note that if the interesting octet is not the fourth octet, all octets after the interesting octet must be set to 0 for the subnet address.

6. The usable range of addresses for the subnet in question extends from one higher than the subnet address to one less than the broadcast address, making the range for the subnet in question 192.168.10.33 through 192.168.10.62. As you can see, 192.168.10.50/27 definitely falls within the subnet 192.168.10.32/27.

Identifying Class B Subnet Characteristics

Using the steps in the previous section, find the subnet in which the address 172.16.76.12 with a mask of 255.255.240.0 belongs.

1. The corresponding CIDR notation prefix length is /20.

2. The next multiple of 8 that is greater than 20 is 24. 24/8 = 3. Octet 3 is interesting.

3. 24 – 20 = 4, so the incremental value is 2^4 = 16.

4. The increments in the third octet are 0, 16, 32, 48, 64, 80, and so on.

5. The increments of 64 and 80 bracket the address's third-octet value of 76, making the subnet in question 172.16.64.0, after setting all octets after the interesting octet to 0. This subnet's broadcast address is 172.16.79.255, which comes right before the next subnet address of 172.16.80.0.

6. The usable address range then extends from 172.16.64.1 through 172.16.79.254.

Identifying Class A Subnet Characteristics

Try it one more time with 10.6.127.255/14. Combine some of the related steps if possible:

1. The prefix length is 14. The next multiple of 8 that is greater than or equal to 14 is 16. 16/8 = 2, so the second octet is interesting.

2. 16 – 14 = 2, so the incremental value in the second octet is 2^2 = 4.

3. The corresponding second-octet value of 6 in the address falls between the 4 and 8 increments. This means that the subnet in question is 10.4.0.0 (setting octets after the second one to 0) and its broadcast address is 10.7.255.255.

4. The usable address range is from 10.4.0.1 through 10.7.255.254.

DETERMINING QUANTITIES OF SUBNETS AND HOSTS

The general technique described in the previous sections is also useful when trying to determine the total number of subnets and hosts produced by a given mask with respect to the default mask of the class of address in question.

For example, consider the Class B address 172.16.0.0 with a subnet mask of 255.255.254.0.

This is a prefix length of 23 bits. When you subtract the default prefix length for a Class B address of 16 from 23, you get the value 7. Raising 2 to the 7th power results in the value 128, which is the number of subnets you get when you subnet a Class B address with the 255.255.254.0 mask.

Determining the number of hosts available in each of these 128 subnets is simple because you always subtract the prefix length that the subnet mask produces, 23 in this example, from the value 32, which represents the total number of bits in any IP address. The difference, 9, represents the remaining number of 0s, or host bits, in the subnet mask. Raising 2 to this value produces the total possible number of host IDs per subnet that this subnet mask allows.

Remember to subtract 2 from this result to account for the subnet and broadcast addresses for each subnet. This gives you the actual number of usable host IDs per subnet. In this case, this value is $2^9 - 2 = 510$.

Repeated practice with this technique will reduce your time to obtain the desired answer to mere seconds, leaving time for the more challenging tasks in each question.

Supernetting

Let's take a look at a different type of subnetting. Class B addresses give you 65,534 addresses, but let's say that you have 1,000 users. Would you really need a Class B address? Not if you use supernetting.

Supernetting allows you to have two or more blocks of contiguous subnetwork addresses. So, what does that actually mean? Class C addresses give you 254 usable addresses. So, if you needed 1,000 users, you could set up Supernetting of 4 Class C addresses that are contiguous.

Example:

192.168.16.0
192.168.17.0
192.168.18.0
192.168.19.0

When you set up supernetting for a Class C, you would use a Class B subnet mask. When you set up supernetting for a Class B, you would use a Class A subnet mask. This allows you to use multiple classes to get a larger number of hosts without taking up an entire class.

So, the subnet mask for the above example would be 255.255.252.0 or /22. The reason we used this subnet mask is because a 252 subnet mask allows for 4 subnets. Each of the above Class C numbers would equal one subnet on this network.

Understanding IPv6

Internet Protocol version 6 (IPv6) is the first major revamping of IP since RFC 791 was accepted in 1981. Yes, the operation of IP has improved, and there have been a few bells and whistles added (such as NAT, for example), but the basic structure is still being used as it was originally intended. IPv6 has actually been available to use in Microsoft operating systems since NT 4.0, but it always had to be manually enabled. Windows Vista was the first Microsoft operating system to have it enabled by default. It is also enabled by default in Windows 7, Windows 10, Windows 11, Windows Server 2008, Windows Server 2008 R2, 2012, 2012 R2, 2016, 2019 and Windows Server 2022, and it probably will be in all Microsoft operating systems from this point on.

TCP and UDP—as well as the IP applications, such as HTTP, FTP, SNMP, and the rest—are still being used in IPv4. So, you might ask, why change to the new version? What does IPv6 bring to your networking infrastructure? What is the structure of an IPv6 address? How is it implemented and used within Windows Server 2022? I'll answer all of those questions and more in the following sections.

IPv6 History and Need

In the late 1970s, as the IP specifications were being put together, the vision of the interconnected devices was limited compared to what we actually have today. To get an idea of the growth of the Internet, take a look at Hobbes' Internet Timeline in RFC 2235 (www.faqs.org/rfcs/

rfc2235.html). As you can see, in 1984, the number of hosts finally surpassed 1,000—two years after TCP and IP were introduced. With 32 bits of addressing available in IPv4, it handled the 1,000+ hosts just fine. And even with the number of hosts breaking the 10,000 mark in 1987 and then 100,000 in 1989, there were still plenty of IP addresses to go around. But when the number of hosts exceeded 2 million in 1992 and 3 million in 1994, concern in the industry started to build. So in 1994, a working group was formed to come up with a solution to the quickly dwindling usable address availability in the IPv4 space. Internet Protocol next generation (IPng) was started.

Have you heard of IP address depletion being a problem today? Probably not as much. When the working group realized that it could not have IPv6 standardized before the available addresses might run out, they developed and standardized *Network Address Translation (NAT)* as an interim solution. NAT, or more specifically an implementation of NAT called *Port Address Translation (PAT)*, took care of a big portion of the problem.

NAT works very well, but it does have some limitations, including issues of peer-to-peer applications with their IPv4 addresses embedded in the data, issues of end-to-end traceability, and issues of overlapping addresses when two networks merge. Because all devices in an IPv6 network will have a unique address and no network address translation will take place, the global addressing concept of IPv4 will be brought back (the address put on by the source device will stay all the way to the destination). Thus, with the new-and-improved functionality of IPv6, the drawbacks of NAT and the limitations of IPv4 will be eliminated.

New and Improved IPv6 Concepts

Several elements of the IPv4 protocol could use some enhancements. Fortunately, IPv6 incorporates those enhancements as well as new features directly into the protocol specification to provide better and additional functionality.

The following list includes new concepts and new implementations of old concepts in IPv6:

◆ Larger address space (128-bit vs. 32-bit).

◆ Autoconfiguration of Internet-accessible addresses with or without DHCP. (Without DHCP, it's called *stateless autoconfiguration*.)

◆ More efficient IP header (fewer fields and no checksum).

◆ Fixed-length IP header (the IPv4 header is variable length) with extension headers beyond the standard fixed length to provide enhancements.

◆ Built-in IP mobility and security. (Although available in IPv4, the IPv6 implementation is a much better implementation.)

◆ Built-in transition schemes to allow integration of the IPv4 and IPv6 spaces.

◆ ARP broadcast messages replaced with multicast request.

Here are more details about these features:

128-Bit Address Space   The new 128-bit address space will provide unique addresses for the foreseeable future. Although I would like to say that we will never use up all of the addresses, history may prove me wrong. The number of unique addresses in the IPv6 space is 2^{128}, or 3.4 × 10^{38}, addresses. How big is that number? It's enough for toasters and refrigerators (and maybe even cars) to all have their own addresses.

As a point of reference, the nearest black hole to Earth is 1,600 light years away. If you were to stack 4mm BB pellets from here to the nearest black hole and back, you would need 1.51×10^{22} BBs. This means you could uniquely address each BB from Earth to the black hole and back and still have quite a few addresses left over.

Another way to look at it is that the IPv6 address space is big enough to provide more than 1 million addresses per square inch of the surface area of the Earth (oceans included).

Autoconfiguration and Stateless Autoconfiguration   Autoconfiguration is another added/improved feature of IPv6. We've used DHCP for a while to assign IP addresses to client machines. You should even remember that APIPA can be used to assign addresses automatically to Microsoft DHCP client machines in the absence of a DHCP server. The problem with APIPA is that it confines communication between machines to a local LAN (no default gateway). What if a client machine could ask whether there was a router on the LAN and what network it was on? If the client machine knew that, it could not only assign itself an address, it could also choose the appropriate network and default gateway. The stateless autoconfiguration functionality of IPv6 allows the clients to do this.

Improved IPv6 Header   The IPv6 header is more efficient than the IPv4 header because it is fixed length (with extensions possible) and has only a few fields. The IPv6 header consists of a total of 40 bytes:

32 bytes   Source and destination IPv6 addresses

8 bytes   Version field, traffic class field, flow label field, payload length field, next header field, and hop limit field

You don't have to waste your time with a checksum validation anymore, and you don't have to include the length of the IP header (it's fixed in IPv6; the IP header is variable length in IPv4, so the length must be included as a field).

IPv6 Mobility   IPv6 is only a replacement of the OSI layer 3 component, so you'll continue to use the TCP (and UDP) components as they currently exist. IPv6 addresses a TCP issue, though. Specifically, TCP is connection oriented, meaning that you establish an end-to-end communication path with sequencing and acknowledgments before you ever send any data, and then you have to acknowledge all of the pieces of data sent. You do this through a combination of an IP address, port number, and port type (socket).

If the source IP address changes, the TCP connection may be disrupted. But then how often does this happen? Well, it happens more and more often because more people are walking around with a wireless laptop or a wireless Voice over IP (VoIP) telephone. IPv6 mobility establishes a TCP connection with a home address and, when changing networks, it continues to communicate with the original endpoint from a care-of address as it changes LANs, which sends all traffic back through the home address. The handing off of network addresses does not disrupt the TCP connection state (the original TCP port number and address remain intact).

Improved Security   Unlike IPv4, IPv6 has security built in. *Internet Protocol Security (IPsec)* is a component used today to authenticate and encrypt secure tunnels from a source to a destination. This can be from the client to the server or between gateways. IPv4 lets you do this by enhancing IP header functionality (basically adding a second IP header while encrypting everything behind it). In IPv6, you add this as standard functionality by using extension headers. Extension headers are inserted into the packet only if they are needed. Each header has a "next header" field, which identifies the next piece of information. The extension headers currently identified for IPv6 are Hop-By-Hop Options, Routing, Fragment, Destination Options, Authentication, and Encapsulating Security Payload. The Authentication header and the Encapsulating Security Payload header are the IPsec-specific control headers.

IPv4 to IPv6 Interoperability   Several mechanisms in IPv6 make the IPv4-to-IPv6 transition easy.

◆ A simple dual-stack implementation where both IPv4 and IPv6 are installed and used is certainly an option. In most situations (so far), this doesn't work so well because most of us aren't connected to an IPv6 network and our Internet connection is not IPv6 even if we're using IPv6 internally. Therefore, Microsoft includes other mechanisms that can be used in several different circumstances.

◆ *Intra-Site Automatic Tunnel Addressing Protocol (ISATAP)* is an automatic tunneling mechanism used to connect an IPv6 network to an IPv4 address space (not using NAT). ISATAP treats the IPv4 space as one big logical link connection space.

◆ *6to4* is a mechanism used to transition to IPv4. This method, like ISATAP, treats the IPv4 address space as a logical link layer with each IPv6 space in transition using a 6to4 router to create endpoints using the IPv4 space as a point-to-point connection (kind of like a WAN, eh?). 6to4 implementations still do not work well through a NAT, although a 6to4 implementation using an Application layer gateway (ALG) is certainly doable.

◆ *Teredo* is a mechanism that allows users behind a NAT to access the IPv6 space by tunneling IPv6 packets in UDP.

Pseudo-interfaces are used in these mechanisms to create a usable interface for the operating system. Another interesting feature of IPv6 is that addresses are assigned to interfaces (or pseudo-interfaces), not simply to the end node. Your Windows Server 2022 will have several unique IPv6 addresses assigned.

New Broadcast Methods   IPv6 has moved away from using broadcasting. The three types of packets used in IPv6 are unicast, multicast, and anycast. IPv6 clients then must use one of these types to get the MAC address of the next Ethernet hop (default gateway). IPv6 makes use of multicasting for this along with the new functionality called *neighbor discovery*. Not only does ARP utilize new functionality, but ICMP (also a layer 3 protocol) has been redone and is now known as ICMP6. *ICMP6* is used for messaging (packet too large, time exceeded, and so on) as it was in IPv4, but now it's also used for the messaging of IPv6 mobility. ICMP6 echo request and ICMP6 echo reply are still used for ping.

IPv6 Addressing Concepts

You need to consider several concepts when using IPv6 addressing. For starters, the format of the address has changed. Three types of addresses are used in IPv6, with some predefined values within the address space. You need to get used to seeing these addresses and be able to identify their uses.

IPv6 Address Format

For the design of IPv4 addresses, you present addresses as octets or the decimal (base 10) representation of 8 bits. Four octets add up to the 32 bits required. IPv6 expands the address space to 128 bits, and the representation is for the most part shown in hexadecimal (a notation used to represent 8 bits using the values 0–9 and A–F). Figure 5.13 compares IPv4 to IPv6.

FIGURE 5.13
IPv4/IPv6 comparison

A full IPv6 address looks like this example:

2001:0DB8:0000:0000:1234:0000:A9FE:133E

You can tell the implementation of DNS will make life a lot easier even for those who like to ping the address in lieu of the name. Fortunately, DNS already has the ability to handle IPv6 addresses with the use of an AAAA record. (*A* is short for *alias*.) An A record in IPv4's addressing space is 32 bits, so an AAAA record, or four *A*s, is 128 bits. The Windows Server 2022 DNS server handles the AAAA and the reverse pointer (PTR) records for IPv6.

IPv6 Address Shortcuts

There are several shortcuts for writing an IPv6 address. These are described in the following list:

◆ :0: stands for :0000:.

◆ You can omit preceding 0s in any 16-bit word. For example, :DB8: and :0DB8: are equivalent.

◆ :: is a variable standing for enough zeros to round out the address to 128 bits. :: can be used only once in an address.

You can use these shortcuts to represent the example address 2001:0DB8:0000:0000:1234:0000 :A9FE:133E, as shown here:

◆ Compress :0000: into :0::
2001:0DB8:0000:0000:1234:0:A9FE:133E

◆ Eliminate preceding zeros:

2001:DB8:0000:0000:1234:0:A9FE:133E

◆ Use the special variable shortcut for multiple 0s:

2001:DB8::1234:0:A9FE:133E

You now also use prefix notation or slash notation when discussing IPv6 networks. For example, the network of the previous address can be represented as 2001:DB8:0000:0000:0000:0000:0000:0000. This can also be expressed as 2001:DB8:: /32. The /32 indicates 32 bits of network, and 2001:DB8: is 32 bits of network.

IPv6 Address Assignment

So, do you subnet IPv6? The answer depends on your definition of subnetting. If you are given 32 bits of network from your ISP, you have 96 bits with which to work. If you use some of the 96 bits to route within your network infrastructure, then you are subnetting. In this context, you do subnet IPv6. However, given the huge number of bits you have available, you will no longer need to implement VLSM. For example, Microsoft has a network space of 2001:4898:: /32. That gives the administrators a space of 96 bits (2^{96} = 79,228,162,514,264,337,593,543,950,336 unique addresses using all 96 bits) with which to work.

You can let Windows Server 2022 dynamically/automatically assign its IPv6 address, or you can still assign it manually (see Figure 5.14). With dynamic/automatic assignment, the IPv6 address is assigned either by a DHCPv6 server or by the Windows Server 2022 machine. If no DHCPv6 server is configured, the Windows Server 2022 machine can query the local LAN segment to find a router with a configured IPv6 interface. If so, the server will assign itself an address on the same IPv6 network as the router interface and set its default gateway to the router interface's IPv6 address. Figure 5.14 shows that you have the same dynamic and manual choices as you do in IPv4; however, the input values for IPv6 must conform to the new format.

FIGURE 5.14
TCP/IPv6
Properties window

To see your configured IP addresses (IPv4 and IPv6), you can still use the `ipconfig` command. For example, I have configured a static IPv4 address and an IPv6 address on my server. The IPv6 address is the same as the one used in the earlier IPv6 example address. Figure 5.15 shows the result of this command on Windows Server 2022 for my server.

FIGURE 5.15
IPv6 configuration as seen from the command prompt

```
Administrator: C:\Windows\system32\cmd.exe
Ethernet adapter Local Area Connection:

    Connection-specific DNS Suffix  . :
    Description . . . . . . . . . . . : Intel 21140-Based PCI Fast Ethernet Adapt
er (Emulated)
    Physical Address. . . . . . . . . : 00-03-FF-11-02-CD
    DHCP Enabled. . . . . . . . . . . : No
    Autoconfiguration Enabled . . . . : Yes
    IPv6 Address. . . . . . . . . . . : 2001:db8::1234:0:a9fe:133e(Preferred)
    Link-local IPv6 Address . . . . . : fe80::a425:ab9d:7da4:ccba%10(Preferred)
    IPv4 Address. . . . . . . . . . . : 192.168.1.200(Preferred)
    Subnet Mask . . . . . . . . . . . : 255.255.255.0
    Default Gateway . . . . . . . . . : 2001:db8::1234:0:0:1
                                        0.0.0.0
                                        192.168.1.1
    DNS Servers . . . . . . . . . . . : ::1
                                        192.168.1.1
    NetBIOS over Tcpip. . . . . . . . : Enabled
```

IPv6 Address Types

As stated earlier, there are three types of addresses in IPv6: anycast, unicast, and multicast. A description of each of these types of IPv6 addresses follows.

NOTE Note the absence of the broadcast type, which is included in IPv4. You can't use broadcasts in IPv6; they've been replaced with multicasts.

Anycast Addresses Anycast addresses are not really new. The concept of anycast existed in IPv4 but was not widely used. An *anycast address* is an IPv6 address assigned to multiple devices (usually different devices). When an anycast packet is sent, it is delivered to one of the devices, usually the closest one.

Unicast Addresses A *unicast packet* uniquely identifies an interface of an IPv6 device. The interface can be a virtual interface or pseudo-interface or a real (physical) interface.
Unicast addresses come in several types, as described in the following list:

Global Unicast Address As of this writing, the global unicast address space is defined as 2000:: /3. The 2001::/32 networks are the IPv6 addresses currently being issued to business entities. As mentioned, Microsoft has been allocated 2001:4898:: /32. A Microsoft DHCPv6 server would be set up with scopes (ranges of addresses to be assigned) within this address space. There are some special addresses and address formats that you will see in use as well. You'll find most example addresses listed as 2001:DB8:: /32; this space has been reserved for documentation. Do you remember the loopback address in IPv4, 127.0.0.1? In IPv6 the loopback address is ::1 (or 0:0:0:0:0:0:0:0001). You may also see an address with dotted-decimal used. A dual-stack Windows Server 2022 machine may also show you FE80::5EFE:192.168.1.200. This address form is used in an integration/migration model of IPv6 (or if you just can't leave the dotted-decimal era, I suppose).

Link-Local Address Link-local addresses are defined as FE80:: /10. If you refer to Figure 5.15 showing the `ipconfig` command, you will see the link-local IPv6 address as fe80::a425:ab9d:7da4:ccba. The last 8 bytes (64 bits) are random to ensure a high probability of randomness for the link-local address. The link-local address is to be used on a single link (network segment) and should never be routed.

There is another form of the local-link IPv6 address called the *Extended User Interface 64-bit (EUI-64)* format. This is derived by using the MAC address of the physical interface and inserting an FFFE between the third and fourth bytes of the MAC. The first byte is also made 02 (this sets the universal/local, or U/L, bit to 1 as defined in IEEE 802 frame specification). Again looking at Figure 5.15, the EUI-64 address would take the physical (MAC) address 00-03-FF-11-02-CD and make the link-local IPv6 address FE80::0203:FFFF:FE11:02CD. (I've left the preceding zeros in the link-local IPv6 address to make it easier for you to pick out the MAC address with the FFFE inserted.)

AnonymousAddress   Microsoft Server 2022 uses the random address by default instead of EUI-64. The random value is called the *AnonymousAddress* in Microsoft Server 2022. It can be modified to allow the use of EUI-64.

Unique Local Address   The *unique local address* can be Fc00 or FD00, and it is used like the private address space of IPv4. RFC 4193 describes unique local addresses. They are not expected to be routable on the global Internet. They are used for private routing within an organization.

Multicast Address   *Multicast addresses* are one-to-many communication packets. Multicast packets are identifiable by their first byte (most significant byte, leftmost byte, leftmost 2 nibbles, leftmost 8 bits, and so on). A multicast address is defined as FF00::/8.

In the second byte shown (the 00 of FF00), the second 0 is what's called the *scope*. Interface-local is 01, and link-local is 02. FF01:: is an interface-local multicast.

There are several well-known (already defined) multicast addresses. For example, if you want to send a packet to all nodes in the link-local scope, you send the packet to FF02::1 (also shown as FF02:0:0:0:0:0:0:1). The all-routers multicast address is FF02::2.

You can also use multicasting to get the logical link layer address (MAC address) of a device with which you are trying to communicate. Instead of using the ARP mechanism of IPv4, IPv6 uses the ICMPv6 neighbor solicitation (NS) and neighbor advertisement (NA) messages. The NS and NA ICMPv6 messages are all part of the new *Neighbor Discovery Protocol (NDP)*. This new ICMPv6 functionality also includes router solicitation and router advertisements as well as redirect messages (similar to the IPv4 redirect functionality).

Table 5.7 outlines the IPv6 address space known prefixes and some well-known addresses.

UNICAST VS. ANYCAST

Unicast and anycast addresses look the same and may be indistinguishable from each other; it just depends on how many devices have the same address. If only one device has a globally unique IPv6 address, it's a unicast address. If more than one device has the same address, it's an anycast address. Both unicast and anycast are considered one-to-one communication, although you could say that anycast is one-to-"one of many."

TABLE 5.7:   IPv6 address space known prefixes and addresses

ADDRESS PREFIX	SCOPE OF USE
2000:: /3	Global unicast space prefix
FE80:: /10	Link-local address prefix
FC00:: /7	Unique local unicast prefix
FD00:: /8	Unique local unicast prefix
FF00:: /8	Multicast prefix
2001:DB8:: /32	Global unicast prefix used for documentation
::1	Reserved local loopback address
2001:0000: /32	Teredo prefix (discussed later in this chapter)
2002:: /16	6to4 prefix

IPv6 Integration/Migration

It's time to get into the mindset of integrating IPv6 into your existing infrastructure with the longer goal of migrating to IPv6. In other words, this is not going to be an "OK, Friday the Internet is changing over" rollout. You have to bring about the change as a controlled implementation. It could easily take three to five years before a solid migration occurs and probably longer. I think the migration will take slightly less time than getting the world to migrate to the metric system on the overall timeline. The process of integration/migration consists of several mechanisms.

Dual Stack   Simply running both IPv4 and IPv6 on the same network, utilizing the IPv4 address space for devices using only IPv4 addresses and utilizing the IPv6 address space for devices using IPv6 addresses.

Tunneling   Using an encapsulation scheme for transporting one address space inside another

Address Translation   Using a higher-level application to change one address type (IPv4 or IPv6) to the other transparently so that end devices are unaware one address space is talking to another.

I elaborate on these three mechanisms in the following sections.

IPv6 DUAL STACK

The default implementation in Windows Server 2022 is an enabled IPv6 configuration along with IPv4; this is dual stack. The implementation can be dual IP layer or dual TCP/IP stack. Windows Server 2022 uses the dual IP layer implementation (see Figure 5.16). When an application queries a DNS server to resolve a hostname to an IP address, the DNS server may respond with an IPv4 address or an IPv6 address. If the DNS server responds with both, Windows Server 2022 will prefer the IPv6 address. Windows Server 2022 can use both IPv4 and IPv6 addresses as necessary for network communication. When looking at the output of the `ipconfig` command, you will see both address spaces displayed.

FIGURE 5.16
IPv6 dual IP
layer diagram

IPv6 Tunneling

Windows Server 2022 includes several tunneling mechanisms for tunneling IPv6 through the IPv4 address space. They include the following:

- ◆ Intra-Site Automatic Tunnel Addressing Protocol (ISATAP), which is used for unicast IPv6 communication across an IPv4 infrastructure. ISATAP is enabled by default in Windows Server 2022.

- ◆ 6to4, which is used for unicast IPv6 communication across an IPv4 infrastructure.

- ◆ Teredo, which is used for unicast IPv6 communication with an IPv4 NAT implementation across an IPv4 infrastructure.

With multiple tunneling protocols available and enabled by default, you might ask, what's the difference, and why is one used over the others? They all allow you to tunnel IPv6 packets through the IPv4 address space (a really cool thing if you're trying to integrate/migrate). Here are the details of these tunneling mechanisms:

ISATAP   *Intra-Site Automatic Tunnel Addressing Protocol (ISATAP)* is the automatic tunnel addressing protocol providing IPv6 addresses based on the IPv4 address of the end interface (node). The IPv6 address is automatically configured on the local device, and the dual stack machine can use either its IPv4 or IPv6 address to communicate on the local network (within the local network infrastructure). ISATAP can use the neighbor discovery mechanism to determine the router ID and network prefix where the device is located, thus making intrasite communication possible even in a routed infrastructure.

The format of an ISATAP address is as follows:

[64 bits of prefix] [32 bits indicating ISATAP] [32 bits IPv4 address]

The center 32 bits indicating ISATAP are actually 0000:5EFE (when using private IPv4 addresses). The ISATAP address of the example Windows Server 2022 machine using the link-local IPv6 address is FE80::5EFE:192.168.1.200. Each node participating in the ISATAP infrastructure must support ISATAP. If you're routing through an IPv4 cloud, a border router (a router transitioning from an IPv6 to IPv4 space) must support ISATAP. Windows Server 2022 can be configured as a border router, and it will forward ISATAP packets. ISATAP is experimental and is defined in RFC 4214.

6to4   *6to4* specifies a procedure for IPv6 networks to communicate with each other through an IPv4 space without the IPv6 nodes having to know what's happening. The IPv6 nodes do not need to be dual stacked to make this happen. The border router is the device responsible for knowing about the IPv6-to-IPv4 transition. The IPv6 packets are encapsulated at the border router (and decapsulated at the other end or on the way back). There is an assigned prefix for the 6to4 implementation: 2002:: /16. 6to4 is defined in RFC 3056.

Teredo   *Teredo* (named after a kind of shipworm that drills holes in the wood of ships) is a protocol designed to allow IPv6 addresses to be available to hosts through one or more layers of NAT. Teredo uses a process of tunneling packets through the IPv4 space using UDP. The Teredo service encapsulates the IPv6 data within a UDP segment (packet) and uses IPv4 addressing to get through the IPv4 cloud. Having layer 4 (Transport layer) available to use as translation functionality is what gives you the ability to be behind a NAT. Teredo provides host-to-host communication and dynamic addressing for IPv6 nodes (dual stack), allowing the nodes to have access to resources in an IPv6 network and the IPv6 devices to have access to the IPv6 devices that have only connectivity to the IPv4 space (like home users who have an IPv6-enabled operating system connecting to IPv6 resources while their home ISP has only IPv4 capabilities). Teredo is defined in RFC 4380.

In Windows Server 2022, an IPv4 Teredo server is identified and configured (using the `netsh` command interface). The Teredo server provides connectivity resources (address) to the Teredo client (the node that has access to the IPv4 Internet and needs access to an IPv6 network/Internet). A Teredo relay is a component used by the IPv6 router to receive traffic destined for Teredo clients and forward the traffic appropriately. The defined prefix for a Teredo address is 2001:0000:: /32. Teredo does add overhead like all the other implementations discussed. It is generally accepted that you should use the simplest model available. However, in the process of integration/migration for most of us behind a NAT, Teredo will be the process to choose.

From Windows Server 2022, use the `ipconfig /all` command to view the default configurations including IPv4 and IPv6. You may notice a notation that I didn't discuss, the percent sign at the end of the IPv6 address (see Figure 5.17). The number after the percent sign is the virtual interface identifier used by Windows Server 2022.

FIGURE 5.17
IPv6 interface identifier
for `ipconfig` display

```
Link-local IPv6 Address . . . . . : fe80::a425:ab9d:7da4:ccba%10
```

Useful IPv6 Information Commands

You can use numerous commands to view, verify, and configure the network parameters of Windows Server 2022. Specifically, you can use the `netsh` command set and the `route` command set as well as the standard `ping` and `tracert` functions.

Use the `netsh` command interface (as well as the provided dialog boxes, if you want) to examine and configure IPv6 functionality. The `netsh` command issued from the command interpreter changes into a network shell (`netsh`) where you can configure and view both IPv4 and IPv6 components.

Don't forget to use the ever-popular `route print` command to see the Windows Server 2022 routing tables (IPv4 and IPv6). The other diagnostic commands are still available for IPv4 as well as IPv6. In previous versions of Microsoft operating systems, `ping` was the IPv4 command, and `ping6` was the IPv6 command. This has changed in Windows Server 2022; `ping` works for both IPv4 and IPv6 to test layer 3 connectivity to remote devices. The IPv4 `tracert` command was `tracert6` for IPv6. The command is now `tracert` for both IPv4 and IPv6, and it will show you every layer 3 (IP) hop from source to destination. (This assumes that all of the administrators from here to there want you to see the hops and are not blocking ICMP. It also assumes that there are no IP tunnels, which your packets are traversing; you won't see the router hops in the tunnel either.)

Overall, the consortium of people developing the Internet and the Internet Protocol have tried to make all of the changes to communication infrastructures easy to implement. (This is a daunting task with the many vendors and various infrastructures currently in place.) The goal is not to daze and confuse administrators; it's designed to provide maximum flexibility with the greatest functionality. IPv6 is going to provide the needed layer 3 (Network layer, global addressing layer, logical addressing layer. . .call it what you like) functionality for the foreseeable future.

IPv6 Address Breakdown

The final thing that you need to understand about IPv6 is how the address breaks down. As I have stated previously, there are different sections of an IPv6 address. For example, the first group of numbers can show you the site prefix and what type of message that you are dealing with. The ending part of the IPv6 address shows the computer's Interface ID. So, let's take a look at an IPv6 address and how each section shows you about the network and computer system.

2001:0db8:6d4c:2116:0000:0000:1996:5acb

In this IPv6 address, there are actually multiple sections. As I have stated, an IPv6 address is 128 bits. The first 64 bits explain the Site Prefix and Subnet ID and the final 64 bits shows the Interface ID.

So, using the previous IPv6 address, let's break down the sections.

2001:0db8:6d4c:2116 :	0000:0000:1996:5acb
64 bits	64 bits

2001:0db8:6d4c :	2116 :	0000:0000:1996:5acb
Site Prefix	Subnet ID	Interface ID

The Bottom Line

Understand subnetting and when to use it. If an organization is large and has many computers or if its computers are geographically dispersed, it's sensible to divide its large network into smaller ones connected by routers. These smaller networks are called subnets.

Master It You are an administrator of a large network. All computers are on the same network and the network only has a single router (connecting the network to the Internet). You notice that there is a lot of broadcast traffic on the network. You want to reduce some of the broadcast traffic.

Understand subnet masks. For the subnet address scheme to work, every machine on the network must know which part of the host address will be used as the subnet address. The network administrator creates a 32-bit subnet mask consisting of 1s and 0s. The 1s in the subnet mask represent the positions that refer to the network or subnet addresses. The 0s represent the positions that refer to the host portion of the address.

Master It You are the administrator of an organization that has multiple subnets. You think that one of the computers is set with an IP address from a different subnet.

Chapter 6

Implementing DNS

As we move closer to connecting your onsite network with Azure, we still have features and services required to make this happen. That brings us to DNS.

The Domain Name System (DNS) is one of the most important networking services that you can put on your network, and it's also one of the key topics that you'll need to understand if you plan to take any of the Microsoft Azure exams.

By the end of this chapter, you should have a deeper understanding of how DNS works, how to set it up properly, how to configure DNS, proper management of the DNS server, and how to troubleshoot DNS issues quickly and easily in Microsoft Windows Server 2022.

IN THIS CHAPTER YOU'LL LEARN

◆ Understand DNS

◆ Understand DNS records

◆ Understand Dynamic Updates

Introducing DNS

The *Domain Name System (DNS)* is a service that allows you to resolve a hostname to an Internet Protocol (IP) address. One of the inherent complexities of operating in networked environments is working with multiple protocols and network addresses. Owing largely to the tremendous rise in the popularity of the Internet, however, most environments have transitioned to use *Transmission Control Protocol/Internet Protocol (TCP/IP)* as their primary networking protocol. Microsoft is no exception when it comes to supporting TCP/IP in its workstation and server products. All current versions of Microsoft's operating systems support TCP/IP, as do most other modern operating systems.

An easy way to understand DNS is to think about making a telephone call. If you wanted to call Microsoft and did not know the phone number, you could call information, tell the operator the name (Microsoft), and get the telephone number. You would then make the call. Now think about trying to connect to Server1. You don't know the TCP/IP number (the computer's telephone number), so your computer asks DNS (information) for the number of Server1. DNS returns the number, and your system makes the connection (call). DNS is your network's 411, or information, and it returns the TCP/IP data for your network.

TCP/IP is actually a collection of different technologies (protocols and services) that allow computers to function together on a single, large, and heterogeneous network. Some of the major advantages of this protocol include widespread support for hardware, software, and network devices; reliance on a system of standards; and scalability. TCP handles tasks such as sequenced acknowledgments. IP involves many jobs, such as logical subnet assignment and routing.

HOSTS File

Nowadays, most computer users are quite familiar with navigating to DNS-based resources, such as www.willpanek.com. To resolve these "friendly" names to TCP/IP addresses that the network stack can use, you need a method for mapping them. Originally, ASCII flat files (often called *HOSTS files*, as shown in Figure 6.1) were used for this purpose. In some cases, they are still used today in small networks, and they can be useful in helping to troubleshoot name resolution problems.

FIGURE 6.1
HOSTS file

```
 hosts - Notepad                                                  —  □  ×
File  Edit  Format  View  Help
# This is a sample HOSTS file used by Microsoft TCP/IP for Windows.
#
# This file contains the mappings of IP addresses to host names. Each
# entry should be kept on an individual line. The IP address should
# be placed in the first column followed by the corresponding host name.
# The IP address and the host name should be separated by at least one
# space.
#
# Additionally, comments (such as these) may be inserted on individual
# lines or following the machine name denoted by a '#' symbol.
#
# For example:
#
#      102.54.94.97     rhino.acme.com          # source server
#      38.25.63.10      x.acme.com              # x client host

# localhost name resolution is handled within DNS itself.
#      127.0.0.1        localhost
#      ::1              localhost
```

As the number of machines and network devices grew, it became unwieldy for administrators to manage all of the manual updates required to enter new mappings to a master HOSTS file and distribute it. Clearly, a better system was needed.

As you can see from the sample HOSTS file in Figure 6.1, you can conduct a quick test of the email server's name resolution as follows:

1. Open the HOSTS file: `C:\Windows\Systems32\drivers\etc`.

2. Add the IP-address-to-hostname mapping.

3. Try to ping the server using the hostname to verify that you can reach it using an easy-to-remember name.

Following these steps should drive home the concept of DNS for you because you can see it working to make your life easier. Now you don't have to remember 10.0.0.10; you only need to remember exchange03. However, you can also see how this method can become unwieldy if you have many hosts that want to use easy-to-remember names instead of IP addresses to locate resources on your network.

When dealing with large networks, users and network administrators must be able to locate the resources they require with minimal searching. Users don't care about the actual physical or logical network address of the machine; they just want to be able to connect to it using a simple name that they can remember.

From a network administrator's standpoint, however, each machine must have its own logical address that makes it part of the network on which it resides. Therefore, some scalable and easy-to-manage method for resolving a machine's logical name to an IP address and then to a domain name is required. DNS was created just for this purpose.

DNS is a hierarchically distributed database. In other words, its layers are arranged in a definite order, and its data is distributed across a wide range of machines, each of which can exert control over a portion of the database. DNS is a standard set of protocols that defines the following:

◆ A mechanism for querying and updating address information in the database

◆ A mechanism for replicating the information in the database among servers

◆ A schema of the database

DNS was originally developed in the early days of the Internet (called ARPAnet at the time) when it was a small network created by the Department of Defense for research purposes. Before DNS, computer names, or hostnames, were manually entered into a HOSTS file located on a centrally administered server. Each site that needed to resolve hostnames outside of its organiza-tion had to download this file. As the number of computers on the Internet grew, so did the size of this HOSTS file—and along with it the problems of its management. The need for a new system that would offer features such as scalability, decentralized administration, and support for various data types became more and more obvious. DNS, introduced in 1984, became this new system.

With DNS, the hostnames reside in a database that can be distributed among multiple servers, decreasing the load on any one server and providing the ability to administer this naming system on a per-partition basis. DNS supports hierarchical names and allows for the registration of various data types in addition to the hostname-to-IP-address mapping used in HOSTS files. Database performance is ensured through its distributed nature as well as through caching.

The DNS distributed database establishes an inverted logical tree structure called the *domain namespace*. Each node, or domain, in that space has a unique name. At the top of the tree is the root. This may not sound quite right, which is why the DNS hierarchical model is described as being an inverted tree, with the root at the top. The root is represented by the null set: "". When written, the root node is represented by a single dot (.).

Each node in the DNS can branch out to any number of nodes below it. For example, below the root node are a number of other nodes, commonly referred to as *top-level domains (TLDs)*. These are the familiar .com, .net, .org, .gov, .edu, and other such names. Table 6.1 lists some of these TLDs.

TABLE 6.1: Common top-level DNS domains

DOMAIN NAME	TYPE OF ORGANIZATION
com	Commercial (for example, `stormwind.com` for StormWind Training Corporation).
edu	Educational (for example, `gatech.edu` for the Georgia Institute of Technology).
gov	Government (for example, `whitehouse.gov` for the White House in Washington, D.C.).
int	International organizations (for example, `nato.int` for NATO); this top-level domain is fairly rare.
mil	Military organizations (for example, `usmc.mil` for the Marine Corps); there is a separate set of root name servers for this domain.
net	Networking organizations and Internet providers (for example, `hiwaay.net` for HiWAAY Information Systems); many commercial organizations have registered names under this domain too.
org	Noncommercial organizations (for example, `fidonet.org` for FidoNet).
au	Australia.
uk	United Kingdom.
ca	Canada.
us	United States.
jp	Japan.

Each of these nodes then branches out into another set of domains, and they combine to form what we refer to as *domain names*, such as `microsoft.com`. A domain name identifies the domain's position in the logical DNS hierarchy in relation to its parent domain by separating each branch of the tree with a dot. Figure 6.2 shows a few of the top-level domains, where the Microsoft domain fits, and a host called Tigger within the `microsoft.com` domain. If someone wanted to contact that host, they would use the *fully qualified domain name (FQDN)*, `tigger.microsoft.com`.

An FQDN includes the trailing dot (`.`) to indicate the root node, but it's commonly left off in practice.

As previously stated, one of the strengths of DNS is the ability to delegate control over portions of the DNS namespace to multiple organizations. For example, the Internet Corporation for Assigned Names and Numbers (ICANN) assigns the control over TLDs to one or more organizations. In turn, those organizations delegate portions of the DNS namespace to other organizations. For example, when you register a domain name, let's call it `example.com`, you control the DNS for the portion of the DNS namespace within `example.com`. The registrar controlling the `.com` TLD has delegated control over the `example.com` node in the DNS tree. No other node can be named `example` directly below the `.com` within the DNS database.

FIGURE 6.2

The DNS hierarchy

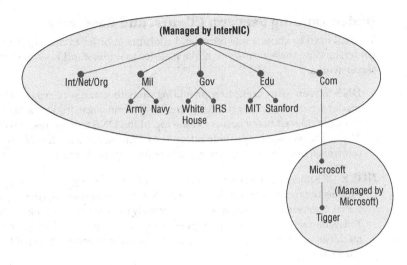

Within the portion of the domain namespace that you control (example.com), you could create host and other records (more on these later). You could also further subdivide example.com and delegate control over those divisions to other organizations or departments. These divisions are called *subdomains*. For example, you might create subdomains named for the cities in which the company has branch offices and then delegate control over those subdomains to the branch offices. The subdomains might be named losangeles.example.com, chicago.example.com, portsmouth.example.com, and so on.

Each domain (or delegated subdomain) is associated with DNS name servers. In other words, for every node in the DNS, one or more servers can give an authoritative answer to queries about that domain. At the root of the domain namespace are the root servers, which I'll cover later in the chapter.

NOTE   Domain names and hostnames must contain only characters a to z, A to Z, 0 to 9, and – (hyphen). Other common and useful characters, such as the & (ampersand), / (slash), . (period), and _ (underscore) characters, are not allowed. This is in conflict with NetBIOS's naming restrictions. However, you'll find that Windows Server 2022 is smart enough to take a NetBIOS name, like Server_1, and turn it into a legal DNS name, like server1.example.com.

DNS servers work together to resolve hierarchical names. If a server already has information about a name, it simply fulfills the query for the client. Otherwise, it queries other DNS servers for the appropriate information. The system works well because it distributes the authority over separate parts of the DNS structure to specific servers. A DNS zone is a portion of the DNS namespace over which a specific DNS server has authority. (DNS zone types are discussed in detail later in this chapter.)

Within a given DNS zone, resource records (RRs) contain the hosts and other database information that make up the data for the zone. For example, an RR might contain the host entry for www.example.com, pointing it to the IP address 192.168.1.10.

Understanding Servers, Clients, and Resolvers

You will need to know a few terms and concepts in order to manage a DNS server. Understanding these terms will make it easier to understand how the Windows Server 2022 DNS server works:

DNS Server Any computer providing domain name services is a *DNS name server*. No matter where the server resides in the DNS namespace, it's still a DNS name server. For example, 13 root name servers at the top of the DNS tree are responsible for delegating the TLDs. The *root servers* provide referrals to name servers for the TLDs, which in turn provides referrals to an authoritative name server for a given domain.

NOTE The Berkeley Internet Name Domain (BIND) was originally the only software available for running the root servers on the Internet. However, a few years ago the organizations responsible for the root servers undertook an effort to diversify the software running on these important machines. Today, root servers run multiple types of name server software. BIND is still primarily on Unix-based machines, and it is also the most popular for Internet providers. None of the root servers run Windows DNS.

Any DNS server implementation supporting Service Location Resource Records (see RFC 2782) and Dynamic Updates (RFC 2136) is sufficient to provide the name service for any operating system running Windows 2003 software and newer.

DNS Client A *DNS client* is any machine that issues queries to a DNS server. The client hostname may or may not be registered in a DNS database. Clients issue DNS requests through processes called *resolvers*. You'll sometimes see the terms *client* and *resolver* used synonymously.

Resolver *Resolvers* are software processes, sometimes implemented in software libraries, which handles the actual process of finding the answers to queries for DNS data. The resolver is also built into many larger pieces of software so that external libraries don't have to be called to make and process DNS queries. Resolvers can be what you'd consider client computers or other DNS servers attempting to resolve an answer on behalf of a client (for example, Edge).

Query A *query* is a request for information sent to a DNS server. Three types of queries can be made to a DNS server: recursive, inverse, and iterative. I'll discuss the differences between these query types in the section "DNS Queries" a bit later in the chapter.

Understanding the DNS Process

To help you understand the DNS process, I will start by covering the differences between Dynamic DNS and Non-Dynamic DNS. During this discussion, you will learn how Dynamic DNS populates the DNS database. You'll also see how to implement security for Dynamic DNS. I will then talk about the workings of different types of DNS queries. Finally, I will discuss caching and time to live (TTL). You'll learn how to determine the best setting for your organization.

Dynamic DNS and Non-Dynamic DNS

To understand Dynamic DNS and Non-Dynamic DNS, you must go back in time (here is where the TV screen always used to get wavy). Many years ago when we all worked on NT 3.51 and NT 4.0, most networks used Windows Internet Name Service (WINS) to do their TCP/IP name resolution. Windows versions 95/98 and NT 4.0 Professional were all built on the idea of using WINS. This worked out well for administrators because WINS was dynamic (which meant that once it was installed, it automatically built its own database). Back then, there was no such thing as Dynamic DNS; administrators had to enter DNS records into the server manually. This is important to know even today. If you have clients still running any of these older operating systems (95/98 or NT 4), these clients cannot use Dynamic DNS.

Now let's move forward in time to the release of Windows Server 2000. Microsoft announced that DNS was going to be the name resolution method of choice. Many administrators (me included) did not look forward to the switch. Because there was no such thing as Dynamic DNS, most administrators had nightmares about manually entering records. However, luckily for us, when Microsoft released Windows Server 2000, DNS had the ability to operate dynamically. Now when you're setting up Windows Server 2022 DNS, you can choose what type of dynamic update you would like to use, if any. Let's talk about why you would want to choose one over the other.

The *Dynamic DNS (DDNS) standard*, described in RFC 2136, allows DNS clients to update information in the DNS database files. For example, a Windows Server 2022 DHCP server can automatically tell a DDNS server which IP addresses it has assigned to what machines. Windows 2000 (and higher) and Windows 7 (and higher) DHCP clients can do this too. For security reasons, however, it's better to let the DHCP server do it. The result: IP addresses and DNS records stay in sync so that you can use DNS and DHCP together seamlessly. Because DDNS is a proposed Internet standard, you can even use the Windows Server 2022 DDNS-aware parts with Unix/Linux-based DNS servers.

Non-Dynamic DNS (NDDNS) does not automatically populate the DNS database. The client systems do not have the ability to update to DNS. If you decide to use Non-Dynamic DNS, an administrator will need to populate the DNS database manually. Non-Dynamic DNS is a reasonable choice if your organization is small to midsize and you do not want extra network traffic (clients updating to the DNS server) or if you need to enter the computer's TCP/IP information manually because of strict security measures.

NOTE Dynamic DNS has the ability to be secure, and the chances are slim that a rogue system (a computer that does not belong in your DNS database) could update to a secure DNS server. Nevertheless, some organizations have to follow stricter security measures and are not allowed to have dynamic updates.

The major downside to entering records into DNS manually occurs when the organization is using the *Dynamic Host Configuration Protocol (DHCP)*. When using DHCP, it is possible for users to end up with different TCP/IP addresses every day. This means that an administrator has to update DNS manually each day to keep it accurate.

If you choose to allow Dynamic DNS, you need to decide how you want to set it up. When setting up dynamic updates on your DNS server, you have three choices (see Figure 6.3).

FIGURE 6.3
Setting the Dynamic
Updates option

None   This means your DNS server is Non-Dynamic.

Nonsecure and Secure   This means that any machine (even if it does not have a domain
account) can register with DNS. Using this setting could allow rogue systems to enter records
into your DNS server.

Secure Only   This means that only machines with accounts in Active Directory can register
with DNS. Before DNS registers any account in its database, it checks Active Directory to
make sure that account is an authorized domain computer.

How Dynamic DNS Populates the DNS Database

TCP/IP is the protocol used for network communications on a Microsoft Windows Server
2022 network. Users have two ways to receive a TCP/IP number:

♦   Static (administrators manually enter the TCP/IP information)

♦   Dynamic (using DHCP)

When an administrator sets up TCP/IP, DNS can also be configured.

Once a client gets the address of the DNS server, if that client is allowed to update with DNS,
the client sends a registration to DNS or requests DHCP to send the registration. DNS then does
one of two things, depending on which Dynamic Updates option is specified:

♦   Check with Active Directory to see if that computer has an account (Secure Only updates)
and, if it does, enter the record into the database.

♦   Enter the record into its database (nonsecure and secure updates).

What if you have clients that cannot update DNS? Well, there is a solution—DHCP. In the DNS tab of the IPv4 Properties window, check the option labeled "Dynamically update DNS records for DHCP clients that do not request updates (for example, clients running Windows NT 4.0)," which is shown in Figure 6.4.

FIGURE 6.4
DHCP settings for DNS

DHCP, along with Dynamic DNS clients, allows an organization to update its DNS database dynamically without the time and effort of having an administrator manually enter DNS records.

DNS QUERIES

As stated earlier, a client can make three types of queries to a DNS server: recursive, inverse, and iterative. Remember that the client of a DNS server can be a resolver (what you'd normally call a client) or another DNS server.

Iterative Queries

Iterative queries are the easiest to understand: A client asks the DNS server for an answer, and the server returns the best answer. This information likely comes from the server's cache. The server never sends out an additional query in response to an iterative query. If the server doesn't know the answer, it may direct the client to another server through a referral.

Recursive Queries

In a *recursive query*, the client sends a query to a name server, asking it to respond either with the requested answer or with an error message. The error states one of two things:

◆ The server can't come up with the right answer.

◆ The domain name doesn't exist.

In a recursive query, the name server isn't allowed to just refer the client to some other name server. Most resolvers use recursive queries. In addition, if your DNS server uses a forwarder, the requests sent by your server to the forwarder will be recursive queries.

Figure 6.5 shows an example of both recursive and iterative queries. In this example, a client within the Microsoft Corporation is querying its DNS server for the IP address for www .whitehouse.gov.

FIGURE 6.5
A sample DNS query

Here's what happens to resolve the request:

1. The resolver sends a recursive DNS query to its local DNS server asking for the IP address of www.whitehouse.gov. The local name server is responsible for resolving the name, and it cannot refer the resolver to another name server.

2. The local name server checks its zones, and it finds no zones corresponding to the requested domain name.

3. The root name server has authority for the root domain and will reply with the IP address of a name server for the .gov top-level domain.

4. The local name server sends an iterative query for www.whitehouse.gov to the Gov name server.

5. The Gov name server replies with the IP address of the name server servicing the whitehouse.gov domain.

6. The local name server sends an iterative query for www.whitehouse.gov to the whitehouse.gov name server.

7. The whitehouse.gov name server replies with the IP address corresponding to www .whitehouse.gov.

8. The local name server sends the IP address of www.whitehouse.gov back to the original resolver.

Inverse Queries

Inverse queries use pointer (PTR) records. Instead of supplying a name and then asking for an IP address, the client first provides the IP address and then asks for the name. Because there's no direct correlation in the DNS namespace between a domain name and its associated IP address, this search would be fruitless without the use of the in-addr.arpa domain. Nodes in the in-addr.arpa domain are named after the numbers in the dotted-octet representation of IP addresses. However, because IP addresses get more specific from left to right and domain names get less specific from left to right, the order of IP address octets must be reversed when building the in-addr.arpa tree. With this arrangement, administration of the lower limbs of the DNS in-addr.arpa tree can be given to companies as they are assigned their Class A, B, or C subnet address or delegated even further down thanks to Variable Length Subnet Masking (VLSM).

Once the domain tree is built into the DNS database, a special PTR record is added to associate the IP addresses with the corresponding hostnames. In other words, to find a hostname for the IP address 206.131.234.1, the resolver would query the DNS server for a PTR record for 1.234.131.206.in-addr.arpa. If this IP address is outside the local domain, the DNS server will start at the root and sequentially resolve the domain nodes until arriving at 234.131.206.in-addr.arpa, which would contain the PTR record for the desired host.

Caching and Time to Live

When a name server is processing a recursive query, it may be required to send out several queries to find the definitive answer. Name servers, acting as resolvers, are allowed to cache all of the received information during this process; each record contains information called *time to live (TTL)*. The TTL specifies how long the record will be held in the local cache until it must be resolved again. If a query comes in that can be satisfied by this cached data, the TTL that's returned with it equals the current amount of time left before the data is flushed.

There is also a negative cache TTL. The *negative cache TTL* is used when an authoritative server responds to a query indicating that the record queried doesn't exist, and it indicates the amount of time that this negative answer may be held. Negative caching is quite helpful in preventing repeated queries for names that don't exist.

The administrator for the DNS zone sets TTL values for the entire zone. The value can be the same across the zone, or the administrator can set a separate TTL for each RR within the zone. Client resolvers also have data caches and honor the TTL value so that they know when to flush. Users also have the ability to manually flush the DNS cache by running the Ipconfig / flushDNS command.

Introducing DNS Database Zones

As mentioned earlier in this chapter, a DNS zone is a portion of the DNS namespace over which a specific DNS server has authority. Within a given DNS zone, there are resource records that define the hosts and other types of information that make up the database for the zone. You can choose from several different zone types. Understanding the characteristics of each will help you choose which is right for your organization.

NOTE The DNS zones discussed in this book are all Microsoft Windows Server 2022 zones. Non-Windows (for example, Unix) systems set up their DNS zones differently.

In the following sections, I will discuss the different zone types and their characteristics.

Understanding Primary Zones

When you're learning about zone types, things can get a bit confusing. But it's really not difficult to understand how they work and why you would want to choose one type of zone over another. Zones are databases that store records. By choosing one zone type over another, you are basically just choosing how the database works and how it will be stored on the server.

The primary zone is responsible for maintaining all of the records for the DNS zone. It contains the primary copy of the DNS database. All record updates occur on the primary zone. You will want to create and add primary zones whenever you create a new DNS domain.

There are two types of primary zones:

- ◆ Primary zone

- ◆ Primary zone with Active Directory Integration (Active Directory DNS)

NOTE From this point forward, I refer to a primary zone with Active Directory Integration as an *Active Directory Integrated DNS*. When I use only the term *primary zone*, Active Directory is not included.

To install DNS as a primary zone, first you must install DNS using the Server Manager MMC. Once DNS is installed and running, you create a new zone and specify it as a primary zone.

NOTE The process of installing DNS and its zones will be discussed later in this chapter. In addition, there will be step-by-step exercises to walk you through how to install these components.

Primary zones have advantages and disadvantages. Knowing the characteristics of a primary zone will help you decide when you need the zone and when it fits into your organization.

LOCAL DATABASE

Primary DNS zones get stored locally in a file (with the suffix .dns) on the server. This allows you to store a primary zone on a domain controller or a member server. In addition, by loading DNS onto a member server, you can help a small organization conserve resources. Such an organization may not have the resources to load DNS on an Active Directory domain controller.

Unfortunately, the local database has many disadvantages:

Lack of Fault Tolerance Think of a primary zone as a contact list on your smartphone. All of the contacts in the list are the records in your database. The problem is that if you lose your phone or the phone breaks, you lose your contact list. Until your phone gets fixed or you swap out your phone card, the contacts are unavailable.

It works the same way with a primary zone. If the server goes down or you lose the hard drive, DNS records on that machine are unreachable. An administrator can install a secondary zone (explained in the next section), and that provides temporary fault tolerance. Unfortunately, if the primary zone is down for an extended period of time, the secondary server's information will no longer be valid.

Additional Network Traffic Let's imagine that you are looking for a contact number for John Smith. John Smith is not listed in your cell phone directory, but he is listed in your partner's cell phone. You have to contact your partner to get the listing. You cannot directly access your partner's cell contacts.

When a resolver sends a request to DNS to get the TCP/IP address for Jsmith (in this case Jsmith is a computer name) and the DNS server does not have an answer, it does not have the ability to check the other server's database directly to get an answer. Thus, it forwards the request to another DNS. When DNS servers are replicating zone databases with other DNS servers, this causes additional network traffic.

No Security Staying with the cell phone example, let's say that you call your partner looking for John Smith's phone number. When your partner gives you the phone number over your wireless phone, someone with a scanner can pick up your conversation. Unfortunately, wireless telephone calls are not very secure.

Now a resolver asks a primary zone for the Jsmith TCP/IP address. If someone on the network has a packet sniffer, they can steal the information in the DNS packets being sent over the network. The packets are not secure unless you implement some form of secondary security. Also, the DNS server has the ability to be dynamic. A primary zone accepts all updates from DNS servers. You cannot set it to accept secure updates only.

Understanding Secondary Zones

In Windows Server 2022 DNS, you have the ability to use secondary DNS zones. Secondary zones are noneditable copies of the DNS database. You use them for *load balancing* (also referred to as *load sharing*), which is a way of managing network overloads on a single server. A secondary zone gets its database from a primary zone.

A *secondary zone* contains a database with all of the same information as the primary zone, and it can be used to resolve DNS requests. Secondary zones have the following advantages:

◆ A secondary zone provides fault tolerance, so if the primary zone server becomes unavailable, name resolution can still occur using the secondary zone server.

◆ Secondary DNS servers can also increase network performance by offloading some of the traffic that would otherwise go to the primary server.

Secondary servers are often placed within the parts of an organization that have high-speed network access. This prevents DNS queries from having to run across slow wide area network (WAN) connections. For example, if there are two remote offices within the stormwind.com organization, you may want to place a secondary DNS server in each remote office. This way, when clients require name resolution, they will contact the nearest server for this IP address information, thus preventing unnecessary WAN traffic.

NOTE Having too many secondary zone servers can actually cause an increase in network traffic because of replication (especially if DNS changes are fairly frequent). Therefore, you should always weigh the benefits and drawbacks and properly plan for secondary zone servers.

CONFIGURE ZONE DELEGATION

One advantage of DNS is the ability of turning a namespace into one or more zones. These zones can be replicated to each other or other DNS servers. As an administrator, you must decide when you want to break your DNS into multiple zones. When considering this option, there are a few things to think about:

◆ You want the management of your DNS namespace to be delegated by another location or department in your organization.

◆ You want to load-balance your traffic among multiple servers by turning a large zone into many smaller zones. This will help improve performance and create redundancy among your DNS servers.

◆ You have remote offices opening up, and you want to expand your DNS namespace.

To create a new zone delegation, you would complete the following steps:

1. Open the DNS console.

2. In the console tree, right-click the applicable subdomain and then click New Delegation.

3. Follow the instructions provided in the New Delegation Wizard to finish creating the newly delegated domain.

Understanding Active Directory Integrated DNS

Windows Server 2000 introduced *Active Directory Integrated DNS* to the world. This zone type was unique, and it was a separate choice during setup. In Windows Server 2003, this zone type became an add-on to a primary zone. In Windows Server 2022, it works the same way. After choosing to set up a primary zone, you check the box Store The Zone In Active Directory (see Figure 6.6).

FIGURE 6.6
Setting up an Active Directory Integrated zone

Change Zone Type ×

Select a zone type:

◉ Primary zone
Stores a copy of the zone that can be updated directly.

○ Secondary zone
Stores a copy of an existing zone. This option helps balance the processing load of primary servers and provides fault tolerance.

○ Stub zone
Stores a copy of a zone containing only NS, SOA, and possibly glue A records. A server containing a stub zone is not authoritative for that zone.

☑ Store the zone in Active Directory (available only if DNS server is a domain controller)

OK   Cancel

DISADVANTAGES OF ACTIVE DIRECTORY INTEGRATED DNS

The main disadvantage of Active Directory Integrated DNS is that it has to reside on a domain controller because the DNS database is stored in Active Directory. As a result, you cannot load this zone type on a member server, and small organizations might not have the resources to set up a dedicated domain controller.

ADVANTAGES OF ACTIVE DIRECTORY INTEGRATED DNS

The advantages of using an Active Directory Integrated DNS zone well outweigh the disadvantages just discussed. The following are some of the major advantages to an Active Directory Integrated zone:

Full Fault Tolerance Think of an Active Directory Integrated zone as a database on your server that stores contact information for all your clients. If you need to retrieve John Smith's phone number, as long as it was entered, you can look it up on the software.

If John Smith's phone number was stored only on your computer and your computer stopped working, no one could access John Smith's phone number. But since John Smith's phone number is stored in a database to which everyone has access, if your computer stops working, other users can still retrieve John Smith's phone number.

An Active Directory Integrated zone works the same way. Since the DNS database is stored in Active Directory, all Active Directory DNS servers can have access to the same data. If one server goes down or you lose a hard drive, all other Active Directory DNS servers can still retrieve DNS records.

No Additional Network Traffic As previously discussed, an Active Directory Integrated zone is stored in Active Directory. Since all records are now stored in Active Directory, when a resolver needs a TCP/IP address for Jsmith, any Active Directory DNS server can access Jsmith's address and respond to the resolver.

When you choose an Active Directory Integrated zone, DNS zone data can be replicated automatically to other DNS servers during the normal Active Directory replication process.

DNS Security An Active Directory Integrated zone has a few security advantages over a primary zone:

- An Active Directory Integrated zone can use secure dynamic updates.

- As explained earlier, the Dynamic DNS standard allows secure-only updates or dynamic updates, not both.

- If you choose secure updates, then only machines with accounts in Active Directory can register with DNS. Before DNS registers any account in its database, it checks Active Directory to make sure that it is an authorized domain computer.

- An Active Directory Integrated zone stores and replicates its database through Active Directory replication. Because of this, the data gets encrypted as it is sent from one DNS server to another.

Background Zone Loading Background zone loading (discussed in more detail later in this chapter) allows an Active Directory Integrated DNS zone to load in the background. As a result, a DNS server can service client requests while the zone is still loading into memory.

Understanding Stub Zones

Stub zones work a lot like secondary zones—the database is a noneditable copy of a primary zone. The difference is that the stub zone's database contains only the information necessary (three record types) to identify the authoritative DNS servers for a zone (see Figure 6.7). You should not use stub zones to replace secondary zones, nor should you use them for redundancy and load balancing.

FIGURE 6.7
DNS stub zone type

Change Zone Type   ×

Select a zone type:

○ Primary zone
Stores a copy of the zone that can be updated directly.

○ Secondary zone
Stores a copy of an existing zone. This option helps balance the processing load of primary servers and provides fault tolerance.

● Stub zone
Stores a copy of a zone containing only NS, SOA, and possibly glue A records. A server containing a stub zone is not authoritative for that zone.

☐ Store the zone in Active Directory (available only if DNS server is a domain controller)

OK   Cancel

NOTE   Stub zone databases contain only three record types: name server (NS), start of authority (SOA), and glue host (A) records. Understanding these records will help you on the Microsoft certification exams. Microsoft asks many questions about stub zones on all DNS-related exams.

WHEN TO USE STUB ZONES

Stub zones become particularly useful in a couple of different scenarios. Consider what happens when two large companies merge: example.com and example.net. In most cases, the DNS zone information from both companies must be available to every employee. You could set up a new zone on each side that acts as a secondary for the other side's primary zone, but administrators tend to be very protective of their DNS databases and probably wouldn't agree to this plan.

A better solution is to add to each side a stub zone that points to the primary server on the other side. When a client in example.com (which you help administer) makes a request for a name in example.net, the stub zone on the example.com DNS server would send the client to the primary DNS server for example.net without actually resolving the name. At this point, it would be up to example.net's primary server to resolve the name.

An added benefit is that even if the administrators over at example.net change their configuration, you won't have to do anything because the changes will automatically replicate to the stub zone, just as they would for a secondary server.

Stub zones can also be useful when you administer two domains across a slow connection. Let's change the previous example a bit and assume that you have full control over example.com and `example.net` but they connect through a 56 Kbps line. In this case, you wouldn't necessarily mind using secondary zones because you personally administer the entire network. However, it could get messy to replicate an entire zone file across that slow line. Instead, stub zones would refer clients to the appropriate primary server at the other site.

GlobalName Zones

Earlier in this chapter, I talked about organizations using WINS to resolve NetBIOS names (also referred to as *computer names*) to TCP/IP addresses. Even today, many organizations still use WINS along with DNS for name resolution. Unfortunately, WINS is slowly becoming obsolete.

To help organizations move forward with an all-DNS network, Microsoft Windows Server 2022 DNS supports *GlobalName zones*. These use single-label names (DNS names that do not contain a suffix such as `.com`, `.net`, and so on). GlobalName zones are not intended to support peer-to-peer networks and workstation name resolution, and they don't support dynamic DNS updates.

GlobalName zones are designed to be used with servers. Because GlobalName zones are not dynamic, an administrator has to enter the records into the zone database manually. In most organizations, the servers have static TCP/IP addresses, and this works well with the GlobalName zone design. GlobalName zones are usually used to map single-label CNAME (alias) resource records to an FQDN.

Zone Transfers and Replication

DNS is such an important part of the network that you should not just use a single DNS server. With a single DNS server, you also have a single point of failure and in fact, many domain registrars encourage the use of more than two name servers for a domain. Secondary servers or multiple primary Active Directory Integrated servers play an integral role in providing DNS information for an entire domain.

As previously stated, secondary DNS servers receive their zone databases through zone transfers. When you configure a secondary server for the first time, you must specify the primary server that is authoritative for the zone and will send the zone transfer. The primary server must also permit the secondary server to request the zone transfer.

Zone transfers occur in one of two ways: *full zone transfers (AXFR)* and *incremental zone transfers (IXFR)*.

When a new secondary server is configured for the first time, it receives a full zone transfer from the primary DNS server. The full zone transfer contains all of the information in the DNS database. Some DNS implementations always receive full zone transfers.

After the secondary server receives its first full zone transfer, subsequent zone transfers are incremental. The primary name server compares its zone version number with that of the secondary server, and it sends only the changes that have been made in the interim. This significantly reduces network traffic generated by zone transfers.

The secondary server typically initiates zone transfers when the refresh interval time for the zone expires or when the secondary or stub server boots. Alternatively, you can configure notify lists on the primary server that send a message to the secondary or stub servers whenever any changes to the zone database occur.

When you consider your DNS strategy, you must carefully consider the layout of your network. If you have a single domain with offices in separate cities, you want to reduce the number of zone transfers across the potentially slow or expensive WAN links, although this is becoming less of a concern because of continuous increases in bandwidth.

Active Directory Integrated zones do away with traditional zone transfers altogether with other DNS integrated zones. Instead, they replicate across Active Directory with all of the other AD information. This replication is secure and encrypted because it uses the Active Directory security. AD Integrated zones can still do database transfers to DNS servers that are setup as a secondary zone.

How DNS Notify Works

Windows Server 2022 supports DNS Notify. *DNS Notify* is a mechanism that allows the process of initiating notifications to secondary servers when zone changes occur (RFC 1996). DNS Notify uses a push mechanism for communicating to a select set of secondary zone servers when their zone information is updated. (DNS Notify does not allow you to configure a notify list for a stub zone.)

After being notified of the changes, secondary servers can then start a pull zone transfer and update their local copies of the database.

NOTE   Many different mechanisms use the push/pull relationship. Normally, one object pushes information to another, and the second object pulls the information from the first. Most applications push replication on a change value and pull it on a time value. For example, a system can push replication after 10 updates, or it can be pulled every 30 minutes.

To configure the DNS Notify process, you create a list of secondary servers to notify. List the IP address of the server in the primary master's Notify dialog box (see Figure 6.8). The Notify dialog box is located under the Zone Transfers tab, which is located in the zone Properties dialog box (see Figure 6.9).

FIGURE 6.8
DNS Notify dialog box

FIGURE 6.9
DNS Zone Transfers tab

CONFIGURING STUB ZONE TRANSFERS WITH ZONE REPLICATION

In the preceding section, I talked about how to configure secondary server zone transfers. What if you wanted to configure settings for stub zone transfers? This is where zone replication scope comes in.

Only Active Directory–integrated primary and stub zones can configure their replication scope. Secondary servers do not have this ability.

You can configure zone replication scope configurations in two ways. An administrator can set configuration options through the DNS snap-in or through a command-line tool called DNSCmd.

To configure zone replication scope through the DNS snap-in, follow these steps:

1. Click Start ➢ Administrative Tools ➢ DNS.

2. Right-click the zone that you want to set up.

3. Choose Properties.

4. In the Properties dialog box, click the Change button next to Replication (see Figure 6.10).

5. Choose the replication scope that fits your organization.

FIGURE 6.10
DNS zone replica-
tion scope

Advantages of DNS in Windows Server 2022

DNS in Microsoft Windows Server 2022 has some great advantages over many other versions of Microsoft DNS. Here are some of the improvements of DNS in Windows Server 2022 (some of these became available in previous versions of Windows Server):

- Background zone loading
- Support for TCP/IP version 6 (IPv6)
- Read-only domain controllers
- GlobalName zone
- DNS socket pools
- DNS cache locking
- Response Rate Limiting (RRL)
- Unknown Record Support
- IPv6 Root Hints
- DNS Security Extensions (DNSSEC)
- DNS devolution
- Record weighting

- ◆ Netmask ordering
- ◆ DnsUpdateProxy group
- ◆ DNS Policies

Background Zone Loading

If an organization had to restart a DNS server with an extremely large Active Directory Integrated DNS zones database in the past, DNS had a common problem with an Active Directory Integrated DNS zone. After the DNS restart, it could take hours for DNS data to be retrieved from Active Directory. During this time, the DNS server was unable to service any client requests.

Microsoft Windows Server 2008 DNS addressed this problem by implementing background zone loading, and Windows Server 2022 has taken it a step further. As the DNS restarts, the Active Directory zone data populates the database in the background. This allows the DNS server to service client requests for data from other zones almost immediately after a restart.

Background zone loading accomplishes this task by loading the DNS zone using separate threads. This allows a DNS server to service requests while still loading the rest of the zone. If a client sends a request to the DNS server for a computer that has not yet loaded into memory, the DNS server retrieves the data from Active Directory and updates the record.

Support for IPv6 Addresses

Over the past few years, the Internet has starting running into a problem that was not foreseen when it was first created—it started running out of TCP/IP addresses. As you probably know, when the Internet was created, it was used for government and academic purposes only. Then, seemingly overnight, it grew to be the information superhighway. Nowadays, asking someone for their email address is almost more common than asking for their phone number.

Version 4 (IPv4) was the common version of TCP/IP. The release of TCP/IP version 6 (IPv6) has solved the lack-of-IP-addresses problem. IPv4 addresses are 32 bits long, but IPv6 addresses are 128 bits in length. The longer lengths allow for a much greater number of globally unique TCP/IP addresses.

Microsoft Windows Server 2022 DNS has built-in support to accommodate both IPv4 and IPv6 address records (DNS records are explained later in this chapter). DHCP can also issue IPv6 addresses, which lets administrators allow DHCP to register the client with DNS, or the IPv6 client can register their address with the DNS server.

Support for Read-Only Domain Controllers

Windows Server 2008 introduced a new type of domain controller called the *read-only domain controller (RODC)*. This is a full copy of the Active Directory database without the ability to write to Active Directory. The RODC gives an organization the ability to install a domain controller in a location (onsite or offsite) where security is a concern.

Microsoft Windows Server 2022 DNS has implemented a type of zone to help support an RODC. A primary read-only zone allows a DNS server to receive a copy of the application partition (including ForestDNSZones and DomainDNSZones) that DNS uses. This allows DNS to support an RODC because DNS now has a full copy of all DNS zones stored in Active Directory.

A primary, read-only zone is just what it says—a read-only zone; so to make any changes to it, you have to change the primary zones server. Read-only zones cannot have any changes made directly to the read-only server.

DNS Socket Pools

If your server is running Windows Server 2022, you will be able to take advantage of DNS socket pools. *DNS socket pools* allow source port randomization to protect against DNS cache-poisoning attacks.

If you choose to use source port randomization, when the DNS service starts, the DNS server will randomly pick a source port from a pool of available sockets. This is an advantage because instead of DNS using a well-known source port when issuing queries, the DNS server uses a random port selected from the socket pool. This helps guard against attacks because a hacker must correctly access the source port of the DNS query. The socket pool is automatically enabled in DNS with the default settings.

When using the DNS socket pool, the default size of the DNS socket pool is 2,500. When configuring the socket pool, you have the ability to choose a size value from 0 to 10,000. The larger the value, the greater the protection you will have against DNS spoofing attacks. If you decide to configure your socket pool size with a zero value, only a single socket for remote DNS queries will be used.

DNS Cache Locking

Windows Server 2022 *DNS cache locking* allows cached DNS records to remain safe for the duration of the record's time to live (TTL) value. This means that the cached DNS records cannot be overwritten or changed. Because of this DNS feature, it's tougher for hackers to perform cache-poisoning attacks against your DNS server.

DNS administrators can set how long a record will remain safe in cache. The configuration is based on a percent value. For example, if you set your cache locking value to 50 percent, then the cached records cannot be overwritten until half of the TTL has been reached. DNS cache locking is set to 100 percent by default. This means that the cached records never get overwritten.

Response Rate Limiting

Response Rate Limiting (RRL) allows an administrator to help prevent the possibility of hackers using your corporate DNS servers to initiate a denial of service attack on your corporate DNS clients.

Administrators have the ability to configure their RRL settings so that they can control how requests are responded to by DNS servers when these servers receive multiple requests by the same clients. When an administrator configures these settings, it helps prevent hackers from sending a denial of service (DoS) attack using your corporate DNS servers. When configuring RRL, an administrator can manipulate the following settings:

Responses Per Second   This setting allows administrators to set the maximum number of times the same response will be given to a client per second.

Errors Per Second   This setting allows administrators to set the maximum number of times an error response will be sent to the same client per second.

Window   This setting allows administrators to set the number of requests that are made by a client. This setting sets the number of seconds for which responses to a client will be suspended if too many requests are made.

Leak Rate   This setting allows administrators to set how often the DNS server will respond to a query during the suspended time responses. For example, if the DNS server suspends a response to a client for 20 seconds and the leak rate is 10, then the server will still respond to one query for every 10 queries sent. This will ensure that the appropriate clients get responses even when the DNS server is applying response rate limiting.

TC Rate   Administrators can set this setting to inform clients who are trying to connect using TCP when responses to the client are suspended. For example, if the TC rate is 3 and the DNS server suspends responses to a client, the server will issue a request for TCP connection for every three queries. Administrators want to set the value of the TC rate lower than the leak rate. This gives clients the option to connect using TCP before the leak rate applies.

Maximum Responses   This setting allows administrators to set the maximum number of responses a DNS server will issue to a client while responses are suspended.

White List Domains   Administrators can set the list of domains that are to be excluded from RRL settings.

White List Subnets   Administrators can set the list of subnets that are to be excluded from RRL settings.

White List Server Interfaces   Administrators can set the list of DNS server interfaces that are to be excluded from RRL settings.

Unknown Record Support

There are times when a DNS server does not recognize the RDATA format of a resource record. These resource records are known as Unknown Records.

Windows Server 2022 now supports Unknown Records (RFC 3597). This now means that administrators can add these unsupported record types into the Windows DNS server zone. Administrators can add these records using the binary on-wire supported format.

Windows caching resolvers already have the ability to support these unknown record types but DNS servers do not do any processing of these unknown records. What happens is after administrators add the unknown record types to the DNS zone, the DNS servers will respond back to the clients when queries are received.

IPv6 Root Hints

Windows Server 2022 DNS now supports root hints as published by the IANA. DNS name queries now have the ability to use IPv6 root servers for completing name resolution.

DNS Security Extensions

One major issue that you must always look at is keeping your DNS safe. Think about it: DNS is a database of computer names and IP addresses. As a hacker, if I control DNS, I can control your company. In organizations that do not support extra security like IPsec, DNS security is even more important. This is where *Domain Name System Security Extensions (DNSSEC)* can help.

Windows Server 2022 can use a suite of extensions that will help add security to DNS, and that suite is called DNSSEC, which was introduced in Windows Server 2008 R2. The DNSSEC protocol allows your DNS servers to be secure by validating DNS responses. DNSSEC secures your DNS resource records by accompanying the records with a digital signature.

To allow your DNS resource records to receive digital signatures, DNSSEC is applied to your DNS server by a procedure called *zone signing*. This process begins when a DNS resolver initiates a DNS query for a resource record in a signed DNS zone. When a response is returned, a digital signature (RRSIG) accompanies the response, and this allows the response to be verified. If the verification is successful, then the DNS resolver knows that the data has not been modified or tampered with in any way.

Once you implement a zone with DNSSEC, all of the records that are contained within that zone get individually signed. Since all of the records in the zone get individually signed, this gives administrators the ability to add, modify, or delete records without re-signing the entire zone. The only requirement is to re-sign any updated records.

DNS-based Authentication of Named Entities

Another RFC that deals with DNS security is RFC 6698. RFC 6698 explains DNS-based Authentication of Named Entities (DANE). DANE is a protocol that is based on Transport Layer Security Authentication (TLSA). The TLSA records then provide information to DNS clients telling the clients which CA server they should expect their certificate from. By knowing your CA, hackers can't corrupt your DNS cache. Man in the middle attackers can change your cache. This would then point you to their websites. DANE stops these types of attacks. DANE support is now included with Windows Server 2022.

Trust Anchors

Trust anchors are an important part of the DNSSEC process because trust anchors allow the DNS servers to validate the DNSKEY resource records. *Trust anchors* are preconfigured public keys that are linked to a DNS zone. For a DNS server to perform validation, one or more trust anchors must be configured. If you are running an Active Directory Integrated zone, trust anchors can be stored in the Active Directory Domain Services directory partition of the forest. If you decide to store the trust anchors in the directory partition, then all DNS servers that reside on a domain controller get a copy of this trust anchor. On DNS servers that reside on stand-alone servers, trust anchors are stored in a file called TrustAnchors.dns.

If your servers are running Windows Server 2022, then you can view trust anchors in the DNS Manager Console tree in the Trust Points container. You can also use Windows PowerShell or Dnscmd.exe to view trust anchors. Windows PowerShell is the recommended command-line method for viewing trust anchors. The following line is a PowerShell command to view the trust anchors for Contoso.com:

```
get-dnsservertrustanchor sec.contoso.com
```

DNSSEC Clients

Windows 7, Windows 8/8.1, Windows 10, Windows 11, Windows Server 2008/2008 R2, and Windows Server 2012/R2, Server 2016, 2019, and Server 2022 are all DNS clients that receive a response to a DNS query, examine the response, and then evaluate whether the response has been validated by a DNS server. The DNS client itself is nonvalidating, and the DNS client relies on the local DNS server to indicate that validation was successful. If the server doesn't perform validation, then the DNS client service can be configured to return no results.

DNS Devolution

Using *DNS devolution*, if a client computer is a member of a child namespace, the client computer will be able to access resources in the parent namespace without the need to explicitly provide the fully qualified domain name of the resource. DNS devolution removes the leftmost label of the namespace to get to the parent suffix. DNS devolution allows the DNS resolver to create the new FQDNs. DNS devolution works by appending the single-label, unqualified domain name with the parent suffix of the primary DNS suffix name.

Record Weighting

Weighting DNS records will allow an administrator to place a value on DNS SRV records. Clients will then randomly choose SRV records proportional to the weight value assigned.

Netmask Ordering

If round robin is enabled, when a client requests name resolution, the first address entered in the database is returned to the resolver, and it is then sent to the end of the list. The next time a client attempts to resolve the name, the DNS server returns the second name in the database (which is now the first name) and then sends it to the end of the list, and so on. Round robin is enabled by default.

Netmask ordering is a part of the round robin process. When an administrator configures netmask ordering, the DNS server will detect the subnet of the querying client. The DNS server will then return a host address available for the same subnet. Netmask ordering is enabled through the DNS Manager console on the Advanced tab of the server Properties dialog box.

DnsUpdateProxy Group

As mentioned previously, the DHCP server can be configured to register host (A) and pointer (PTR) resource records dynamically on behalf of DHCP clients. Because of this, the DNS server can end up with stale resources. To help solve this issue, an administrator can use the built-in security group called *DnsUpdateProxy*.

To use the DnsUpdateProxy group, an administrator must first create a dedicated user account and configure the DHCP servers with its credentials. This will protect against the creation of unsecured records. Also, when you create the dedicated user account, members of the DnsUpdateProxy group will be able to register records in zones that allow only secured dynamic updates. Multiple DHCP servers can use the same credentials of one dedicated user account.

DNS Policies

One of the best advantages to Windows Server 2022 DNS is the ability to set up DNS Policies. Administrators can set up policies based on location, time of day, deployment types, queries, application load balancing, and more. The following are just some of the items that you can configure:

Application Load Balancing There are many times in a corporate environment when you have multiple copies of the same application running in different locations. Application Load Balancing allows DNS to pass client requests for the same applications (even when they are in different locations) to multiple servers hosting that application. This allows DNS to give an application load balancing.

Location Based Traffic Management Administrators can set DNS to work off of locations and help direct users to resources that are closer to their location. Administrators can set up DNS policies so that a DNS server will respond to a DNS client's query based on geographic location of the client and the IP address of the nearest requested resource.

Split Brain DNS Another DNS policy that an administrator can set up is the ability to have DNS split zones. Split zones allow a DNS server to respond to a client based on whether the clients are internal or external clients. Active Directory zones or stand-alone DNS servers can be configured as Split Brain DNS servers.

Filtering Administrators now have the ability to set up policies to create query filters that are based on criteria that an administrator supplies. Query filters allow an administrator to set up the DNS server to send a custom response based on a specific type of DNS query and/or DNS client.

Forensics Administrators also have the ability to set up a DNS honeypot. A honeypot allows a DNS server to redirect a malicious DNS client to an IP address that does not exist.

Time of Day Based Redirection Administrators can set up a DNS policy to distribute application traffic between different locations. DNS will be able to do this because the policy that you set for an application will be based on the time of day. So for example, when it's 1:00 p.m., a server that has a copy of the application gets all client requests, and at 7:00 p.m., a different server that has a copy of the application gets all of the client requests.

Now that you have learned about some of the features of Windows Server 2022 DNS, let's take a look at some of the DNS record types.

Introducing DNS Record Types

No matter where your zone information is stored, you can rest assured that it contains a variety of DNS information. Although the DNS snap-in makes it unlikely that you'll ever need to edit these files by hand, it's good to know exactly what data is contained there.

As stated previously, zone files consist of a number of resource records. You need to know about several types of resource records to manage your DNS servers effectively. They are discussed in the following sections.

Start of Authority (SOA) Records

The first record in a database file is the *start of authority (SOA) record*. The SOA defines the general parameters for the DNS zone, including the identity of the authoritative server for the zone.

The SOA appears in the following format:

```
@ IN SOA primary_mastercontact_e-mailserial_number
refresh_timeretry_timeexpiration_timetime_to_live
```

Here is a sample SOA from the domain `example.com`:

```
@ IN SOA win2k3r2.example.com. hostmaster.example.com. (
                        5            ; serial number
                        900          ; refresh
                        600          ; retry
                        86400        ; expire
                        3600         ) ; default TTL
```

Table 6.2 lists the attributes stored in the SOA record.

TABLE 6.2:   The SOA record structure

FIELD	MEANING
Current zone	The current zone for the SOA. This can be represented by an @ symbol to indicate the current zone or by naming the zone itself. In the example, the current zone is `example.com`. The trailing dot (`.com.`) indicates the zone's place relative to the root of the DNS.
Class	This will almost always be the letters *IN* for the Internet class.
Type of record	The type of record follows. In this case, it's SOA.
Primary master	The primary master for the zone on which this file is maintained.
Contact email	The Internet email address for the person responsible for this domain's database file. There is no @ symbol in this contact email address because @ is a special character in zone files. The contact email address is separated by a single dot (`.`). So, the email address of root@example.com would be represented by `root.example.com` in a zone file.
Serial number	This is the "version number" of this database file. It increases each time the database file is changed.
Refresh time	The amount of time (in seconds) that a secondary server will wait between checks to its master server to see whether the database file has changed and a zone transfer should be requested.
Retry time	The amount of time (in seconds) that a secondary server will wait before retrying a failed zone transfer.
Expiration time	The amount of time (in seconds) that a secondary server will spend trying to download a zone. Once this time limit expires, the old zone information will be discarded.
Time to live	The amount of time (in seconds) that another DNS server is allowed to cache any resource records from this database file. This is the value that is sent out with all query responses from this zone file when the individual resource record doesn't contain an overriding value.

Name Server Records

Name server (NS) records list the name servers for a domain. This record allows other name servers to look up names in your domain. A zone file may contain more than one name server record. The format of these records is simple:

```
example.com.    IN      NS      Hostname.example.com
```

Table 6.3 explains the attributes stored in the NS record.

TABLE 6.3:   The NS record structure

FIELD	MEANING
Name	The domain that will be serviced by this name server. In this case I used `example.com`.
AddressClass	Internet (IN)
RecordType	Name server (NS)
Name Server Name	The FQDN of the server responsible for the domain

NOTE   Any domain name in the database file that is not terminated with a period will have the root domain appended to the end. For example, an entry that just has the name *sales* will be expanded by adding the root domain to the end, whereas the entry `sales.example.com.` won't be expanded.

Host Record

A *host record* (also called an *A record* for IPv4 and *AAAA record* for IPv6) is used to associate statically a host's name to its IP addresses. The format is pretty simple:

```
host_nameoptional_TTL IN  A  IP_Address
```

Here's an example from my DNS database:

```
www  IN  A  192.168.0.204
SMTP IN  A  192.168.3.144
```

The A or AAAA record ties a hostname (which is part of an FQDN) to a specific IP address. This makes these records suitable for use when you have devices with statically assigned IP addresses. In this case, you create these records manually using the DNS snap-in. As it turns out, if you enable DDNS, your DHCP server can create these for you. This automatic creation is what enables DDNS to work.

Notice that an optional TTL field is available for each resource record in the DNS. This value is used to set a TTL that is different from the default TTL for the domain. For example, if you wanted a 60-second TTL for the www A or AAAA record, it would look like this:

```
www 60 IN  A  192.168.0.204
```

Alias Record

Closely related to the host record is the *alias record,* or *canonical name (CNAME) record.* The syntax of an alias record is as follows:

```
aliasoptional_TTL  IN  CNAME  hostname
```

Aliases are used to point more than one DNS record toward a host for which an A record already exists. For example, if the hostname of your web server was actually chaos, you would likely have an A record such as this:

```
chaos IN A 192.168.1.10
```

Then you could make an alias or CNAME for the record so that www.example.com would point to chaos:

```
www IN CNAME chaos.example.com.
```

Note the trailing dot (.) on the end of the CNAME record. This means the root domain is not appended to the entry.

Pointer Record

A or AAAA records are probably the most visible component of the DNS database because Internet users depend on them to turn FQDNs like www.microsoft.com into the IP addresses that browsers and other components require to find Internet resources. However, the host record has a lesser-known but still important twin: the *pointer (PTR) record.* The format of a PTR record appears as follows:

```
reversed_address.in-addr.arpa. optional_TTL IN PTR targeted_domain_name
```

The A or AAAA record maps a hostname to an IP address, and the PTR record does just the opposite—mapping an IP address to a hostname through the use of the in-addr.arpa zone.

The PTR record is necessary because IP addresses begin with the least-specific portion first (the network) and end with the most-specific portion (the host), whereas hostnames begin with the most-specific portion at the beginning and the least-specific portion at the end.

Consider the example 192.168.1.10 with a subnet mask 255.255.255.0. The portion 192.168.1 defines the network and the final .10 defines the host, or the most-specific portion of the address. DNS is just the opposite: The hostname www.example.com. defines the most-specific portion, www, at the beginning and then traverses the DNS tree to the least-specific part, the dot (.), at the root of the tree.

Reverse DNS records, therefore, need to be represented in this most-specific-to-least-specific manner. The PTR record for mapping 192.168.1.10 to www.example.com would look like this:

```
10.1.168.192.in-addr.arpa. IN PTR www.example.com.
```

Now a DNS query for that record can follow the logical DNS hierarchy from the root of the DNS tree all the way to the most-specific portion.

Mail Exchanger Record

The *mail exchanger (MX) record* is used to specify which servers accept mail for this domain. Each MX record contains two parameters—a preference and a mail server, as shown in the following example:

```
domain IN MX preference mailserver_host
```

The MX record uses the preference value to specify which server should be used if more than one MX record is present. The preference value is a number. The lower the number, the more preferred the server. Here's an example:

```
example.com.    IN  MX  0  mail.example.com.
example.com.    IN  MX  10 backupmail.example.com.
```

In the example, `mail.example.com` is the default mail server for the domain. If that server goes down for any reason, the `backupmail.example.com` mail server is used by emailers.

Service Record

Windows Server 2022 depends on some other services, like the Lightweight Directory Access Protocol (LDAP) and Kerberos. Using a service record, which is another type of DNS record, a Windows 2000, XP, Vista, Windows 7, Windows 8 / 8.1, or Windows 10, Windows 11 client can query DNS servers for the location of a domain controller. This makes it much easier (for both the client and the administrator) to manage and distribute logon traffic in large-scale networks. For this approach to work, Microsoft has to have some way to register the presence of a service in DNS. Enter the service (SRV) record.

Service (SRV) records tie together the location of a service (like a domain controller) with information about how to contact the service. SRV records provide seven items of information. Let's review an example to help clarify this powerful concept. (Table 6.4 explains the fields in the following example.)

```
ldap.tcp.example.com.  86400 IN SRV  10  100  389  hsv.example.com
ldap.tcp.example.com.  86400 IN SRV  20  100  389  msy.example.com
```

TABLE 6.4:   The SRV record structure

FIELD	MEANING
Domain name	Domain for which this record is valid (`ldap.tcp.example.com.`).
TTL	Time to live (86,400 seconds).
Class	This field is always IN, which stands for Internet.
Record type	Type of record (SRV).
Priority	Specifies a preference, similar to the Preference field in an MX record. The SRV record with the lowest priority is used first (`10`).

TABLE 6.4:   The SRV record structure   *(CONTINUED)*

FIELD	MEANING
Weight	Service records with equal priority are chosen according to their weight (100).
Port number	The port where the server is listening for this service (389).
Target	The FQDN of the host computer (`hsv.example.com` and `msy.example.com`).

NOTE   You can define other types of service records. If your applications support them, they can query DNS to find the services they need.

Configuring DNS

In the following sections, you'll begin to learn about the actual DNS server. You will start by installing DNS. Then I will talk about different zone configuration options and what they mean. Finally, you'll complete an exercise that covers configuring Dynamic DNS, delegating zones, and manually entering records.

Installing DNS

If DNS is already installed onto your server, you can skip this exercise. But if you have not installed DNS, let's start by installing DNS. Installing DNS is an important part of running a network. Exercise 6.1 walks you through the installation of a DNS server.

NOTE   If you are using a Dynamic TCP/IP address, please change your TCP/IP number to static.

EXERCISE 6.1   Installing and Configuring the DNS Service

1. Open Server Manager.

2. On the Server Manager dashboard, click the Add Roles And Features link.

3. If a Before You Begin screen appears, click Next.

4. On the Selection type page, choose Role-Based Or Feature-Based Installation and click Next.

5. Click the Select A Server From The Server Pool radio button and choose the server under the Server Pool section. Click Next.

6. Click the DNS Server Item in the Server Role list. If a pop-up window appears telling you that you need to add additional features, click the Add Features button. Click Next to continue.

7. On the Add Features page, just click Next.

8. Click Next on the DNS Server information screen.

9. On the Confirm Installation screen, choose the Restart The Destination Server Automatically If Required check box and then click the Install button.

10. At the Installation progress screen, click Close after the DNS server is installed.

11. Close Server Manager.

Load Balancing with Round Robin

Like other DNS implementations, the Windows Server 2022 implementation of DNS supports load balancing through the use of round robin. Load balancing distributes the network load among multiple network hosts if they are available. You set up round-robin load balancing by creating multiple resource records with the same hostname but different IP addresses for multiple computers. Depending on the options that you select, the DNS server responds with the addresses of one of the host computers.

If round robin is enabled, when a client requests name resolution, the first address entered in the database is returned to the resolver and is then sent to the end of the list. The next time a client attempts to resolve the name, the DNS server returns the second name in the database (which is now the first name) and then sends it to the end of the list, and so on. Round robin is enabled by default.

Configuring a Caching-Only Server

Although all DNS name servers cache queries that they have resolved, caching-only servers are DNS name servers that only perform queries, cache the answers, and return the results. They are not authoritative for any domains, and the information that they contain is limited to what has been cached while resolving queries. Accordingly, they don't have any zone files, and they don't participate in zone transfers. When a caching-only server is first started, it has no information in its cache; the cache is gradually built over time.

Caching-only servers are easy to configure. After installing the DNS service, simply make sure the root hints are configured properly. One advantage to Windows Server 2022 is the ability to also support IPv6 root hints.

1. Right-click your DNS server and choose the Properties command.

2. When the Properties dialog box appears, switch to the Root Hints tab (see Figure 6.11).

3. If your server is connected to the Internet, you should see a list of root hints for the root servers maintained by ICANN and the Internet Assigned Numbers Authority (IANA). If not, click the Add button to add root hints as defined in the cache.dns file.

   You can obtain current cache.dns files on the Internet by using a search engine. Just search for *cache.dns* and download one. (I always try to get cache.dns files from a university or a company that manages domain names.)

Setting Zone Properties

There are six tabs on the Properties dialog box for a forward or reverse lookup zone. You only use the Security tab to control who can change properties and to make dynamic updates to records on that zone. The other tabs are discussed in the following sections.

NOTE Secondary zones don't have a Security tab, and their SOA tab shows you the contents of the master SOA record, which you can't change.

FIGURE 6.11
The Root Hints tab of
the DNS server's
Properties dialog box

GENERAL TAB

The General tab includes the following:

- The Status indicator and the associated Pause button let you see and control whether this zone can be used to answer queries. When the zone is running, the server can use it to answer client queries; when it's paused, the server won't answer any queries it gets for that particular zone.

- The Type indicator and its Change button allow you to select the zone type. The options are Standard Primary, Standard Secondary, and AD-Integrated. (See "Introducing DNS Database Zones" earlier in this chapter.) As you change the type, the controls you see below the horizontal dividing line change too. For primary zones, you'll see a field that lets you select the zone filename; for secondary zones, you'll get controls that allow you to specify the IP addresses of the primary servers. But the most interesting controls are the ones you see for AD Integrated zones. When you change to the AD Integrated zones, you have the ability to make the dynamic zones Secure Only.

- The Replication indicator and its Change button allow you to change the replication scope if the zone is stored in Active Directory. You can choose to replicate the zone data to any of the following:

  - All DNS servers in the Active Directory forest
  - All DNS servers in a specified domain

- All domain controllers in the Active Directory domain (required if you use Windows 2000 domain controllers in your domain)

- All domain controllers specified in the replication scope of the application directory partition

- The Dynamic Updates field gives you a way to specify whether you want to support Dynamic DNS updates from compatible DHCP servers. As you learned earlier in the section "Dynamic DNS and Non-Dynamic DNS," the DHCP server or DHCP client must know about and support Dynamic DNS in order to use it, but the DNS server has to participate too. You can turn dynamic updates on or off, or you can require that updates be secured.

START OF AUTHORITY (SOA) TAB

The following options in the Start Of Authority (SOA) tab, shown in Figure 6.12, control the contents of the SOA record for this zone.

FIGURE 6.12
The Start Of Authority
(SOA) tab of the zone
Properties dialog box

- The Serial Number field indicates which version of the SOA record the server currently holds. Every time you change another field, you should increment the serial number so that other servers will notice the change and get a copy of the updated record.

- The Primary Server and Responsible Person fields indicate the location of the primary name server for this zone and the email address of the administrator responsible for the maintenance of this zone, respectively. The standard username for this is hostmaster.

- The Refresh Interval field controls how often any secondary zones of this zone must contact the primary zone server and get any changes that have been posted since the last update.

- The Retry Interval field controls how long secondary servers will wait after a zone transfer fails before they try again. They'll keep trying at the interval you specify (which should be shorter than the refresh interval) until they eventually succeed in transferring zone data.

- The Expires After field tells the secondary servers when to throw away zone data. The default of 1 day (24 hours) means that a secondary server that hasn't gotten an update in 24 hours will delete its local copy of the zone data.

- The Minimum (Default) TTL field sets the default TTL for all RRs created in the zone. You can assign specific TTLs to individual records if you want.

- The TTL For This Record field controls the TTL for the SOA record itself.

NAME SERVERS TAB

The *name server (NS) record* for a zone indicates which name servers are authoritative for the zone. That normally means the zone primary server and any secondary servers you've configured for the zone. (Remember, secondary servers are authoritative read-only copies of the zone.) You edit the NS record for a zone using the Name Servers tab (see Figure 6.13). The tab shows you which servers are currently listed, and you use the Add, Edit, and Remove buttons to specify which name servers you want included in the zone's NS record.

FIGURE 6.13
The Name Servers tab of the zone Properties dialog box

WINS TAB

The WINS tab allows you to control whether this zone uses WINS forward lookups or not. These lookups pass on queries that DNS can't resolve to WINS for action. This is a useful setup if you're still using WINS on your network. You must explicitly turn this option on with the Use WINS Forward Lookup check box in the WINS tab for a particular zone.

ZONE TRANSFERS TAB

Zone transfers are necessary and useful because they're the mechanism used to propagate zone data between primary and secondary servers. For primary servers (whether AD Integrated or not), you can specify whether your servers will allow zone transfers and, if so, to whom.

You can use the following controls on the Zone Transfers tab to configure these settings per zone:

◆ The Allow Zone Transfers check box controls whether the server answers zone transfer requests for this zone at all—when it's not checked, no zone data is transferred. The Allow Zone Transfers selections are as follows:

◆ To Any Server allows any server anywhere on the Internet to request a copy of your zone data.

◆ Only To Servers Listed On The Name Servers Tab (the default) limits transfers to servers you specify. This is a more secure setting than To Any Server because it limits transfers to other servers for the same zone.

◆ Only To The Following Servers allows you to specify exactly which servers are allowed to request zone transfers. This list can be larger or smaller than the list specified on the Name Servers tab.

◆ The Notify button is for setting up automatic notification triggers that are sent to secondary servers for this zone. Those triggers signal the secondary servers that changes have occurred on the primary server so that the secondary servers can request updates sooner than their normally scheduled interval. The options in the Notify dialog box are similar to those in the Zone Transfers tab. You can enable automatic notification and then choose either Servers Listed On The Name Servers Tab or The Following Servers.

Configuring Zones for Dynamic Updates

In Exercise 6.2, you will create and then modify the properties of a forward lookup zone. In addition, you'll configure the zone to allow dynamic updates.

EXERCISE 6.2   Configuring a Zone for Dynamic Updates

1. Open the DNS management snap-in by selecting Server Manager. Once in Server Manager, click DNS on the left side. In the Servers window (center screen), right-click your server name and choose DNS Manager.

2. Click the DNS server to expand it and then click the Forward Lookup Zones folder. Right-click the Forward Lookup Zones folder and choose New Zone.

---

3. At the New Zone Welcome screen, click Next.

4. At the Zone Type screen, choose the Primary Zone option. If your DNS server is also a domain controller, do not check the box to store the zone in Active Directory. Click Next when you are ready.

5. Enter a new zone name in the Zone Name field and click Next. (I used my last name—-Panek.com.)

6. Leave the default zone filename and click Next.

7. Select the Do Not Allow Dynamic Updates radio button and click Next.

8. Click Finish to end the wizard.

9. Right-click the zone you just created and choose the Properties command.

10. Click the down arrow next to Dynamic Updates. Notice that there are only two options (None and Nonsecure And Secure). The Secure Only option is not available because you are not using Active Directory Integrated. Make sure Nonsecure And Secure is chosen.

11. Click OK to close the Properties box.

12. Close the DNS management snap-in.

13. Close the Server Manager snap-in.

Delegating Zones for DNS

DNS provides the ability to divide the namespace into one or more zones, which can then be stored, distributed, and replicated to other DNS servers. When deciding whether to divide your DNS namespace to make additional zones, consider the following reasons to use additional zones:

◆ A need to delegate management of part of your DNS namespace to another location or department within your organization

◆ A need to divide one large zone into smaller zones for distributing traffic loads among multiple servers, for improving DNS name-resolution performance, or for creating a more fault-tolerant DNS environment

◆ A need to extend the namespace by adding numerous subdomains at once, such as to accommodate the opening of a new branch or site

Each newly delegated zone requires a primary DNS server just as a regular DNS zone does. When delegating zones within your namespace, be aware that for each new zone you create, you need to place delegation records in other zones that point to the authoritative DNS servers for the new zone. This is necessary both to transfer authority and to provide correct referral to other DNS servers and clients of the new servers being made authoritative for the new zone.

In Exercise 6.3, you'll create a delegated subdomain of the domain you created in Exercise 6.2. Note that the name of the server to which you want to delegate the subdomain must be stored in an A or CNAME record in the parent domain.

EXERCISE 6.3   Creating a Delegated DNS Zone

1. Open the DNS management snap-in by selecting Server Manager. Once in Server Manager, click DNS on the left side. In the Servers window (center screen), right-click your server name and choose DNS Manager.

2. Expand the DNS server and locate the zone you created in Exercise 6.2.

3. Right-click the zone and choose the New Delegation command.

4. The New Delegation Wizard appears. Click Next to dismiss the initial wizard page.

5. Enter **ns1** (or whatever other name you like) in the Delegated Domain field of the Delegated Domain Name page. This is the name of the domain for which you want to delegate authority to another DNS server. It should be a subdomain of the primary domain (for example, to delegate authority for farmington.example.net, you'd enter **farmington** in the Delegated Domain field). Click Next to complete this step.

6. When the Name Servers page appears, click the Add button to add the names and IP addresses of the servers that will be hosting the newly delegated zone. For the purpose of this exercise, enter the server name you used in Exercise 6.2. Click the Resolve button to resolve this domain name's IP address automatically into the IP address field. Click OK when you are finished. Click Next to continue with the wizard.

7. Click the Finish button. The New Delegation Wizard disappears, and you'll see the new zone you just created appear beneath the zone you selected in step 3. The newly delegated zone's folder icon is drawn in gray to indicate that control of the zone is delegated.

DNS Forwarding

If a DNS server does not have an answer to a DNS request, it may be necessary to send that request to another DNS server. This is called *DNS forwarding*. You need to understand the two main types of forwarding:

External Forwarding   When a DNS server forwards an external DNS request to a DNS server outside of your organization, this is considered *external forwarding*. For example, a resolver requests the host www.microsoft.com. Most likely, your internal DNS server is not going to have Microsoft's web address in its DNS database. So, your DNS server is going to send the request to an external DNS (most likely your ISP) or use the setup root hints.

Conditional Forwarding   *Conditional forwarding* is a lot like external forwarding except that you are going to forward requests to specific DNS servers based on a condition. Usually this is an excellent setup for internal DNS resolution. For example, let's say that you have two companies, stormwind.com and stormtest.com. If a request comes in for Stormwind.com, it gets forwarded to the Stormwind DNS server, and any requests for Stormtest.com will get forwarded to the Stormtest DNS server. Requests are forwarded to a specific DNS server depending on the condition that an administrator sets up.

Manually Creating DNS Records

From time to time you may find it necessary to add resource records manually to your Windows Server 2022 DNS servers. Although Dynamic DNS frees you from the need to fiddle with A and PTR records for clients and other such entries, you still have to create other resource types (including MX records, required for the proper flow of SMTP email) manually. You can manually create A, PTR, MX, SRV, and many other record types.

There are only two important things to remember for manually creating DNS records:

◆ You must right-click the zone and choose either the New Record command or the Other New Records command.

◆ You must know how to fill in the fields of whatever record type you're using.

For example, to create an MX record, you need three pieces of information (the domain, the mail server, and the priority). To create an SRV record, however, you need several more pieces of information.

In Exercise 6.4, you will manually create an MX record for a mailtest server in the zone you created in Exercise 6.2.

EXERCISE 6.4   Manually Creating DNS RRs

1. Open the DNS management snap-in by selecting Server Manager. Once in Server Manager, click DNS on the left side. In the Servers window (center screen), right-click your server name and choose DNS Manager.

2. Expand your DNS server, right-click its zone, and choose New Host (A record).

3. Enter **mailtest** in the Name field. Enter a TCP/IP number in the IP Address field. (You can use any number for this exercise, such as, for example, 192.168.1.254.) Click the Add Host button.

4. A dialog box appears stating that the host record was created successfully. Click OK. Click Done.

5. Right-click your zone name and choose New Mail Exchanger (MX).

6. Enter **mailtest** in the Host Or Child Domain field and enter **mailtest.yourDomain.com** (or whatever domain name you used in Exercise 6.2) in the Fully-Qualified Domain Name (FQDN) Of Mail Server field and then click OK. Notice that the new record is already visible.

7. Next create an alias (or CNAME) record to point to the mail server. (It is assumed that you already have an A record for **mailtest** in your zone.) Right-click your zone and choose New Alias (CNAME).

8. Type **mail** into the Alias Name field.

9. Type **mailtest.yourDomain.com** into the Fully-Qualified Domain Name (FQDN) For Target Host field.

10. Click the OK button.

11. Close the DNS management snap-in.

DNS Aging and Scavenging

When using dynamic updates, computers (or DHCP) will register a resource record with DNS. These records get removed when a computer is shut down properly. A major problem in the industry is that laptops are frequently removed from the network without a proper shutdown. Therefore, their resource records continue to live in the DNS database.

Windows Server 2022 DNS supports two features called *DNS aging* and *DNS scavenging*. These features are used to clean up and remove stale resource records. DNS zone or DNS server aging and scavenging flag old resource records that have not been updated in a certain amount of time (determined by the scavenging interval). These stale records will be scavenged at the next cleanup interval. DNS uses time stamps on the resource records to determine how long they have been listed in the DNS database.

By default, DNS aging and scavenging are disabled by default. Microsoft states that these features should only be enabled if you have users that are not logging off the network properly. If your users are all using desktops or if your users log off the network properly every day, you should keep these features disabled.

The issue that you can run into if this feature is enabled and DNS deletes records that should not be deleted, then that can stop users from accessing resources on the network because their DNS records have been deleted improperly.

If you decide that you want to enable DNS aging and scavenging, you must enable these features on both at the DNS server and on the zone.

DNS aging and scavenging is done by using time stamps. Time stamps are a date and time value that is used by the DNS server. The date and time is used to determine removal of the resource record when it performs the aging and scavenging operations.

DNS PowerShell Commands

When talking about PowerShell commands for DNS, I must let you know that there are dozens of commands that you can use to configure and maintain a DNS server. Before I show you the table of DNS PowerShell commands, let's look at two commands first.

When we install DNS onto a server, we can use PowerShell to do the install. But when we are talking about Nano server, the PowerShell commands are a bit different.

Let's first look at how you install DNS on a regular Windows server using PowerShell. The following command is the command used to install DNS on a Windows Server.

```
Install-WindowsFeature DNS -IncludeManagementTools
```

Now let's take a look at the PowerShell command for installing DNS on a Nano server. The following commands are used to install DNS on a Nano server. The first command downloads DNS to the Nano server and the second command installs it on the server.

```
Install-NanoServerPackage Microsoft-NanoServer-DNS-Package -Culture en-us
Enable-WindowsOptionalFeature -Online -FeatureName DNS-Server-Full-Role
```

Nano servers have no GUI interface and all installations have to be done using remote tools or PowerShell commands. There are dozens of possible PowerShell commands. Nano servers are excellent servers to use as DNS servers. Just be sure that you know what Roles can be installed onto a Nano server and which Roles can't be installed on a Nano server (like DHCP).

In Table 6.5, I will show you just some of the possible PowerShell commands that are available for DNS.

NOTE For a complete list of DNS PowerShell commands, please visit Microsoft's website at

```
https://docs.microsoft.com/en-us/powershell/module/dnsserver/?view=windowsse
rver2022-ps.
```

TABLE 6.5:   PowerShell Commands for DNS

POWERSHELL COMMAND	DESCRIPTION
Add-DnsServerClientSubnet	This command allows an administrator to add a client subnet to a DNS server.
Add-DnsServerConditionalForwarderZone	Administrators can use this command to add a conditional forwarder to a DNS server.
Add-DnsServerForwarder	This command allows an administrator to add forwarders to a DNS server.
Add-DnsServerPrimaryZone	Administrators can use this command to add a primary zone to a DNS server.
Add-DnsServerQueryResolutionPolicy	This command allows an administrator to add a query resolution policy to DNS.
Add-DnsServerResourceRecord	Administrators can use this command to add a resource record to a DNS zone.
Add-DnsServerResourceRecordA	This command allows an administrator to add an A record to a DNS zone.
Add-DnsServerResourceRecordAAAA	This command allows an administrator to add an AAAA record to a DNS zone.
Add-DnsServerResourceRecordCName	This command allows an administrator to add a CNAME record to a DNS zone.
Add-DnsServerResourceRecordDnsKey	Administrators can use this command to add a DNSKEY record to a DNS zone.
Add-DnsServerResourceRecordDS	This command allows an administrator to add a DS record to a DNS zone.
Add-DnsServerResourceRecordMX	This command allows an administrator to add an MX record to a DNS zone.
Add-DnsServerResourceRecordPtr	This command allows an administrator to add a PTR record to a DNS zone.

TABLE 6.5: PowerShell Commands for DNS *(CONTINUED)*

POWERSHELL COMMAND	DESCRIPTION
Add-DnsServerSecondaryZone	Administrators can use this command to add a secondary zone.
Add-DnsServerSigningKey	This command adds a KSK or ZSK to a signed zone.
Add-DnsServerStubZone	This command adds a stub zone to a DNS server.
Add-DnsServerTrustAnchor	Admins can use this command to add a trust anchor to a DNS server.
Add-DnsServerZoneDelegation	This command allows an administrator to add a new delegated DNS zone to an existing zone.
Clear-DnsServerCache	Administrators use this command to clear resource records from a DNS cache.
ConvertTo-DnsServerPrimaryZone	This command converts a zone to a primary zone.
Get-DnsServer	This command retrieves configuration information for a DNS server.
Get-DnsServerDsSetting	This command allows you to gather information about DNS Active Directory settings.
Get-DnsServerRootHint	Administrators use this command to view root hints on a DNS server.
Get-DnsServerScavenging	Administrators use this command to view DNS aging and scavenging settings.
Get-DnsServerSetting	This command allows you to view DNS server settings.
Get-DnsServerSigningKey	This command allows you to view zone signing keys.
Import-DnsServerResourceRecordDS	This command allows an administrator to import DNS resource record from a file.
Import-DnsServerRootHint	This command imports root hints from a DNS server.
Remove-DnsServerZone	Administrators use this command to remove a DNS zone from a server.
Resume-DnsServerZone	This command allows you to resume resolution on a suspended zone.
Set-DnsServer	Administrators can use this command to set the DNS server configuration.

TABLE 6.5:   PowerShell Commands for DNS *(CONTINUED)*

POWERSHELL COMMAND	DESCRIPTION
Set-DnsServerRootHint	This command allows an administrator to replace a server's root hints.
Set-DnsServerSetting	Administrators can use this command to change DNS server settings.
Test-DnsServer	This command allows an administrator to test a functioning DNS server.

The Bottom Line

Understand DNS.   DNS was designed to be a robust, scalable, and high-performance system for resolving friendly names to TCP/IP host addresses. Microsoft's DNS is based on a widely accepted set of industry standards. Because of this, Microsoft's DNS can work with both Windows- and non-Windows-based networks.

Master It   You are an administrator of a large network. All computers are on the same network. You need to configure a Windows service that allows you to turn hostnames into IP addresses.

Understand DNS records.   Understanding which DNS records to use for each server, computer, host, and service is one of the most important ways to best set up your network. Setting up the proper DNS records will ensure that your connection to Azure will work seamlessly.

Master It   You are the administrator of an organization that has decided to use cloud-based services. You need to be sure that your DNS records are set properly and that you use the proper record for each component.

Understand Dynamic Updates.   As an IT administrator, you have the ability to configure all of the DNS records manually or you can use Dynamic Updates. Configuring DNS records manually will work for an organization where IP addresses are manually assigned to hosts. But if your network automatically assigns IP addresses to host names, this can be a very difficult task because IP addresses can change daily.

Master It   You are the administrator of an organization that has 1,000 hosts on the network. You need to set up the DNS server and clients to update the DNS database automatically.

Chapter 7

Understanding Active Directory

One of the most important tasks that you will complete on a network is setting up your domain. To set up your domain properly, you must know how to install and configure your domain controllers.

Once you understand how to plan properly for your domain environment, you will learn how to install Active Directory, which you will accomplish by promoting a Windows Server 2022 computer to a domain controller. We will look at the difference between setting up Active Directory on a Server Core machine vs. Windows Server 2022 with the Desktop Experience.

I will also discuss a feature in Windows Server 2022 called a *read-only domain controller (RODC)*, and I will show you how to install Active Directory using Windows PowerShell.

IN THIS CHAPTER YOU'LL LEARN

◆ Know the prerequisites for promoting a server to a domain controller

◆ Understand domains, trees, and forests

NOTE   For the exercises in this chapter, I assume you are creating a Windows Server 2022 machine in a test environment and not on a live network.

Verifying the File System

When you're planning your Active Directory deployment, the file system that the operating system uses is an important concern for two reasons. First, the file system can provide the ultimate level of security for all the information (that is, data) stored on the server itself. Second, it is responsible for managing and tracking all of this data. The Windows Server 2022 platform supports three file systems:

◆ File Allocation Table 32 (FAT32)

◆ Windows NT File System (NTFS)

◆ Resilient File System (ReFS)

Although ReFS was new to Windows Server 2012, NTFS has been around for many years, and NTFS in Windows Server 2022 has been improved for better performance.

If you have been working with servers for many years, you may have noticed a few changes to the server file system choices. For example, in Windows Server 2003, you could choose between FAT, FAT32, and NTFS. In Windows Server 2022, you can choose between FAT32, NTFS, and ReFS (see Figure 7.1).

FIGURE 7.1
Format options on
Windows Server 2022

New Simple Volume Wizard ✕

Format Partition
To store data on this partition, you must format it first.

Choose whether you want to format this volume, and if so, what settings you want to use.

○ Do not format this volume

● Format this volume with the following settings:

File system:	NTFS ▾
Allocation unit size:	FAT32 / **NTFS** / ReFS
Volume label:	New Volume

☑ Perform a quick format

☐ Enable file and folder compression

< Back   Next >   Cancel

Resilient File System (ReFS)

Windows Server 2022 includes a file system called *Resilient File System (ReFS)*. ReFS was created to help Windows Server maximize the availability of data and online operation. ReFS allows the Windows Server 2022 system to continue to function despite some errors that would normally cause data to be lost or the system to go down. ReFS uses data integrity to protect your data from errors and also to make sure that all of your important data is online when that data is needed.

One of the issues that IT members have had to face over the years is the problem of rapidly growing data sizes. As we continue to rely more and more on computers, our data continues to get larger and larger. This is where ReFS can help an IT department. ReFS was designed specifically with the issues of scalability and performance in mind, which resulted in some of the following ReFS features:

Availability   If your hard disk becomes corrupt, ReFS has the ability to implement a salvage strategy that removes the data that has been corrupted. This feature allows the healthy data to continue to be available while the unhealthy data is removed. All of this can be done without taking the hard disk offline.

Scalability   One of the main advantages of ReFS is the ability to support volume sizes up to 2^{78} bytes using 16 KB cluster sizes, while Windows stack addressing allows 2^{64} bytes. ReFS also supports file sizes of $2^{64}-1$ bytes, 2^{64} files in a directory, and the same number of directories in a volume.

Robust Disk Updating   ReFS uses a disk updating system referred to as an *allocate-on-write transactional model* (also known as *copy on write*). This model helps to avoid many hard disk issues while data is written to the disk because ReFS updates data using disk writes to multiple locations in an atomic manner instead of updating data in place.

Data Integrity   ReFS uses a check-summed system to verify that all data that is being written and stored is accurate and reliable. ReFS always uses allocate-on-write for updates to the data, and it uses checksums to detect disk corruption.

Application Compatibility   ReFS allows for most NTFS features and also supports the Win32 API. Because of this, ReFS is compatible with most Windows applications.

NTFS

Let's start with some of the features of NTFS. There are many benefits to using NTFS, including support for the following:

Disk Quotas   To restrict the amount of disk space used by users on the network, system administrators can establish *disk quotas*. By default, Windows Server 2022 supports disk quota restrictions at the volume level. That is, you can restrict the amount of storage space that a specific user uses on a single disk volume. Third-party solutions that allow more granular quota settings are also available.

File System Encryption   One of the fundamental problems with network operating systems (NOSs) is that system administrators are often given full permission to view all files and data stored on hard disks, which can be a security and privacy concern. In some cases, this is necessary. For example, to perform backup, recovery, and disk management functions, at least one user must have all permissions. Windows Server 2022 and NTFS address these issues by allowing for *file system encryption*. Encryption essentially scrambles all of the data stored within files before they are written to the disk. When an authorized user requests the files, they are transparently decrypted and provided. By using encryption, you can prevent the data from being used in case it is stolen or intercepted by an unauthorized user—even a system administrator.

Dynamic Volumes   Protecting against disk failures is an important concern for production servers. Although earlier versions of Windows NT supported various levels of Redundant Array of Independent Disks (RAID) technology, software-based solutions had some shortcomings. Perhaps the most significant was that administrators needed to perform server reboots to change RAID configurations. Also, you could not make some configuration changes without completely reinstalling the operating system. With Windows Server 2022 support for *dynamic volumes*, system administrators can change RAID and other disk configuration settings without needing to reboot or reinstall the server. The result is greater data protection, increased scalability, and increased uptime. Dynamic volumes are also included with ReFS.

Mounted Drives   By using *mounted drives*, system administrators can map a local disk drive to an NTFS directory name. This helps them organize disk space on servers and increase manageability. By using mounted drives, you can mount the `C:\Users` directory to an actual physical disk. If that disk becomes full, you can copy all of the files to another, larger drive without changing the directory path name or reconfiguring applications.

Remote Storage   System administrators often notice that as soon as they add more space, they must plan the next upgrade. One way to recover disk space is to move infrequently used files to external hard drives. However, backing up and restoring these files can be quite difficult and time-consuming. System administrators can use the *remote storage* features supported by NTFS to off-load seldom-used data automatically to a backup system or other devices. The files, however, remain available to users. If a user requests an archived file, Windows Server 2022 can automatically restore the file from a remote storage device and make it available. Using remote storage like this frees up system administrators' time and allows them to focus on tasks other than micromanaging disk space.

Self-Healing NTFS   In previous versions of the Windows Server operating system, if you had to fix a corrupted NTFS volume, you used a tool called Chkdsk.exe. The disadvantage of this tool is that the Windows Server's availability was disrupted. If this server was your domain controller, that could stop domain logon authentication.

To help protect the Windows Server 2022 NTFS file system, Microsoft now uses a feature called self-healing NTFS. *Self-healing NTFS* attempts to fix corrupted NTFS file systems without taking them offline. Self-healing NTFS allows an NTFS file system to be corrected without running the Chkdsk.exe utility. New features added to the NTFS kernel code allow disk inconsistencies to be corrected without system downtime.

Security   NTFS allows you to configure not only folder-level security but also file-level security. NTFS security is one of the biggest reasons most companies use NTFS. ReFS also allows folder- and file-level security.

SETTING UP THE NTFS PARTITION

Although the features mentioned in the previous section likely compel most system administrators to use NTFS, additional reasons make using it mandatory. The most important reason is that the Active Directory data store must reside on an NTFS partition. Therefore, before you begin installing Active Directory, make sure you have at least one NTFS partition available. Also, be sure you have a reasonable amount of disk space available (at least 4 GB). Because the size of the Active Directory data store will grow as you add objects to it, also be sure that you have adequate space for the future.

Exercise 7.1 shows you how to use the administrative tools to view and modify disk configuration.

WARNING   Before you make any disk configuration changes, be sure you completely understand their potential effects; then perform the test in a lab environment and make sure you have good, verifiable backups handy. Changing partition sizes and adding and removing partitions can result in a total loss of all information on one or more partitions.

If you want to convert an existing partition from FAT or FAT32 to NTFS, you need to use the CONVERT command-line utility. For example, the following command converts the C: partition from FAT to NTFS:

```
CONVERT c: /fs:ntfs
```

EXERCISE 7.1   Viewing the Disk Configurations

1. Right-click on the Start button and then choose Computer Management.

2. Under Storage, click Disk Management (see Figure 7.2).

FIGURE 7.2
Disk Management

The Disk Management program shows you the logical and physical disks that are currently configured on your system.

3. Use the View menu to choose various depictions of the physical and logical drives in your system.

4. To see the available options for modifying partition settings, right-click any of the disks or partitions. This step is optional.

5. Close Computer Management.

Verifying Network Connectivity

Although a Windows Server 2022 computer can be used by itself without connecting to a network, you will not harness much of the potential of the operating system without network connectivity. Because the fundamental purpose of a network operating system is to provide resources to users, you must verify network connectivity.

Basic Connectivity Tests

Before you begin to install Active Directory, you should perform several checks of your current configuration to ensure that the server is configured properly on the network. You should test the following:

Network Adapter   At least one network adapter should be installed and properly configured on your server. A quick way to verify that a network adapter is properly installed is to use the Computer Management administrative tool. Under Device Manager, Network Adapters branch, you should have at least one network adapter listed. If you do not, use the Add Hardware icon in Control Panel to configure hardware.

TCP/IP   Make sure that TCP/IP is installed, configured, and enabled on any necessary network adapters. The server should also be given a valid IP address and subnet mask. Optionally, you may need to configure a default gateway, DNS servers, WINS servers, and other network settings. If you are using DHCP, be sure that the assigned information is correct. It is always a good idea to use a static IP address for servers because IP address changes can cause network connectivity problems if they are not handled properly.

Internet Access   If the server should have access to the Internet, verify that it is able to connect to external web servers and other machines outside of the local area network (LAN). If the server is unable to connect, you might have a problem with the TCP/IP configuration.

LAN Access   The server should be able to view other servers and workstations on the network. If other machines are not visible, make sure that the network and TCP/IP configurations are correct for your environment.

Client Access   Network client computers should be able to connect to your server and view any shared resources. A simple way to test connectivity is to create a share and test whether other machines are able to see files and folders within it. If clients cannot access the machine, make sure that both the client and the server are configured properly.

Wide Area Network Access   If you're working in a distributed environment, you should ensure that you have access to any remote sites or users who will need to connect to this machine. Usually, this is a simple test that can be performed by a network administrator.

Tools and Techniques for Testing Network Configuration

In some cases, verifying network access can be quite simple. You might have some internal and external network resources with which to test. In other cases, it might be more complicated. You can use several tools and techniques to verify that your network configuration is correct.

Using the Ipconfig Utility   By typing **ipconfig/all** at the command prompt, you can view information about the TCP/IP settings of a computer. Figure 7.3 shows the types of information you'll receive.

Using the Ping Command   The ping command was designed to test connectivity to other computers. You can use the command simply by typing **ping** and then an IP address or hostname at the command line. The following are some steps for testing connectivity using the ping command.

> **Ping the router on the Same Subnet**   You should start by pinging the router's IP address on the network to check for a response. If you receive one, then you have connectivity to the network/subnet.

FIGURE 7.3
Viewing TCP/IP
information with the
ipconfig utility

```
Administrator: Windows PowerShell                                    —    □    ×
PS C:\Users\Administrator> ipconfig

Windows IP Configuration


Ethernet adapter Ethernet:

   Connection-specific DNS Suffix  . : dts
   Link-local IPv6 Address . . . . . : fe80::2080:e2c1:15d4:7173%6
   IPv4 Address. . . . . . . . . . . : 192.168.0.14
   Subnet Mask . . . . . . . . . . . : 255.255.255.0
   Default Gateway . . . . . . . . . : 192.168.0.1
PS C:\Users\Administrator>
```

Next check to see whether you can ping another machine using its hostname. If this
works, then local name resolution works properly.

Ping Computers on Different Subnets To ensure that routing is set up properly, you
should attempt to ping computers that are on other subnets (if any exist) on your network.
If this test fails, try pinging the default gateway. Any errors may indicate a problem in the
network configuration or a problem with a router.

WHEN YOU DON'T RECEIVE A RESPONSE

Some firewalls, routers, or servers on your network or on the Internet might prevent you from
receiving a successful response from a ping command. This is usually for security reasons (malicious users might attempt to disrupt network traffic using excessive pings as well as redirects and
smurf attacks). If you do not receive a response, do not assume that the service is not available.
Instead, try to verify connectivity in other ways. For example, you can use the TraceRT command
to demonstrate connectivity beyond your subnet, even if other routers ignore Internet Control
Message Protocol (ICMP) responses. Because the display of a second router implies connectivity, the
path to an ultimate destination shows success even if it does not display the actual names and
addresses.

Using the TraceRT Command The TraceRT command works just like the ping command
except that the TraceRT command shows you every hop along the way. So, if one router or
switch is down, the TraceRT command will show you where the trace stops.

Browsing the Network To ensure that you have access to other computers on the network,
be sure that they can be viewed by clicking Network. This verifies that your name resolution
parameters are set up correctly and that other computers are accessible. Also, try connecting
to resources (such as file shares or printers) on other machines.

Browsing the Internet You can quickly verify whether your server has access to the Internet by visiting a known website, such as www.microsoft.com. Success ensures that you have access outside of your network. If you do not have access to the Web, you might need to verify your proxy server settings (if applicable) and your DNS server settings.

By performing these simple tests, you can ensure that you have a properly configured network connection and that other network resources are available.

Understanding Active Directory

The first thing that you need to understand about Active Directory is that Active Directory is just a database. When you think about Active Directory this way, it makes Active Directory easier to understand and not such a scary proposition.

Now, even though it's just a database, it's one of the most important databases that you will ever set up. This is a database that controls all the objects in your network.

The first step when setting up Active Directory is to understand the different ways you can set it up. During the installation process, you need to understand the difference between a Domain, Tree or Forest. These options will be asked during the Active Directory setup. If you choose the wrong option, you may setup your network incorrectly. So, this is where we need to start.

Domains

There is one question that I frequently get from new IT people or people who work for a company. What is a domain? Most IT have heard this term, but it can be a difficult thing to explain to people.

Domains are LOGICAL groupings of objects. You may hear people say that a domain is a logical grouping of security objects. But this is not really true because not all objects in a domain are security objects.

So why did I stress the word *LOGICAL*? Domains are logical groupings and not physical groupings. For example, Microsoft.com is worldwide. Their network has offices all over the world. They are not all located in the same physical location. That's why domains are logical. They can stretch across multiple geographic locations.

When you are reading one of my books or reading about domains on Microsoft's website, you will notice that domains are represented by a Triangle. So, when you are seeing a drawing of a domain, the Triangle represents that single domain.

When you name your first domain, for example, StormWindAD.net you are establishing a Tree. So let's look at how Trees work.

Trees

Trees are one or more domains that follow the same contiguous namespace. For example, I have a domain called StormWindAD.net. If I decide to create a child domain called Florida. The full name of that domain name is Florida.StormWindAD.net.

Think about when you were born. When my parents named me William, I took on my parent's last name. So, I became William Panek. Domains in Tree work the same way. When you create a child domain, its takes on the name of the parent.

We can even take it a step further. Let's create another child domain under Florida called Orlando. The full name would be `Orlando.Florida.StormWindAD.net`. This allows you to setup child domains for any reason if you need them.

I have worked with companies that create child domains based on geographic location, department names or even the resources held in the domain. This gives you a lot of flexibility on how you setup your network.

Most small to mid-size companies will only have a single tree in their Active Directory structure. But there may be times that you want to create a second tree. For example, StormWind buys out `WillPanek.com`. StormWind may choose to create a second Tree with the parent name of `WillPanek.com`.

Now we have two Trees: `StormWindAD.net` and `WillPanek.com`. All of the child domains will follow the parent name of which ever Tree they are created in.

Forests

So now that you understand Trees, let's talk about Forests. Let's take a look at the example I gave you in the last section under Trees. We have two Trees: `StormWindAD.com` and `WillPanek.com`. These two trees are part of the same Active Directory. This is our Forest.

A Forest is one or more Trees that are part of the same Active Directory structure. So, if you have only one Tree, you still have a Forest (one or more Trees). If I have three Trees in my Active Directory, all three are part of the same Forest.

Now don't get me wrong. You can have multiple Forests in a company. For example. If `StormWindAD.net` buys out `WillPanek.com` but StormWind does not want the WillPanek network to be part of their Active Directory Forest, they can leave it as two separate Forests.

The downside to this is that Forests do NOT work together by default. Most companies have their own Forest and you would not want your network to automatically work with someone else's network. That's not a partnership, that's just hacking.

So, if you own two separate Forests, you will need to do extra work to make them work together. This can be done in many different ways but it will require extra work.

This is why it is so important to understand what Domains, Trees, and Forests do. Because if I setup a network and I set each company department as their own Forest, none of my departments will be able to work with each other unless I do a lot of work to make it happen.

During the Active Directory installation, you will have the option to do the following:

- Add an additional Domain Controller to an existing Domain
- Add a new domain to an existing Tree
- Add a new Tree to an existing Forest
- Add a new Forest

So, it is important to understand each of these components so that you setup your Active Directory network properly for your organization.

Understanding Domain and Forest Functionality

Windows Server 2022 Active Directory uses a concept called *domain and forest functionality*. The functional level that you choose during the Active Directory installation determines which features your domain can use. Since Windows Server 2022 is built on the Windows Server 2016 frame, the highest function level you can choose is Windows Server 2016.

About the Domain Functional Level

Windows Server 2022 will support the following domain functional levels:

◆ Windows Server 2008

◆ Windows Server 2008 R2

◆ Windows Server 2012

◆ Windows Server 2012 R2

◆ Windows Server 2016

Which function level you use depends on the domain controllers you have installed on your network. This is an important fact to remember. You can use any version of Windows Server as long as those servers are member servers only. You can only use Domain Controllers as low as your function level.

For example, if the Domain Function Level is Windows Server 2012 R2, then all domain controllers must be running Windows Server 2012 R2 or higher. You can have Windows Server 2008 R2 member servers but all of your domain controllers need to be at least 2012 R2.

NOTE Windows Server 2022 no longer supports the Windows Server 2003 function levels. With Windows Server 2003 being no longer supported, the Windows Server 2003 function levels have been removed.

Table 7.1 shows the features available in Windows Server 2008, Windows Server 2008 R2, Windows Server 2012, Windows Server 2012 R2, and Windows Server 2016 domain function levels.

TABLE 7.1 Comparing domain functional levels

DOMAIN FUNCTIONAL FEATURE	WINDOWS SERVER 2008	WINDOWS SERVER 2008 R2	WINDOWS SERVER 2012	WINDOWS SERVER 2012 R2	WINDOWS SERVER 2016
Privileged access management	Disabled	Disabled	Disabled	Enabled	Enabled
Authentication assurance	Disabled	Enabled	Enabled	Enabled	Enabled
Fine-grained password policies	Enabled	Enabled	Enabled	Enabled	Enabled
Last interactive logon information	Enabled	Enabled	Enabled	Enabled	Enabled

Domain Functional Feature	Windows Server 2008	Windows Server 2008 R2	Windows Server 2012	Windows Server 2012 R2	Windows Server 2016
Advanced Encryption Services (AES 128 and 256) support for the Kerberos protocol	Enabled	Enabled	Enabled	Enabled	Enabled
Distributed File System replication support for Sysvol	Enabled	Enabled	Enabled	Enabled	Enabled
Read-only domain controller (RODC)	Enabled	Enabled	Enabled	Enabled	Enabled
Ability to redirect the Users and Computers containers	Enabled	Enabled	Enabled	Enabled	Enabled
Ability to rename domain controllers	Enabled	Enabled	Enabled	Enabled	Enabled
Logon time stamp updates	Enabled	Enabled	Enabled	Enabled	Enabled
Kerberos KDC key version numbers	Enabled	Enabled	Enabled	Enabled	Enabled
Passwords for InetOrgPerson objects	Enabled	Enabled	Enabled	Enabled	Enabled
Converts NT groups to domain local and global groups	Enabled	Enabled	Enabled	Enabled	Enabled
SID history	Enabled	Enabled	Enabled	Enabled	Enabled
Group nesting	Enabled	Enabled	Enabled	Enabled	Enabled
Universal groups	Enabled	Enabled	Enabled	Enabled	Enabled

About Forest Functionality

Windows Server 2022 forest functionality applies to all of the domains in a forest. All domains have to be upgraded to Windows Server 2016 /2019 /2022 before the forest can be upgraded to Windows Server 2016.

There are five levels of forest functionality:

◆ Windows Server 2008

◆ Windows Server 2008 R2

- Windows Server 2012

- Windows Server 2012 R2

- Windows Server 2016

Windows Server 2008, Windows Server 2008 R2, Windows Server 2012, Windows Server 2012 R2, and Windows Server 2022 have many of the same forest features. Some of these features are described in the following list:

Global Catalog Replication Enhancements   When an administrator adds a new attribute to the global catalog, only those changes are replicated to other global catalogs in the forest. This can significantly reduce the amount of network traffic generated by replication.

Defunct Schema Classes and Attributes   You can never permanently remove classes and attributes from the Active Directory schema. However, you can mark them as defunct so that they cannot be used. With Windows Server 2003, Windows Server 2008/2008 R2, Windows Server 2012/2012 R2, and Windows Server 2022 forest functionality, you can redefine the defunct schema attribute so that it occupies a new role in the schema.

Forest Trusts   Previously, system administrators had no easy way of granting permission on resources in different forests. Windows Server 2003, Windows Server 2008/2008 R2, Windows Server 2012/2012 R2, and Windows Server 2022 resolve some of these difficulties by allowing trust relationships between separate Active Directory forests. Forest trusts act much like domain trusts, except that they extend to every domain in two forests. Note that all forest trusts are intransitive.

Linked Value Replication   Windows Server 2003, Windows Server 2008/2008 R2, Windows Server 2012/2012 R2, and Windows Server 2022 use a concept called *linked value replication*. With linked value replication, only the user record that has been changed is replicated (not the entire group). This can significantly reduce network traffic associated with replication.

Renaming Domains   Although the Active Directory domain structure was originally designed to be flexible, there were several limitations. Because of mergers, acquisitions, corporate reorganizations, and other business changes, you may need to rename domains. In Windows Server 2008/2008 R2, Windows Server 2012/2012 R2, and Windows Server 2016 / 2019 / 2022 you can change the DNS and NetBIOS names for any domain. Note that this operation is not as simple as just issuing a `rename` command. Instead, there's a specific process that you must follow to make sure the operation is successful. Fortunately, when you properly follow the procedure, Microsoft supports domain renaming even though not all applications support it.

Other Features   Windows Server 2008 and higher also support the following features:

- Improved replication algorithms and dynamic auxiliary classes are designed to increase performance, scalability, and reliability.

- *Active Directory Federation Services (AD FS)*, also known as *Trustbridge*, handles federated identity management. *Federated identity management* is a standards-based information technology process that enables distributed identification, authentication, and authorization across organizational and platform boundaries. The ADFS solution in Windows Server 2008, Windows Server 2008 R2, Windows Server 2012, Windows Server 2012 R2, and Windows Server 2016/2019/2022 helps administrators address these challenges by enabling organizations to share a user's identity information securely.

◆ *Active Directory Lightweight Directory Services (AD LDS)* was developed for organizations that require flexible support for directory-enabled applications. AD LDS, which uses the Lightweight Directory Access Protocol (LDAP), is a directory service that adds flexibility and helps organizations avoid increased infrastructure costs.

◆ Active Directory Recycle Bin (Windows Server 2008 R2 Forest level or higher) provides administrators with the ability to restore deleted objects in their entirety while AD DS is running. Before this, if you deleted an Active Directory object, you needed to recover it from a backup. Now you can recover the object from the AD recycle bin.

Planning the Domain Structure

Once you have verified the technical configuration of your server for Active Directory, it's time to verify the Active Directory configuration for your organization. Since the content of this chapter focuses on installing the first domain in your environment, you really need to know only the following information prior to beginning setup:

◆ The DNS name of the domain

◆ The computer name or the NetBIOS name of the server (which will be used by previous versions of Windows to access server resources)

◆ The domain functional level in which the domain will operate

◆ Whether other DNS servers are available on the network

◆ What type of and how many DNS servers are available on the network

However, if you will be installing additional domain controllers in your environment or will be attaching to an existing Active Directory structure, you should also have the following information:

◆ If this domain controller will join an existing domain, you should know the name of that domain. You will also either require a password for a member of the Enterprise Administrators group for that domain or have someone with those permissions create a domain account before promotion.

◆ You should know whether the new domain will join an existing tree and, if so, the name of the tree it will join.

◆ You should know the name of a forest to which this domain will connect (if applicable).

Installing Active Directory

Installing Active Directory is an easy and straightforward process as long as you plan adequately and make the necessary decisions beforehand. There are many ways that you can install Active Directory.

You can install Active Directory by using the Windows Server 2022 installation disk (Install from Media, or IFM), using Server Manager, or using Windows PowerShell. But before you can do the actual installation, you must first make sure that your network is ready for the install.

In the following sections, you'll look at the benefits and required steps to install the first domain controller in a given environment.

Improved Active Directory Features

As with any new version of Windows Server, Microsoft has made some improvements to Active Directory. The following improvements have been made to Windows Server 2016/2019/2022 Active Directory:

Privileged Access Management Privileged access management (PAM) allows you to alleviate security concerns about the Active Directory environment. Some of these security issues include credential theft techniques (pass-the-hash and spear phishing) along with other types of similar attacks. PAM allows an administrator to create new access solutions that can be configured by using Microsoft Identity Manager (MIM).

Azure AD Join Azure Active Directory Join allows you to set up an Office 365 based Azure network and then easily join your end-users systems to that domain.

Microsoft Passport Microsoft Passport allows your users to setup a key-based authentication that allows your users to authenticate by using more than just their password (biometrics or PIN numbers). Your users would then logon to their systems using a biometric or PIN number that is linked to a certificate or an asymmetrical key pair.

Read-Only Domain Controllers

Windows Server 2022 supports another type of domain controller called the *read-only domain controller (RODC)*. This is a full copy of the Active Directory database without the ability to write to Active Directory. The RODC gives an organization the ability to install a domain controller in a location (onsite or offsite) where security is a concern.

RODCs need to get their Active Directory database from another domain controller. If there are no domain controllers set up yet for a domain, RODCs will not be available (the option will be grayed out). Implementing an RODC is the same as adding another domain controller to a domain. The installation is exactly the same except that when you get to the screen to choose Domain Controller options, you check the box for RODC. Again, this is ONLY available if there are other domain controllers already in the domain.

Active Directory Prerequisites

Before you install Active Directory into your network, you must first make sure your network and the server meet some minimum requirements. Table 7.2 will show you the requirements needed for Active Directory.

The Installation Process

Windows Server 2022 computers are configured as either member servers (if they are joined to a domain) or stand-alone servers (if they are part of a workgroup). The process of converting a

TABLE 7.2 Active Directory requirements

REQUIREMENT	DESCRIPTION
Adprep	When adding the first Windows Server 2022 domain controller to an existing Active Directory domain, Adprep commands run automatically as needed.
Credentials	When installing a new AD DS forest, the administrator must be set to local Administrator on the first server. To install an additional domain controller in an existing domain, you need to be a member of the Domain Admins group.
DNS	Domain Name System needs to be installed for Active Directory to function properly. You can install DNS during the Active Directory installation.
NTFS	The Windows Server 2022 drives that store the database, log files, and SYSVOL folder must be placed on a volume that is formatted with the NTFS file system.
RODCs	Read Only Domain Controllers can be installed as long as another domain controller (Windows Server 2008 or newer) already exists on the domain.
TCP/IP	You must configure the appropriate TCP/IP settings on your domain, and you must configure the DNS server addresses.

server to a domain controller is known as *promotion*. Through the use of a simple and intuitive wizard in Server Manager, system administrators can quickly configure servers to be domain controllers after installation. Administrators also have the ability to promote domain controllers using Windows PowerShell.

The first step in installing Active Directory is promoting a Windows Server 2022 computer to a domain controller. The first domain controller in an environment serves as the starting point for the forest, trees, domains, and the operations master roles.

Exercise 7.2 shows the steps you need to follow to promote an existing Windows Server 2022 computer to a domain controller. To complete the steps in this exercise, you must have already installed and configured a Windows Server 2022 computer. You also need a DNS server that supports SRV records. If you do not have a DNS server available, the Active Directory Installation Wizard automatically configures one for you.

EXERCISE 7.2 Promoting a Domain Controller

1. Install the Active Directory Domain Services by clicking the Add Roles And Features link in Server Manager's Dashboard view.

2. At the Before You Begin screen, click Next.

3. The Select Installation Type screen will be next. Make sure that the Role-Based radio button is selected and click Next.

4. At the Select Destination Server screen, choose the local machine. Click Next.

5. At the Select Server Roles screen, click the check box for Active Directory Domain Services.

6. After you check the Active Directory Domain Services box, a pop-up menu will appear asking you to install additional features. Click the Add Features button.

7. Click Next.

8. At the Select Features screen, accept the defaults and click Next.

9. Click Next at the information screen.

10. Click the Install button at the Confirmation Installation screen.

11. The Installation Progress screen will show you how the installation is progressing.

12. After the installation is complete, click the Close button.

13. On the left-side window, click the AD DS link.

14. Click the More link (see Figure 7.4) next to Configuration Required for Active Directory Domain Services.

FIGURE 7.4
New Forest screen

15. Under the Post-Deployment Configuration section, click the Promote This Server To A Domain Controller link.

16. At this point, you will configure this domain controller. You are going to install a new domain controller in a new domain in a new forest. At the Deployment Configuration screen, choose the Add A New Forest radio button. You then need to add a root domain name. In this exercise, I will use StormWindAD.com (see Figure 7.5). Click Next.

FIGURE 7.5
New Forest screen

17. At the Domain Controller Options screen, set the following options (see Figure 7.6):

- Function levels: Windows Server 2012 R2 (for both; we will upgrade them later).

- Verify that the DNS and Global Catalog check boxes are checked. Notice that the RODC check box is grayed out. This is because RODCs need to get their Active Directory database from another domain controller. Since this is the first domain controller in the forest, RODCs are not possible. If you need an RODC, complete the previous steps on a member server in a domain where domain controllers already exist.

- Enter **P@ssw0rd** for the password (do not use P@ssw0rd for a live server).

   Then click Next.

FIGURE 7.6
Domain
Controller Options

18. At the DNS screen, click Next.

19. At the additional options screen, accept the default NetBIOS domain name and click Next.

20. At the Paths screen, accept the default file locations and click Next.

21. At the Review Options screen (see Figure 7.7), verify your settings and click Next. At this screen, there is a View Script button. This button allows you to grab a PowerShell script based on the features you have just set up.

FIGURE 7.7
Review Options screen

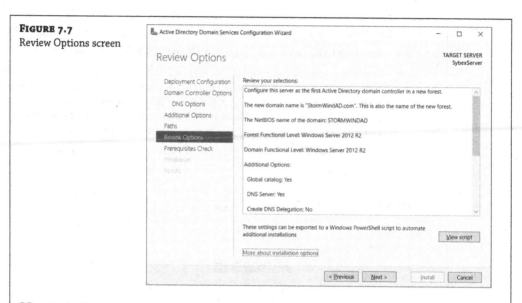

22. At the Prerequisites Check screen, click the Install button (as long as there are no errors). Warnings are OK just as long as there are no errors (see Figure 7.8).

FIGURE 7.8
Prerequisites
Check screen

23. After the installation completes, the machine will automatically reboot. Log in as the administrator.

24. Close Server Manager.

25. Click the Start button on the keyboard and choose Administrative Tools.

26. You should see new MMC snap-ins for Active Directory.

27. Close the Administrative Tools window.

In Exercise 7.3, you will learn how to install Active Directory on a Server Core installation. You will use Windows Server 2022 Datacenter Server Core. Before actually installing AD DS, you will learn how to configure the computer name, the time, the administrator password, and a static TCP/IP address, and then you will install DNS.

Exercise 7.3 will have you install Active Directory onto a Datacenter Server Core server using Microsoft PowerShell. If you need to install Active Directory onto any Windows Server 2022 server using PowerShell, it's the same steps in this exercise.

EXERCISE 7.3 Installing AD DS on Server Core Using PowerShell

1. At the Server Core command prompt, type **cd\windows\system32** and press Enter.
2. Type **timedate.cpl** and set your date, local time zone, and time. Click OK.
3. Type **Netsh** and press Enter.
4. Type **Interface**, and press Enter.
5. Type **IPv4,** and press Enter.
6. Type **Show IP** and press Enter. This will show you the current TCP/IP address and the interface with which the TCP/IP address is associated.
7. On my setup, interface 12 is my Ethernet interface. To change this interface, type the following command and press Enter:

   ```
   Set address name="12" source=static address=192.168.0.165 mask=255.255.255.0
   gateway=192.168.0.1
   ```

   I used 192.168.0.x for my address. You can replace the address, mask, and gateway based on your local settings.

8. Type **Show IP** and press Enter. You should see that the new address is now manual and set to the IP address you set.
9. Type **Exit** and press Enter.
10. Type **Net User Administrator** * and press Enter.
11. Type in your password and then confirm the password. I used P@ssw0rd for my password.
12. Type the following command and press Enter:

    ```
    Netdom renamecomputer %computername% /newname:ServerA
    ```

13. Type **Y** and press Enter.
14. Type **Shutdown /R /T 0** and press Enter. This will reboot the machine. After the reboot, log back into the system.
15. Type **PowerShell** and press Enter.
16. At the PowerShell prompt, type **Add-WindowsFeature DNS** and press Enter. This will add DNS to the server.
17. At the PowerShell prompt, type **Add-WindowsFeature AD-Domain-Services** and press Enter.

18. At the PowerShell prompt, type **Import-Module ADDSDeployment**.

19. At the PowerShell prompt, type **Install-ADDSForest**.

20. Type in your domain name and press Enter. I used Sybex.com.

21. Next you will be asked for your Safe mode administrator password. Type in **P@ssw0rd** and then confirm it.

22. Type **Y** and press Enter.

Active Directory will install, and the machine will automatically reboot.

Now that we have installed Active Directory onto two different types of systems, let's take a look at how to install an RODC. In Exercise 7.4 I will show you how to add a RODC to a domain. To do this exercise, you need another domain controller in the domain.

EXERCISE 7.4   Creating an RODC Server

1. Install the Active Directory Domain Services by clicking the Add Roles And Features link in Server Manager's Dashboard view.

2. At the Before You Begin screen, click Next.

3. The Select Installation Type screen will be next. Make sure that the Role-Based radio button is selected and click Next.

4. At the Select Destination Server screen, choose the local machine. Click Next.

5. At the Select Server Roles screen, click the check box for Active Directory Domain Services.

6. After you check the Active Directory Domain Services box, a pop-up menu will appear asking you to install additional features. Click the Add Features button.

7. Click Next.

8. At the Select Features screen, accept the defaults and click Next.

9. Click Next at the information screen.

10. Click the Install button at the Confirmation Installation screen.

11. The Installation Progress screen will show you how the installation is progressing.

12. After the installation is complete, click the Close button.

13. On the left side window, click the AD DS link.

14. Click the More link next to Configuration Required for Active Directory Domain Services.

15. Under the Post-Deployment Configuration section, click the Promote This Server To A Domain Controller link.

16. At this point, you will configure this domain controller. You are going to install a new domain controller in an existing domain. At the Deployment Configuration screen, choose Add A Domain Controller To An Existing Domain. You then need to add the name of another domain controller in that domain.

17. At the Domain Controller Options screen, set the following options:

- Verify that the RODC check box is checked.

- Password: **P@ssw0rd**

  Then click Next.

18. At the Paths screen, accept the default file locations and click Next.

19. At the Review Options screen, verify your settings and click Next. At this screen, there is a View Script button. This button allows you to grab a PowerShell script based on the features you have just set up.

20. At the Prerequisites Check screen, click the Install button (as long as there are no errors). Warnings are OK just as long as there are no errors.

21. After the installation completes, the machine will automatically reboot. Log in as the administrator.

22. Close Server Manager.

Installing Additional Domain Controllers by Using Install from Media

There may be times when you need to install additional domain controllers without having a lot of additional replication traffic. When you can install a domain controller without the need for additional replication traffic, the installation is much quicker. This is the perfect time to install an additional domain controller by using the install from media (IFM) method.

Windows Server 2022 allows you to install a domain controller using the IFM method by using the Ntdsutil or PowerShell utility. The Ntdsutil and PowerShell utilities allow you to create installation media for an additional domain controller in a domain. One issue that you must remember is that any objects that were created, modified, or deleted since the IFM was created must be replicated. Creating the IFM close (timewise) to the installation of the domain controller guarantees that all objects will be created at the time the domain controller is installed.

One other way that you can also create the IFM is by restoring a backup of a similar domain controller in the same domain to another location.

Verifying Active Directory Installation

Once you have installed and configured Active Directory, you'll want to verify that you have done so properly. In the following sections, you'll look at methods for doing this.

Using Event Viewer

The first (and perhaps most informative) way to verify the operations of Active Directory is to query information stored in the Windows Server 2022 event log. You can do this using the Windows Server 2022 Event Viewer. Exercise 7.5 walks you through this procedure. Entries seen with the Event Viewer include errors, warnings, and informational messages.

NOTE To complete the steps in Exercise 7.5, you must have configured the local machine as a domain controller.

EXERCISE 7.5 Viewing the Active Directory Event Log

1. Open Administrative Tools by pressing the Windows key and choosing Administrative Tools.

2. Open the Event Viewer snap-in from the Administrative Tools program group.

3. In the left pane, under Applications And Services Logs, select Directory Service.

4. In the right pane, you can sort information by clicking column headings. For example, you can click the Source column to sort by the service or process that reported the event.

5. Double-click an event in the list to see the details for that item. Note that you can click the Copy button to copy the event information to the Clipboard. You can then paste the data into a document for later reference. Also, you can move between items using the up and down arrows. Click OK when you have finished viewing an event.

6. Filter an event list by right-clicking the Directory Service item in the left pane and selecting Filter Current Log. Note that filtering does not remove entries from the event logs—it only restricts their display.

7. To verify Active Directory installation, look for events related to the proper startup of Active Directory, such as Event ID 1000 (Active Directory Startup Complete) and 1394 (Attempts To Update The Active Directory Database Are Succeeding). Also, be sure to examine any error or warning messages because they could indicate problems with DNS or other necessary services.

8. When you've finished viewing information in the Event Viewer, close the application.

GAINING INSIGHT THROUGH EVENT VIEWER

Despite its simple user interface and somewhat limited GUI functionality, the Event Viewer tool can be your best ally in isolating and troubleshooting problems with Windows Server 2022. The Event Viewer allows you to view information that is stored in various log files that are maintained by the operating system. This includes information from the following logs:

Application Stores messages generated by programs running on your system. For example, SQL Server 2012 might report the completion of a database backup job within the Application log.

Security Contains security-related information as defined by your auditing settings. For example, you could see when users have logged onto the system or when particularly sensitive files have been accessed.

System Contains operating system-related information and messages. Common messages might include a service startup failure or information about when the operating system was last rebooted.

Directory Service Stores messages and events related to how Active Directory functions. For example, you might find details related to replication here.

DNS Server Contains details about the operations of the DNS service. This log is useful for troubleshooting replication or name-resolution problems.

Other Log Files Contain various features of Windows Server 2022 and the applications that may run on this operating system, which can create additional types of logs. These files allow you to view more information about other applications or services through the familiar Event Viewer tool.

Additionally, developers can easily send custom information from their programs to the Application log. Having all of this information in one place really makes it easy to analyze operating system and application messages. Also, many third-party tools and utilities are available for analyzing log files.

Although the Event Viewer GUI does a reasonably good job of letting you find the information you need, you might want to extract information to analyze other systems or applications. One especially useful feature of the Event Viewer is its ability to save a log file in various formats. You can access this feature by clicking Action ➤ Save As. You'll be given the option of saving in various formats, including tab- and comma-delimited text files. You can then open these files in other applications (such as Microsoft Excel) for additional data analysis.

Overall, in the real world, the Event Viewer can be an excellent resource for monitoring and troubleshooting your important servers and workstations.

In addition to providing information about the status of events related to Active Directory, the Event Viewer shows you useful information about other system services and applications. You should routinely use this tool.

Using Active Directory Administrative Tools

After a server has been promoted to a domain controller, you will see that various tools are added to the Administrative Tools program group, including the following:

Active Directory Administrative Center   This is a *Microsoft Management Console (MMC)* snap-in that allows you to accomplish many Active Directory tasks from one central location. This MMC snap-in allows you to manage your directory services objects, including doing the following tasks:

- ◆ Reset user passwords

- ◆ Create or manage user accounts

- ◆ Create or manage groups

- ◆ Create or manage computer accounts

- ◆ Create or manage organizational units (OUs) and containers

- ◆ Connect to one or several domains or domain controllers in the same instance of Active Directory Administrative Center

- ◆ Filter Active Directory data

Active Directory Domains and Trusts   Use this tool to view and change information related to the various domains in an Active Directory environment. This MMC snap-in also allows you to set up shortcut trusts.

Active Directory Sites and Services   Use this tool to create and manage Active Directory sites and services to map to an organization's physical network infrastructure.

Active Directory Users and Computers   User and computer management is fundamental for an Active Directory environment. The Active Directory Users and Computers tool allows you to set machine- and user-specific settings across the domain. This tool is discussed throughout this book.

Active Directory Module for Windows PowerShell *Windows PowerShell* is a command-line shell and scripting language. The Active Directory Module for Windows PowerShell is a group of cmdlets used to manage your Active Directory domains, Active Directory Lightweight Directory Services (AD LDS) configuration sets, and Active Directory Database Mounting Tool instances in a single, self-contained package. The Active Directory Module for Windows PowerShell is a normal PowerShell window. The only difference is that the Active Directory PowerShell module is pre-loaded when you choose the Active Directory Module for Windows PowerShell.

A good way to make sure that Active Directory is accessible and functioning properly is to run the Active Directory Users and Computers tool. When you open the tool, you should see a configuration similar to that shown in Figure 7.9. Specifically, you should make sure the name of the domain you created appears in the list. You should also click the Domain Controllers folder and make sure that the name of your local server appears in the right pane. If your configuration passes these two checks, Active Directory is present and configured.

FIGURE 7.9
Viewing Active Directory information using the Active Directory Users and Computers tool

Testing from Clients

The best test of any solution is simply to verify that it works the way you had intended in your environment. When it comes to using Active Directory, a good test is to ensure that clients can view and access the various resources presented by Windows Server 2022 domain controllers. In the following sections, you'll look at several ways to verify that Active Directory is functioning properly.

VERIFYING CLIENT CONNECTIVITY

If you are unable to see the recently promoted server on the network, there is likely a network configuration error. If only one or a few clients are unable to see the machine, the problem is probably related to client-side configuration. To fix this, make sure that the client computers have the appropriate TCP/IP configuration (including DNS server settings) and that they can see other computers on the network.

If the new domain controller is unavailable from any of the other client computers, you should verify the proper startup of Active Directory using the methods mentioned earlier in this chapter. If Active Directory has been started, ensure that the DNS settings are correct. Finally, test network connectivity between the server and the clients by accessing the network or by using the ping command.

JOINING A DOMAIN

If Active Directory has been properly configured, clients and other servers should be able to join the domain. Exercise 7.6 outlines the steps you need to take to join a Windows 7, Windows 8/8.1, or Windows 10 computer to the domain.

To complete this exercise, you must have already installed and properly configured at least one Active Directory domain controller and a DNS server that supports SRV records in your environment. In addition to the domain controller, you need at least one other computer, not configured as a domain controller, running one of the following operating systems: Windows 7, Windows 8, Windows 8.1, Windows 10, Windows 11, Windows Server 2008, Windows Server 2008 R2, Windows Server 2012, Windows Server 2012 R2, or Windows Server 2016/2019/2022.

Once clients are able to join the domain successfully, they should be able to view Active Directory resources using the Network icon. This test validates the proper functioning of Active Directory and ensures that you have connectivity with client computers.

NOTE Exercise 7.6 is being done from a Windows 10 Enterprise computer.

EXERCISE 7.6   Joining a Computer to an Active Directory Domain

1. Right-click on the Start menu and choose System.

2. Go to the section called Computer Name. On the right side, click the Change Settings link.

3. Next to the section To Rename This Computer Or Change Its Domain Or Workgroup, click the Change button.

4. In the Member Of section, choose the Domain option. Type the name of the Active Directory domain that this computer should join. Click OK.

5. When prompted for the username and password of an account that has permission to join computers to the domain, enter the information for an administrator of the domain. Click OK to commit the changes. If you successfully joined the domain, you will see a dialog box welcoming you to the new domain.

6. You will be notified that you must reboot the computer before the changes take place. Select Yes when prompted to reboot.

Creating and Configuring Application Data Partitions

Organizations store many different kinds of information in various places. For the IT departments that support this information, it can be difficult to ensure that the right information is available when and where it is needed. Windows Server 2022 uses a feature called *application data partitions*, which allows system administrators and application developers to store custom information within Active Directory. The idea behind application data partitions is that since you already have a directory service that can replicate all kinds of information, you might as well use it to keep track of your own information.

Developing distributed applications that can, for example, synchronize information across an enterprise is not a trivial task. You have to come up with a way to transfer data between remote sites (some of which are located across the world), and you have to ensure that the data is properly replicated. By storing application information in Active Directory, you can take advantage of its storage mechanism and replication topology. Application-related information stored on domain controllers benefits from having fault-tolerance features and availability.

Consider the following simple example to understand how this can work. Suppose your organization has developed a customer Sales Tracking and Inventory application. The company needs to make the information that is stored by this application available to all of its branch offices and users located throughout the world. However, the goal is to do this with the least amount of IT administrative effort. Assuming that Active Directory has already been deployed throughout the organization, developers can build support into the application for storing data within Active Directory. They can then rely on Active Directory to store and synchronize the information among various sites. When users request updated data from the application, the application can obtain this information from the nearest domain controller that hosts a replica of the Sales Tracking and Inventory data.

Other types of applications can also benefit greatly from the use of application data partitions. Now that you have a good understanding of the nature of application data partitions, let's take a look at how you can create and manage them using Windows Server 2022 and Active Directory.

Creating Application Data Partitions

By default, after you create an Active Directory environment, you will not have any customer application data partitions. Therefore, the first step in making this functionality available is to create a new application data partition. You can use several tools to do this:

Third-Party Applications or Application-Specific Tools   Generally, if you are planning to install an application that can store information in the Active Directory database, you'll receive some method of administering and configuring that data along with the application. For example, the setup process for the application might assist you in the steps you need to take to set up a new application data partition and to create the necessary structures for storing data.

NOTE   Creating and managing application data partitions are advanced Active Directory–related functions. Be sure that you have a solid understanding of the Active Directory schema, Active Directory replication, LDAP, and your applications' needs before you attempt to create new application data partitions in a live environment.

Active Directory Service Interfaces   ADSI is a set of programmable objects that can be accessed through languages such as Visual Basic Scripting Edition (VBScript), Visual C#, Visual Basic .NET, and many other language technologies that support the Component Object Model (COM) standard. Through the use of ADSI, developers can create, access, and update data stored in Active Directory and in any application data partitions.

The LDP Tool   You can view and modify the contents of the Active Directory schema using LDAP-based queries. The LDP tool allows you to view information about application data partitions.

Ldp.exe is a graphical user interface (GUI) tool that allows an administrator to configure the Lightweight Directory Access Protocol (LDAP) directory service. Administrators have the ability to use the LDP tool to administer an Active Directory Lightweight Directory Services (AD LDS) instance. To use the LDP tool, you must be an administrator or equivalent.

Ntdsutil   The ntdsutil utility is the main method by which system administrators create and manage application data partitions on their Windows Server 2022 domain controllers. This utility's specific commands are covered later in this chapter.

NOTE   Creating and managing application data partitions can be fairly complex. Such a project's success depends on the quality of the architecture design. This is a good example of where IT staff and application developers must cooperate to ensure that data is stored effectively and that it is replicated efficiently.

You can create an application data partition in one of three different locations within an Active Directory forest:

◆   As a new tree in an Active Directory forest.

◆   As a child of an Active Directory domain partition.

For example, you can create an Accounting application data partition within the Finance .MyCompany.com domain.

◆   As a child of another application data partition.

This method allows you to create a hierarchy of application data partitions.

As you might expect, you must be a member of the Enterprise Admins or Domain Admins group to be able to create application data partitions. Alternatively, you can be delegated the appropriate permissions to create new partitions.

Now that you have a good idea of the basic ways in which you can create application data partitions, let's look at how replicas (copies of application data partition information) are handled.

Managing Replicas

A *replica* is a copy of any data stored within Active Directory. Unlike the basic information that is stored in Active Directory, application partitions cannot contain security principals. Also, not all domain controllers automatically contain copies of the data stored in an application data partition. System administrators can define which domain controllers host copies of the application data. This is an important feature because, if replicas are used effectively, administrators can find a good balance between replication traffic and data consistency. For example, suppose that three of your organization's 30 locations require up-to-date accounting-related information. You might choose to replicate the data only to domain controllers located in the places that require the data. Limiting replication of this data reduces network traffic.

Replication is the process by which replicas are kept up-to-date. Application data can be stored and updated on designated servers in the same way basic Active Directory information (such as users and groups) is synchronized between domain controllers. Application data partition replicas are managed using the *Knowledge Consistency Checker (KCC)*, which ensures that the designated domain controllers receive updated replica information. Additionally, the KCC uses all Active Directory sites and connection objects that you create to determine the best method to handle replication.

Removing Replicas

When you perform a *demotion* on a domain controller, that server can no longer host an application data partition. If a domain controller contains a replica of application data partition information, you must remove the replica from the domain controller before you demote it. If a domain controller is the last machine that hosts a replica of the application data partition, then the entire application data partition is removed and will be permanently lost. Generally, you want to do this only after you're absolutely sure that your organization no longer needs access to the data stored in the application data partition.

Using *ntdsutil* to Manage Application Data Partitions

The primary method by which system administrators create and manage application data partitions is through the `ntdsutil` command-line tool. You can launch this tool simply by entering **ntdsutil** at a command prompt. The `ntdsutil` command is both interactive and context sensitive. That is, once you launch the utility, you'll see an `ntdsutil` command prompt. At this prompt, you can enter various commands that set your context within the application. For example, if you enter the `domain management` command, you'll be able to use domain-related commands. Several operations also require you to connect to a domain, a domain controller, or an Active Directory object before you perform a command.

NOTE   For complete details on using `ntdsutil`, see the Windows Server 2022 Help and Support Center.

Table 7.3 describes the domain management commands supported by the `ntdsutil` tool. You can access this information by typing in the following sequence of commands at a command prompt:

```
ntdsutil
domain management
Help
```

TABLE 7.3   ntdsutil domain management commands

ntdsutil DOMAIN MANAGEMENT COMMAND	PURPOSE
Help or ?	Displays information about the commands that are available within the Domain Management menu of the ntdsutil command.
Connection or Connections	Allows you to connect to a specific domain controller. This will set the context for further operations that are performed on specific domain controllers.
Create NC *PartitionDistinguishedName DNSName*	Creates a new application directory partition.
Delete NC *PartitionDistinguishedName*	Removes an application data partition.
List NC Information *PartitionDistinguishedName*	Shows information about the specified application data partition.
List NC Replicas *PartitionDistinguishedName*	Returns information about all replicas for the specific application data partition.
Precreate*PartitionDistinguishedNameServerDNSName*	Pre-creates cross-reference application data partition objects. This allows the specified DNS server to host a copy of the application data partition.
Remove NC Replica *PartitionDistinguishedName DCDNSName*	Removes a replica from the specified domain controller.
Select Operation Target	Selects the naming context that will be used for other operations.
Set NC Reference Domain *PartitionDistinguishedName DomainDistinguishedName*	Specifies the reference domain for an application data partition.
Set NC Replicate NotificationDelay *PartitionDistinguishedName FirstDCNotificationDelay OtherDCNotificationDelay*	Defines settings for how often replication will occur for the specified application data partition.

NOTE   The ntdsutil commands are all case insensitive. Mixed case was used in the table to make them easier to read. NC in commands stands for "naming context," referring to the fact that this is a partition of the Active Directory schema.

Configuring DNS Integration with Active Directory

There are many benefits to integrating Active Directory and DNS services:

◆ You can configure and manage replication along with other Active Directory components.

◆ You can automate much of the maintenance of DNS resource records through the use of dynamic updates.

◆ You will be able to set specific security options on the various properties of the DNS service.

Exercise 7.7 shows the steps that you must take to ensure that these integration features are enabled. You'll look at the various DNS functions that are specific to interoperability with Active Directory.

Before you begin this exercise, make sure that the local machine is configured as an Active Directory domain controller and that DNS services have been properly configured. If you instructed the Active Directory Installation Wizard to configure DNS automatically, many of the settings mentioned in this section may already be enabled. However, you should verify the configuration and be familiar with how the options can be set manually.

EXERCISE 7.7   Configuring DNS Integration with Active Directory

1. Open Administrative Tools by pressing the Windows key and choosing Administrative Tools.

2. Open the DNS snap-in from the Administrative Tools program group.

3. Right-click the icon for the local DNS server and select Properties. Click the Security tab. Notice that you can now specify which users and groups have access to modify the configuration of the DNS server. Make any necessary changes and click OK.

4. Expand the local server branch and the Forward Lookup Zones folder.

5. Right-click the name of the Active Directory domain you created and select Properties.

6. On the General tab (see Figure 7.10), verify that the type is Active Directory–Integrated and that the Data Is Stored In Active Directory message is displayed. If this option is not currently selected, you can change it by clicking the Change button next to Type and choosing the Store The Zone In Active Directory check box on the bottom.

FIGURE 7.10
General Tab of DNS zone properties

StormWindAD.com Properties   ?   ✕

| WINS | Zone Transfers | Security |
| General | Start of Authority (SOA) | Name Servers |

Status: Running   [Pause]

Type: Active Directory-Integrated   [Change...]

Replication: All DNS servers in this domain   [Change...]

Data is stored in Active Directory.

Dynamic updates: [Secure only ⌄]

⚠ Allowing nonsecure dynamic updates is a significant security vulnerability because updates can be accepted from untrusted sources.

To set aging/scavenging properties, click Aging.   [Aging...]

[OK]   [Cancel]   [Apply]   [Help]

7. Verify that the Dynamic Updates option is set to Secure Only. This ensures that all updates to the DNS resource records database are made through authenticated Active Directory accounts and processes.

   The other options are Nonsecure And Secure (accepts all updates) and None (to disallow dynamic updates).

8. Finally, notice that you can define the security permissions at the zone level by clicking the Security tab. Make any necessary changes and click OK.

The Bottom Line

Know the prerequisites for promoting a server to a domain controller. You should understand the tasks that you must complete before you attempt to upgrade a server to a domain controller. Also, you should have a good idea of the information you need in order to complete the domain controller promotion process.

Master It You are an administrator of a large network. You need to install Windows Server 2022 Active Directory on your network.

Understand Domains, Trees, and Forests. Understanding which way to setup Active Directory is one of the most important tasks that you will undertake. If you choose the wrong option, you may need to manually build connections between your networks instead of Active Directory doing it for you.

Master It You are the administrator of an organization that has decided to buy out a company called Sybex.com. You want Sybex.com to be part of your current Active Directory structure. But it is important that Sybex.com keeps its own naming structure.

## Chapter 8

Administering Active Directory

In previous chapters, you learned how to install Active Directory, but you still haven't been introduced to the lower-level objects that exist in Active Directory.

In this chapter, you will look at the structure of the various components within a domain. You'll see how an organization's business structure can be mirrored within Active Directory through the use of organizational units for ease of use and to create a seamless look and feel. Because the concepts related to organizational units are quite simple, some system administrators may underestimate their importance and not plan to use them accordingly. Make no mistake: one of the fundamental components of a successful Active Directory installation is the proper design and deployment of organizational units.

You'll also see in this chapter the actual steps you need to take to create common Active Directory objects and then learn how to configure and manage them. Finally, you'll look at ways to publish resources and methods for creating user accounts automatically.

IN THIS CHAPTER YOU'LL LEARN

◆ Understand the Purpose of OUs

◆ Know Groups and Group Strategies

Active Directory Overview

One of the fundamental design goals for Active Directory is to define a single, centralized repository of users and information resources. Active Directory records information about all of the users, computers, and resources on your network. Each domain acts as a logical boundary, and members of the domain (including workstations, servers, and domain controllers) share information about the objects within them.

The information stored within Active Directory determines which resources are accessible to which users. Through the use of permissions that are assigned to Active Directory objects, you can control all aspects of network security.

Let's start by looking at the various components of network security, which include working with security principals and managing security and permissions, access control lists (ACLs), and access control entries (ACEs).

Understanding Active Directory Features

Active Directory is the heart and soul of a Microsoft domain, and I can never talk enough about the roles and features included with Active Directory. Let's take a look at some of the advantages of Windows Server 2022 and Active Directory.

Active Directory Certificate Services   Active Directory Certificate Services (AD CS) provides a customizable set of services that allows you to issue and manage public key infrastructure (PKI) certificates. These certificates can be used in software security systems that employ public key technologies.

Active Directory Domain Services   Active Directory Domain Services (AD DS) includes new features that make deploying domain controllers simpler and lets you implement them faster. AD DS also makes the domain controllers more flexible, both to audit and to authorize access to files. Moreover, AD DS has been designed to make performing administrative tasks easier through consistent graphical and scripted management experiences.

Active Directory Rights Management Services   Active Directory Rights Management Services (AD RMS) provides management and development tools that let you work with industry security technologies, including encryption, certificates, and authentication. Using these technologies allows organizations to create reliable information protection solutions.

Kerberos Authentication   Windows Server 2022 uses the Kerberos authentication protocol and extensions for password-based and public-key authentication. The Kerberos client is installed as a security support provider (SSP), and it can be accessed through the Security Support Provider Interface (SSPI).

Kerberos Constrained Delegation   Kerberos constrained delegation (KCD) is an authentication protocol that administrators can set up for delegating client credentials for specific service accounts. For example, KCD may be a requirement for services in SharePoint. If you are planning on using SharePoint Analysis Services and Power Pivot data, you will need to configure KCD. KCD allows a service account to impersonate another service account and this allows access to specific resources.

Managed Service Accounts   The *Managed Service Accounts* is a Windows Server 2022 account that is managed by Active Directory. Regular service accounts are accounts that are created to run specific services such as Exchange and SQL Server. Normally when an administrator creates a service account, it's up to that administrator to maintain the account (including changing the password). Managed Service Accounts are accounts that administrators create but the accounts are managed by Active Directory (including password changes). To create Managed Service Accounts, you must use the `New-ADServiceAccount` PowerShell command. You must use PowerShell in order to create a Managed Service Account.

Group Managed Service Accounts   The group Managed Service Account (gMSA) provides the same functionality within the domain as Managed Service Accounts, but gMSAs extend their functionality over multiple servers. These accounts are very useful when a service account needs to work with multiple servers, as with a server farm (for Network Load Balancing).

There are times when the authentication process requires that all instances of a service use the same service account. This is where gMSAs are used. Once group Managed Service

Account are used, Windows Server 2022 will automatically manage the password for the service account. The network administrator will no longer be responsible to manage the service account password.

Security Auditing   Security auditing gives an organization the ability to help maintain the security of an enterprise. By using security audits, you can verify authorized or unauthorized access to machines, resources, applications, and services. One of the best advantages of security audits is to verify regulatory compliance.

TLS/SSL (Schannel SSP)   Schannel is a security support provider (SSP) that uses the Secure Sockets Layer (SSL) and Transport Layer Security (TLS) Internet standard authentication protocols together. The Security Support Provider Interface (SSPI) is an API used by Windows systems to allow security-related functionality, including authentication.

Understanding Security Principals

Security principals are Active Directory objects that are assigned *security identifiers (SIDs)*. An SID is a unique identifier that is used to manage any object to which permissions can be assigned. Security principals are assigned permissions to perform certain actions and access certain network resources.

The following basic types of Active Directory objects serve as security principals:

User Accounts   User accounts identify individual users on your network by including information such as the user's name and their password. User accounts are the fundamental unit of security administration.

Groups   There are two main types of groups: security groups and distribution groups. Both types can contain user accounts. System administrators use security groups to ease the management of security permissions. They use distribution groups, on the other hand, solely to send email. Distribution groups are not security principals.

Computer Accounts   Computer accounts identify which client computers are members of particular domains. Because these computers participate in the Active Directory database, system administrators can manage security settings that affect the computer. They use computer accounts to determine whether a computer can join a domain and for authentication purposes.

Note that other objects—such as OUs—do not function as security principals. What this means is that you can apply certain settings (such as Group Policy) on all of the objects within an OU; however, you cannot specifically set permissions of an object (like a file or folder) using an OU itself. The purpose of OUs is to organize other Active Directory objects logically based on business needs, add a needed level of control for security, and create an easier way to delegate.

You can manage security by performing the following actions with security principals:

◆   You can assign them permissions to access various network resources.

◆   You can give them user rights.

◆   You can track their actions through auditing (covered later in this chapter).

The major types of security principals—user accounts, groups, and computer accounts—form the basis of the Active Directory security architecture. As a system administrator, you will likely spend a portion of your time managing permissions for these objects.

TIP   It is important to understand that, since a unique SID defines each security principal, deleting a security principal is an irreversible process. For example, if you delete a user account and then later re-create one with the same name, you'll need to reassign permissions and group membership settings for the new account. Once a user account is deleted, its SID is deleted. This is why you should always consider disabling accounts instead of deleting them or enabling the Active Directory Recycle Bin.

An Overview of OUs

An *organizational unit (OU)* is a logical group of Active Directory objects, just as the name implies. OUs serve as containers (see Figure 8.1) within which Active Directory objects can be created, but they do not form part of the DNS namespace. They are used solely to create organization within a domain.

FIGURE 8.1
Active Directory OUs

OUs can contain the following types of Active Directory objects:

◆   Users

◆   Groups

◆   Computers

◆   Shared Folder objects

◆   Contacts

◆   Printers

◆   InetOrgPerson objects

◆   Microsoft Message Queuing (MSMQ) Queue aliases

◆   Other OUs

Perhaps the most useful feature of OUs is that they can contain other OU objects. As a result, system administrators can hierarchically group resources and objects according to business practices. The OU structure is extremely flexible and, as you will see later in this chapter, can easily be rearranged to reflect business reorganizations.

Another advantage of OUs is that each can have its own set of policies. Administrators can create individual and unique Group Policy objects (GPOs) for each OU. GPOs are rules or policies that can apply to all of the objects within the OU.

Each type of object has its own purpose within the organization of Active Directory domains. Later in this chapter, you'll look at the specifics of User, Computer, Group, and Shared Folder objects. For now, let's focus on the purpose and benefits of using OUs.

The Purpose of OUs

OUs are mainly used to organize the objects within Active Directory. Before you dive into the details of OUs, however, you must understand how OUs, users, and groups interact. Most important, you should understand that OUs are simply containers that you can use to group various objects logically. They are not, however, groups in the classical sense. That is, they are not used for assigning security permissions. Another way of stating this is that the user accounts, computer accounts, and group accounts that are contained in OUs are considered security principals while the OUs themselves are not.

OUs do not take the place of standard user and group permissions. A good general practice is to assign users to groups and then place the groups within OUs. This enhances the benefits of setting security permissions and of using the OU hierarchy for making settings.

An OU contains objects only from within the domain in which it resides. As you'll see in the section "Delegating Administrative Control" later in this chapter, the OU is the finest level of granularity used for group policies and other administrative settings.

Benefits of OUs

There are many benefits to using OUs throughout your network environment:

- OUs are the smallest unit to which you can assign directory permissions.

- You can easily change the OU structure, and it is more flexible than the domain structure.

- The OU structure can support many different levels of hierarchy.

- Child objects can inherit OU settings.

- You can set Group Policy settings on OUs.

- You can easily delegate the administration of OUs and the objects within them to the appropriate users and groups.

Now that you have a good idea of why you should use OUs, take a look at some general practices you can use to plan the OU structure.

Planning the OU Structure

One of the key benefits of Active Directory is the way in which it can bring organization to complex network environments. Before you can begin to implement OUs in various configurations, you must plan a structure that is compatible with business and technical needs. In the following sections, you'll learn about several factors that you should consider when planning for the structure of OUs.

Logical Grouping of Resources

The fundamental purpose of using OUs is to group resources (which exist within Active Directory) hierarchically. Fortunately, hierarchical groups are quite intuitive and widely used in most businesses. For example, a typical manufacturing business might divide its various operations into different departments as follows:

◆ Sales

◆ Marketing

◆ Engineering

◆ Research and Development

◆ Support

◆ Information Technology (IT)

Each of these departments usually has its own goals and mission. To make the business competitive, individuals within each of the departments are assigned to various roles. The following role types might be used:

◆ Managers

◆ Clerical staff

◆ Technical staff

◆ Planners

Each of these roles usually entails specific job responsibilities. For example, managers should provide direction to general staff members. Note that the very nature of these roles suggests that employees may fill many different positions. That is, one employee might be a manager in one department and a member of the technical staff in another. In the modern workplace, such situations are quite common.

All of this information helps you plan how to use OUs. First, the structure of OUs within a given network environment should map well to the business's needs, including the political and logical structure of the organization as well as its technical needs. Figure 8.2 shows how a business organization might be mapped to the OU structure within an Active Directory domain.

When naming OUs for your organization, you should keep several considerations and limitations in mind:

Keep the Names and Descriptions Simple The purpose of OUs is to make administering and using resources simple. Therefore, it's always a good idea to keep the names of your objects simple and descriptive. Sometimes, finding a balance between these two goals can be a challenge. For example, although a printer name like "The LaserJet located near Bob's cube" might seem descriptive, it is certainly difficult to type. Also, imagine the naming changes that you might have to make if Bob moves (or leaves the company)!

FIGURE 8.2
Mapping a business
organization to an OU
structure

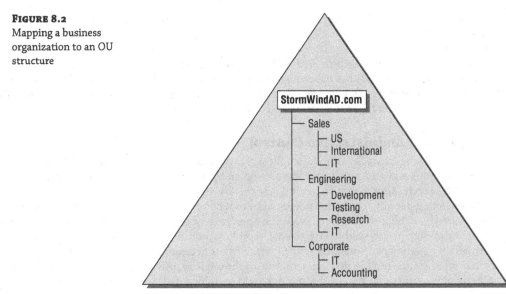

StormWindAD.com Domain

Pay Attention to Limitations The maximum length for the name of an OU is 64 characters. In most cases, this should adequately describe the OU. Remember, the name of an OU does not have to describe the object uniquely because the OU is generally referenced only as part of the overall hierarchy. For example, you can choose to create an OU named "IT" within two different parent OUs. Even though the OUs have the same name, users and administrators are able to distinguish between them based on their complete pathname.

Pay Attention to the Hierarchical Consistency The fundamental basis of an OU structure is its position in a hierarchy. From a design standpoint, this means you cannot have two OUs with the same name at the same level. However, you can have OUs with the same name at different levels. For example, you could create an OU named "Corporate" within the North America OU and another one within the South America OU. This is because the fully qualified domain name includes information about the hierarchy. When an administrator tries to access resources in a Corporate OU, they must specify which Corporate OU they mean.

For example, if you create a North America OU, the Canada OU should logically fit under it. If you decide that you want to separate the North America and Canada OUs into completely different containers, then you might want to use other, more appropriate names. For example, you could change North America to "U.S." Users and administrators depend on the hierarchy of OUs within the domain, so make sure that it remains logically consistent.

Based on these considerations, you should have a good idea of how best to organize the OU structure for your domain.

Understanding OU Inheritance

When you rearrange OUs within the structure of Active Directory, you can change several settings. When they are moving and reorganizing OUs, system administrators must pay careful attention to automatic and unforeseen changes in security permissions and other configuration options. By default, OUs inherit the permissions of their new parent container when they are moved.

By using the built-in tools provided with Windows Server 2022 and Active Directory, you can move or copy OUs only within the same domain. You cannot use the Active Directory Users and Computers tool to move OUs between domains. To do this, use the *Active Directory Migration Tool (ADMT)*. This is one of the many Active Directory support tools.

Delegating Administrative Control

I already mentioned that OUs are the smallest component within a domain to which administrative permissions and group policies can be assigned by administrators. Now you'll take a look specifically at how administrative control is set on OUs.

Businesses generally have a division of labor that handles all of the tasks involved in keeping the company's networks humming. Network operating systems (NOSs), however, often make it difficult to assign just the right permissions; in other words, they do not support very granular permission assignments. Sometimes, fine granularity is necessary to ensure that only the right permissions are assigned. A good general rule of thumb is to provide users and administrators with the minimum permissions they require to do their jobs. This way, you can ensure that accidental, malicious, and otherwise unwanted changes do not occur.

In the world of Active Directory, you delegate to define responsibilities for OU administrators. As a system administrator, you will occasionally be tasked with having to delegate responsibility to others—you can't do it all, although sometimes administrators believe that they can. You understand the old IT logic of doing all of the tasks yourself for job security, but this can actually make you look worse.

NOTE   You can delegate control only at the OU level and not at the object level within the OU.

If you do find yourself in a role where you need to delegate, remember that Windows Server 2022 was designed to offer you the ability to do so. In its simplest definition, *delegation* allows a higher administrative authority to grant specific administrative rights for containers and subtrees to individuals and groups. What this essentially does is eliminate the need for domain administrators with sweeping authority over large segments of the user population. You can break up this control over branches within your tree, within each OU you create.

NOTE   To understand delegation and rights, you should first understand the concept of *access control entries (ACEs)*. ACEs grant specific administrative rights on objects in a container to a user or group. A container's access control list (ACL) is used to store ACEs.

When you are considering implementing delegation, keep these two concerns in mind:

Parent-Child Relationships   The OU hierarchy you create will be important when you consider the maintainability of security permissions. OUs can exist in a parent-child relationship, which means that permissions and group policies set on OUs higher up in the hierarchy (parents) can interact with objects in lower-level OUs (children). When it comes to delegating permissions, this is extremely important. You can allow child containers to inherit the permissions set on parent containers automatically. For example, if the North America division of your organization contains 12 other OUs, you could delegate permissions to all of them at once (saving time and reducing the likelihood of human error) by placing security permissions on the North America division. This feature can greatly ease administration, especially in larger organizations, but it is also a reminder of the importance of properly planning the OU structure within a domain.

Inheritance Settings   Now that you've seen how you can use parent-child relationships for administration, you should consider *inheritance*, the process in which child objects take on the permissions of a parent container. When you set permissions on a parent container, all of the child objects are configured to inherit the same permissions. You can override this behavior, however, if business rules do not lend themselves well to inheritance.

Applying Group Policies

One of the strengths of the Windows operating system is that it offers users a great deal of power and flexibility. From installing new software to adding device drivers, users can make many changes to their workstation configurations. However, this level of flexibility is also a potential problem. For instance, inexperienced users might inadvertently change settings, causing problems that can require many hours to fix.

In many cases (and especially in business environments), users require only a subset of the complete functionality the operating system provides. In the past, however, the difficulty associated with implementing and managing security and policy settings has led to lax security policies. Some of the reasons for this are technical—it can be tedious and difficult to implement and manage security restrictions. Other problems have been political—users and management might feel that they should have full permissions on their local machines, despite the potential problems this might cause.

That's where the idea of group policies comes in. Simply defined, *group policies* are collections of rules that you can apply to objects within Active Directory. Specifically, Group Policy settings are assigned at the site, domain, and OU levels, and they can apply to user accounts and computer accounts. For example, a system administrator can use group policies to configure the following settings:

- Restricting users from installing new programs
- Disallowing the use of the Control Panel
- Limiting choices for display and Desktop settings

Creating OUs

Now that you have looked at several different ways in which OUs can be used to bring organization to the objects within Active Directory, it's time to look at how you can create and manage them.

Through the use of the *Active Directory Users and Computers administrative tool*, also called the *MMC (Microsoft Management Console)*, you can quickly and easily add, move, and change OUs. This graphical tool makes it easy to visualize and create the various levels of hierarchy an organization requires.

Figure 8.3 shows a geographically based OU structure that a multinational company might use. Note that the organization is based in North America and that it has a corporate office located there. In general, the other offices are much smaller than the corporate office located in North America.

FIGURE 8.3
A geographically based
OU structure

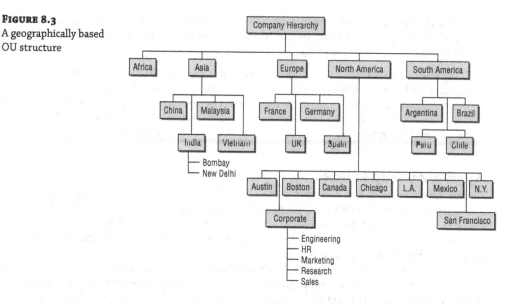

It's important to note that this OU structure could have been designed in several different ways. For example, I could have chosen to group all of the offices located in the United States within an OU named "U.S." However, because of the large size of these offices, I chose to place these objects at the same level as the Canada and Mexico OUs. This prevents an unnecessarily deep OU hierarchy while still logically grouping the offices.

One nice feature when creating an OU is the ability to protect the OU from being accidentally deleted. When you create an OU, you can check the Protect Container From Accidental Deletion check box. This check box protects against an administrator deleting the OU. To delete the OU, you must go into the advanced view of the OU and uncheck the box.

Exercise 8.1 walks you through the process of creating several OUs for a multinational business. You'll be using this OU structure in later exercises within this chapter.

NOTE To perform the exercises included in this chapter, you must have administrative access to a Windows Server 2022 domain controller.

EXERCISE 8.1 Creating an OU Structure

1. Open Active Directory Users and Computers by clicking Start ➢ Administrative Tools ↺ Active Directory Users And Computers.

2. Right-click the name of the local domain and choose New ➢ Organizational Unit.

3. Type **North America** for the name of the first OU (see Figure 8.4). Uncheck the box Protect Container From Accidental Deletion and click OK to create this object.

4. Create the following top-level OUs by right-clicking the name of the domain and choosing New ↺ Organizational Unit. Also make sure to uncheck Protect Container From Accidental Deletion for all OUs in these exercises because you'll be deleting some of these OUs in later ones.

FIGURE 8.4
New OU dialog box

Africa

Asia

Europe

South America

Note that the order in which you create the OUs is not important. In this exercise, you are simply using a method that emphasizes the hierarchical relationship.

5. Create the following second-level OUs within the North America OU by right-clicking the North America OU and selecting New ⇨ Organizational Unit:

Austin

Boston

Canada

Chicago

Corporate

Los Angeles

Mexico

New York

San Francisco

6. Create the following OUs under the Asia OU:

China

India

Malaysia

Vietnam

7. Create the following OUs under the Europe OU:

France

Germany

Spain

UK

8. Create the following OUs under the South America OU:

Argentina

Brazil

Chile

Peru

9. Create the following third-level OUs under the India OU by right-clicking India within the Asia OU and selecting New ⇨ Organizational Unit:

Bombay

New Delhi

10. Within the North America Corporate OU, create the following OUs:

Engineering

HR

Marketing

Research

Sales

11. When you have completed creating the OUs, close Active Directory.

Managing OUs

Managing network environments would still be challenging, even if things rarely changed. However, in the real world, business units, departments, and employee roles change frequently. As business and technical needs change, so should the structure of Active Directory.

Fortunately, changing the structure of OUs within a domain is a relatively simple process. In the following sections, you'll look at ways to delegate control of OUs and make other changes.

Moving, Deleting, and Renaming OUs

The process of moving, deleting, and renaming OUs is a simple one. Exercise 8.2 shows how you can easily modify and reorganize OUs to reflect changes in the business organization. The specific scenario covered in this exercise includes the following changes:

- The Research and Engineering departments have been combined to form a department known as Research and Development (RD).

- The Sales department has been moved from the Corporate headquarters office to the New York office.

- The Marketing department has been moved from the Corporate headquarters office to the Chicago office.

This exercise assumes you have already completed the steps in Exercise 8.1.

EXERCISE 8.2 Modifying OU Structure

1. Open Active Directory Users and Computers by clicking Start ⇨ Administrative Tools ⇨ Active Directory Users And Computers.

2. Right-click the Engineering OU (located within North America ⇨ Corporate) and click Delete. When you are prompted for confirmation, click Yes. Note that if this OU contained objects, they would have all been automatically deleted as well.

3. Right-click the Research OU and select Rename. Type **RD** to change the name of the OU and press Enter.

4. Right-click the Sales OU and select Move. In the Move dialog box, expand the North America branch and click the New York OU. Click OK to move the OU.

5. You will use an alternate method to move the Marketing OU. Drag the Marketing OU and drop it onto the Chicago OU.

6. When you have finished, close the Active Directory Users and Computers administrative tool.

Administering Properties of OUs

Although OUs are primarily created for organizational purposes within the Active Directory environment, they have several settings that you can modify. To modify the properties of an OU using the Active Directory Users and Computers administrative tool, right-click the name of any OU and select Properties. When you do, the OU Properties dialog box appears. In the example shown in Figure 8.5, you'll see the options on the General tab.

FIGURE 8.5
The General tab of the
OU's Properties
dialog box

In any organization, it helps to know who is responsible for managing an OU. You can set this information on the Managed By tab (see Figure 8.6). The information specified on this tab is convenient because it is automatically pulled from the contact information on a user record. You should consider always having a contact for each OU within your organization so that other system administrators know whom to contact if they need to make any changes.

FIGURE 8.6
The Managed By tab of
the OU's Properties
dialog box

Delegating Control of OUs

In simple environments, one or a few system administrators may be responsible for managing all of the settings within Active Directory. For example, a single system administrator could manage all users within all OUs in the environment. In larger organizations, however, roles and responsibilities may be divided among many different individuals. A typical situation is one in which a system administrator is responsible for objects within only a few OUs in an Active Directory domain. Alternatively, one system administrator might manage User and Group objects while another is responsible for managing file and print services.

Fortunately, using the Active Directory Users and Computers tool, you can quickly and easily ensure that specific users receive only the permissions they need. In Exercise 8.3, you will use the Delegation of Control Wizard to assign permissions to individuals. To complete these steps successfully, first you must have created the objects in the previous exercises of this chapter.

EXERCISE 8.3   Using the Delegation of Control Wizard

1. Open Active Directory Users and Computers by clicking Start ⇨ Administrative Tools ⇨ Active Directory Users And Computers.

2. Right-click the Corporate OU within the North America OU and select Delegate Control. This starts the Delegation of Control Wizard. Click Next to begin configuring security settings.

3. In the Users Or Groups page, click the Add button. In the Enter The Object Names To Select field, enter **Account Operators** and click the Check Names button. Click OK. Click Next to continue.

4. In the Tasks To Delegate page, select Delegate The Following Common Tasks and place a check mark next to the following items:

   Create, Delete, And Manage User Accounts

   Reset User Passwords And Force Password Change At Next Logon

   Read All User Information

   Create, Delete, And Manage Groups

   Modify The Membership Of A Group

5. Click Next to continue.

6. The Completing The Delegation Of Control Wizard page then provides a summary of the operations you have selected. To implement the changes, click Finish.

Although the common tasks available through the wizard are sufficient for many delegation operations, you may have cases in which you want more control. For example, you might want to give a particular system administrator permission to modify only Computer objects. Exercise 8.4 uses the Delegation of Control Wizard to assign more granular permissions. To complete these steps successfully, you must have completed the previous exercises in this chapter.

EXERCISE 8.4 Delegating Custom Tasks

1. Open Active Directory Users and Computers by clicking Start ⇨ Administrative Tools ⇨ Active Directory Users And Computers.

2. Right-click the Corporate OU within the North America OU and select Delegate Control. This starts the Delegation of Control Wizard. Click Next to begin making security settings.

3. In the Users Or Groups page, click the Add button. In the Enter The Object Names To Select field, enter **Server Operators** and click the Check Names button. Click OK and then click Next to continue.

4. In the Tasks To Delegate page, select the Create A Custom Task To Delegate radio button and click Next to continue.

5. In the Active Directory Object Type page, choose Only The Following Objects In The Folder and place a check mark next to the following items. (You will have to scroll down to see them all.)

   User Objects

   Computer Objects

   Contact Objects

   Group Objects

   Organizational Unit Objects

   Printer Objects

6. Click Next to continue.

7. In the Permissions page, place a check mark next to the General option and make sure the other options are not checked. Note that if the various objects within your Active Directory schema had property-specific settings, you would see those options here. Place a check mark next to the following items:

   Create All Child Objects

   Read All Properties

   Write All Properties

   This gives the members of the Server Operators group the ability to create new objects within the Corporate OU and the permissions to read and write all properties for these objects.

8. Click Next to continue.

9. The Completing The Delegation Of Control Wizard page provides a summary of the operations you have selected. To implement the changes, click Finish.

Creating and Managing Active Directory Objects

Now that you are familiar with the task of creating OUs, you should find creating and managing other Active Directory objects quite simple. The following sections will examine the details.

Overview of Active Directory Objects

When you install and configure a domain controller, Active Directory sets up an organizational structure for you, and you can create and manage several types of objects.

ACTIVE DIRECTORY ORGANIZATION

When you are looking at your Active Directory structure, you will see objects that look like folders in Windows Explorer. These objects are containers, or *organizational units (OUs)*. The difference is that an OU is a container to which you can link a GPO. Normal containers cannot have a GPO linked to them. That's what makes an OU a special container.

By default, after you install and configure a domain controller, you will see the following organizational sections within the Active Directory Users and Computers tool (they look like folders):

Built-In The *Built-In container* includes all of the standard groups that are installed by default when you promote a domain controller. You can use these groups to administer the servers in your environment. Examples include the Administrators group, Backup Operators group, and Print Operators group.

Computers By default, the *Computers container* contains a list of the workstations in your domain. From here, you can manage all of the computers in your domain.

Domain Controllers The *Domain Controllers OU* includes a list of all the domain controllers for the domain.

Foreign Security Principals In environments that have more than one domain, you may need to grant permissions to users who reside in multiple domains. Generally, you manage this using Active Directory trees and forests. However, in some cases, you may want to provide resources to users who belong to domains that are not part of the forest.

Active Directory uses the concept of foreign security principals to allow permissions to be assigned to users who are not part of an Active Directory forest. This process is automatic and does not require the intervention of system administrators. You can then add the foreign security principals to domain local groups for which, in turn, you can grant permissions for resources within the domain. You can view a list of foreign security principals by using the Active Directory Users and Computers tool.

Foreign security principals containers are any objects to which security can be assigned and that are not part of the current domain. Security principals are Active Directory objects to which permissions can be applied, and they can be used to manage permissions in Active Directory.

Managed Service Accounts The Managed Service Accounts container is a Windows Server 2022 container. Service accounts are accounts created to run specific services such as Exchange and SQL Server. Having a Managed Service Accounts container allows you to control the service accounts better and thus allows for better service account security. To create Managed Service Accounts, you must use the `New-ADServiceAccount` PowerShell command.

Users The *Users container* includes all the security accounts that are part of the domain. When you first install the domain controller, there will be several groups in this container.

For example, the Domain Admins group and the administrator account are created in this container.

You want to be sure to protect the administrator account. You should rename the admin account and make sure the password is complex. Protected admin accounts can make your network safer. Every hacker knows that there is an administrator account on the server by default. Be sure to make your network safer by protecting the admin account.

ACTIVE DIRECTORY OBJECTS

You can create and manage several different types of Active Directory objects. The following are specific object types:

Computer *Computer objects* represent workstations that are part of the Active Directory domain. All computers within a domain share the same security database, including user and group information. Computer objects are useful for managing security permissions and enforcing Group Policy restrictions.

Contact *Contact objects* are usually used in OUs to specify the main administrative contact. Contacts are not security principals like users. They are used to specify information about individuals outside the organization.

Group *Group objects* are logical collections of users primarily for assigning security permissions to resources. When managing users, you should place them into groups and then assign permissions to the group. This allows for flexible management without the need to set permissions for individual users.

InetOrgPerson The *InetOrgPerson object* is an Active Directory object that defines attributes of users in Lightweight Directory Access Protocol (LDAP) and X.500 directories.

MSIMaging-PSPs *MSIMaging-PSPs* is a container for all Enterprise Scan Post Scan Process objects.

MSMQ Queue Alias An *MSMQ Queue Alias object* is an Active Directory object for the MSMQ-Custom-Recipient class type. The Microsoft Message Queuing (MSMQ) Queue Alias object associates an Active Directory path and a user-defined alias with a public, private, or direct single-element format name. This allows a queue alias to be used to reference a queue that might not be listed in Active Directory Domain Services (AD DS).

Organizational Unit An *OU object* is created to build a hierarchy within the Active Directory domain. It is the smallest unit that can be used to create administrative groupings, and it can be used to assign group policies. Generally, the OU structure within a domain reflects a company's business organization.

Printer *Printer objects* map to printers.

Shared Folder *Shared Folder objects* map to server shares. They are used to organize the various file resources that may be available on file/print servers. Often, Shared Folder objects are used to give logical names to specific file collections. For example, system administrators might create separate shared folders for common applications, user data, and shared public files.

User A *User object* is the fundamental security principal on which Active Directory is based. User accounts contain information about individuals as well as password and other permission information.

Creating Objects Using the Active Directory Users and Computers Tool

Exercise 8.5 walks you through the steps necessary to create various objects within an Active Directory domain. In this exercise, you create some basic Active Directory objects. To complete this exercise, you must have access to at least one Active Directory domain controller, and you should have also completed the previous exercises in this chapter.

EXERCISE 8.5   Creating Active Directory Objects

1. Open Active Directory Users and Computers by clicking Start ⇨ Administrative Tools ⇨ Active Directory Users And Computers.

2. Expand the current domain to list the objects currently contained within it. For this exercise, you will use the second- and third-level OUs contained within the North America top-level OU.

3. Right-click the Corporate OU and select New ⇨ User. Fill in the following information:

    First Name: **Maria**

    Initial: **D**

    Last Name: **President**

    Full Name: (leave as default)

    User Logon Name: **mdpresident** (leave default domain)

    Click Next to continue.

4. Enter **P@ssw0rd** for the password for this user and then confirm it. Note that you can also make changes to password settings here. Click Next.

5. You will see a summary of the user information. Click Finish to create the new user.

6. Click the RD container and create another user in that container with the following information:

    First Name: **John**

    Initial: **Q**

    Last Name: **Adams**

    Full Name: (leave as default)

    User Logon Name: **jqadams** (leave default domain)

    Click Next to continue.

7. Assign the password **P@ssw0rd**. Click Next and then click Finish to create the user.

8. Right-click the RD OU and select New ⇨ Contact. Use the following information to fill in the properties of the Contact object:

    First Name: **Jane**

    Initials: **R**

Last Name: **Admin**

Display Name: **jradmin**

Click OK to create the new Contact object.

9. Right-click the RD OU and select New ↳ Shared Folder. Enter **Software** for the name and \\ **server1\applications** for the network path (also known as the Universal Naming Convention [UNC] path). Note that you can create the object even though this resource (the physical server) does not exist. Click OK to create the Shared Folder object.

10. Right-click the HR OU and select New ↳ Group. Type **All Users** for the group name. Do not change the value in the Group Name (Pre–Windows 2000) field. For Group Scope, select Global, and for Group Type, select Security. To create the group, click OK.

11. Right-click the Sales OU and select New ↳ Computer. Type **Workstation1** for the name of the computer. Notice that the pre–Windows 2000 name is automatically populated and that, by default, the members of the Domain Admins group are the only ones who can add this computer to the domain. Place a check mark in the Assign This Computer Account As A Pre-Windows 2000 Computer box and then click OK to create the Computer object.

12. Close the Active Directory Users and Computers tool.

Configuring the User Principal Name

When you log into a domain, your logon name looks like an email address (for example, wpanek@ willpanek.com). This is called your *user principal name (UPN)*. A UPN is the username followed by the @ sign and the domain name. At the time the user account is created, the UPN suffix is generated by default. The UPN is created as *userName@DomainName*, but an administrator can alter or change the default UPN. If your forest has multiple domains and you need to change the UPN to a different domain, you have that ability. To change the UPN suffix, in Active Directory Users and Computers, choose a user and go into their properties. Choose the Attribute Editor tab. Scroll down to the userPrincipalName attribute and make your changes. These changes then get replicated to the global catalog.

NOTE   If your organization has multiple forests set up by a trust, you can't change the UPN to a domain in the other forest. Global catalogs are used to log on users. Because UPNs get replicated to the local forest global catalog servers, you cannot log onto other forests using the UPN.

Using Templates

Now you are going to dive into user templates. *User templates* allow an Active Directory administrator to create a default account (for example, template_sales) and use that account to create all of the other users who match it (all the salespeople).

If you are creating multiple accounts, this can save you a lot of time and resources. For example, if you need to add 35 new salespeople to your company, you'll create one template for sales and use a copy of that template for all of the other new accounts. This saves you the trouble of filling out many of the same fields over and over again. When you copy a template, some of the information does *not* get copied over. This is because it is user-specific information. Here are some of the fields that do not get copied over from a template:

◆ Name

◆ Logon Name

◆ Password

◆ Email

◆ Phone Numbers

◆ Description

◆ Office

◆ Web Page

Many of the important fields such as Member Of (groups to which the user belongs), Profile Path, Department, and Company all get copied over. There is one important item that needs to be done when creating a template: the template account needs to be disabled after creation. You do not want anyone using this account to access your network. In Exercise 8.6, you will create a Sales template to use for your Sales department.

EXERCISE 8.6   Creating a User Template

1. Open Active Directory Users and Computers by clicking Start ⇨ Administrative Tools ⇨ Active Directory Users And Computers.

2. Expand the current domain to list the objects contained within it. For this exercise, you will use the Sales OU. Right-click the Sales OU and choose New ⇨ User.

3. Use the following properties:

   First Name: **Sales**

   Last Name: **Template**

   Username: **sales_template**

   Password: **P@ssw0rd**

4. Click Next and then click Finish.

5. In the right window, double-click the Sales Template user to open the properties.

6. On the General tab, complete the following items:

   Description: **Template Account**

   Office: **Corporate**

   Telephone: **999-999-9999**

   Email: **Sales@abc.com**

   Web: **www.abc.com**

---

7. Click the Profile tab. In the Profile Path field, type **\\ServerA\%username%**.

8. On the Members Of tab, click the Add button. At the Enter The Object Name To Select box, type **Administrator** and click the Check Names button. (Normally you would not add salespeople to the Administrators group, but you are doing so just for this exercise.) Click OK.

9. Click the Account tab. Scroll down in the Account Options box and check the Account Is Disabled check box.

10. Click OK in the user's Properties window to go back to the Sales OU.

11. Right-click the Sales Template account and choose Copy.

12. Enter the following information:

    First Name: **Jenny**

    Last Name: **Sales**

    Username: **jsales**

    Password: **P@ssw0rd**

          Uncheck the Account Is Disabled check box.

13. In the right window, double-click the Jenny Sales user to open the properties.

14. Take a look at the Members Of tab, the General tab, and the Profile tab, and you will see that some of the fields are prefilled (including the Administrators group).

15. Close Jenny Sales Properties and exit Active Directory Users and Computers.

Importing Objects from a File

In Exercise 8.5, you created an account using the Active Directory Users and Computers tool. But what if you need to bulk import accounts? There are two main applications for doing bulk imports of accounts: the ldifde.exe utility and the csvde.exe utility. Both utilities import accounts from files.

The ldifde utility imports from line-delimited files. This utility allows an administrator to export and import data, thus allowing batch operations such as Add, Modify, and Delete to be performed in Active Directory. Windows Server 2022 includes ldifde.exe to help support batch operations.

The csvde.exe utility performs the same export functions as ldifde.exe, but csvde.exe uses a comma-separated value file format. The csvde.exe utility does not allow administrators to modify or delete objects. It only supports adding objects to Active Directory.

Active Directory Migration Tool

Another tool that administrators have used in the past is *Active Directory Migration Tool (ADMT)*. ADMT allows an administrator to migrate users, groups, and computers from a previous version of the server to a current version of the server.

Administrators also used ADMT to migrate users, groups, and computers between Active Directory domains in different forests (interforest migration) and between Active Directory domains in the same forest (intraforest migration).

At the time this book was written, Microsoft had not yet released a new version of ADMT that is supported by Windows Server 2022. The reason I even mention it in this book is because Microsoft may be releasing a version of it soon and I wanted you to understand what it can do. Continue to check the Microsoft website to see whether a new version has been released.

Offline Domain Join of a Computer

Offline domain join gives administrators the ability to preprovision computer accounts in the domain to prepare operating systems for deployments. At startup, computers can then join the domain without the need to contact a domain controller. This helps reduce the time it takes to deploy computers in a datacenter.

Let's say your datacenter needs to have multiple virtual machines deployed. This is where offline domain join can be useful. Upon initial startup after the operating system is installed, offline domain join allows the virtual machines to join the domain automatically. No additional steps or restarts are needed.

The following are some of the benefits of using offline domain join:

♦ There is no additional network traffic for Active Directory state changes.

♦ There is no additional network traffic for computer state changes to the domain controller.

♦ Changes for both the Active Directory state and the computer state can be completed at a different times.

Managing Object Properties

Once you've created the necessary Active Directory objects, you'll probably need to make changes to their default properties. In addition to the settings you made when you were creating Active Directory objects, you can configure several more properties. You can also access object properties by right-clicking any object and selecting Properties from the pop-up menu.

Each object type contains a unique set of properties.

USER OBJECT PROPERTIES

The following list describes some of the properties of a User object (see Figure 8.7):

General   General account information about this user

Address   Physical location information about this user

Account   User logon name and other account restrictions, such as workstation restrictions and logon hours

Profile   Information about the user's roaming profile settings

Telephones   Telephone contact information for the user

Organization   The user's title, department, and company information

Member Of   Group membership information for the user

Dial-In   Remote Access Service (RAS) permissions for the user

Environment   Logon and other network settings for the user

Sessions   Session limits, including maximum session time and idle session settings

Remote Control   Remote control options for this user's session

Remote Desktop Services Profile   Information about the user's profile for use with Remote Desktop Services

Personal Virtual Desktop   Allows you to assign a user a specific virtual machine to use as a personal virtual desktop

COM+   Specifies a COM+ partition set for the user

FIGURE 8.7
User Properties

COMPUTER OBJECT PROPERTIES

Computer objects have different properties than User objects. Computer objects refer to the systems that clients are operating to be part of a domain. The following list describes some Computer object properties:

General   Information about the name of the computer, the role of the computer, and its description

(You can enable an option to allow the Local System account of this machine to request services from other servers. This is useful if the machine is a trusted and secure computer.)

Operating System   The name, version, and service pack information for the operating system running on the computer

Member Of   Active Directory groups of which this Computer object is a member

Delegation   Allows you to set services that work on behalf of another user

Location   A description of the computer's physical location

Managed By   Information about the User or Contact object that is responsible for managing this computer

Dial-In   Sets dial-in options for the computer

SETTING PROPERTIES FOR ACTIVE DIRECTORY OBJECTS

Now that you have seen the various properties that can be set for the Active Directory objects, let's complete an exercise on how to configure some of these properties. Exercise 8.7 walks you through how to set various properties for Active Directory objects. To complete the steps in this exercise, first you must have completed Exercises 8.1 and 8.5.

TIP   Although it may seem a bit tedious, it's always a good idea to enter as much information as you know about Active Directory objects when you create them. Although the name Printer1 may be meaningful to you, users will appreciate the additional information, such as location, when they are searching for objects.

EXERCISE 8.7   Managing Object Properties

1. Open Active Directory Users and Computers by clicking Start ➪ Administrative Tools ➪ Active Directory Users And Computers.

2. Expand the name of the domain and select the RD container. Right-click the John Q. Adams user account and select Properties.

3. Here you will see the various Properties tabs for the User account. Make some configuration changes based on your personal preferences. Click OK to continue.

4. Select the HR OU. Right-click the All Users group and click Properties. In the All Users Properties dialog box, you will be able to modify the membership of the group.

   Click the Members tab and then click Add. Add the Maria D. President and John Q. Admin user accounts to the group. Click OK to save the settings and then OK to accept the group modifications.

5. Select the Sales OU. Right-click the Workstation1 Computer object. Notice that you can choose to disable the account or reset it (to allow another computer to join the domain under that same name). From the context menu, choose Properties. You'll see the properties for the Computer object.

   Examine the various options and make changes based on your personal preference. After you have examined the available options, click OK to continue.

---

6. Select the Corporate OU. Right-click the Maria D. President user account and choose Reset Password. You will be prompted to enter a new password, and then you'll be asked to confirm it. Note that you can also force the user to change this password upon the next logon, and you can also unlock the user's account from here. For this exercise, do not enter a new password; just click Cancel.

7. Close the Active Directory Users and Computers tool.

By now, you have probably noticed that Active Directory objects have a lot of common options. For example, Group and Computer objects both have a Managed By tab.

Windows Server 2022 allows you to manage many User objects at once. For instance, you can select several User objects by holding down the Shift or Ctrl key while selecting. You can then right-click any one of the selected objects and select Properties to display the properties that are available for multiple users. Notice that not every user property is available because some properties are unique to each user. You can configure the Description field for multiple object selections that include both users and nonusers, such as computers and groups.

NOTE An important thing to think about when it comes to accounts is the difference between disabling an account and deleting an account. When you delete an account, the security ID (SID) gets deleted. Even if you later create an account with the same username, it will have a different SID number, and therefore it will be a different account. It is sometimes better to disable an account and place it into a nonactive OU called *Disabled*. This way, if you ever need to reaccess the account, you can do so.

Another object management task is the process of deprovisioning. *Deprovisioning* is the management of Active Directory objects in the container. When you remove an object from an Active Directory container, the deprovisioning process removes the object and synchronizes the container to stay current.

Understanding Groups

Now that you know how to create user accounts, it's time to learn how to create group accounts. As an instructor, I am always amazed when students (who work in the IT field) have no idea why they should use groups. This is something every organization should be using.

To illustrate their usefulness, let's say you have a Sales department user by the name of wpanek. Your organization has 100 resources shared on the network for users to access. Because wpanek is part of the Sales department, he has access to 50 of the resources. The Marketing department uses the other 50. If the organization is not using groups and wpanek moves from Sales to Marketing, how many changes do you have to make? The answer is 100. You have to move him out of the 50 resources he currently can use and place his account into the 50 new resources that he now needs.

Now let's say that you use groups. The Sales group has access to 50 resources, and the Marketing group has access to the other 50. If wpanek moves from Sales to Marketing, you need to make only two changes. You just have to take wpanek out of the Sales group and place him in the Marketing group. Once this is done, wpanek can access everything he needs to do his job.

GROUP PROPERTIES

Now that you understand why you should use groups, let's go over setting up groups and their properties (see Figure 8.8). When you are creating groups, it helps to understand some of the options that you need to use.

FIGURE 8.8

New Group dialog box

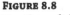

New Object - Group   ✕

    Create in: StormWindAD.com/Arizona

Group name:

Group name (pre-Windows 2000):

Group scope   Group type
○ Domain local   ● Security
● Global   ○ Distribution
○ Universal

                  OK   Cancel

Group Type   You can choose from two group types: security groups and distribution groups.

Security Groups   These groups can have rights and permissions placed on them. For example, if you want to give a certain group of users access to a particular printer but you want to control what they are allowed to do with this printer, you'd create a security group and then apply certain rights and permissions to this group.

Security groups can also receive emails. If someone sent an email to the group, all users within that group would receive it (as long as they have a mail system that allows for mail-enabled groups, like Exchange).

Distribution Groups   These groups are used for email *only* (as long as they have a mail system that allows for mail-enabled groups, like Exchange). You cannot place permissions and rights for objects on this group type.

Group Scope   When it comes to group scopes, you have three choices.

Domain Local Groups   Domain local groups are groups that remain in the domain in which they were created. You use these groups to grant permissions within a single domain. For example, if you create a domain local group named HPLaser, you cannot use that group in any other domain, and it has to reside in the domain in which you created it.

Global Groups Global groups can contain other groups and accounts from the domain in which the group is created. In addition, you can give them permissions in any domain in the forest.

Universal Groups Universal groups can include other groups and accounts from any domain in the domain tree or forest. You can give universal groups permissions in any domain in the domain tree or forest.

CREATING GROUP STRATEGIES

When you are creating a group strategy, think of this acronym that Microsoft likes to use in the exam: AGDLP (or AGLP). This acronym stands for a series of actions you should perform. Here is how it expands:

A Accounts (Create your user accounts.)

G Global groups (Put user accounts into global groups.)

DL Domain local groups (Put global groups into domain local groups.)

P Permissions (Assign permissions such as Deny or Apply on the domain local group.)

Another acronym that stands for a strategy you can use is AGUDLP (or AULP). Here is how it expands:

A Accounts (Create your user accounts.)

G Global groups (Put user accounts into global groups.)

U Universal groups (Put the global groups into universal groups.)

DL Domain local groups (Put universal groups into domain local groups.)

P Permissions (Place permissions on the local group.)

CREATING A GROUP

To create a new group, open the Active Directory Users and Computers snap-in. Click the OU where the group is going to reside. Right-click and choose New and then Group. After you create the group, just click the Members tab and choose Add. Add the users you want to reside in that group, and that's all there is to it.

Filtering and Advanced Active Directory Features

The Active Directory Users and Computers tool has a couple of other features that come in quite handy when you are managing many objects. You can access the Filter Options dialog box by clicking the View menu in the MMC and choosing Filter Options. You'll see a dialog box similar to the one shown in Figure 8.9. Here you can choose to filter objects by their specific types within the display. For example, if you are an administrator who works primarily with user accounts and groups, you can select those specific items by placing check marks in the list. In addition, you can create more complex filters by choosing Create Custom. Doing so provides you with an interface that looks similar to that of the Find command.

FIGURE 8.9
The Filter Options
dialog box

Another option in the Active Directory Users and Computers tool is to view advanced options. You can enable the advanced options by choosing Advanced Features in the View menu. This adds some top-level folders to the list under the name of the domain. Let's take a look at a couple of the new top-level folders.

The System folder (shown in Figure 8.10) provides additional features that you can configure to work with Active Directory. You can configure settings for the Distributed File System (DFS), IP Security (IPsec) policies, the File Replication Service (FRS), and more. In addition to the System folder, you'll see the LostAndFound folder. This folder contains any files that may not have been replicated properly between domain controllers. You should check this folder periodically for any files so that you can decide whether you need to move them or copy them to other locations.

As you can see, managing Active Directory objects is generally a simple task. The Active Directory Users and Computers tool allows you to configure several objects. Let's move on to look at one more common administration function: moving objects.

Moving, Renaming, and Deleting Active Directory Objects

One of the extremely useful features of the Active Directory Users and Computers tool is its ability to move users and resources easily.

Exercise 8.8 walks you through the process of moving Active Directory objects. In this exercise, you will make several changes to the organization of Active Directory objects. To complete this exercise, first you must have completed the previous exercises in this chapter before you begin this exercise.

In addition to moving objects within Active Directory, you can easily rename them by right-clicking an object and selecting Rename. Note that this option does not apply to all objects. You can remove objects from Active Directory by right-clicking them and choosing Delete.

FIGURE 8.10

Advanced Features in the System folder of the Active Directory Users and Computers tool

Name	Type	Description
AdminSDHo...	Container	
BCKUPKEY_...	secret	
BCKUPKEY_...	secret	
BCKUPKEY_...	secret	
BCKUPKEY_...	secret	
ComPartitions	Container	
ComPartitio...	Container	
Default Dom...	Domain Policy	
Dfs-Configu...	dfsConfigurati...	
DFSR-Global...	msDFSR-Globa...	
DomainUpd...	Container	
File Replicati...	FRS Settings	
FileLinks	fileLinkTracking	
IP Security	Container	
Meetings	Container	
MicrosoftDNS	Container	
Password Se...	msDS-Passwor...	
Policies	Container	
PSPs	msImaging-PS...	
RAS and IAS ...	Container	
RID Manager$	rIDManager	
RpcServices	RPC Services	
Server	samServer	
WinsockServ...	Container	
WMIPolicy	Container	

Tree pane:
- Active Directory Users and Com
  - Saved Queries
  - StormWindAD.com
    - Arizona
    - Builtin
    - Computers
    - Domain Controllers
    - Florida
    - ForeignSecurityPrincipal:
    - Keys
    - LostAndFound
    - Managed Service Accoun
    - North America
    - Program Data
    - System
    - Users
    - NTDS Quotas
    - TPM Devices

EXERCISE 8.8 Moving Active Directory Objects

1. Open Active Directory Users and Computers by clicking Start ⇨ Administrative Tools ⇨ Active Directory Users And Computers.

2. Expand the name of the domain.

3. Select the Sales OU (under the New York OU), right-click Workstation1, and select Move. A dialog box appears. Select the RD OU and click OK to move the Computer object to that container.

4. Click the RD OU and verify that Workstation1 was moved.

5. Close the Active Directory Users and Computers tool.

Resetting an Existing Computer Account

Every computer on the domain establishes a discrete channel of communication with the domain controller at logon time. The domain controller stores a randomly selected password (different from the user password) for authentication across the channel. The password is updated every 30 days.

Sometimes the computer's password and the domain controller's password don't match and communication between the two machines fails. Without the ability to reset the computer account, you wouldn't be able to connect the machine to the domain. Fortunately, you can use the Active Directory Users and Computers tool to reestablish the connection.

Exercise 8.9 shows you how to reset an existing computer account. You should have completed the previous exercises in this chapter before you begin this exercise.

EXERCISE 8.9   Resetting an Existing Computer Account

1. Open Active Directory Users and Computers by clicking Start ⇨ Administrative Tools ⇨ Active Directory Users And Computers.

2. Expand the name of the domain.

3. Click the RD OU and then right-click the Workstation1 computer account.

4. Select Reset Account from the context menu. Click Yes to confirm your selection. Click OK at the success prompt.

5. When you reset the account, you break the connection between the computer and the domain. So, after performing this exercise, reconnect the computer to the domain if you want it to continue working on the network.

Throughout this book, I have tried to show you the PowerShell way of doing a task shown previously using an MMC snap-in. Well, this is going to be no different.

This example shows you how to reset the secure connection between the local computer and the domain to which it is joined using a PowerShell command. In this example, the domain controller that performs the operation is specified as StormDC1.StormWindAD.com. To execute this PowerShell command, you must run this command on the local computer:

```
Test-ComputerSecureChannel -Repair -Server StormDC1.StormWindAD.com
```

Understanding Dynamic Access Control

One of the advantages of Windows Server 2022 is the ability to apply data governance to your file server. This will help control who has access to information and auditing. You get these advantages through the use of *Dynamic Access Control (DAC)*. Dynamic Access Control allows you to identify data by using data classifications (both automatic and manual) and then control access to these files based on these classifications.

DAC also gives administrators the ability to control file access by using a central access policy. This central access policy will also allow an administrator to set up audit access to files for reporting and forensic investigation.

DAC allows an administrator to set up Active Directory Rights Management Service encryption for Microsoft Office documents. For example, you can set up encryption for any documents that contain financial information.

Dynamic Access Control gives an administrator the flexibility to configure file access and auditing to domain-based file servers. To do this, DAC controls claims in the authentication token, resource properties, and conditional expressions within permission and auditing entries.

Administrators have the ability to give users access to files and folders based on Active Directory attributes. For example, a user named Dana is given access to the file server share because in the user's Active Directory (department attribute) properties, the value contains the value Sales.

Managing Security and Permissions

Now that you understand the basic issues, terms, and Active Directory objects that pertain to security, it's time to look at how you can apply this information to secure your network resources. The general practice for managing security is to assign users to groups and then grant permissions and logon parameters to the groups so that they can access certain resources.

For management ease and to implement a hierarchical structure, you can place groups within OUs. You can also assign Group Policy settings to all of the objects contained within an OU. By using this method, you can combine the benefits of a hierarchical structure (through OUs) with the use of security principals.

The primary tool you use to manage security permissions for users, groups, and computers is the Active Directory Users and Computers tool. Using this tool, you can create and manage Active Directory objects and organize them based on your business needs. Common tasks for many system administrators might include the following:

◆ Resetting a user's password (for example, in cases where they forget their password)

◆ Creating new user accounts (when, for instance, a new employee joins the company)

◆ Modifying group memberships based on changes in job requirements and functions

◆ Disabling user accounts (when, for example, users will be out of the office for long periods of time and will not require network resource access)

Once you've properly grouped your users, you need to set the actual permissions that affect the objects within Active Directory. The actual permissions that are available vary based on the type of object. Table 8.1 provides an example of some of the permissions that you can apply to various Active Directory objects and an explanation of what each permission does.

TABLE 8.1　　Permissions of Active Directory objects

PERMISSION	EXPLANATION
Control Access	Changes security permissions on the object
Create Child	Creates objects within an OU (such as other OUs)
Delete Child	Deletes child objects within an OU
Delete Tree	Deletes an OU and the objects within it
List Contents	Views objects within an OU
List Object	Views a list of the objects within an OU
Read	Views properties of an object (such as a username)
Write	Modifies properties of an object

Publishing Active Directory Objects

One of the main goals of Active Directory is to make resources easy to find. Two of the most commonly used resources in a networked environment are server file shares and printers. These are so common, in fact, that most organizations have dedicated file and print servers. When it comes to managing these types of resources, Active Directory makes it easy to determine which files and printers are available to users.

With that being said, take a look at how Active Directory manages to publish shared folders and printers.

Making Active Directory Objects Available to Users

An important aspect of managing Active Directory objects is that a system administrator can control which objects users can see. The act of making an Active Directory object available is known as *publishing*. The two main types of publishable objects are Printer objects and Shared Folder objects.

The general process for creating server shares and shared printers has remained unchanged from previous versions of Windows: you create the various objects (a printer or a file system folder) and then enable them for sharing. To make these resources available via Active Directory, however, there's an additional step: you must publish the resources. Once an object has been published in Active Directory, clients will be able to use it.

When you publish objects in Active Directory, you should know the server name and share name of the resource. When system administrators use Active Directory objects, they can change the resource to which the object points, without having to reconfigure or even notify clients. For example, if you move a share from one server to another, all you need to do is to update the Shared Folder object's properties to point to the new location. Active Directory clients still refer to the resource with the same path and name that they used before.

Publishing Printers

Printers can be published easily within Active Directory. This makes them available to users in your domain.

Exercise 8.10 walks you through the steps you need to take to share and publish a Printer object by having you create and share a printer. To complete the printer installation, you need access to the Windows Server 2022 installation media (via the hard disk, a network share, or the CD-ROM drive).

EXERCISE 8.10   Creating and Publishing a Printer

1. Click the Windows key on the keyboard and choose Control Panel.
2. Click Devices And Printers ⇨ Add A Printer. This starts the Add Printer Wizard. Then click the Next button.
3. In the Choose A Local Or Network Printer page, select Add A Local Printer. This should automatically take you to the next page. If it does not, click Next.
4. On the Choose A Printer Port page, select Use An Existing Port. From the drop-down list beside that option, make sure LPT1: (Printer Port) is selected. Click Next.

---

5. On the Install The Printer Driver page, select Generic for the manufacturer. For the printer, highlight Generic/Text Only. Click Next.

6. On the Type A Printer Name page, type **Text Printer**. Uncheck the Set As The Default Printer box and then click Next.

7. The Installing Printer screen appears. After the system is finished, the Printer Sharing page appears. Make sure the box labeled "Share this printer so that others on your network can find and use it" is selected, and accept the default share name of Text Printer.

8. In the Location section, type **Building 203**, and in the Comment section, add the following comment: **This is a text-only Printer**. Click Next.

9. On the You've Successfully Added Text Printer page, click Finish.

10. Next you need to verify that the printer will be listed in Active Directory. Right-click the Text Printer icon and select Printer Properties.

11. Select the Sharing tab and make sure that the List In The Directory box is checked. Note that you can also add additional printer drivers for other operating systems using this tab. Click OK to accept the settings.

Note that when you create and share a printer this way, an Active Directory Printer object is not displayed within the Active Directory Users and Computers tool. The printer is actually associated with the Computer object to which it is connected.

Publishing Shared Folders

Now that you've created and published a printer, you'll see how the same thing can be done to shared folders.

Exercise 8.11 walks through the steps required to create a folder, share it, and then publish it in Active Directory. This exercise assumes you are using the C: partition; however, you may want to change this based on your server configuration. You should have completed the previous exercises in this chapter before you begin this exercise.

EXERCISE 8.11   Creating and Publishing a Shared Folder

1. Create a new folder in the root directory of your C: partition and name it Test Share. To do this, click the File Explorer link on the toolbar.

2. Right-click the Test Share folder. Choose Share With ➪ Specific People.

3. In the File Sharing dialog box, enter the names of users with whom you want to share this folder. In the upper box, enter **Everyone** and then click Add. Note that Everyone appears in the lower box. Click in the Permission Level column next to Everyone and choose Read/Write from the pop-up menu. Then click Share.

4. You'll see a message that your folder has been shared. Click Done.

5. Click the Windows key on the keyboard and choose Administrative Tools.

6. Open the Active Directory Users and Computers tool. Expand the current domain and right-click the RD OU. Select New ➪ Shared Folder.

7. In the New Object - Shared Folder dialog box, type **Shared Folder Test** for the name of the folder. Then type the UNC path to the share (for example, **\\server1\Test Share**). Click OK to create the share.

Once you have created and published the Shared Folder object, clients can use the My Network Places icon to find it. The Shared Folder object will be organized based on the OU in which you created it. When you use publication, you can see how this makes it easy to manage shared folders.

PowerShell for Active Directory

Table 8.2 will show you just some of the available PowerShell commands for maintaining Active Directory. These PowerShell commands can help you do everything from unlocking disabled accounts to doing password resets.

NOTE   To see a complete list of PowerShell commands for Active Directory, please visit Microsoft's website at

https://docs.microsoft.com/en-us/powershell/module/activedirectory/?view=wind
owsserver2019-ps

TABLE 8.2   PowerShell commands for Active Directory

COMMAND	EXPLANATION
Add-ADComputerServiceAccount	This command allows an administrator to add service accounts to Active Directory.
Add-ADGroupMember	This command allows you to add users to an Active Directory group.
Disable-ADAccount	Administrators can use this command to disable an Active Directory account.
Enable-ADAccount	Administrators can use this command to enable an Active Directory account.
Get-ADComputer	This command allows you to view one or more Active Directory computers.
Get-ADDomain	Administrators can use this command to view an Active Directory domain.
Get-ADFineGrainedPasswordPolicy	This command allows you to view the Active Directory fine-grained password policies.
Get-ADGroup	Administrators can use this command to view Active Directory groups.
Get-ADGroupMember	This command allows you to view the users in an Active Directory group.
Get-ADServiceAccount	Administrators can use this command to view the Active Directory service accounts.

TABLE 8.2:   PowerShell commands for Active Directory   *(CONTINUED)*

COMMAND	EXPLANATION
Get-ADUser	This command allows you to view one or more Active Directory users.
New-ADComputer	Administrators can use this command to create a new Active Directory computer.
New-ADGroup	Administrators can use this command to create a new Active Directory group.
New-ADServiceAccount	This command is the *only* way that you can create a new Managed Service Account.
New-ADUser	Administrators can use this command to create a new Active Directory user.
Set-ADAccountPassword	This command allows you to modify the password of an Active Directory account.
Unlock-ADAccount	Administrators can use this command to unlock an Active Directory account.

The Bottom Line

Understand the Purpose of OUs.   You should understand that OUs are used to create a hierarchical, logical organization for objects within an Active Directory domain. They are like storage containers for objects, but you can put rules on those containers.

Master It   You are an administrator of a large network. You need to set up your Active Directory users by geographic location.

Know Groups and Group Strategies.   You can build and use three groups: domain local, global, and universal. Understand the group strategies and when they apply. Understand when to us Security groups vs. Distributed groups.

Master It   You are the administrator of an organization that has decided to buy out a company called Sybex.com. You need to create groups that stay in their tree only.

Chapter 9

Configuring DHCP

In this chapter, I will show you the different methods of setting up an IP address network. If you want systems to be able to share network resources, the computers must all talk the same type of language. This is where DHCP comes into play.

DHCP allows your users to get the required information so that they can properly communicate on the network. I will show you how to install and configure DHCP. I will also show you the advantages of using DHCP and how DHCP can save you hours of configuration time.

IN THIS CHAPTER YOU'LL LEARN

- ◆ Understand DHCP
- ◆ Know how to verify authorization of a DHCP server

Understanding DHCP

When you're setting up a network, the computers need to communicate with each other using the same type of computer language. This is referred to as a protocol. TCP/IP is the priority protocol for Windows Server 2022. For all of your machines to work using TCP/IP, each system must have its own unique IP address. There are two ways to have clients and servers get TCP/IP addresses:

- ◆ You can manually assign the addresses.
- ◆ The addresses can be assigned automatically.

Manually assigning addresses is a fairly simple process. An administrator goes to each of the machines on the network and assigns TCP/IP addresses. The problem with this method arises when the network becomes midsized or larger. Think of an administrator trying to individually assign 4,000 TCP/IP addresses, subnet masks, default gateways, and all other configuration options needed to run the network.

DHCP's job is to centralize the process of IP address and option assignment. You can configure a DHCP server with a range of addresses (called a *pool*) and other configuration information and let it assign all of the IP parameters—addresses, default gateways, DNS server addresses, and so on.

One of the nice advantages of DHCP is that you can install DHCP onto a Server Core server. DHCP is one of the roles that can be deployed onto a Server Core server. At the time this book was written, DHCP was not supported on a Nano server. So you can NOT load DHCP on a Windows Server 2022 Nano server.

NOTE DHCP is defined by a series of Request for Comments documents, notably 2131 and 2132.

Introducing the DORA Process

An easy way to remember how DHCP works is to learn the acronym DORA. *DORA* stands for Discover, Offer, Request, and Acknowledge. In brief, here is DHCP's DORA process:

1. *Discover*: When IP networking starts up on a DHCP-enabled client, a special message called a DHCPDISCOVER is broadcast within the local physical subnet.

2. *Offer*: Any DHCP server that hears the request checks its internal database and replies with a message called a DHCPOFFER, which contains an available IP address.

   The contents of this message depend on how the DHCP server is configured—there are numerous options aside from an IP address that you can specify to pass to the client on a Windows Server DHCP server.

3. *Request*: The client receives one or more DHCPOFFERs (depending on how many DHCP servers exist on the local subnet), chooses an address from one of the offers, and sends a DHCPREQUEST message to the server to signal acceptance of the DHCPOFFER.

   This message might also request additional configuration parameters.

   Other DHCP servers that sent offers take the request message as an acknowledgment that the client didn't accept their offer.

4. *Acknowledge*: When the DHCP server receives the DHCPREQUEST, it marks the IP address as being in use (that is, usually, though it's not required). Then it sends a DHCPACK to the client.

   The acknowledgment message might contain requested configuration parameters.

   If the server is unable to accept the DHCPREQUEST for any reason, it sends a DHCPNAK message. If a client receives a DHCPNAK, it begins the configuration process over again.

5. When the client accepts the IP offer, the address is assigned to the client for a specified period of time, called a *lease*. After receiving the DHCPACK message, the client performs a final check on the parameters (sometimes it sends an ARP request for the offered IP address) and makes note of the duration of the lease. The client is now configured. If the client detects that the address is already in use, it sends a DHCPDECLINE.

If the DHCP server has given out all of the IP addresses in its pool, it won't make an offer. If no other servers make an offer, the client's IP network initialization will fail, and the client will use Automatic Private IP Addressing (APIPA).

DHCP LEASE RENEWAL

No matter how long the lease period, the client sends a new lease request message directly to the DHCP server when the lease period is half over (give or take some randomness required by

RFC 2131). This period goes by the name *T1* (not to be confused with the T1 type of network connection). If the server hears the request message and there's no reason to reject it, it sends a DHCPACK to the client. This resets the lease period.

If the DHCP server isn't available, the client realizes that the lease can't be renewed. The client continues to use the address, and once 87.5 percent of the lease period has elapsed (again, give or take some randomness), the client sends out another renewal request. This interval is known as T2. At that point, any DHCP server that hears the renewal can respond to this *DHCP request message* (which is a request for a lease renewal) with a DHCPACK and renew the lease. If at any time during this process the client gets a negative DHCPNACK message, it must stop using its IP address immediately and start the leasing process over from the beginning by requesting a new lease.

When a client initializes its IP networking, it always attempts to renew its old address. If the client has time left on the lease, it continues to use the lease until its end. If the client is unable to get a new lease by that time, the client will swap over to using an APIPA address and that client would only be able to talk to the local segment with other computers using an APIPA address.

DHCP Lease Release

Although leases can be renewed repeatedly, at some point they might run out. Furthermore, the lease process is "at will." That is, the client or server can cancel the lease before it ends. In addition, if the client doesn't succeed in renewing the lease before it expires, the client loses its lease and reverts to APIPA. This release process is important for reclaiming extinct IP addresses used by systems that have moved or switched to a non-DHCP address.

Advantages and Disadvantages of DHCP

DHCP was designed from the start to simplify network management. It has some significant advantages, but it also has some drawbacks.

Advantages of DHCP

The following are advantages of DHCP:

- Configuration of large and even midsized networks is much simpler. If a DNS server address or some other change is necessary to the client, the administrator doesn't have to touch each device in the network physically to reconfigure it with the new settings.

- Once you enter the IP configuration information in one place—the server—it's automatically propagated to clients, eliminating the risk that a user will misconfigure some parameters and require you to fix them.

- IP addresses are conserved because DHCP assigns them only when requested.

- IP configuration becomes almost completely automatic. In most cases, you can plug in a new system (or move one) and then watch as it receives a configuration from the server. For example, when you install new network changes, such as a gateway or DNS server, the client configuration is done at only one location—the DHCP server.

- It allows a preboot execution environment (PXE) client to get a TCP/IP address from DHCP. PXE clients (also called Microsoft Windows Deployment Services [WDS] clients) can get an IP address without needing to have an operating system installed. This allows WDS clients to connect to a WDS server through the TCP/IP protocol and download an operating system remotely.

DISADVANTAGES OF DHCP

Unfortunately, there are a few drawbacks with DHCP:

◆ DHCP can become a single point of failure for your network. If you have only one DHCP server and it's not available, clients can't request or renew leases.

◆ If the DHCP server contains incorrect information, the misinformation will automatically be delivered to all of your DHCP clients.

◆ If you want to use DHCP on a multisegment network, you must put either a DHCP server or a relay agent on each segment, or you must ensure that your router can forward Bootstrap Protocol (BOOTP) broadcasts.

Ipconfig Lease Options

The ipconfig command-line tool is useful for working with network settings. Its /renew and /release switches make it particularly handy for DHCP clients. These switches allow you to request renewal of, or give up, your machine's existing address lease. You can do the same thing by toggling the Obtain An IP Address Automatically button in the Internet Protocol (TCP/IP) Properties dialog box, but the command-line option is useful especially when you're setting up a new network.

For example, I spend about a third of my time teaching MCSA or MCSE classes, usually in temporary classrooms set up at conferences, hotels, and so on. Laptops are used in these classes, with one brawny one set up as a DNS/DHCP/DC server. Occasionally, a client will lose its DHCP lease (or not get one, perhaps because a cable has come loose). The quickest way to fix it is to pop open a command-line window and type **ipconfig /renew**.

You can configure DHCP to assign options only to certain classes. *Classes*, defined by an administrator, are groups of computers that require identical DHCP options. The /setclassid-*classID* switch of ipconfig is the only way to assign a machine to a class.

More specifically, the switches do the following:

ipconfig /renew   Instructs the DHCP client to request a lease renewal. If the client already has a lease, it requests a renewal from the server that issued the current lease. This is equivalent to what happens when the client reaches the half-life of its lease. Alternatively, if the client doesn't currently have a lease, it is equivalent to what happens when you boot a DHCP client for the first time.

ipconfig /release   Forces the client to give up its lease immediately by sending the server a DHCP release notification. The server updates its status information and marks the client's old IP address as "available," leaving the client with no address bound to its network interface. When you use this command, most of the time it will be immediately followed by ipconfig/renew. The combination releases the existing lease and gets a new one, probably with a different address. (It's also a handy way to force your client to get a new set of settings from the server before the lease expiration time.)

`ipconfig /setclassidclassID` Sets a new class ID for the client. You will see how to configure class options later in the section "Setting Scope Options for IPv4." For now, you should know that the only way to add a client machine to a class is to use this command. Note that you need to renew the client lease for the class assignment to take effect.

If you have multiple network adapters in a single machine, you can provide the name of the adapter (or adapters) upon which you want the command to work, including an asterisk (*) as a wildcard. For example, one of my servers has two network cards: an Intel EtherExpress (ELNK1) and a generic 100 Mbps card. If you want to renew DHCP settings for both adapters, you can type `ipconfig /renew *`. If you just want to renew the Intel EtherExpress card, you can type `ipconfig /renew ELNK1`.

Understanding Scope Details

By now you should have a good grasp of what a lease is and how it works. To learn how to configure your servers to hand out those leases, however, you need to have a complete understanding of some additional topics: scopes, superscopes, exclusions, reservations, address pool, and relay agents.

SCOPE

Let's start with the concept of a *scope*, which is a contiguous range of addresses. There's usually one scope per physical subnet, and a scope can cover a Class A, Class B, or Class C network address or a TCP/IP v6 address. DHCP uses scopes as the basis for managing and assigning IP addressing information.

Each scope has a set of parameters, or scope options, that you can configure. *Scope options* control what data is delivered to DHCP clients when they're completing the DHCP negotiation process with a particular server. For example, the DNS server name, default gateway, and default network time server are all separate options that can be assigned. These settings are called *option types*. You can use any of the types provided with Windows Server 2022, or you can specify your own.

SUPERSCOPE

A *superscope* enables the DHCP server to provide addresses from more than one scope to clients on the same physical subnet. This is helpful when clients within the same subnet have more than one IP network and thus need IPs from more than one address pool. Microsoft's DHCP snap-in allows you to manage IP address assignment in the superscope, though you must still configure other scope options individually for each child scope.

EXCLUSIONS AND RESERVATIONS

The scope defines what IP addresses could potentially be assigned, but you can influence the assignment process in two additional ways by specifying exclusions and reservations:

Exclusions These are IP addresses within the range that you never want automatically assigned. These excluded addresses are off-limits to DHCP. You'll typically use exclusions to tag any addresses that you never want the DHCP server to assign at all. You might use exclusions to set aside addresses that you want to assign permanently to servers that play a vital role in your organization.

Reservations These are IP addresses within the range for which you want a permanent DHCP lease. They essentially reserve a particular IP address for a particular device. The device still goes through the DHCP process (that is, its lease expires and it asks for a new one), but it always obtains the same addressing information from the DHCP server.

TIP *Exclusions are useful for addresses that you don't want to participate in DHCP at all. Reservations* are helpful for situations in which you want a client to get the same settings each time they obtain an address.

TIP An address cannot be simultaneously reserved and excluded. Be aware of this fact for the exam, possibly relating to a troubleshooting question.

Real World Scenario

USING RESERVATIONS AND EXCLUSIONS

Deciding when to assign a reservation or exclusion can sometimes be confusing. In practice, you'll find that certain computers in the network greatly benefit by having static IP network information. Servers such as DNS servers, the DHCP server itself, SMTP servers, and other low-level infrastructure servers are good candidates for static assignment. There are usually so few of these servers that the administrator is not overburdened if a change in network settings requires going out to reconfigure each individually. Even in large installations, I find it preferable to manage these vital servers by hand rather than to rely on DHCP.

Reservations are also appropriate for application servers and other special but nonvital infrastructure servers. With a reservation in DHCP, the client device will still go through the DHCP process but will always obtain the same addressing information from the DHCP server. The premise behind this strategy is that these nonvital servers can withstand a short outage if DHCP settings change or if the DHCP server fails.

ADDRESS POOL

The range of IP addresses that the DHCP server can assign is called its *address pool*. For example, let's say you set up a new DHCP scope covering the 192.168.1 subnet. That gives you 254 usable IP addresses in the pool. After adding an exclusion from 192.168.1.241 to 192.168.1.254, you're left with 240 (254 – 14) IP addresses in the pool. That means (in theory, at least) that you can service 240 unique clients at a time before you run out of IP addresses.

DHCP RELAY AGENT

By design, DHCP is intended to work with clients and servers on a single IP network. But RFC 1542 sets out how BOOTP (on which DHCP is based) should work in circumstances in which the client and server are on different IP networks. If no DHCP server is available on the client's network, you can use a DHCP relay agent to forward DHCP broadcasts from the client's network to the DHCP server. The relay agent acts like a radio repeater, listening for DHCP client requests and retransmitting them through the router to the server.

Installing and Authorizing DHCP

Installing DHCP is easy using the Windows Server 2022/2012 R2 installation mechanism. Unlike some other services discussed in this book, the installation process installs just the service and its associated snap-in, starting it when the installation is complete. At that point, it's not delivering any DHCP service, but you don't have to reboot.

Installing DHCP

Exercise 9.1 shows you how to install a DHCP Server using Server Manager. This exercise was completed on a Windows Server 2022 Member Server since Active Directory is not installed yet.

EXERCISE 9.1   Installing the DHCP Service

1. Choose Server Manager by clicking the Server Manager icon on the Taskbar.

2. Click Add Roles And Features.

3. Choose role-based or feature-based installation and click Next.

4. Choose your server and click Next.

5. Choose DHCP Server (as shown in Figure 9.1) and click Next.

FIGURE 9.1
Choosing DHCP

---

6. At the Features screen, click Next.

7. Click Next at the DHCP screen.

8. At the DHCP confirmation screen, click the Install button.

9. When the installation is complete, click the Close button.

10. On the left side, click the DHCP link.

11. Click the More link next to Configuration Required For DHCP Server.

12. Under Action, click Complete DHCP Configuration.

13. At the DHCP Description page, click Commit.

14. Click Close at the Summary screen.

15. Close Server Manager.

Introducing the DHCP Snap-In

When you install the DHCP server, the DHCP snap-in is also installed. You can open it by selecting Administrative Tools ➤ DHCP. Figure 9.2 shows the DHCP management snap-in option.

FIGURE 9.2
DHCP snap-in

As you can see, the snap-in follows the standard MMC model. The left pane displays IPv4 and IPv6 sections and which servers are available; you can connect to servers other than the one to which you're already connected. A `Server Options` folder contains options that are specific to a particular DHCP server. Each server contains subordinate items grouped into folders. Each scope has a folder named after the scope's IP address range. Within each scope, four subordinate views show you interesting things about the scope, such as the following:

- The Address Pool view shows what the address pool looks like.

- The Address Leases view shows one entry for each current lease. Each lease shows the computer name to which the lease was issued, the corresponding IP address, and the current lease expiration time.

- The Reservations view shows the IP addresses that are reserved and which devices hold them.

- The Scope Options view lists the set of options you've defined for this scope.

Authorizing DHCP for Active Directory

Authorization creates an Active Directory object representing the new server. It helps keep unauthorized servers off your network. Unauthorized servers can cause two kinds of problems. They may hand out bogus leases, or they may fraudulently deny renewal requests from legitimate clients.

When you install a DHCP server using Windows Server 2022 and Active Directory is present on your network, the server won't be allowed to provide DHCP services to clients until it has been authorized. If you install DHCP on a member server in an Active Directory domain or on a stand-alone server, you'll have to authorize the server manually. When you authorize a server, you're adding its IP address to the Active Directory object that contains the IP addresses of all authorized DHCP servers.

At start time, each DHCP server queries the directory, looking for its IP address on the "authorized" list. If it can't find the list or if it can't find its IP address on the list, the DHCP service fails to start. Instead, it adds a message to the event log, indicating that it couldn't service client requests because the server wasn't authorized.

Exercise 9.2 and Exercise 9.3 show you how to authorize and unauthorize a DHCP server onto a network with Active Directory. If you installed DHCP onto a network with a domain, you can complete the following two exercises, but if you are still on a Stand-Alone server, you *cannot* do these exercises. Also, if you install the DHCP server on a Domain Controller, at the time this book was written, the DHCP server will auto Authorize. These steps are here to show you how to do it after you have Active Directory on your network or you install DHCP onto a Member server.

EXERCISE 9.2 Authorizing a DHCP Server

1. From Administrative Tools, choose DHCP to open the DHCP snap-in.

2. Right-click the server you want to authorize and choose the Authorize command (see Figure 9.3).

FIGURE 9.3
Choosing Authorize

3. Wait a few seconds and then hit F5. This will refresh the server. You should now see that the red down arrows are now green.

EXERCISE 9.3 Unauthorizing a DHCP Server

1. From Administrative Tools, choose DHCP to open the DHCP snap-in.

2. Right-click the server you want to authorize and choose the Unauthorize command (as shown in Figure 9.4).

FIGURE 9.4
Choosing Unauthorize

3. Wait a few seconds and then hit F5. This will refresh the server. You should now see that the green arrows are now red.

4. Now let's reauthorize the server. Right-click the server and choose the Authorize command. Wait a few seconds and hit F5.

Creating and Managing DHCP Scopes

You can use any number of DHCP servers on a single physical network if you divide the range of addresses that you want assigned into multiple scopes. Each scope contains a number of useful pieces of data, but before you can understand them, you need to know some additional terminology.

You can perform the following management tasks on DHCP scopes:

- Create a scope
- Configure scope properties
- Configure reservations and exclusions
- Set scope options
- Activate and deactivate scopes
- Create a superscope
- Create a multicast scope
- Integrate Dynamic DNS and DHCP

I will cover each task in the following sections.

Creating a New Scope in IPv4

Like many other things in Windows Server 2022, a wizard drives the process of creating a new scope. You will most likely create a scope while installing DHCP, but you may need to create more than one. The overall process is simple, as long as you know beforehand what the wizard is going to ask. If you think about what defines a scope, you'll be well prepared. You need to know the following:

- The IP address range for the scope you want to create.
- Which IP addresses, if any, you want to exclude from the address pool.
- Which IP addresses, if any, you want to reserve.
- Values for the DHCP options you want to set, if any. This item isn't strictly necessary for creating a scope. However, to create a useful scope, you'll need to have some options to specify for the clients.

To create a scope, under the server name, right-click the IPv4 option in the DHCP snap-in, and use the Action ⇨ New Scope command. This starts the New Scope Wizard (see Figure 9.5). You will look at each page of the wizard in the following sections.

FIGURE 9.5
Welcome page of the
New Scope Wizard

SETTING THE SCREEN NAME

The Scope Name page allows you to enter a name and description for your scope. These will be displayed by the DHCP snap-in.

TIP   It's a good idea to pick sensible names for your scopes so that other administrators will be able to figure out the purpose of the scope. For example, the name DHCP is likely not very helpful, whereas a name like 1st Floor Subnet is more descriptive and can help in troubleshooting.

DEFINING THE IP ADDRESS RANGE

The IP Address Range page (see Figure 9.6) is where you enter the start and end IP addresses for your range. The wizard does minimal checking on the addresses you enter, and it automatically calculates the appropriate subnet mask for the range. You can modify the subnet mask if you know what you're doing.

ADDING EXCLUSIONS AND DELAY

The Add Exclusions And Delay page (see Figure 9.7) allows you to create exclusion ranges. Exclusions are TCP/IP numbers that are in the pool, but they do not get issued to clients. To exclude one address, put it in the Start IP Address field. To exclude a range, also fill in the End IP Address field. The delay setting is a time duration by which the server will delay the transmission of a DHCPOFFER message.

TIP   Although you can always add exclusions later, it's best to include them when you create the scope so that no excluded addresses are ever passed out to clients.

FIGURE 9.6
IP Address Range page
of the New Scope Wizard

New Scope Wizard

IP Address Range
You define the scope address range by identifying a set of consecutive IP addresses.

Configuration settings for DHCP Server

Enter the range of addresses that the scope distributes.

Start IP address:　　10 . 10 . 16 . 1

End IP address:　　10 . 10 . 31 . 254

Configuration settings that propagate to DHCP Client

Length:　　20

Subnet mask:　　255 . 255 . 240 . 0

< Back　　Next >　　Cancel

FIGURE 9.7
Add Exclusions And
Delay page of the New
Scope Wizard

New Scope Wizard

Add Exclusions and Delay
Exclusions are addresses or a range of addresses that are not distributed by the
server. A delay is the time duration by which the server will delay the transmission of a
DHCPOFFER message.

Type the IP address range that you want to exclude. If you want to exclude a single
address, type an address in Start IP address only.

Start IP address:　　End IP address:

Add

Excluded address range:

10.10.20.1 to 10.10.20.250　　Remove

Subnet delay in milli second:

< Back　　Next >　　Cancel

SETTING A LEASE DURATION

The Lease Duration page (see Figure 9.8) allows you to set how long a device gets to use an assigned IP address before it has to renew its lease. The default lease duration is eight days. You may find that a shorter or longer duration makes sense for your network. If your network is highly dynamic, with lots of arrivals, departures, and moving computers, set a shorter lease duration; if it's less active, make it longer.

FIGURE 9.8
Lease Duration page of the New Scope Wizard

> **New Scope Wizard**
>
> **Lease Duration**
> The lease duration specifies how long a client can use an IP address from this scope.
>
> Lease durations should typically be equal to the average time the computer is connected to the same physical network. For mobile networks that consist mainly of portable computers or dial-up clients, shorter lease durations can be useful. Likewise, for a stable network that consists mainly of desktop computers at fixed locations, longer lease durations are more appropriate.
>
> Set the duration for scope leases when distributed by this server.
>
> Limited to:
>
> Days: Hours: Minutes:
> 8   0   0
>
> < Back   Next >   Cancel

TIP Remember that renewal attempts begin when approximately half of the lease period is over (give or take a random interval) or when a system restarts, so don't set them too short. For example, leases that are set too short can cause renewal traffic in the middle of the work day and this can cause network delays while all of the machines try to renew their addresses.

CONFIGURING BASIC DHCP OPTIONS

The Configure DHCP Options page (see Figure 9.9) allows you to choose whether you want to set up basic DHCP options such as default gateway and DNS settings. The options are described in the following sections. If you choose not to configure options, you can always do so later. However, you should not activate the scope until you've configured the options you want assigned.

Configuring a Router

The first option configuration page is the Router (Default Gateway) page (see Figure 9.10), in which you enter the IP addresses of one or more routers (more commonly referred to as *default gateways*) that you want to use for outbound traffic. After entering the IP addresses of the routers, use the Up and Down buttons to order the addresses. Clients will use the routers in the order specified when attempting to send outgoing packets.

FIGURE 9.9
Configure DHCP
Options page of the New
Scope Wizard

New Scope Wizard

Configure DHCP Options
You have to configure the most common DHCP options before clients can use the scope.

When clients obtain an address, they are given DHCP options such as the IP addresses of routers (default gateways), DNS servers, and WINS settings for that scope.

The settings you select here are for this scope and override settings configured in the Server Options folder for this server.

Do you want to configure the DHCP options for this scope now?

⦿ Yes, I want to configure these options now

◯ No, I will configure these options later

< Back | Next > | Cancel

FIGURE 9.10
Router (Default
Gateway) page of the
New Scope Wizard

New Scope Wizard

Router (Default Gateway)
You can specify the routers, or default gateways, to be distributed by this scope.

To add an IP address for a router used by clients, enter the address below.

IP address:

[. . .] Add

10.10.1.1 | Remove

Up

Down

< Back | Next > | Cancel

Providing DNS Settings

On the Domain Name And DNS Servers page (see Figure 9.11), you specify the set of DNS servers and the parent domain you want passed down to DHCP clients. Normally, you'll want to specify at least one DNS server by filling in its DNS name or IP address. You can also specify the domain suffix that you want clients to use as the base domain for all connections that aren't fully qualified. For example, if your clients are used to navigating based on server name alone rather than the fully qualified domain name (FQDN) of server.willpanek.com, then you'll want to place your domain here.

FIGURE 9.11
Domain Name And DNS
Servers page of the New
Scope Wizard

Providing WINS Settings

If you're still using Windows Internet Name Service (WINS) on your network, you can configure DHCP so that it passes WINS server addresses to your Windows clients. (If you want the Windows clients to honor it, you'll also need to define the WINS/NBT Node Type option for the scope.) As on the DNS server page, on the WINS Servers page (see Figure 9.12) you can enter the addresses of several servers and move them into the order in which you want clients to try them. You can enter the DNS or NetBIOS name of each server, or you can enter an IP address.

Here are some of the more common options you can set on a DHCP server:

003 Router   Used to provide a list of available routers or default gateways on the same subnet.

006 DNS Servers   Used to provide a list of DNS servers.

015 DNS Domain Name   Used to provide the DNS suffix.

FIGURE 9.12
WINS Servers page of
the New Scope Wizard

FIGURE 9.12
WINS Servers page of
the New Scope Wizard

028 Broadcast Address Used to configure the broadcast address, if different than the default, based on the subnet mask.

44 WINS/NBNS Servers Used to configure the IP addresses of WINS servers.

46 WINS/NBT Node Type Used to configure the preferred NetBIOS name resolution method. There are four settings for node type:

B node (0x1)   Broadcast for NetBIOS resolution

P node (0x2)   Peer-to-peer (WINS) server for NetBIOS resolution

M node (0x4)   Mixed node (does a B node and then a P node)

H node (0x8) Hybrid node (does a P node and then a B node)

051 Lease Used to configure a special lease duration.

Activating the Scope

The Activate Scope page (see Figure 9.13) gives you the option to activate the scope immediately after creating it. By default, the wizard assumes that you want the scope activated unless you select the No, I Will Activate This Scope Later radio button, in which case the scope will remain dormant until you activate it manually.

WARNING   Be sure to verify that there are no other DHCP servers assigned to the address range you choose!

FIGURE 9.13
Activate Scope page of
the New Scope Wizard

New Scope Wizard

Activate Scope
Clients can obtain address leases only if a scope is activated.

Do you want to activate this scope now?

(•) Yes, I want to activate this scope now

( ) No, I will activate this scope later

< Back | Next > | Cancel

In Exercise 9.4, you will create a new scope for the 192.168.0.x private Class C network. First you need to complete Exercise 9.1 before beginning this exercise.

EXERCISE 9.4   Creating a New Scope

1. Open the DHCP snap-in by selecting Administrative Tools ⇨ DHCP.

2. Right-click the IPv4 folder and choose New Scope. The New Scope Wizard appears.

3. Click the Next button on the welcome page.

4. Enter a name and a description for your new scope and click the Next button.

5. On the IP Address Range page, enter **192.168.0.2** as the start IP address for the scope and **192.168.0.250** as the end IP address. Leave the subnet mask controls alone (though when creating a scope on a production network, you might need to change them). Click the Next button.

6. On the Add Exclusions And Delay page, click Next without adding any excluded addresses or delays.

7. On the Lease Duration page, set the lease duration to 3 days and click the Next button.

8. On the Configure DHCP Options page, click the Next button to indicate you want to configure default options for this scope.

9. On the Router (Default Gateway) page, enter **192.168.0.1** for the router IP address and then click the Add button. Once the address is added, click the Next button.

10. On the Domain Name And DNS Servers page, enter the IP address of a DNS server on your network in the IP Address field (for example, you might enter **192.168.0.251**) and click the Add button. Click the Next button.

11. On the WINS Servers page, click the Next button to leave the WINS options unset.

12. On the Activate Scope page, if your network is currently using the 192.168.0.*x* range, select Yes, I Want To Activate This Scope Now. Click the Next button.

13. When the wizard's summary page appears, click the Finish button to create the scope.

Creating a New Scope in IPv6

Now that you have seen how to create a new scope in IPv4, I'll go through the steps to create a new scope in IPv6.

To create a scope, right-click the IPv6 option in the DHCP snap-in under the server name and select the Action ⇨ New Scope command. This starts the New Scope Wizard. Just as with creating a scope in IPv4, the welcome page of the wizard tells you that you've launched the New Scope Wizard. You will look at each page of the wizard in the following sections.

SETTING THE SCREEN NAME

The Scope Name page (see Figure 9.14) allows you to enter a name and description for your scope. These will be displayed by the DHCP snap-in.

FIGURE 9.14
IPv6 Scope Name page
of the New Scope Wizard

TIP It's a good idea to pick a sensible name for your scopes so that other administrators will be able to figure out what the scope is used for.

SCOPE PREFIX

The Scope Prefix page (see Figure 9.15) gets you started creating the IPv6 scope. IPv6 has three types of addresses, which can be categorized by type and scope.

FIGURE 9.15
Scope Prefix page of the
New Scope Wizard

Unicast Addresses *One-to-one.* A packet from one host is delivered to another host. The following are some examples of IPv6 unicast:

- The unicast prefix for site-local addresses is FEC0::/48.

- The unicast prefix for link-local addresses is FE80::/64.

The 6to4 address allows communication between two hosts running both IPv4 and IPv6. The way to calculate the 6to4 address is by combining the global prefix 2002::/16 with the 32 bits of a public IPv4 address of the host. This gives you a 48-bit prefix. 6to4 is described in RFC 3056.

Multicast addresses *One-to-many.* A packet from one host is delivered to multiple hosts (but not everyone). The prefix for multicast addresses is FF00::/8.

Anycast addresses A packet from one host is delivered to the nearest of multiple hosts (in terms of routing distance).

ADDING EXCLUSIONS

As with the IPv4 New Scope Wizard, the Add Exclusions page allows you to create exclusion ranges. *Exclusions* are TCP/IP numbers that are in the pool but do not get issued to clients. To exclude one address, put it in the Start IPv6 Address field. To exclude a range, also fill in the End IPv6 Address field.

SETTING A LEASE DURATION

The Scope Lease page allows you to set how long a device gets to use an assigned IP address before it has to renew its lease. You can set two different lease durations. The section labeled Non Temporary Address (IANA) is the lease time for your more permanent hosts (such as printers and server towers). The one labeled Temporary Address (IATA) is for hosts that might disconnect at any time, such as laptops.

ACTIVATING THE SCOPE

The Completing The New Scope Wizard page gives you the option to activate the scope immediately after creating it. By default, the wizard will assume you want the scope activated. If you want to wait to activate the scope, choose No in the Activate Scope Now box.

Changing Scope Properties (IPv4 and IPv6)

Each scope has a set of properties associated with it. Except for the set of options assigned by the scope, you can find these properties on the General tab of the scope's Properties dialog box (see Figure 9.16). Some of these properties, such as the scope name and description, are self-explanatory. Others require a little more explanation.

FIGURE 9.16
General tab of the scope's Properties dialog box for an IPv4 scope

◆ The Start IP Address and End IP Address fields allow you to set the range of the scope.

◆ For IPv4 scopes, the settings in the section Lease Duration For DHCP Clients control how long leases in this scope are valid.

The IPv6 scope dialog box includes a Lease tab where you set the lease properties.

TIP When you make changes to these properties, they have no effect on existing leases. For example, say you create a scope from 172.30.1.1 to 172.30.1.199. You use that scope for a while and then edit its properties to reduce the range from 172.30.1.1 to 172.30.1.150. If a client has been assigned the address 172.30.1.180, which was part of the scope before you changed it, the client will retain that address until the lease expires but will not be able to renew it.

Changing Server Properties

Just as each scope has its own set of properties, so too does the server itself. You access the server properties by right-clicking the IPv4 or IPv6 object within the DHCP management console and selecting Properties.

IPv4 SERVER PROPERTIES

Figure 9.17 shows the IPv4 Properties dialog box.

FIGURE 9.17
General tab of the IPv4
Properties dialog box for
the server

The IPv4 Properties dialog box has five tabs: General, DNS, Filters, Failover, and Advanced. The Advanced tab, shown in Figure 9.18, contains the following configuration parameters:

◆ Conflict Detection Attempts specifies how many ICMP echo requests (pings) the server sends for an address it is about to offer. The default is 0. Conflict detection is a way to verify that the DHCP server is not issuing IP addresses that are already being used on the network.

◆ Audit Log File Path is where you enter the location for log files.

◆ Change Server Connection Bindings allows an administrator to choose which of the network adapters will be used by the DHCP server for both IPv4 and IPv6 addresses.

◆ DNS Dynamic Update Registration Credentials allows an administrator to put in user credentials so that DHCP can update DNS if DNS is using Secure only dynamic updates.

FIGURE 9.18
Advanced tab of the IPv4 Properties dialog box for the server

IPv6 SERVER PROPERTIES

The IPv6 Properties dialog box for the server has two tabs: General and Advanced. On the General tab, you can configure the following settings:

◆ Frequency with which statistics are updated

◆ DHCP auditing

The Advanced tab allows you to configure the following settings:

- Database path for the audit log file path.
- Connection bindings.
- Registration credentials for dynamic DNS. The registration credential is the user account that DHCP will use to register clients with Active Directory.

Managing Reservations and Exclusions

After defining the address pool for your scope, the next step is to create reservations and exclusions, which reduce the size of the pool. In the following sections, you will learn how to add and remove exclusions and reservations.

ADDING AND REMOVING EXCLUSIONS

When you want to exclude an entire range of IP addresses, you need to add that range as an exclusion. Ordinarily, you'll want to do this before you enable a scope because that prevents any of the IP addresses you want excluded from being leased before you have a chance to exclude them. In fact, you can't create an exclusion that includes a leased address—you have to get rid of the lease first.

Adding an Exclusion Range

Here's how to add an exclusion range:

1. Open the DHCP snap-in and find the scope to which you want to add an exclusion (either IPv4 or IPv6).
2. Expand the scope so that you can see its Address Pool item for IPv4 or the Exclusion section for IPv6.
3. Right-click the Address Pool or Exclusion section and choose the New Exclusion Range command.
4. When the Add Exclusion dialog box appears, enter the IP addresses you want to exclude. To exclude a single address, type it in the Start IP Address field. To exclude a range of addresses, also fill in the End IP Address field.
5. Click the Add button to add the exclusion.

When you add exclusions, they appear in the Address Pool node, which is under the Scope section for IPv4 and under the Exclusion section of IPv6.

Removing an Exclusion Range

To remove an exclusion, just right-click it and choose the Delete command. After confirming your command, the snap-in removes the excluded range and the addresses become immediately available for issuance.

ADDING AND REMOVING RESERVATIONS

Adding a reservation is simple as long as you have the MAC address of the device for which you want to create a reservation. Because reservations belong to a single scope, you create and remove them within the Reservations node beneath each scope.

Adding a Reservation

To add a reservation, perform the following tasks:

1. Right-click the scope and select New Reservation.

   This displays the New Reservation dialog box, shown in Figure 9.19.

FIGURE 9.19
New Reservation dialog
boxes for IPv4 and IPv6

2. Enter the IP address and MAC address or ID for the reservation.

TIP To find the MAC address of the local computer, use the `ipconfig` command. To find the MAC address of a remote machine, use the `nbtstat -a computername` command.

3. If you want, you can also enter a name and description.

4. For IPv4, in the Supported Types section, choose whether the reservation will be made by DHCP only, BOOTP only (useful for remote-access devices), or both.

Removing a Reservation

To remove a reservation, right-click it and select Delete. This removes the reservation but does nothing to the client device.

NOTE There's no way to change a reservation once it has been created. If you want to change any of the associated settings, you'll have to delete and re-create the reservation.

Setting Scope Options for IPv4

Once you've installed a server, authorized it in Active Directory, and fixed up the address pool, the next step is to set scope options that you want sent out to clients, such as router (that is, default gateway) and DNS server addresses. You must configure the options you want sent out before you activate a scope. If you don't, clients may register in the scope without getting any options, rendering them virtually useless. Thus, configure the scope options, along with the IP address and subnet mask that you configured earlier in this chapter.

In the following sections, you will learn how to configure and assign scope options on the DHCP server.

UNDERSTANDING OPTION ASSIGNMENT

You can control which DHCP options are doled out to clients in five (slightly overlapping) ways:

Predefined Options   *Predefined options* are templates that are available in the Server, Scope, or Client Options dialog box.

Server Options   *Server options* are assigned to all scopes and clients of a particular server. That means if there's some setting you want all clients of a DHCP server to have, no matter what scope they're in, this is where you assign it. Specific options (those that are set at the class, scope, or client level) will override server-level options. That gives you an escape valve; it's a better idea, though, to be careful about which options you assign if your server manages multiple scopes.

Scope Options   If you want a particular option value assigned only to those clients in a certain subnet, you should assign it as a *scope option*. For example, it's common to specify different routers for different physical subnets; if you have two scopes corresponding to different subnets, each scope would probably have a separate value for the router option.

Class Options   You can assign different options to clients of different types, that is, *class options*. For example, Windows 2000, XP, Vista, Windows 7, Windows 8/8.1, Windows 10, Windows 11, Server 2003, Server 2003 R2, Server 2008, Server 2008 R2, and Server 2022/2012 R2, Server 2016, Server 2019, and Server 2022 machines recognize a number of DHCP options that Windows 98, Windows NT, and Mac OS machines ignore, and vice versa. By defining a Windows 2000 or newer class (using the `ipconfig/setclassid` command you saw earlier), you could assign those options only to machines that report themselves as being in that class.

Client Options   If a client is using DHCP reservations, you can assign certain options to that specific client. You attach *client options* to a particular reservation. Client options override scope, server, and class options. The only way to override a client option is to configure the client manually. The DHCP server manages client options.

NOTE   Client options override class options, class options override scope options, and scope options override server options.

ASSIGNING OPTIONS

You can use the DHCP snap-in to assign options at the scope, server, reserved address, or class level. The mechanism you use to assign these options is the same for each; the only difference is where you set the options.

When you create an option assignment, remember that it applies to all of the clients in the server or the scope from that point forward. Option assignments aren't retroactive, and they don't migrate from one scope to another.

Creating and Assigning a New Option

To create a new option and have it assigned, follow these steps:

1. Select the scope or server where you want the option assigned.

2. Select the corresponding Options node and choose Action ⇨ Configure Options.

   To set options for a reserved client, right-click its entry in the Reservations node and select Configure Options.

   Then you'll see the Scope Options dialog box, which lists all of the options that you might want to configure.

3. To select an individual option, check the box next to it and then use the controls in the Data Entry control group to enter the value you want associated with the option.

4. Continue to add options until you've specified all of the ones you want attached to the server or scope. Then click OK.

Configuring the DHCP Server for Classes

Now it is time for you to learn how to configure the DHCP server to recognize your customized classes and configure options for them. In Exercise 9.5, you will create a new user class and configure options for the new class. Before you begin, make sure that the computers you want to use in the class have been configured with the `ipconfig/setclassid` command.

EXERCISE 9.5 Configuring User Class Options

1. Open the DHCP snap-in by selecting Administrative Tools ⇨ DHCP.

2. Right-click the IPv4 item and select Define User Classes.

3. Click the Add button in the DHCP User Classes dialog box.

4. In the New Class dialog box, enter a descriptive name for the class in the Display Name field. Enter a class ID in the ID field. (Typically, you will enter the class ID in the ASCII portion of the ID field.) When you have finished, click OK.

5. The new class appears in the DHCP User Classes dialog box. Click the Close button to return to the DHCP snap-in.

6. Right-click the Scope Options node and select Configure Options.

7. Click the Advanced tab. Select the class you defined in step 4 from the User Class pop-up menu.

8. Configure the options you want to set for the class. Click OK when you have finished. Notice that the options you configured (and the class with which they are associated) appear in the right pane of the DHCP window.

About the Default Routing and Remote Access Predefined User Class

Windows Server 2022 includes a predefined user class called the *Default Routing and Remote Access class*. This class includes options important to clients connecting to Routing and Remote Access, notably the 051 Lease option.

NOTE Be sure to know that the 051 Lease option is included within this class and that it can be used to assign a shorter lease duration for clients connecting to Routing and Remote Access.

Activating and Deactivating Scopes

When you've completed the steps in Exercise 9.4 and you're ready to unleash your new scope so that it can be used to make client assignments, the final required step is activating the scope. When you activate a scope, you're just telling the server that it's OK to start handing out addresses from that scope's address pool. As soon as you activate a scope, addresses from its pool may be assigned to clients. Of course, this is a necessary precondition to getting any use out of your scope.

If you later want to stop using a scope, you can, but be aware that it's a permanent change. When you deactivate a scope, DHCP tells all clients registered with the scope that they need to release their leases immediately and renew them someplace else—the equivalent of a landlord who evicts tenants when the building is condemned!

WARNING Don't deactivate a scope unless you want clients to stop using it immediately.

Creating a Superscope for IPv4

A *superscope* allows the DHCP server to provide multiple logical subnet addresses to DHCP clients on a single physical network. You create superscopes with the New Superscope command, which triggers the New Superscope Wizard.

NOTE You can have only one superscope per server.

The steps in Exercise 9.6 take you through the process of creating a superscope.

EXERCISE 9.6 Creating a Superscope

1. Open the DHCP snap-in by selecting Administrative Tools ⇨ DHCP.

2. Follow the instructions in Exercise 9.4 to create two scopes: one for 192.168.0.2 through 192.168.0.127 and one for 192.168.1.12 through 192.168.1.127.

3. Right-click IPv4 and choose the New Superscope command. The New Superscope Wizard appears. Click the Next button.

4. On the Superscope Name page, name your superscope and click the Next button.

5. The Select Scopes page appears, listing all scopes on the current server. Select the two scopes you created in step 2 and then click the Next button.

6. The wizard's summary page appears. Click the Finish button to create your scope.

7. Verify that your new superscope appears in the DHCP snap-in.

DELETING A SUPERSCOPE

You can delete a superscope by right-clicking it and choosing the Delete command. A superscope is just an administrative convenience, so you can safely delete one at any time—it doesn't affect the "real" scopes that make up the superscope.

ADDING A SCOPE TO A SUPERSCOPE

To add a scope to an existing superscope, find the scope you want to add, right-click it, and choose Action ⇨ Add To Superscope. A dialog box appears, listing all of the superscopes known to this server. Pick the one to which you want the current scope appended and click the OK button.

REMOVING A SCOPE FROM A SUPERSCOPE

To remove a scope from a superscope, open the superscope and right-click the target scope. The pop-up menu provides a Remove From Superscope command that will do the deed.

ACTIVATING AND DEACTIVATING SUPERSCOPES

Just as with regular scopes, you can activate and deactivate superscopes. The same restrictions and guidelines apply. You must activate a superscope before it can be used, and you must not deactivate it until you want all of your clients to lose their existing leases and be forced to request new ones.

To activate or deactivate a superscope, right-click the superscope name and select Activate or Deactivate, respectively, from the pop-up menu.

Creating IPv4 Multicast Scopes

Multicasting occurs when one machine communicates to a network of subscribed computers rather than specifically addressing each computer on the destination network. It's much more efficient to multicast a video or audio stream to multiple destinations than it is to unicast it to the same number of clients, and the increased demand for multicast-friendly network hardware has resulted in some head scratching about how to automate the multicast configuration.

In the following sections, you will learn about MADCAP, the protocol that controls multicasting, and about how to build and configure a multicast scope.

UNDERSTANDING THE MULTICAST ADDRESS DYNAMIC CLIENT ALLOCATION PROTOCOL

DHCP is usually used to assign IP configuration information for *unicast* (or one-to-one) network communications. With multicast, there's a separate type of address space assigned from 224.0.0.0 through 239.255.255.255. Addresses in this space are known as *Class D addresses*, or simply *multicast addresses*. Clients can participate in a multicast just by knowing (and using) the multicast address for the content they want to receive. However, multicast clients also need to have an ordinary IP address.

How do clients know what address to use? Ordinary DHCP won't help because it's designed to assign IP addresses and option information to one client at a time. Realizing this, the Internet Engineering Task Force (IETF) defined a new protocol: *Multicast Address Dynamic Client Allocation*

Protocol (MADCAP). MADCAP provides an analog to DHCP but for multicast use. A MADCAP server issues leases for multicast addresses only. MADCAP clients can request a multicast lease when they want to participate in a multicast.

DHCP and MADCAP have some important differences. First you have to realize that the two are totally separate. A single server can be a DHCP server, a MADCAP server, or both; no implied or actual relation exists between the two. Likewise, clients can use DHCP and/or MADCAP at the same time—the only requirement is that every MADCAP client has to get a unicast IP address from somewhere.

TIP Remember that DHCP can assign options as part of the lease process but MADCAP cannot. The only thing MADCAP does is dynamically assign multicast addresses.

BUILDING MULTICAST SCOPES

Most of the steps you go through when creating a multicast scope are identical to those required for an ordinary unicast scope. Exercise 9.7 highlights the differences.

EXERCISE 9.7 Creating a New Multicast Scope

1. Open the DHCP snap-in by selecting Administrative Tools ⇨ DHCP.

2. Right-click IPv4 and choose New Multicast Scope. The New Multicast Scope Wizard appears. Click the Next button on the welcome page.

3. In the Multicast Scope Name page, name your multicast scope (and add a description if you'd like). Click the Next button.

4. The IP Address Range page appears. Enter a start IP address of **224.0.0.0** and an end IP address of **224.255.0.0**. Adjust the TTL to 1 to make sure that no multicast packets escape your local network segment. Click the Next button when you're finished.

5. The Add Exclusions page appears; click its Next button.

6. The Lease Duration page appears. Since multicast addresses are used for video and audio, you'd ordinarily leave multicast scope assignments in place somewhat longer than you would with a regular unicast scope, so the default lease length is 30 days (instead of 8 days for a unicast scope). Click the Next button.

7. The wizard asks you if you want to activate the scope now. Click the No radio button and then the Next button.

8. The wizard's summary page appears; click the Finish button to create your scope.

9. Verify that your new multicast scope appears in the DHCP snap-in.

SETTING MULTICAST SCOPE PROPERTIES

Once you create a multicast scope, you can adjust its properties by right-clicking the scope name and selecting Properties.

The Multicast Scope Properties dialog box has two tabs. The General tab allows you to change the scope's name, its start and end addresses, its Time To Live (TTL) value, its lease duration, and its description—in essence, all of the settings you provided when you created it in the first place.

The Lifetime tab allows you to limit how long your multicast scope will be active. By default, a newly created multicast scope will live forever, but if you're creating a scope to provide MADCAP assignments for a single event (or a set of events of limited duration), you can specify an expiration time for the scope. When that time is reached, the scope disappears from the server but not before making all of its clients give up their multicast address leases. This is a nice way to make sure that the lease cleans up after itself when you're finished with it.

Integrating Dynamic DNS and IPv4 DHCP

DHCP integration with Dynamic DNS is a simple concept but powerful in action. By setting up this integration, you can pass addresses to DHCP clients while still maintaining the integrity of your DNS services.

The DNS server can be updated in two ways. One way is for the DHCP client to tell the DNS server its address. Another way is for the DHCP server to tell the DNS server when it registers a new client.

Neither of these updates will take place, however, unless you configure the DNS server to use Dynamic DNS. You can make this change in two ways:

♦ If you change it at the scope level, it will apply only to the scope.

♦ If you change it at the server level, it will apply to all scopes and superscopes served by the server.

Which of these options you choose depends on how widely you want to support Dynamic DNS; most of the sites I visit have enabled DNS updates at the server level.

To update the settings at either the server or scope level, you need to open the scope or server properties by right-clicking the appropriate object and choosing Properties. The DNS tab of the Properties dialog box (see Figure 9.20) includes the following options:

FIGURE 9.20
DNS tab of the scope's
IPv4 Properties
dialog box

Enable DNS Dynamic Updates According To The Settings Below This check box controls whether this DHCP server will attempt to register lease information with a DNS server. It must be checked to enable Dynamic DNS.

Dynamically Update DNS A And PTR Records Only If Requested By The DHCP Clients This radio button (which is on by default) tells the DHCP server to register the update only if the DHCP client asks for DNS registration. When this button is active, DHCP clients that aren't hip to DDNS won't have their DNS records updated. However, Windows 2000, XP, Vista, Windows 7, Windows 8/8.1, Windows 10, Windows 11, Server 2003/2003 R2, Server 2008/2008 R2, Server 2022/2012 R2, Server 2016, Server 2019, and Server 2022 DHCP clients are smart enough to ask for the updates.

Always Dynamically Update DNS A And PTR Records This radio button forces the DHCP server to register any client to which it issues a lease. This setting may add DNS registrations for DHCP-enabled devices that don't really need them, such as print servers. However, it allows other clients (such as Mac OS, Windows NT, and Linux machines) to have their DNS information automatically updated.

Discard A And PTR Records When Lease Is Deleted This check box has a long name but a simple function. When a DHCP lease expires, what should happen to the DNS registration? Obviously, it would be nice if the DNS record associated with a lease vanished when the lease expired. When this check box is checked (as it is by default), that's exactly what happens. If you uncheck this box, your DNS will contain entries for expired leases that are no longer valid. When a particular IP address is reissued on a new lease, the DNS will be updated, but in between leases you'll have incorrect data in your DNS—something that's always best to avoid.

Dynamically Update DNS A And PTR Records For DHCP Clients That Do Not Request Updates This check box lets you handle these older clients graciously by making the updates using a separate mechanism.

In Exercise 9.8, you will enable a scope to participate in Dynamic DNS updates.

EXERCISE 9.8 Enabling DHCP-DNS Integration

1. Open the DHCP snap-in by selecting Administrative Tools ⇨ DHCP.

2. Right-click the IPv4 item and select Properties.

3. The Server Properties dialog box appears. Click the DNS tab.

4. Verify that the check box labeled Enable DNS Dynamic Updates According To The Settings Below is checked and verify that the radio button labeled Dynamically Update DNS A And PTR Records Only If Requested By The DHCP Clients is selected.

5. Verify that the check box labeled Discard A And PTR Records When Lease Is Deleted is checked. If not, then check it.

6. Click the OK button to apply your changes and close the Server Properties dialog box.

Using DHCP Failover Architecture

DHCP can become a single point of failure within a network if there is only one DHCP server. If that server becomes unavailable, clients will not be able to obtain new leases or renew existing leases. For this reason, it is recommended that you have more than one DHCP server in the network. However, more than one DHCP server can create problems if they both are configured to use the same scope or set of addresses. Microsoft recommends the 80/20 rule for redundancy of DHCP services in a network.

Implementing the 80/20 rule calls for one DHCP server to make approximately 80 percent of the addresses for a given subnet available through DHCP while another server makes the remaining 20 percent of the addresses available. For example, with a /24 network of 254 addresses, say 192.168.1.1 to 192.168.1.254, you might have Server 1 offer 192.168.1.10 to 192.168.1.210 while Server 2 offers 192.168.1.211 to 192.168.254.

DHCP LOAD SHARING

Load sharing is the normal default way that you use multiple DHCP servers. Both servers cover the same subnets (remember that a DHCP server can handle multiple subnets at the same time) simultaneously, and both servers assign IP addresses and options to clients on the assigned subnets. The client requests are load balanced and shared between the two servers.

This is a good option for a company that has multiple DHCP servers in the same physical location. The DHCP servers are set up in a failover relationship at the same site, and both servers respond to all DHCP client requests from the subnets to which they are associated. The DHCP server administrator can set the load distribution ratio between the multiple DHCP servers.

DHCP HOT STANDBY

When thinking of a DHCP hot standby setup, think of the old server failover cluster. You have two servers where one server does all of the work and the other server is a standby server in the event that the first server crashes or goes down.

In a DHCP hot standby situation, the two DHCP servers operate in a failover relationship where one server acts as an active server and is responsible for leasing IP addresses to all clients in a scope or subnet. The secondary DHCP server assumes the standby role, and it is ready to go in the event that the primary DHCP server becomes unavailable. If the primary server becomes unavailable, the secondary DHCP server is given the role of the primary DHCP server and takes over all the responsibilities of the primary DHCP server.

This failover situation is best suited to DHCP deployments where a company has DHCP servers in multiple locations.

Working with the DHCP Database Files

DHCP uses a set of database files to maintain its knowledge of scopes, superscopes, and client leases. These files, which live in the *systemroot*\System32\DHCP folder, are always open when the DHCP service is running. DHCP servers use Joint Engine Technology (JET) databases to maintain their records.

WARNING You shouldn't modify or alter the DHCP database files when the service is running.

The primary database file is dhcp.mdb—it has all of the scope data in it. The following files are also part of the DHCP database:

Dhcp.tmp This is a backup copy of the database file created during reindexing of the database. You normally won't see this file, but if the service fails during reindexing, it may not remove the file when it should.

J50.log This file (plus a number of files named J50*xxxxx*.log, where *xxxxx* stands for 00001, 00002, 00003, and so on) is a log file that stores changes before they're written to the database. The DHCP database engine can recover some changes from these files when it restarts.

J50.chk This is a checkpoint file that tells the DHCP engine which log files it still needs to recover.

In the following sections, you will see how to manipulate the DHCP database files.

REMOVING THE DATABASE FILES

If you're convinced that your database is corrupt because the lease information that you see doesn't match what's on the network, the easiest repair mechanism is to remove the database files and start over with an empty database.

TIP If you think the database is corrupt because the DHCP service fails at startup, you should check the event log.

To start over, follow these steps:

1. Stop the DHCP service by typing **net stop dhcpserver** at the command prompt.

2. Remove all of the files from the *systemroot*\system32\DHCP folder.

3. Restart the service (at command prompt, type **net start dhcpserver**).

4. Reconcile the scope.

CHANGING THE DATABASE BACKUP INTERVAL

By default, the DHCP service backs up its databases every 60 minutes. You can adjust this setting by editing the Backup Interval value under HKEY_LOCAL_MACHINE\SYSTEM\CurrentControlSet\ Services\DHCPServer\Parameters. This allows you to make backups either more frequently (if your database changes a lot or if you seem to have ongoing corruption problems) or less often (if everything seems to be on an even keel).

MOVING THE DHCP DATABASE FILES

You may find that you need to dismantle or change the role of your DHCP server and offload the DHCP functions to another computer. Rather than spend the time re-creating the DHCP database on the new machine by hand, you can copy the database files and use them directly. This is especially helpful if you have a complicated DHCP database with lots of reservations and option assignments.

By copying the files, you also minimize the amount of human error that could be introduced by reentering the information by hand.

COMPACTING THE DHCP DATABASE FILES

There may be a time when you need to compact the DHCP database. Microsoft has a utility called `jetpack.exe` that allows you to compact the JET database. Microsoft JET databases are used for WINS and DHCP databases. If you wanted to use the `jetpack` command, the proper syntax is

```
JETPACK.EXE <database name><temp database name>
```

After you compact the database, you rename the temp database to `dhcp.mdb`.

Working with Advanced DHCP Configuration Options

DHCP makes the life of an administrator easy when it comes to managing the IP addresses of devices within an organization. Could you imagine having to keep track of each device and that device's IP manually? With Windows Server 2022's DHCP high availability and load balancing options available, life gets even easier. The next few sections will cover how to implement advanced DHCP solutions in detail.

Implement DHCPv6

In Windows Server 2022, administrators can create and manage both IPv4 and IPv6 DHCP scopes for their organization. Even though they are managed separately, they have the same capabilities of being able to configure reservations, exclusions, and other DHCP options. Unlike an IPv4 client, a DHCPv6 client uses a device unique identifier (DUID) instead of a MAC address to get an IP address from the DHCP server.

DHCPv6 supports both stateful address configuration and stateless address configuration. An easy way to think of the difference between a stateful configuration and a stateless configuration is that, with a stateful configuration, the DHCPv6 client receives its IPv6 address and its additional DHCP options from the DHCPv6 server. With a stateless configuration, the IPv6 client can automatically assign itself an IPv6 address without ever having to communicate with the DHCPv6 server. The stateless configuration process is also known as *DHCPv6 autoconfiguration*. Exercise 9.9 will walk you through the process of creating and activating a new DHCPv6 scope.

EXERCISE 9.9   Creating and Activating a New DHCPv6 Scope

1. Open the DHCP Management Console.
2. Right-click IPv6 and choose the New Scope command. The New Scope Wizard appears. Click the Next button.
3. On the Welcome To The New Scope Wizard page, click the Next button.
4. On the Scope Name page, provide a name and description for your new DHCPv6 scope. Click the Next button.

---

5. On the Scope Prefix page, input the corresponding prefix for your organization's IPv6 network settings. In the event that you have more than one DHCPv6 server, you can set a preference value that will indicate your server priority. The lower the preference value, the higher the server priority. Click Next.

6. On the Add Exclusions page of the wizard, you can configure either a single IP exclusion or a range of IPs to exclude from obtaining an address automatically. Exclusions should include any device or range of devices that have been manually set with a static IP on that particular scope. Click Next.

7. Keep the default selections on the Scope Lease page. Click Next.

8. Make sure the Activate Scope Now radio button is toggled to Yes. Click Finish to complete the creation and activation of your new DHCPv6 scope.

9. Verify that your new scope appears in the DHCP Management Console to complete this exercise.

Configure High Availability for DHCP, Including DHCP Failover and Split Scopes

DHCP failover provides load balancing and redundancy for DHCP services, enabling administrators to deploy a highly resilient DHCP service for their organization. The idea is to share your DHCP IPV4 scopes between two Windows Server 2022 servers so that if one of the failover partners goes down, then the other failover partner will continue providing DHCP services throughout the environment. DHCP failover supports large-scale DHCP deployments without the challenges of a split-scope DHCP environment.

Here are a few of the benefits that DHCP failover provides:

Multisite   DHCP failover supports a deployment architecture that includes multiple sites. DHCP failover partner servers do not need to be located at the same physical site.

Flexibility   DHCP failover can be configured to provide redundancy in hot standby mode; or, with load balancing mode, client requests can be distributed between two DHCP servers.

Seamless   DHCP servers share lease information, allowing one server to assume the responsibility for servicing clients if the other server is unavailable. DHCP clients can keep the same IP address when a lease is renewed, even if a different DHCP server issues the lease.

Simplicity   A wizard is provided to create DHCP failover relationships between DHCP servers. The wizard automatically replicates scopes and settings from the primary server to the failover partner.

CONFIGURING DHCP FAILOVER

One of the nice things about DHCP failover is that the configured scope is replicated between both clustered DHCP nodes whether or not you are running the cluster in hot standby or load balancing mode. If one server fails, the other can manage the entire pool of IP addresses on behalf of the environment. Exercise 9.10 provides step-by-step DHCP failover configuration in Windows Server 2022.

EXERCISE 9.10   Configuring DHCP Failover

1. Open the DHCP Management Console.

2. Right-click IPv4 and choose the Configure Failover command to launch the Configure Failover Wizard. Click Next on the Introduction page.

3. On the Specify The Partner Server To Use For Failover page, select your partner DHCP server from the drop-down menu or by browsing the Add Server directory. Click Next.

4. On the Create A New Failover Relationship page, provide a relationship name, select the Load Balance mode from the drop-down, and provide a shared secret password that will be used to authenticate the DHCP failover relationship between the two servers in the failover cluster. Click Next.

5. Review your configuration settings and click the Finish button to configure your new DHCP failover configuration. Click Close upon successful completion.

6. After the wizard successfully completes on the primary DHCP server, verify that the new failover scope has been created and activated on the secondary DHCP server in the DHCP Management Console to complete this exercise.

You can always go back in and change the properties of the failover scope if you want. Test both hot standby and load balancing modes to decide which deployment configuration option best suits your organization's needs. Expect to see exam scenarios discussing both DHCP failover configuration modes and the differences between them.

DHCP SPLIT SCOPES

Even though you have the capabilities of DHCP failover in Windows Server 2022, for exam purposes you will need to understand how DHCP split scopes work. Split scopes are configurable only on IPv4 IP addresses and cannot be configured on IPv6 scopes. The idea of DHCP split scopes is to have two stand-alone DHCP servers that are individually responsible for only a percentage of the IP addresses on a particular subnet.

For example, DHCP Server 1 would be responsible for 70 percent of the IP addresses, and DHCP Server 2 would be responsible for the other 30 percent of IP addresses. The two DHCP servers in a split-scope configuration do not share any lease information between one another, and they do not take over for one another in the event that one of the two DHCP servers fails. As you can see, a split-scope configuration is less fault tolerant than a full DHCP failover configuration. However, a split-scope configuration does split the load of DHCP leases and renewals between two servers, providing a basic level of native load balancing in a Windows Server 2022 environment.

DHCP ALLOW AND DENY FILTERING

One of the nice things about DHCP is that administrators can use allow or deny filtering to control which devices get an IP address and which devices do not on your network. DHCP filtering is controlled by recording a client's MAC address in a list and then enabling either the

Allow or Deny filter. One thing to keep in mind about DHCP filtering is that by enabling the allow list, you automatically deny DHCP addresses to any client computer not on the list. In Exercise 9.11, you will configure DHCP filtering by adding a client machine to the Deny filter by MAC address.

EXERCISE 9.11   Configuring DHCP Filtering

1. Open the DHCP Management Console.
2. Expand IPv4 until you reach the Deny filter object in your DHCP hierarchy.
3. Right-click the Deny filter object and select New Filter.
4. Enter the MAC address of the device you want to exclude from your network, provide a description such as Unwanted Device, click Add, and then click Close.
5. Right-click the Deny filter and select Enable to complete this exercise.

One of the good things about these filters is that you can move devices from one filter to the other quite easily at any time by right-clicking the device in the list and selecting either Move To Allow or Move To Deny. Test both Allow and Deny filters thoroughly while preparing for the exam. You will most likely see multiple scenarios surrounding DHCP filtering.

Configure DHCP Name Protection

DHCP name protection is an additional configuration option that administrators should consider when working DHCP within their environment. Name protection protects a DHCP leased machine's name from being overwritten by another machine with the same name during DNS dynamic updates so that you can configure a Windows 2016 and WIndows 2022 DHCP server to verify and update the DNS records of a client machine during the lease renewal process. If the DHCP server detects that a machine's DNS A and PTR records already exist in the environment when a DHCP update occurs, then that DHCP update will fail on that client machine, making sure not to overwrite the existing server name. There are just a few simple steps needed in order to configure DHCP name protection. Exercise 9.12 will walk you through these steps.

EXERCISE 9.12   Enabling DHCP Name Protection

1. Open the DHCP Management Console.
2. Right-click IPv4 and select Properties.
3. The Server Properties dialog box appears. Click the DNS tab.
4. Verify that Enable DNS Dynamic Updates According To The Settings Below is checked, and verify that the radio button labeled Dynamically Update DNS A And PTR Records Only If Requested By The DHCP Clients is selected.
5. Verify that Discard A And PTR Records When Lease Is Deleted is checked. If not, then check it.
6. Click Configure under Name Protection, and select Enable Name Protection.
7. Click OK twice to complete this exercise.

PowerShell Commands

When talking about PowerShell commands for DHCP, I must let you know that there are dozens of commands that you can use to configure and maintain a DHCP server.

In Table 9.1, I will show you just some of the possible PowerShell commands that are available for DHCP.

NOTE The following list includes just some of the PowerShell commands available for DHCP. To see the complete list, visit Microsoft's website at https://docs.microsoft.com/en-us/power-shell/module/dhcpserver/?view=windowsserver2019-ps.

TABLE 9.1   DHCP PowerShell commands

COMMAND	DESCRIPTION
Add-DhcpServerInDC	This command allows an administrator to authorize the DHCP server services in Active Directory.
Add-DhcpServerv4Class	This command allows an administrator to add an IPv4 vendor or user class.
Add-DhcpServerv4ExclusionRange	Administrators can use this command to add an exclusion range to an IPv4 scope.
Add-DhcpServerv4Failover	Administrators can use this command to add an IPv4 failover.
Add-DhcpServerv4Lease	This command allows an administrator to add a new IPv4 address lease.
Add-DhcpServerv4MulticastScope	Administrators use this command to add a multicast scope server.
Add-DhcpServerv4OptionDefinition	This command allows an administrator to add a DHCPv4 option definition.
Add-DhcpServerv4Policy	Admins can use this command to add a new policy to either the server or scope level.
Add-DhcpServerv4Reservation	This command allows an admin to reserve a client IPv4 address in the scope.
Add-DhcpServerv4Scope	This command adds an IPv4 scope.
Add-DhcpServerv6Class	This command allows an administrator to add an IPv6 vendor or user class.
Add-DhcpServerv6ExclusionRange	Administrators can use this command to add an exclusion range to an IPv6 scope.

TABLE 9.1:   DHCP PowerShell commands *(CONTINUED)*

COMMAND	DESCRIPTION
Add-DhcpServerv6Lease	This command allows an administrator to add a new IPv6 address lease.
Add-DhcpServerv6OptionDefinition	This command allows an administrator to add a DHCPv6 option definition.
Add-DhcpServerv6Reservation	This command allows an admin to reserve a client IPv6 address in the scope.
Add-DhcpServerv6Scope	This command adds an IPv6 scope.
Backup-DhcpServer	Administrators can use this command to back up the DHCP database.
Export-DhcpServer	This command allows an administrator to export the DHCP server configuration and lease data.
Get-DhcpServerAuditLog	This command shows you the audit log for the DHCP configuration.
Get-DhcpServerDatabase	Administrators can use this command to view the configuration parameters of the DHCP database.
Get-DhcpServerSetting	This command allows an admin to view the configuration parameters of the DHCP database.
Get-DhcpServerv4Class	Administrators use this command to view the IPv4 vendor or user class settings.
Set-DhcpServerDatabase	This command allows an administrator to modify configuration settings of the DHCP database.
Set-DhcpServerDnsCredential	Administrators can set the credentials of the DHCP Server service, which help register or deregister client records.
Set-DhcpServerSetting	This command allows an administrator to configure the server-level settings.
Set-DhcpServerv4Class	This command allows an administrator to configure the IPv4 vendor class or user class settings.
Set-DhcpServerv4Failover	This command allows an admin to configure the settings for an existing failover relationship.
Set-DhcpServerv4Policy	Administrators can use this command to configure the settings of a DHCP policy.

COMMAND	DESCRIPTION
`Set-DhcpServerv4Reservation`	This command allows an administrator to configure an IPv4 reservation.
`Set-DhcpServerv4Scope`	Admins can use this command to configure the settings of an existing IPv4 scope.
`Set-DhcpServerv6Reservation`	This command allows an administrator to configure an IPv4 reservation.
`Set-DhcpServerv6Scope`	Admins can use this command to configure the settings of an existing IPv6 scope.

The Bottom Line

Understand DHCP. You should understand why you need to install and configure DHCP. DHCP may not always be the best option for small companies, but with large companies, DHCP will help reduce IP configuration errors.

Master It You are an administrator of a large network with 2,000 hosts. You need to easily set up all 2,000 hosts using IPv4.

Know how to verify authorization of a DHCP server. Once you have installed the DHCP role onto a server, you need to verify that the server is authorized in the Active Directory network. This helps ensure that only authorized DHCP servers issue IP address information to your domain users.

Master It You are the administrator of an organization that has decided to install the DHCP role. After you install the DHCP role, what do you need to do next to ensure users only get authorized IP address information?

Chapter 10

Building Group Policies

For many years, making changes to computer or user environments was a time-consuming process. If you wanted to install a service pack or a piece of software, unless you had a third-party utility, you had to use the *sneakernet* (that is, you had to walk from one computer to another with a disk containing the software).

Installing any type of software or company-wide security change was one of the biggest challenges faced by system administrators. It was difficult enough just to deploy and manage workstations throughout the environment. Combine this with the fact that users were generally able to make system configuration changes to their own machines and it quickly became a management nightmare!

For example, consider the case of users who change system settings. Relatively minor changes, such as modifying TCP/IP bindings or Desktop settings, could cause hours of support headaches. Now multiply these (or other common) problems by hundreds (or even thousands) of end users. Clearly, system administrators needed to have a secure way to limit the options available to users of client operating systems.

How do you prevent problems such as these from occurring in a Windows Server 2022 environment? Fortunately, there's a readily available solution delivered with the base operating system that's easy to implement. Two of the most important system administration features in Windows Server 2022 and Active Directory are *Group Policy* and *Security Policy*. By using *Group Policy objects (GPOs)*, administrators can quickly and easily define restrictions on common actions and then apply them at the site, domain, or organizational unit (OU) level. In this chapter, you will see how group and security policies work.

IN THIS CHAPTER YOU'LL LEARN

◆ Understand the purpose of GPOs

◆ Understand user and computer settings

◆ Know the interactions between Group Policy objects and Active Directory

Introducing Group Policy

One of the strengths of Windows-based operating systems is their flexibility. End users and system administrators can configure many different options to suit the network environment and their personal tastes. However, this flexibility comes at a price—generally, end users on a network should not change many of these options. For example, TCP/IP configuration and security policies should remain consistent for all client computers. In fact, end users really don't need to be able to change these types of settings in the first place because many of them do not understand the purpose of these settings.

Windows Server 2022 *group policies* are designed to provide system administrators with the ability to customize end-user settings and to place restrictions on the types of actions that users can perform. Group policies can be easily created by system administrators and then later applied to one or more users or computers within the environment. Although they ultimately do affect Registry settings, it is much easier to configure and apply settings through the use of Group Policy than it is to make changes to the Registry manually. To make management easy, Microsoft has set up Windows Server 2022 so that Group Policy settings are all managed from within the Microsoft Management Console (MMC) in the Group Policy Management Console (GPMC).

Group policies have several potential uses. I'll cover the use of group policies for software deployment, and I'll also focus on the technical background of group policies and how they apply to general configuration management.

Let's begin by looking at how group policies function.

Understanding Group Policy Settings

Group Policy settings are based on *Group Policy administrative templates*. These templates provide a list of user-friendly configuration options and specify the system settings to which they apply. For example, an option for a user or computer that reads Require A Specific Desktop Wallpaper Setting would map to a key in the Registry that maintains this value. When the option is set, the appropriate change is made in the Registry of the affected users and computers.

By default, Windows Server 2022 comes with several administrative template files that you can use to manage common settings. Additionally, system administrators and application developers can create their own administrative template files to set options for specific functionality.

Most Group Policy items have three different settings options (see Figure 10.1):

Enabled   Specifies that a setting for this GPO has been configured. Some settings require values or options to be set.

Disabled   Specifies that this option is disabled for client computers. Note that disabling an option *is* a setting. That is, it specifies that the system administrator wants to disallow certain functionality.

Not Configured   Specifies that these settings have been neither enabled nor disabled. Not Configured is the default option for most settings. It simply states that this group policy will not specify an option and that other policy settings may take precedence.

The specific options available (and their effects) will depend on the setting. Often, you will need additional information. For example, when setting the Account Lockout policy, you must specify how many bad login attempts may be made before the account is locked out. With this in mind, let's look at the types of user and computer settings that can be managed.

FIGURE 10.1
Group Policy configura-
tion settings

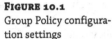

Group Policy settings can apply to two types of Active Directory objects: User objects and
Computer objects. Because both users and computers can be placed into groups and organized
within OUs, this type of configuration simplifies the management of hundreds, or even thousands, of computers.

The main options you can configure within user and computer group policies are as follows:

Software Settings The *Software Settings* options apply to specific applications and software
that might be installed on the computer. System administrators can use these settings to make
new applications available to end users and to control the default configuration for these
applications.

Windows Settings The *Windows Settings* options allow system administrators to customize
the behavior of the Windows operating system. The specific options that are available here are
divided into two types: user and computer. User-specific settings let you configure your
Internet browser (including the default home page and other settings). Computer settings
include security options, such as Account Policy and Event Log options.

Administrative Templates *Administrative templates* are used to configure user and computer
settings further. In addition to using the default options available, system administrators can
create their own administrative templates with custom options.

Group Policy Preferences   The Windows Server 2022 operating system includes *Group Policy preferences (GPPs)*, which give you more than 20 Group Policy extensions. These extensions, in turn, give you a vast range of configurable settings within a Group Policy object. Included in the Group Policy preference extensions are settings for folder options, mapped drives, printers, the Registry, local users and groups, scheduled tasks, services, and the Start menu.

Besides providing easier management, Group Policy preferences give an administrator the ability to deploy settings for client computers without restricting the users from changing the settings. This gives an administrator the flexibility needed to decide which settings to enforce and which not to enforce.

Figure 10.2 shows some of the options you can configure with Group Policy.

FIGURE 10.2
Group Policy options

ADMX Central Store   Another consideration in GPO settings is whether to set up an *ADMX Central Store*. GPO administrative template files are saved as ADMX (.admx) files and AMXL (.amxl) for the supported languages. To get the most benefit out of using administrative templates, you should create an ADMX Central Store.

You create the Central Store in the Sysvol folder on a domain controller. The Central Store is a repository for all of your administrative templates, and the Group Policy tools check it. The Group Policy tools then use any ADMX files that they find in the Central Store. These files then replicate to all domain controllers in the domain.

If you want your clients to be able to edit domain-based GPOs by using the ADMX files that are stored in the ADMX Central Store, you must be using Windows 7 or above and Server 2008 or above.

Security Templates   *Security templates* are used to configure security settings through a GPO. Some of the security settings that can be configured are settings for account policies, local policies, event logs, restricted groups, system services, and the Registry.

Starter GPOs *Starter Group Policy objects* give administrators the ability to store a collection of administrative template policy settings in a single object. Administrators then have the ability to import and export starter GPOs to distribute the GPOs easily to other environments. When a GPO is created from a starter GPO, as with any template, the new GPO receives the settings and values that were defined from the administrative template policy in the starter GPO.

WARNING Group Policy settings do not take effect immediately. You must run the gpupdate command at the command prompt or wait for the regular update cycle in order for the policy changes to take effect.

The Security Settings Section of the GPO

One of the most important sections of a GPO is the Security Settings section. The Security Settings section, under the Windows Settings section, allows an administrator to secure many aspects of the computer and user policies. The following are some of the configurable options for the Security Settings section:

Computer Section Only of the GPO

◆ Account Policies

◆ Local Policies

◆ Event Policies

◆ Restricted Groups

◆ System Services

◆ Registry

◆ File System

◆ Wired Network

◆ Windows Firewall with Advanced Security

◆ Network List Manager Policies

◆ Wireless Networks

◆ Network Access Protection

◆ Application Control Policies

◆ IP Security Policies

◆ Advanced Audit Policy Configuration

Computer and User Sections of the GPO

◆ Public Key Policies

◆ Software Restriction Policy

RESTRICTED GROUPS

The *Restricted Groups* settings allow you to control group membership by using a GPO. The group membership I am referring to is the normal Active Directory groups (domain local, global, and universal). The settings offer two configurable properties: Members and Members Of.

The users on the Members list do not belong to the restricted group. The users on the Members Of list do belong to the restricted group. When you configure a Restricted Groups policy, members of the restricted group that are not on the Members list are removed. Users who are on the Members list who are not currently a member of the restricted group are added.

SOFTWARE RESTRICTION POLICY

Software Restriction Policies (SRP) are a Group Policy based feature that allows administrators to identify software and to control its ability to run on the user's local computer, organizational unit, domain, or site. This prevents users from installing unauthorized software. Software Restriction Policy is discussed in greater detail later in this chapter in the section "Implementing Software Deployment."

Client-Side Extensions

In Windows Server, group policies are designed using both server-side extensions (SSEs) and client-side extensions (CSEs). The server-side elements include a user interface for creating each Group Policy Object (GPO). When a Windows client system logs into the Active Directory network, the client-side extensions (normally a series of DLL files) receive their GPOs and the GPOs make changes to the Windows client systems.

Within GPOs, there are computer policies that exist for each CSE. The policies normally include a maximum of three options: Allow Processing Across A Slow Network Connection, Do Not Apply During Periodic Background Processing, and Process Even If The Group Policy Objects Have Not Changed.

Group Policy Objects

So far, I have discussed what group policies are designed to do. Now it's time to drill down to determine exactly how you can set up and configure them.

To make them easier to manage, group policies may be placed in items called *Group Policy objects (GPOs)*. GPOs act as containers for the settings made within Group Policy files, which simplifies the management of settings. For example, as a system administrator, you might have different policies for users and computers in different departments. Based on these requirements, you could create a GPO for members of the Sales department and another for members of the Engineering department. Then you could apply the GPOs to the OU for each department. Another important concept you need to understand is that Group Policy settings are hierarchical; that is, system administrators can apply Group Policy settings at four different levels. These levels determine the GPO processing priority.

Local Every Windows operating system computer has one Group Policy object that is stored locally. This GPO functions for both the computer and user Group Policy processing.

Sites At the highest level, system administrators can configure GPOs to apply to entire sites within an Active Directory environment. These settings apply to all of the domains and servers that are part of a site. Group Policy settings managed at the site level may apply to more than one domain within the same forest. Therefore, they are useful when you want to make settings that apply to all of the domains within an Active Directory tree or forest.

Domains   Domains are the third level to which system administrators can assign GPOs. GPO settings placed at the domain level will apply to all of the User and Computer objects within the domain. Usually, system administrators make master settings at the domain level.

Organizational Units   The most granular level of settings for GPOs is the OU level. By configuring Group Policy options for OUs, system administrators can take advantage of the hierarchical structure of Active Directory. If the OU structure is planned well, you will find it easy to make logical GPO assignments for various business units at the OU level.

Based on the business need and the organization of the Active Directory environment, system administrators might decide to set up Group Policy settings at any of these four levels. Because the settings are cumulative by default, a User object might receive policy settings from the site level, from the domain level, and from the OUs in which it is contained.

NOTE   You can also apply Group Policy settings to the local computer (in which case Active Directory is not used at all), but this limits the manageability of the Group Policy settings.

Group Policy Inheritance

In most cases, Group Policy settings are cumulative. For example, a GPO at the domain level might specify that all users within the domain must change their password every 60 days, and a GPO at the OU level might specify the default desktop background for all users and computers within that OU. In this case, both settings apply, so users within the OU are forced to change their password every 60 days and have the default Desktop setting.

What happens if there's a conflict in the settings? For example, suppose you create a scenario where a GPO at the site level specifies that users are to use red wallpaper and another GPO at the OU level specifies that they must use green wallpaper. The users at the OU layer would have green wallpaper by default. Although hypothetical, this raises an important point about *inheritance*. By default, the settings at the most specific level (in this case, the OU that contains the User object) override those at more general levels. As a friend of mine from Microsoft always says, "Last one to apply wins."

Although the default behavior is for settings to be cumulative and inherited, system administrators can modify this behavior. They can set two main options at the various levels to which GPOs might apply.

Block Policy Inheritance   The *Block Policy Inheritance* option specifies that Group Policy settings for an object are not inherited from its parents. You might use this, for example, when a child OU requires completely different settings from a parent OU. Note, however, that you should manage blocking policy inheritance carefully because this option allows other system administrators to override the settings made at higher levels.

Force Policy Inheritance   The *Enforced option* (sometimes referred as *No Override*) can be placed on a parent object, and it ensures that all lower-level objects inherit these settings. In some cases, system administrators want to ensure that Group Policy inheritance is not blocked at other levels. For example, suppose it is corporate policy that all network accounts are locked out after five incorrect password attempts. In this case, you would not want lower-level system administrators to override the option with other settings.

System administrators generally use this option when they want to enforce a specific setting globally. For example, if a password expiration policy should apply to all users and computers within a domain, a GPO with the *Force Policy Inheritance* option enabled could be created at the domain level.

You must consider one final case: If a conflict exists between the computer and user settings, the user settings take effect. If, for instance, a system administrator applies a default desktop setting for the Computer policy and a different default desktop setting for the User policy, the one they specify in the User policy takes effect. This is because the user settings are more specific and they allow system administrators to make changes for individual users regardless of the computer they're using.

Planning a Group Policy Strategy

Through the use of Group Policy settings, system administrators can control many different aspects of their network environment. As you'll see throughout this chapter, system administrators can use GPOs to configure user settings and computer configurations. Windows Server 2022 includes many different administrative tools for performing these tasks. However, it's important to keep in mind that, as with many aspects of using Active Directory, a successful Group Policy strategy involves planning.

Because there are thousands of possible Group Policy settings and many different ways to implement them, you should start by determining the business and technical needs of your organization. For example, you should first group your users based on their work functions. You might find, for example, that users in remote branch offices require particular network configuration options. In that case, you might implement Group Policy settings best at the site level. In another instance, you might find that certain departments have varying requirements for disk quota settings. In this case, it would probably make the most sense to apply GPOs to the appropriate department OUs within the domain.

The overall goal should be to reduce complexity (for example, by reducing the overall number of GPOs and GPO links) while still meeting the needs of your users. By taking into account the various needs of your users and the parts of your organization, you can often determine a logical and efficient method of creating and applying GPOs. Although it's rare that you'll come across a right or wrong method of implementing Group Policy settings, you will usually encounter some that are either better or worse than others.

By implementing a logical and consistent set of policies, you'll also be well prepared to troubleshoot any problems that might come up or to adapt to your organization's changing requirements.

Implementing Group Policy

Now that I've covered the basic layout and structure of group policies and how they work, let's look at how you can implement them in an Active Directory environment. In the following sections, you'll start by creating GPOs.

Creating GPOs

In older versions of Windows Server, like Windows Server 2000 and Windows Server 2003, you could create GPOs from many different locations. For example, you could use Active Directory Users and Computers to create GPOs on your OUs along with other GPO tools. In Windows Server 2022, things are simpler. You can create GPOs for OUs in only one location: the Group Policy Management Console (GPMC). You have your choice of three applications for setting up policies on your Windows Server 2022 computers.

Local Computer Policy Tool   This administrative tool allows you to quickly access the Group Policy settings that are available for the local computer. These options apply to the local machine and to users who access it. You must be a member of the local Administrators group to access and make changes to these settings.

Administrators may need the ability to work on multiple local Group Policy Objects (MLGPOs) at the same time. To do this, you would complete the following steps. (You can't configure MLGPOs on domain controllers.)

1. Open the MMC by typing **MMC** in the Run command box.

2. Click File and then click Add/Remove Snap-in.

3. From the available snap-ins list, choose Group Policy Object Editor and click Add.

4. In the Select Group Policy Object dialog box, click the Browse button.

5. Click the Users tab in the Browse For The Group Policy Object dialog box.

6. Click the user or group for which you want to create or edit a local Group Policy and click OK.

7. Click Finish and then click OK.

8. Configure the multiple policy settings.

Group Policy Management Console   You must use the GPMC to manage Group Policy deployment. The GPMC provides a single solution for managing all Group Policy–related tasks, and it is also best suited to handle enterprise-level tasks, such as forest-related work.

The GPMC allows administrators to manage Group Policy and GPOs all from one easy-to-use console whether their enterprise solution spans multiple domains and sites within one or more forests or is local to one site. The GPMC adds flexibility, manageability, and functionality. Using this console, you can also perform other functions, such as backup and restore, importing, and copying.

Auditpol.exe   Auditpol.exe is a command-line utility that works with Windows 7 or above and Windows Server 2008 and above. An administrator has the ability to display information about policies and also to perform some functions to manipulate audit policies. Table 10.1 shows some of the switches available for auditpol.exe.

TABLE 10.1:   Auditpol.exe switches

SWITCH	DESCRIPTION
/?	This is the Auditpol.exe help command.
/get	This allows you to display the current audit policy.
/set	This allows you to set a policy.
/list	This displays selectable policy elements.
/backup	This allows you to save the audit policy to a file.
/restore	This restores a policy from previous backup.
/clear	This clears the audit policy.
/remove	This removes all per-user audit policy settings and disables all system audit policy settings.
/ResourceSACL	This configures the Global Resource SACL.

WARNING   You should be careful when making Group Policy settings because certain options might prevent the proper use of systems on your network. Always test Group Policy settings on a small group of users before you deploy them throughout your organization. You'll probably find that some settings need to be changed to be effective.

Exercise 10.1 walks you through the process of installing the Group Policy Management MMC snap-in for editing Group Policy settings and creating a GPO.

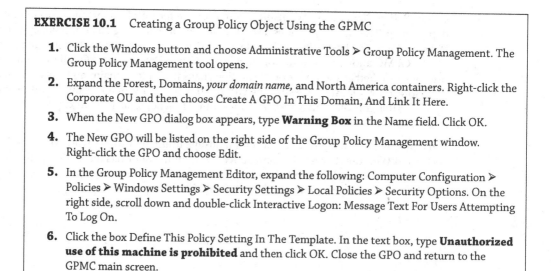

EXERCISE 10.1   Creating a Group Policy Object Using the GPMC

1. Click the Windows button and choose Administrative Tools ➤ Group Policy Management. The Group Policy Management tool opens.

2. Expand the Forest, Domains, *your domain name,* and North America containers. Right-click the Corporate OU and then choose Create A GPO In This Domain, And Link It Here.

3. When the New GPO dialog box appears, type **Warning Box** in the Name field. Click OK.

4. The New GPO will be listed on the right side of the Group Policy Management window. Right-click the GPO and choose Edit.

5. In the Group Policy Management Editor, expand the following: Computer Configuration ➤ Policies ➤ Windows Settings ➤ Security Settings ➤ Local Policies ➤ Security Options. On the right side, scroll down and double-click Interactive Logon: Message Text For Users Attempting To Log On.

6. Click the box Define This Policy Setting In The Template. In the text box, type **Unauthorized use of this machine is prohibited** and then click OK. Close the GPO and return to the GPMC main screen.

7. Under the domain name (in the GPMC), right-click Group Policy Objects and choose New.

8. When the New GPO dialog box appears, type **Unlinked Test GPO** in the Name field. Click OK.

9. On the right side, the new GPO will appear. Right-click Unlinked Test GPO and choose Edit.

10. Under the User Configuration section, click Policies ➤ Administrative Templates ➤ Desktop. On the right side, double-click Hide And Disable All Items On The Desktop and then click Enabled. Click OK and then close the GPMC.

NOTE Note that Group Policy changes may not take effect until the next user logs in (some settings may even require that the machine be rebooted). That is, users who are currently working on the system will not see the effects of the changes until they log off and log in again. GPOs are reapplied every 90 minutes with a 30-minute offset. In other words, users who are logged in will have their policies reapplied every 60 to 120 minutes. Not all settings are reapplied (for example, software settings and password policies).

Linking Existing GPOs to Active Directory

Creating a GPO is the first step in assigning group policies. The second step is to link the GPO to a specific Active Directory object. As mentioned earlier in this chapter, GPOs can be linked to sites, domains, and OUs.

Exercise 10.2 walks you through the steps that you must take to assign an existing GPO to an OU within the local domain. In this exercise, you will link the Test Domain Policy GPO to an OU. To complete the steps in this exercise, you must have completed Exercise 10.1.

EXERCISE 10.2   Linking Existing GPOs to Active Directory

1. Open the Group Policy Management Console.

2. Expand the Forest and Domain containers and right-click the Africa OU.

3. Choose Link An Existing GPO.

4. The Select GPO dialog box appears. Click Unlinked Test GPO and click OK.

5. Close the Group Policy Management Console.

Note that the GPMC tool offers a lot of flexibility in assigning GPOs. You can create new GPOs, add multiple GPOs, edit them directly, change priority settings, remove links, and delete GPOs all from within this interface. In general, creating new GPOs using the GPMC tool is the quickest and easiest way to create the settings you need.

To test the Group Policy settings, you can simply create a user account within the Africa OU that you used in Exercise 10.2. Then, using another computer that is a member of the same domain, you can log on as the newly created user.

Forcing a GPO to Update

There will be times when you need a GPO to get processed immediately. If you are testing a GPO, you will not want to wait for the GPO to process in its own time or you may not want to have to log off the domain and log back onto the domain just to get the GPO processed.

Windows Server 2022 has changed how GPOs get processed. In a Windows Server 2022 domain, when a user logs onto the domain, the latest version of the Group Policy gets downloaded from the domain controller, and it writes that policy to the local store.

If you have your GPOs set up and running in synchronous mode, then the next time the computer restarts, it will use the most recently downloaded GPO from the local store and not download the GPO from the domain. This is a new feature in Windows Server 2022, and it helps to reduce the time it takes to log onto the domain because the GPO policy doesn't need to be downloaded each time.

So, now that you understand how GPOs get processed in Windows Server 2022, let's look at a few different ways that you can force a GPO to get processed immediately.

FORCING THE GPO FROM THE SERVER

Windows Server 2022 has an MMC called Group Policy Management Console (GPMC), and by using this MMC, you can remotely refresh an organizational unit (OU) and force the GPO on all users and computers within that OU. The GPMC remote refresh automatically updates all settings, including security settings, which are configured in the GPO that is linked to the OU. In the OU's context menu, you can choose to refresh remotely the OU and the GPOs associated with that OU. When you remotely refresh an OU, the following steps occur:

1. Windows Server 2022 does an Active Directory query, and that query returns a list of all users and computers that belong to the OU.

2. Windows Management Instrumentation (WMI) queries all users and computers that are currently logged into the domain and creates a list that will be used.

3. Using the list that was created in step 2, a remote scheduled task is created, and a `GPUpdate.exe /force` is executed on all of the users and computers that are logged into the domain. The remote scheduled task is then scheduled to execute with a 10-minute random delay to help decrease the load on network traffic.

NOTE When you are using the GPMC to force a GPO update, you do not have the ability to change the 10-minute random delay, but if you force the GPO through the use of PowerShell, you have the ability to set the delay.

Another way that you can force a GPO to update immediately is to use Windows PowerShell. By using the PowerShell command `Invoke-GPUpdate` cmdlet, you cannot only force the GPO but also set the parameters to be more granular.

FORCING THE GPO FROM THE CLIENT

As an administrator, you have the ability also to force a GPO onto a client machine on which you may be working. The `GPUpdate.exe` command allows you to run a GPO on a client machine. The

GPUpdate command will run on all Windows client machines from Windows Vista to Windows Server 2022. Table 10.2 shows some of the GPUpdate switches you can use.

TABLE 10.2   GPUpdate.exe switches

SWITCH	DESCRIPTION
/target:{Computer | User}	Updates only the User or Computer policy settings for the computer or user specified.
/force	Forces the GPO to reapply all policy settings. By default, only policy settings that have changed are applied.
/wait:<VALUE>	Determines the number of seconds that the system will wait after a policy is processed before returning to the command prompt.
/logoff	The domain user account will automatically log off the computer after the Group Policy settings are updated.
/boot	The computer will automatically restart after the Group Policy settings are applied.
/sync	This switch forces the next available foreground policy application to be done synchronously. Foreground policies are applied when the computer boots up and the user logs in.
/?	Displays help at the command prompt.

Managing Group Policy

Now that you have implemented GPOs and applied them to sites, domains, and OUs within Active Directory, it's time to look at some ways to manage them. In the following sections, you'll look at how multiple GPOs can interact with one another and ways that you can provide security for GPO management. Using these features is an important part of working with Active Directory, and if you properly plan Group Policy, you can greatly reduce the time the help desk spends troubleshooting common problems.

Managing GPOs

One of the benefits of GPOs is that they're modular and can apply to many different objects and levels within Active Directory. This can also be one of the drawbacks of GPOs if they're not managed properly. A common administrative function related to using GPOs is finding all of the Active Directory links for each of these objects. You can do this when you are viewing the Linked Group Policy Objects tab of the site, domain, or OU in the GPMC (shown in Figure 10.3).

In addition to the common action of delegating permissions on OUs, you can set permissions regarding the modification of GPOs. The best way to accomplish this is to add users to the Group Policy Creator/Owners built-in security group. The members of this group are able to modify security policy.

FIGURE 10.3
Viewing GPO links to an
Active Directory OU

WINDOWS MANAGEMENT INSTRUMENTATION

Windows Management Instrumentation (WMI) scripts are used to gather information or to help GPOs deploy better. The best way to explain this is to give an example. Let's say you wanted to deploy Microsoft Office 2016 to everyone in the company. You would first set up a GPO to deploy the Office package.

You can then place a WMI script on the GPO stating that only computers with 10 GB of hard disk space actually deploy Office. Now if a computer has 10 GB of free space, the Office GPO would get installed. If the computer does not have the 10 GB of hard disk space, the GPO will not deploy. You can use WMI scripts to check for computer information such as MAC addresses. WMI is a powerful tool because if you know how to write scripts, the possibilities are endless. The following script is a sample of a WMI script that is checking for at least 10 GB of free space on the C: partition/volume:

```
Select * from Win32_LogicalDisk where FreeSpace > 10737418240 AND Caption = "C:"
```

Security Filtering of a Group Policy

Another method of securing access to GPOs is to set permissions on the GPOs themselves. You can do this by opening the GPMC, selecting the GPO, and clicking the Advanced button in the Delegation tab. The Unlinked Test GPO Security Settings dialog box appears (see Figure 10.4).

The following permissions options are available:

◆ Full Control

◆ Read

◆ Write

◆ Create All Child Objects

◆ Delete All Child Objects

◆ Apply Group Policy

FIGURE 10.4
A GPO's Security
Settings dialog box

You might have to scroll the Permissions window to see the Apply Group Policy item. Of these, the Apply Group Policy setting is particularly important because you use it to filter the scope of the GPO. *Filtering* is the process by which selected security groups are included or excluded from the effects of the GPOs. To specify that the settings should apply to a GPO, you should select the Allow check box for both the Apply Group Policy setting and the Read setting. These settings will be applied only if the security group is also contained within a site, domain, or OU to which the GPO is linked. To disable GPO access for a group, choose Deny for both of these settings. Finally, if you do not want to specify either Allow or Deny, leave both boxes blank. This is effectively the same as having no setting.

In Exercise 10.3, you will filter Group Policy using security groups. To complete the steps in this exercise, you must have completed Exercises 10.1 and 10.2.

EXERCISE 10.3   Filtering Group Policy Using Security Groups

1. Open the Active Directory Users and Computers administrative tool.

2. Create a new OU called **Group Policy Test**.

3. Create two new global security groups within the Group Policy Test OU and name them **PolicyEnabled** and **PolicyDisabled**.

4. Exit Active Directory Users and Computers and open the GPMC.

5. Right-click the Group Policy Test OU and select Link An Existing GPO.

---

6. Choose Unlinked Test GPO and click OK.

7. Expand the Group Policy Test OU so that you can see the GPO (Unlinked Test GPO) underneath the OU.

8. Click the Delegation tab and then click the Advanced button in the lower-right corner of the window.

9. Click the Add button and type **PolicyEnabled** in the Enter The Object Names To Select field. Click the Check Names button. Then click OK.

10. Add a group named **PolicyDisabled** in the same way.

11. Highlight the PolicyEnabled group and select Allow for the Read and Apply Group Policy permissions. This ensures that users in the PolicyEnabled group will be affected by this policy.

12. Highlight the PolicyDisabled group and select Deny for the Read and Apply Group Policy permissions. This ensures that users in the PolicyDisabled group will not be affected by this policy.

13. Click OK. You will see a message stating that you are choosing to use the Deny permission and that the Deny permission takes precedence over the Allow entries. Click the Yes button to continue.

14. When you have finished, close the GPMC tool.

Delegating Administrative Control of GPOs

So far, you have learned about how to use Group Policy to manage user and computer settings. What you haven't done yet is to determine who can modify GPOs. It's important to establish the appropriate security on GPOs themselves for two reasons.

◆ If the security settings aren't set properly, users and system administrators can easily override them. This defeats the purpose of having the GPOs in the first place.

◆ Having many different system administrators creating and modifying GPOs can become extremely difficult to manage. When problems arise, the hierarchical nature of GPO inheritance can make it difficult to pinpoint the problem.

Fortunately, through the use of delegation, determining security permissions for GPOs is a simple task. Exercise 10.4 walks you through the steps that you must take to grant the appropriate permissions to a user account. Specifically, the process involves delegating the ability to manage Group Policy links on an Active Directory object (such as an OU). To complete this exercise, you must have completed Exercises 10.1 and 10.2.

EXERCISE 10.4 Delegating Administrative Control of Group Policy

1. Open the Active Directory Users and Computers tool.

2. Expand the local domain and create a user named **Policy Admin** within the Group Policy Test OU.

3. Exit Active Directory Users and Computers and open the GPMC.

4. Click the Group Policy Test OU and select the Delegation tab.

5. Click the Add button. In the field Enter The Object Name To Select, type **Policy Admin** and click the Check Names button.

6. The Add Group Or User dialog box appears. In the Permissions drop-down list, make sure that the item labeled Edit Settings, Delete, Modify Security is chosen. Click OK.

7. At this point you should be looking at the Group Policy Test Delegation window. Click the Advanced button in the lower-right corner.

8. Highlight the Policy Admin account and check the Allow Full Control box. This user now has full control of these OUs and all child OUs and GPOs for these OUs. Click OK.

   If you just want to give this user individual rights, then in the Properties window (step 8), click the Advanced button and then the Effective Permissions tab. This is where you can also choose a user and give them only the rights that you want them to have.

9. When you have finished, close the GPMC tool.

UNDERSTANDING DELEGATION

Although I have talked about delegation throughout the book, it's important to discuss it again in the context of OUs, Group Policy, and Active Directory.

Once configured, Active Directory administrative delegation allows an administrator to delegate tasks (usually administration related) to specific user accounts or groups. What this means is that if you don't manage it all, the user accounts (or groups) you choose will be able to manage their portions of the tree.

It's important to be aware of the benefits of Active Directory Delegation (AD Delegation). *AD Delegation* will help you manage the assignment of administrative control over objects in Active Directory, such as users, groups, computers, printers, domains, and sites. AD Delegation is used to create more administrators, which essentially saves time.

For example, let's say you have a company whose IT department is small and situated in a central location. The central location connects three other smaller remote sites. These sites do not each warrant a full-time IT person, but the manager on staff (for example) at each remote site can become an administrator for their portion of the tree. If that manager administers the user accounts for the staff at the remote site, this reduces the burden on the system administrator of doing trivial administrative work, such as unlocking user accounts or changing passwords, and thus it reduces costs.

Controlling Inheritance and Filtering Group Policy

Controlling inheritance is an important function when you are managing GPOs. Earlier in this chapter, you learned that, by default, GPO settings flow from higher-level Active Directory objects to lower-level ones. For example, the effective set of Group Policy settings for a user might be based on GPOs assigned at the site level, at the domain level, and in the OU hierarchy. In general, this is probably the behavior you would want.

In some cases, however, you might want to block Group Policy inheritance. You can accomplish this easily by selecting the object to which a GPO has been linked. Right-click the object and choose Block Inheritance. By enabling this option, you are effectively specifying that this object starts with a clean slate; that is, no other Group Policy settings will apply to the contents of this Active Directory site, domain, or OU.

System administrators can also force inheritance. By setting the Enforced option, they can prevent other system administrators from making changes to default policies. You can set the Enforced option by right-clicking the GPO and choosing the Enforced item (see Figure 10.5).

FIGURE 10.5
Setting the Enforced
GPO option

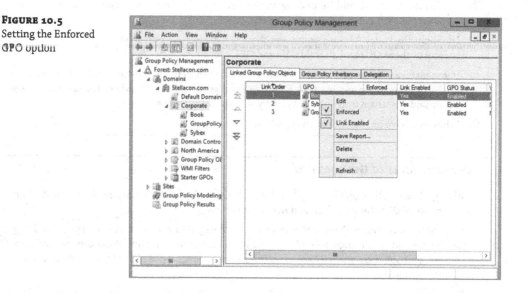

Assigning Script Policies

System administrators might want to make several changes and implement certain settings that would apply while the computer is starting up or the user is logging on. Perhaps the most common operation that logon scripts perform is mapping network drives. Although users can manually map network drives, providing this functionality within login scripts ensures that mappings stay consistent and that users only need to remember the drive letters for their resources.

Script policies are specific options that are part of Group Policy settings for users and computers. These settings direct the operating system to the specific files that should be processed during the startup/shutdown or logon/logoff processes. You can create the scripts by using the *Windows Script Host (WSH)* or with standard batch file commands. WSH allows developers and system administrators to create scripts quickly and easily using Visual Basic Scripting Edition (VBScript) or JScript (Microsoft's implementation of JavaScript). Additionally, WSH can be expanded to accommodate other common scripting languages.

To set script policy options, you simply edit the Group Policy settings. There are two main areas for setting script policy settings.

Startup/Shutdown Scripts   These settings are located within the Computer Configuration ➤ Windows Settings ➤ Scripts (Startup/Shutdown) object (as shown in Figure 10.6).

Logon/Logoff Scripts   These settings are located within the User Configuration ➤ Windows Settings ➤ Scripts (Logon/Logoff) object.

FIGURE 10.6
Viewing Startup/
Shutdown script policy
settings

To assign scripts, simply double-click the setting and its Properties dialog box appears. For instance, if you double-click the Startup setting, the Startup Properties dialog box appears (see Figure 10.7). To add a script filename, click the Add button. When you do, you will be asked to provide the name of the script file (such as `MapNetworkDrives.vbs` or `ResetEnvironment.bat`).

FIGURE 10.7
Setting scripting options

Note that you can change the order in which the scripts are run by using the Up and Down buttons. The Show Files button opens the directory folder in which you should store the Logon script files. To ensure that the files are replicated to all domain controllers, you should be sure you place the files within the Sysvol share.

Understanding the Loopback Policy

There may be times when the user settings of a Group Policy object should be applied to a computer based on its location instead of the User object. Usually, the user Group Policy processing dictates that the GPOs be applied In order during computer startup based on the computers located in their organizational unit. User GPOs, on the other hand, are applied in order during logon, regardless of the computer to which they log on.

In some situations, this processing order may not be appropriate. A good example is a kiosk machine. You would not want applications that have been assigned or published to a user to be installed when the user is logged on to the kiosk machine. *Loopback Policy* allows two ways to retrieve the list of GPOs for any user when they are using a specific computer in an OU.

Merge Mode   The GPOs for the computer are added to the end of the GPOs for the user. Because of this, the computer's GPOs have higher precedence than the user's GPOs.

Replace Mode   In Replace mode, the user's GPOs are not used. Only the GPOs of the Computer object are used.

Managing Network Configuration

Group policies are also useful in network configuration. Although administrators can handle network settings at the protocol level using many different methods, such as Dynamic Host Configuration Protocol (DHCP), Group Policy allows them to set which functions and operations are available to users and computers.

The paths to some of the features that are available for managing Group Policy settings are as follows:

Computer Network Options   These settings are located within the Computer Configuration ➤ Administrative Templates ➤ Network ➤ Network Connections folder.

User Network Options   These settings are located within User Configuration ➤ Administrative Templates ➤ Network, as shown in Figure 10.8.

Here are some examples of the types of settings available:

◆   The ability to allow or disallow the modification of network settings.

In many environments, the improper changing of network configurations and protocol settings is a common cause of help desk calls.

◆   The ability to allow or disallow the creation of Remote Access Service (RAS) connections.

This option is useful, especially in larger networked environments, because the use of modems and other WAN devices can pose a security threat to the network.

◆   The ability to set offline files and folders options.

This is especially useful for keeping files synchronized for traveling users, and it is commonly configured for laptops.

FIGURE 10.8
Viewing Group Policy
User network configura-
tion options

Each setting includes detailed instructions in the description area of the GPO Editor window. By using these configuration options, system administrators can maintain consistency for users and computers and avoid many of the most common troubleshooting calls.

Configuring Network Settings

In Windows Server 2022, you can set a lot of user and network settings by using GPOs. Some of the different settings that can be configured are configure printer preferences, defining network drive mappings, configuring power options, setting custom registry settings, manipulating Control Panel settings, configuring your internet settings, settings for file and folder deployment, setting up shortcut deployments, and configuring item-level targeting.

To configure any of these settings, open the Group Policy Management Console and choose the GPO you want to edit. Once you start editing, you can configure any of these network settings.

Automatically Enrolling User and Computer Certificates in Group Policy

You can also use Group Policy to enroll user and computer certificates automatically, making the entire certificate process transparent to your end users. Before proceeding, you should understand what certificates are and why they are an important part of network security.

Think of a digital certificate as a carrying case for a public key. A certificate contains the public and the private keys and a set of attributes, including the key holder's name and email address. These attributes specify something about the holder: their identity, what they're allowed to do with the certificate, and so on. The attributes and the public key are bound together because the certificate is digitally signed by the entity that issued it. Anyone who wants to verify the certificate's contents can verify the issuer's signature.

Certificates are one part of what security experts call a *public-key infrastructure (PKI)*. A PKI has several different components that you can mix and match to achieve the desired results. Microsoft's PKI implementation offers the following functions:

Certificate Authorities CAs issue certificates, revoke certificates they've issued, and publish certificates for their clients. Big CAs like Thawte and VeriSign do this for millions of users. If you want, you can also set up your own CA for each department or workgroup in your organization. Each CA is responsible for choosing which attributes it will include in a certificate and what mechanism it will use to verify those attributes before it issues the certificate.

Certificate Publishers They make certificates publicly available, inside or outside an organization. This allows widespread availability of the critical material needed to support the entire PKI.

PKI-Savvy Applications These allow you and your users to do useful things with certificates, such as encrypt email or network connections. Ideally, the user shouldn't have to know (or even be aware of) what the application is doing—everything should work seamlessly and automatically. The best-known examples of PKI-savvy applications are web browsers such as Edge and Firefox and email applications such as Outlook.

Certificate Templates These act like rubber stamps. By specifying a particular template as the model you want to use for a newly issued certificate, you're actually telling the CA which optional attributes to add to the certificate as well as implicitly telling it how to fill some of the mandatory attributes. Templates greatly simplify the process of issuing certificates because they keep you from having to memorize the names of all of the attributes you may potentially want to put in a certificate.

LEARN MORE ABOUT PKI

When discussing certificates, it's also important to mention PKI and its definition. The exam doesn't go deeply into PKI, but I recommend you do some extra research on your own because it is an important technology and shouldn't be overlooked. PKI is actually a simple concept with a lot of moving parts. When broken down to its bare essentials, PKI is nothing more than a server and workstations utilizing a software service to add security to your infrastructure. When you use PKI, you are adding a layer of protection. The auto-enrollment Settings policy determines whether users and/or computers are automatically enrolled for the appropriate certificates when necessary. By default, this policy is enabled if a certificate server is installed, but you can make changes to the settings, as shown in Exercise 10.5.

In Exercise 10.5, you will learn how to configure automatic certificate enrollment in Group Policy. You must have first completed the other exercises in this chapter in order to proceed with Exercise 10.5.

EXERCISE 10.5   Configuring Automatic Certificate Enrollment in Group Policy

1. Open the Group Policy Management Console tool.

2. Right-click the North America OU that you created in the previous exercises in this book.

3. Choose Create A GPO In This Domain And Link It Here and name it **Test CA**. Click OK.

4. Right-click the Test CA GPO and choose Edit.

5. Open Computer Configuration ➢ Policies ➢ Windows Settings ➢ Security Settings ➢ Public Key Policies.

6. Double-click Certificate Services Client – Auto-Enrollment in the right pane.

7. The Certificate Services Client – Auto-Enrollment Properties dialog box will appear.

8. For now, don't change anything. Just become familiar with the settings in this dialog box. Click OK to close it.

Redirecting Folders

Another set of Group Policy settings that you will learn about are the *folder redirection settings*. Group Policy provides a means for redirecting the Documents, Desktop, and Start Menu folders, as well as cached application data, to network locations. Folder redirection is particularly useful for the following reasons:

◆ When they are using roaming user profiles, a user's Documents folder is copied to the local machine each time they log on. This requires high bandwidth consumption and time if the Documents folder is large. If you redirect the Documents folder, it stays in the redirected location, and the user opens and saves files directly to that location.

◆ Documents are always available no matter where the user logs on.

◆ Data in the shared location can be backed up during the normal backup cycle without user intervention.

◆ Data can be redirected to a more robust server-side administered disk that is less prone to physical and user errors.

When you decide to redirect folders, you have two options: basic and advanced.

◆ Basic redirection redirects everyone's folders to the same location (but each user gets their own folder within that location).

◆ Advanced redirection redirects folders to different locations based on group membership. For instance, you could configure the Engineers group to redirect their folders to //Engineering1/Documents/ and the Marketing group to //Marketing1/Documents/. Again, individual users still get their own folder within the redirected location.

To configure folder redirection, follow the steps in Exercise 10.6. You must have completed the other exercises in this chapter to proceed with this exercise.

EXERCISE 10.6   Configuring Folder Redirection in Group Policy

1. Open the GPMC tool.
2. Open the North America OU and then edit the Test CA GPO.
3. Open User Configuration ➤ Policies ➤ Windows Settings ➤ Folder Redirection ➤ Documents.
4. Right-click Documents, and select Properties.
5. On the Target tab of the Documents Properties dialog box, choose the Basic – Redirect Everyone's Folder To The Same Location selection from the Settings drop-down list.
6. Leave the default option for the Target Folder Location drop-down list and specify a network path in the Root Path field.
7. Click the Settings tab. All of the default settings are self-explanatory and should typically be left at the default setting. Click OK when you have finished.

FOLDER REDIRECTION FACTS

Try not to mix up the concepts of *folder redirection* and *offline folders*, especially in a world with ever-increasing numbers of mobile users. Folder redirection and offline folders are different features.

Windows Server 2022 folder redirection works as follows: The system uses a pointer that moves the folders you want to a location you specify. Users do not see any of this—it is transparent to them. One problem with folder redirection is that it does not work for mobile users (users who will be offline and who will not have access to files they may need).

Offline folders, however, are copies of folders that were local to you. Files are now available locally to you on the system you have with you. They are also located back on the server where they are stored. The next time you log in, the folders are synchronized so that both folders contain the latest data. This is a perfect feature for mobile users, whereas folder redirection provides no benefit for the mobile user.

Managing GPOs with Windows PowerShell Group Policy Cmdlets

As stated earlier in this book, *Windows PowerShell* is a Windows command-line shell and scripting language. Windows PowerShell can also help an administrator automate many of the same tasks that you perform using the Group Policy Management Console.

Windows Server 2022 helps you perform many of the Group Policy tasks by providing dozens of cmdlets. Each of these cmdlets is a simple, single-function command-line tool.

The Windows PowerShell Group Policy cmdlets can help you perform some of the following tasks for domain-based Group Policy objects:

◆ Maintain, create, remove, back up, and import GPOs

◆ Create, update, and remove GPO links to Active Directory containers

◆ Set Active Directory OUs and domain permissions and inheritance flags

◆ Configure Group Policy registry settings

◆ Create and edit Starter GPOs

The requirement for Windows PowerShell Group Policy cmdlets is Windows Server 2022 on either a domain controller or a member server that has the GPMC installed. Windows 7 or above also have the ability to use Windows PowerShell Group Policy cmdlets if they have Remote Server Administration Tools (RSAT) installed. RSAT includes the GPMC and its cmdlets. PowerShell is also a requirement.

Item-Level Targeting

Administrators have the ability to apply individual preference items only to selected users or computers using a GPO feature called item-level targeting. *Item-level targeting* allows an administrator to select specific items that the GPO will look at and then apply that GPO only to the specific users or computers. Administrators have the ability to include multiple preference items, and each item can be customized for specific users or computers to use.

The target item has a value that belongs to it, and the value can be either true or false. Administrators can get even more granular by using the operation command of AND or OR while building this GPO, and this will allow an administrator to combine the targeted items with the preceding one. Once all of the conditions are executed, if the final value is false, then the GPO is not applied. If the final value is true, the GPO is applied to the users or computers that were previously determined. Administrators have the ability to item-target the following items:

◆ Battery Present Targeting

◆ Computer Name Targeting

◆ CPU Speed Targeting

◆ Date Match Targeting

◆ Disk Space Targeting

◆ Domain Targeting

◆ Environment Variable Targeting

◆ File Match Targeting

◆ IP Address Range Targeting

◆ Language Targeting

◆ LDAP Query Targeting

◆ MAC Address Range Targeting

◆ MSI Query Targeting

◆ Network Connection Targeting

◆ Operating System Targeting

◆ Organizational Unit Targeting

- PCMCIA Present Targeting
- Portable Computer Targeting
- Processing Mode Targeting
- RAM Targeting
- Registry Match Targeting
- Security Group Targeting
- Site Targeting
- Terminal Session Targeting
- Time Range Targeting
- User Targeting
- WMI Query Targeting

Administrators can easily set up item-level targeting by following these steps:

1. Open the Group Policy Management Console. Select the GPO that will contain the new preferences by right clicking the GPO and then choose Edit.

2. In the console tree under Computer Configuration or User Configuration, expand the Preferences folder and then browse to the preference extension.

3. Double-click the node for the preference extension and then right-click the preference item and click Properties.

4. In the Properties dialog box, click the Common tab.

5. Select Item-Level Targeting and then click Targeting.

6. Click New Item. If you are configuring multiple targeted items, on the Item Option menu, click the logical operation (AND or OR). Then click OK when finished.

7. Click the OK button on the Properties dialog box, and you are all set.

Back Up, Restore, Import, Copy, and Migration Tables

One of the biggest advantages of using the Group Policy Management Console is that it is a one-stop shopping utility. You can do everything you need to do for GPOs in one location. The GPMC not only allows you to create and link a GPO but also lets you back up, restore, import, and copy a GPO and use migration tables.

BACKING UP A GPO

Since this book is about Windows Server 2022 and everything you should do to set up the server properly, then you most likely already understand what backups can do for you.

The reason we back up data as an administrator is in case there is a crash or major error that requires us to reload data to the server. Backups should be done daily on all data that is important to your organization. To perform backups, you can either use Windows Server 2022's backup utility or purchase third-party software/hardware to back up your data.

I am an IT Director, and data recoverability is one of the most critical items that I deal with on a daily basis. I use a third-party hardware device from a company called Unitrends. This is just one of many companies that help protect an organization's data.

This hardware device does hourly backups for all of my servers. One of the nice features of the Unitrends box is that it backs up onto the hardware device and then sends my data up to the cloud automatically for an offsite backup. This way, if I need to recover just one piece of data, I can grab it off the hardware device. But if I have a major issue, such as a fire that destroys the entire server room, I have an offsite backup from which I can retrieve my data.

It's the same for GPOs. You need to make sure you back up your GPOs in the event of an issue that requires you to do a reload. To back up your GPOs manually, you can go into the GPMC MMC and under Group Policy Objects, you can right-click and choose Backup All or right click on the specific GPO and choose Backup.

RESTORING A GPO

There may be times when you have to restore a GPO that was previously backed up. There are normally two reasons why you have to restore a GPO—you accidentally deleted the GPO, or you need to restore the GPO to a previous state. (This normally happens if you make changes and it causes an issue.) Restoring a GPO is simple.

1. Open the Group Policy Management Console.

2. In the console tree, right-click Group Policy Objects and choose Manage Backups.

3. Choose the backup you want to restore and click the Restore button.

IMPORTING OR COPYING GPOs

As an administrator, there may be times when you need to import or copy a GPO from one domain to another domain. Administrators do this so that the second domain has the same settings as the first domain.

An administrator can use the import or copy-to-transfer settings from one GPO to another GPO within the same domain, to a GPO in another domain in the same forest, or to a GPO in a domain in a different forest.

Importing or copying a GPO is an easy process. To do this, an administrator completes the following steps:

1. Open the Group Policy Management Console.

2. In the console tree, right-click Group Policy Objects and choose either Import Settings or Copy.

MIGRATION TABLES

One issue that we run into when copying or moving a GPO from one system to another is that when some GPOs are built, they are domain specific. This can be a problem when they are moved to a system in another domain. This is where migration tables can help you out.

Migration tables will tell you how domain-specific settings should be treated when the GPO is moved from the domain in which it was created to another domain.

Migration tables are files that are used to map previous domain information (such as users and groups) to the new domain's object-specific data. Migration tables have mapping entries that map the old data to the new data.

Migration tables store their mapping data in an XML format, and the migration tables have their own extension name, `.migtable`. If you want to create your own migration table, you can use the *Migration Table Editor (MTE)*. The MTE is an easy-to-use utility for configuring or just viewing migration tables.

It does not matter if you decide to copy or import a GPO, migration tables apply to any of the settings within the GPO. However, if you copy a GPO instead of move it, you have the option of bringing the Discretionary Access Control List (DACL) option over with the copy.

If you are looking at using migration tables, there are three settings that can be used:

Do Not Use A Migration Table If an administrator chooses this option, the GPO is copied over exactly as is. All security objects and UNC paths are copied over without any modification.

Use A Migration Table If an administrator chooses this option, the GPO has all of the options that can be in the migration table mapped.

Use A Migration Table Exclusively If an administrator chooses this option, all security principals and UNC path information in the GPO are chosen. If any of this information is not included in the migration table, the operation will fail.

To open the Migration Table Editor, perform the following steps:

1. Open the Group Policy Management Console.

2. In the console tree, right-click Group Policy Objects and choose Open Migration Table Editor.

RESETTING THE DEFAULT GPO

There may be a time when you need to reset the default GPO to its original settings. This is easy to do as long as you understand how to use the DCGPOFix command-line utility. This command-line utility is just what it spells—it fixes the domain controller's GPO. To use this command, you would use the following syntax:

```
DCGPOFix [/ignoreschema] [/target: {Domain | DC | Both}] [/?]
```

So, let's take a look at the switches in the previous command. The /ignoreschema switch ignores the current version of the Active Directory Schema. The reason you use this switch is because this command works only on the same schema version as the Windows version in which the command was shipped. By using this switch, you don't need to worry about what schema you have on the system.

The next switch is [/target: {Domain | DC | Both}]. This switch specifies the GPO you are going to restore. An administrator has the ability to restore the Default Domain Policy GPO, the Default Domain Controllers GPO, or both. The final switch, /?, displays the help for this command.

The Bottom Line

Understand the purpose of GPOs.   System administrators use Group Policy to enforce granular permissions for users in an Active Directory environment.

> **Master It**   You are an administrator of a large network with 3,500 hosts. You need to easily set up a policy to run a script when users log into the domain.

Understand user and computer settings.   Certain Group Policy settings may apply to users, computers, or both. Computer settings affect all users that access the machines to which the policy applies. User settings affect users, regardless of which machines they log on to.

> **Master It**   You are the administrator of an organization that has decided to implement a new domain password policy. This policy will apply to all users on the domain.

Know the interactions between Group Policy objects and Active Directory.   GPOs can be linked to Active Directory objects. This link determines to which objects the policies apply. GPOs can be applied to sites, domains, or OUs. You can set up local policies on Windows systems, but domain-based policies are set on sites, domains, and OUs.

> **Master It**   You are the administrator of an organization that has decided to implement a new policy for a specific set of users.

Chapter 11

Advanced Group Policy Options

Now that you understand how GPOs operate on a network, let's take a closer look at some of the advanced options that you can set using a GPO.

One way that you can use a GPO is for deploying software to all of your end users. With the release of cloud-based services and deploying software using the cloud, you may wonder why we would use GPOs for deploying software. There may be third party applications that can be easily deployed onto your domain using a GPO instead of deploying software using the cloud. Also, another issue with the cloud is that you need Microsoft Endpoint Manager (formally known as Intune Manager) to deploy software. Microsoft Endpoint Manager is not included with the basic Azure subscription. So, if your company decides not to pay the extra money, deploying software through a GPO can be a good option.

I will also talk about some other settings that can help you set up and configure GPOs more effectively.

IN THIS CHAPTER YOU'LL LEARN

- ◆ Know how to use the Resultant Set of Policy (RSoP) tool to troubleshoot and plan Group Policy

- ◆ Understand the difference between publishing and assigning applications

Deploying Software Through a GPO

It's difficult enough to manage applications on a stand-alone computer. It seems that the process of installing, configuring, and uninstalling applications is never finished. Add in the hassle of computer reboots and reinstalling corrupted applications, and the reduction in productivity can be substantial.

Software administrators who manage software in network environments have even more concerns.

- ◆ First, they must determine which applications specific users require.

- ◆ Then, IT departments must purchase the appropriate licenses for the software and acquire any necessary media.

- ◆ Next, the system administrators need to install the applications on users' machines. This process generally involves help desk staff visiting computers, or it requires end users to install the software themselves. Both processes entail several potential problems, including installation inconsistency and lost productivity from downtime experienced when applications were installed.

◆ Finally, software administrators still need to manage software updates and remove unused software.

One of the key design goals for Active Directory was to reduce some of the headaches involved in managing software and configurations in a networked environment. To that end, Windows Server 2022 offers several features that can make the task of deploying software easier and less error prone. Before you dive into the technical details, however, you need to examine the issues related to software deployment.

The Software Management Life Cycle

Although it may seem that the use of a new application requires only the installation of the necessary software, the overall process of managing applications involves many more steps. When managing software applications, there are three main phases to their life cycle, as follows:

Phase 1: Deploying Software   The first step in using applications is to install them on the appropriate client computers. Generally, some applications are deployed during the initial configuration of a PC, and others are deployed when they are requested. In the latter case, this often used to mean that system administrators and help desk staff have to visit client computers and manually walk through the installation process. With Windows Server 2022 and GPOs, the entire process can be automated.

BEFORE YOU INSTALL, STOP

It is important to understand that just because you can easily deploy software, it does not necessarily mean you have the right to do so. Before you install software on client computers, you must make sure you have the appropriate licenses for the software. Furthermore, it's important to take the time to track application installations. As many system administrators have discovered, it's much more difficult to inventory software installations after they've been performed. Another issue you may encounter is that you lack available resources (for instance, your system does not meet the minimum hardware requirements) and that you face problems such as limited hard disk space or memory that may not be able to handle the applications that you want to load and use. You may also find that your user account does not have the permission to install software. It's important to consider not only how you will install software but also whether you can.

Phase 2: Maintaining Software   Once an application is installed and in use on client computers, you need to ensure that the software is maintained. You must keep programs up-to-date by applying changes due to bug fixes, enhancements, and other types of updates. This is normally done with service packs, hot fixes, and updates. As with the initial software deployment, software maintenance can be tedious. Some programs require older versions to be uninstalled before updates are added. Others allow for automatically upgrading over existing installations. Managing and deploying software updates can consume a significant amount of the IT staff's time.

USING WINDOWS UPDATE

Make sure that you learn about Windows Update, a service that allows you to connect to Microsoft's website and download what your system may need to bring it up to compliance. This tool is helpful if you are running a stand-alone system, but if you want to deploy software across the enterprise, the best way to accomplish this is first to test the updates you are downloading and make sure you can use them and that they are not bug ridden. Then you can use a tool such as the Windows Server Update Services (WSUS).

Phase 3: Removing Software   The end of the life cycle for many software products involves the actual removal of unused programs. Removing software is necessary when applications become outdated or when users no longer require their functionality. One of the traditional problems with uninstalling applications is that many of the installed files may not be removed. Furthermore, the removal of shared components can sometimes cause other programs to stop functioning properly. Also, users often forget to uninstall applications that they no longer need, and these programs continue to occupy disk space and consume valuable system resources.

The Microsoft Windows Installer (MSI) manages each of these three phases of the software maintenance life cycle. Now that you have an overview of the process, let's move forward to look at the steps involved in deploying software using Group Policy.

NOTE   The *Microsoft Windows Installer* (sometimes referred to as Microsoft Installer or Windows Installer) is an application installation and configuration service. An instruction file (the Microsoft Installer package) contains information about what needs to be done to install a product. It's common to confuse the two.

The Windows Installer

If you've installed newer application programs (such as Microsoft Office 2016), you've probably noticed the updated setup and installation routines. Applications that comply with the updated standard use the *Windows Installer specification* and MSI software packages for deployment. Each package contains information about various setup options and the files required for installation. Although the benefits may not seem dramatic on the surface, there's a lot of new functionality under the hood.

The Windows Installer was created to solve many of the problems associated with traditional application development. It has several components, including the Installer service (which runs on Windows 7, Windows 8, Windows 10, Windows 11, and Windows Server 2008 and above), the Installer program (`msiexec.exe`) that is responsible for executing the instructions in a *Windows Installer package*, and the specifications third-party developers use to create their own packages. Within each installation package file is a relational structure (similar to the structure of tables in databases) that records information about the programs contained within the package.

To appreciate the true value of the Windows Installer, you'll need to look at some of the problems with traditional software deployment mechanisms and then at how the Windows Installer addresses many of them.

APPLICATION INSTALLATION ISSUES

Before the Windows Installer, applications were installed using a setup program that managed the various operations required for a program to operate. These operations included copying files, changing Registry settings, and managing any other operating system changes that might be required (such as starting or stopping services). However, this method had several problems:

◆ The setup process was not robust, and aborting the operation often left many unnecessary files in the file system.

◆ The process included uninstalling an application (this also often left many unnecessary files in the file system) and remnants in the Windows registry and operating system folders. Over time, these remnants would result in reduced overall system performance and wasted disk space.

◆ There was no standard method for applying upgrades to applications, and installing a new version often required users to uninstall the old application, reboot, and then install the new program.

◆ Conflicts between different versions of *dynamic link libraries (DLLs)*—shared program code used across different applications—could cause the installation or removal of one application to break the functionality of another.

BENEFITS OF THE WINDOWS INSTALLER

Because of the many problems associated with traditional software installation, Microsoft created the *Windows Installer*. This system provides for better manageability of the software installation process and allows system administrators more control over the deployment process. Specifically, the Windows Installer provides the following benefits:

Improved Software Removal The process of removing software is an important one because remnants left behind during the uninstall process can eventually clutter up the Registry and file system. During the installation process, the Windows Installer keeps track of all of the changes made by a setup package. When it comes time to remove an application, all of these changes can then be rolled back.

More Robust Installation Routines If a typical setup program is aborted during the software installation process, the results are unpredictable. If the actual installation hasn't yet begun, then the installer generally removes any temporary files that may have been created. However, if the file copy routine starts before the system encounters an error, it is likely that the files will not be automatically removed from the operating system. In contrast, the Windows Installer allows you to roll back any changes when the application setup process is aborted.

Ability to Use Elevated Privileges Installing applications usually requires the user to have Administrator permissions on the local computer because file system and Registry changes are required. When installing software for network users, system administrators have two options. First, they can log off of the computer before installing the software and then log back on as a user who has Administrator permissions on the local computer. This method is tedious and time-consuming. The second option is to give users Administrator permissions temporarily on their own machines. This method could cause security problems and requires the attention of a system administrator.

Through the use of the Installer service, the Windows Installer is able to use temporarily elevated privileges to install applications. This allows users, regardless of their security settings, to execute the installation of authorized applications. This saves time and preserves security.

Support for Repairing Corrupted Applications   Regardless of how well a network environment is managed, critical files are sometimes lost or corrupted. Such problems can prevent applications from running properly and can cause crashes. Windows Installer packages provide you with the ability to verify the installation of an application and, if necessary, replace any missing or corrupted files. This support saves time and lessens end-user headaches associated with removing and reinstalling an entire application to replace just a few files.

Prevention of File Conflicts   Generally, different versions of the same files should be compatible with each other. In the real world, however, this isn't always the case. A classic problem in the Windows world is the case of one program replacing DLLs that are used by several other programs. Windows Installer accurately tracks which files are used by certain programs and ensures that any shared files are not improperly deleted or overwritten.

Automated Installations   A typical application setup process requires end users or system administrators to respond to several prompts. For example, a user may be able to choose the program group in which icons will be created and the file system location to which the program will be installed. Additionally, they may be required to choose which options are installed. Although this type of flexibility is useful, it can be tedious when you are rolling out multiple applications. By using features of the Windows Installer, however, users are able to specify setup options before the process begins. This allows system administrators to ensure consistency in installations, and it saves users time.

Advertising and On-Demand Installations   One of the most powerful features of the Windows Installer is its ability to perform on-demand software installations. Prior to the Windows Installer, application installation options were quite basic—either a program was installed or it was not. When setting up a computer, system administrators would be required to guess which applications the user might need and install all of them.

The Windows Installer supports a function known as advertising. *Advertising* makes applications appear to be available via the Start menu. However, the programs themselves may not actually be installed on the system. When a user attempts to access an advertised application, the Windows Installer automatically downloads the necessary files from a server and installs the program. The result is that applications are installed only when they are needed, and the process requires no intervention from the end user.

To anyone who has managed many software applications in a network environment, all of these features of the Windows Installer are likely welcome ones. They also make life easier for end users and application developers; they can focus on the "real work" that their jobs demand.

WINDOWS INSTALLER FILE TYPES

When performing software deployment with the Windows Installer in Windows Server 2022, you may encounter several different file types.

Microsoft Windows Installer Packages   To take full advantage of Windows Installer functionality, applications must include Microsoft Windows Installer packages. Third-party application vendors and software developers normally create these packages, and they include the information required to install and configure the application and any supporting files.

Microsoft Transformation Files   *Microsoft Transformation (MST) files* are useful when you are customizing the details of how applications are installed. When a system administrator chooses to assign or publish an application, they may want to specify additional options for the package. For example, if a system administrator wants to allow users to install only the Microsoft Word and Microsoft PowerPoint components of Office 2016, they could specify these options within a transformation file. Then, when users install the application, they will be provided only with the options related to these components.

Microsoft Patches   To maintain software, patches are often required. Patches may make Registry and/or file system changes. *Patch files (MSP)* are used for minor system changes and are subject to certain limitations. Specifically, a patch file cannot remove any installed program components and cannot delete or modify any shortcuts created by the user.

Initialization Files   To provide support for publishing non–Windows Installer applications, *initialization files* can be used. These files provide links to a standard executable file that is used to install an application. An example might be \\server1\software\program1\setup.exe. These files can then be published and advertised, and users can access the *Add Or Remove Programs* icon to install them over the network.

Application Assignment Scripts   *Application assignment scripts (AAS)* store information regarding assigning programs and any settings that the system administrator makes. These files are created when Group Policy is used to create software package assignments for users and computers.

Each of these types of files provides functionality that allows the system administrator to customize software deployment. Windows Installer packages have special properties that you can view by right-clicking the file in Windows Explorer and choosing Properties (see Figure 11.1).

Deploying Applications

The functionality provided by Windows Installer offers many advantages to end users who install their own software. However, that is just the beginning in a networked environment. The various features of Windows Installer and compatible packages allow system administrators to determine centrally applications that users will be able to install.

There are two main methods of making programs available to end users using Active Directory: assigning and publishing. Both assigning and publishing applications greatly ease the process of deploying and managing applications in a network environment.

FIGURE 11.1
Viewing the properties
of an MSI package file

In the following sections, you'll look at how the processes of assigning and publishing applications can make life easier for IT staff and users alike. The various settings for assigned and published applications are managed through the use of GPOs.

Assigning Applications

Software applications can be assigned to users and computers. *Assigning* a software package makes the program available for automatic installation. The applications advertise their availability to the affected users or computers by placing icons within the Apps area on all current versions of Windows.

When applications are assigned to a user, programs will be advertised to the user regardless of which computer they are using. That is, icons for the advertised program will appear regardless of whether the program is installed on that computer. If the user clicks an icon for a program that has not yet been installed on the local computer, the application will automatically be accessed from a server and it will be installed.

When an application is assigned to a computer, the program is made available to any users of the computer. For example, all users who log on to a computer that has been assigned Microsoft Office 2016 will have access to the components of the application. If the user did not previously install Microsoft Office 2016, they will be prompted for any required setup information when the program first runs.

Generally, applications that are required by the vast majority of users should be assigned to computers. This reduces the amount of network bandwidth required to install applications on demand and improves the end-user experience by preventing the delay involved when installing an application the first time it is accessed. Any applications that may be used by only a few users (or those with specific job tasks) should be assigned to users.

PUBLISHING APPLICATIONS

When applications are *published*, they are advertised, but no icons are automatically created. Instead, the applications are made available for installation using the Programs and Features icon in Control Panel.

Implementing Software Deployment

So far, you have become familiar with the issues related to software deployment and management from a theoretical level. Now it's time to drill down into the actual steps required to deploy software using the features of Active Directory and the GPMC. In the following sections, you will walk through the steps required to create an application distribution share point, to publish and assign applications, to update previously installed applications, to verify the installation of applications, and to update Windows operating systems.

Preparing for Software Deployment

Before you can install applications on client computers, you must make sure that the necessary files are available to end users. In many network environments, system administrators create shares on file servers that include the installation files for many applications. Based on security permissions, either end users or system administrators can then connect to these shares from a client computer and install the needed software. The efficient organization of these shares can save the help desk from having to carry around a library of DVDs, and it allows you to install applications easily on many computers at once.

NOTE   One of the problems in network environments is that users frequently install applications whether or not they really need them. They may stumble upon applications that are stored on common file servers and install them out of curiosity. These actions can often decrease productivity and may violate software licensing agreements. You can help avoid this by placing all of your application installation files in hidden shares (for example, software$).

Exercise 11.1 walks you through the process of creating a software distribution share point. In this exercise, you will prepare for software deployment by creating a directory share and placing certain types of files in this directory. To complete the steps in this exercise, you must have access to the Microsoft Office 2016 installation files (via DVD or through a network share) and have 2,000 MB of free disk space. For this exercise, I used Microsoft Office 2016.

EXERCISE 11.1   Creating a Software Deployment Share

1. Using Windows Explorer, create a folder called **Software** that you can use with application sharing. Be sure that the volume on which you create this folder has at least 2,000 MB of available disk space.

2. Create a folder called **Office 2016** within the Software folder.

3. Copy all of the installation files for Microsoft Office 2016 from the DVD or network share containing the files to the Office 2016 folder you created in step 2. If you prefer, you can use switches to install all of the Office 2016 installation files.

4. Right-click the Software folder (created in step 1) and select Share. In the Choose People On Your Network To Share With dialog box, type **Everyone**, and click the Add button. Next click the Share button. When you see a message that the sharing process is complete, click Done.

Software Restriction Policies

One of the biggest problems that we face as IT managers is users downloading and installing software. Many software packages don't cause any issues and are completely safe. Unfortunately, many software packages do have viruses and can cause problems. This is where software restriction policies can help. Software restriction policies help to identify software and to control its ability to run on a local computer, organizational unit, domain, or site.

Software restriction policies give administrators the ability to regulate unknown or untrusted software. Software restriction policies allow you to protect your computers from unwanted software by identifying and also specifying what software packages are allowed to be installed.

When configuring software restriction policies, an administrator is able to define a default security level of Unrestricted (software is allowed) or Disallowed (software is not allowed to run) for a GPO. Administrators can make exceptions to this default security level. They can create software restriction policy rules for specific software.

To create a software policy using the Group Policy Management Console, create a new GPO. In the GPO, expand the Windows Settings for either the user or computer configuration section, expand Security, right-click Software Restriction Policy, and choose New Software Restriction Policy. Set the policy for the level of security that you need.

Using AppLocker

AppLocker is a feature in Windows 7 and above and Windows Server 2012/2012 R2 and above. It is the replacement for software restriction policies. *AppLocker* allows you to configure a Denied list and an Accepted list for applications. Applications that are configured on the Denied list will not run on the system, whereas applications on the Accepted list will operate properly.

The new capabilities and extensions of the AppLocker feature help reduce administrative overhead and help administrators control how users can access and use files, such as EXE files, scripts, Windows Installer files (MSI and MSP files), and DLLs.

Group Policy Slow Link Detection

When setting up GPOs, most of us assume that the connection speeds between servers and clients are going to be fast. In today's world, it is unlikely to see slow connections between locations, but they are still out there. Sometimes connection speeds can cause issues with the deployment of GPOs, specifically ones that are deploying software.

A setting in the Computer and User section of the GPO called *Group Policy Slow Link Detection* defines a slow connection for the purposes of applying and updating GPOs. If the data transfer rate from the domain controller providing the GPO to the computer is slower than what you have specified in this setting, the connection is considered to be a slow connection. If a connection is considered slow, the system response will vary depending on the policy. For example, if a GPO is going to deploy software and the connection is considered slow, the software may not be installed on the client computer. If you configure this option as 0, all connections are considered fast connections.

Publishing and Assigning Applications

As mentioned earlier, system administrators can make software packages available to users by using publishing and assigning operations. Both of these operations allow system administrators to leverage the power of Active Directory and, specifically, GPOs to determine which applications are available to users. Additionally, OUs can provide the organization that can help group users based on their job functions and software requirements.

The general process involves creating a GPO that includes software deployment settings for users and computers and then linking this GPO to Active Directory objects.

Exercise 11.2 walks you through the steps required to publish and assign applications. In this exercise, you will create applications and assign them to specific Active Directory objects using GPOs. To complete the steps in this exercise, you must have completed Exercise 11.1.

EXERCISE 11.2   Publishing and Assigning Applications Using Group Policy

1. Open the Active Directory Users and Computers tool from the Administrative Tools program group (using the Windows key).

2. Expand the domain and create a new top-level OU called **Software**.

3. Within the Software OU, create a user named **Jane User** with a login name of **juser** (choose the defaults for all other options).

4. Exit Active Directory Users and Computers and open the Group Policy Management Console.

5. Right-click the Software OU and choose Create A GPO In This Domain And Link It Here.

6. For the name of the new GPO, type **Software Deployment**.

7. To edit the Software Deployment GPO, right-click it and choose Edit. Expand the Computer Configuration ➢ Policies ➢ Software Settings object.

8. Right-click the Software Installation item and select New ➢ Package.

9. Navigate to the Software share you created in Exercise 11.1.

10. Within the Software share, double-click the Office 2016 folder and select the appropriate MSI file depending on the version of Office 2016 you have. Office 2016 Professional is being used in this example, so you'll see that the OFFICEMUI.MSI file is chosen. Click Open.

11. In the Deploy Software dialog box, choose Advanced. (Note that the Published option is unavailable because applications cannot be published to computers.) Click OK to return to the Deploy Software dialog box.

12. To examine the deployment options of this package, click the Deployment tab. Accept the default settings by clicking OK.

13. Within the Group Policy Object Editor, expand the User Configuration ➢ Software Settings object.

14. Right-click the Software Installation item and select New ➢ Package.

15. Navigate to the Software share you created in Exercise 11.1.

16. Within the Software share, double-click the Office 2016 folder and select the appropriate MSI file. Click Open.

17. For the Software Deployment option, select Published in the Deploy Software dialog box and click OK.

18. Close the GPMC.

The overall process involved with deploying software using Active Directory is quite simple. However, you shouldn't let the intuitive graphical interface fool you—there's a lot of power under the hood of these software deployment features! Once you've properly assigned and published applications, it's time to see the effects of your work.

Applying Software Updates

The steps described in the previous section work only when you are installing a new application. However, software companies often release updates that you need to install on top of existing applications. These updates usually consist of bug fixes or other changes that are required to keep the software up-to-date. You can apply software updates in Active Directory by using the Upgrades tab of the software package Properties dialog box found in the Group Policy Object Editor.

In Exercise 11.3, you will apply a software update to an existing application. You should add the upgrade package to the GPO in the same way you added the original application in steps 8 through 12 of Exercise 11.2. You should also have completed Exercise 11.2 before attempting this exercise.

EXERCISE 11.3   Applying Software Updates

1. Open the Group Policy Management Console from the Administrative Tools program group.

2. Click the Software OU, right-click the Software Deployment GPO, and choose Edit.

3. Expand the Computer Configuration ➢ Policies ➢ Software Settings ➢ Software Installation object.

4. Right-click the software package and select Properties from the context menu to bring up the Properties dialog box.

5. Select the Upgrades tab and click the Add button.

6. Click the Current Group Policy Object (GPO) radio button in the Choose A Package From section of the dialog box or click the Browse button to select the GPO to which you want to apply the upgrade. Consult your application's documentation to see whether you should choose the Uninstall The Existing Package, Then Install The Upgrade Package radio button or the Package Can Upgrade Over The Existing Package radio button.

7. Click Cancel to close the Add Upgrade Package dialog box.

8. Click Cancel and exit the GPMC.

You should understand that not all upgrades make sense in all situations. For instance, if the Panek 2015 files are incompatible with the Panek 2018 application, then your Panek 2015 users might not want you to perform the upgrade without taking additional steps to ensure that they can continue to use their files. In addition, users might have some choice about which version they use when it doesn't affect the support of the network.

Regardless of the underlying reason for allowing this flexibility, you should be aware that there are two basic types of upgrades that are available for administrators to provide to the users:

Mandatory Upgrade   Forces everyone who currently has an existing version of the program to upgrade according to the GPO. Users who have never installed the program for whatever reason will be able to install only the new, upgraded version.

Nonmandatory Upgrade   Allows users to choose whether they would like to upgrade. This upgrade type also allows users who do not have their application installed to choose which version they would like to use.

Verifying Software Installation

To ensure that the software installation settings you make in a GPO have taken place, you can log into the domain from a Windows 10, Windows 11, Windows 8, or Windows 7 computer that is within the OU to which the software settings apply. When you log in, you will notice two changes. First, the application is installed on the computer (if it was not installed already). To access the application, a user needs to click one of the icons within the Program group of the Start menu. Note also that applications are available to any of the users who log on to this machine. Second, the settings apply to any computers that are contained within the OU and to any users who log on to these computers.

If you publish an application to users, the change may not be as evident, but it is equally useful. When you log on to a Windows 8, Windows 7, or Windows 10, or Windows 11 a computer that is a member of the domain, and when you use a user account from the OU where you published the application, you will be able to install any of the published applications automatically. On a Windows 10, Windows 11, Windows 8, or Windows 7 computer, you can do this by accessing the Programs icon in Control Panel. By clicking Add New Programs, you access a display of the applications available for installation. By clicking the Add button in the Add New Programs section of the Programs dialog box, you will automatically begin the installation of the published application.

Configuring Automatic Updates in Group Policy

So far you've seen the advantages of deploying application software in a group policy. Group policies also provide a way to install operating system updates across the network for Windows 7 and above and 2008 and above machines using Windows Update in conjunction with Windows Server Update Service (WSUS). WSUS is the newer version of SUS, and it is used on a Windows Server 2022 system to update systems. As you may remember, WSUS and SUS are patch-management tools that help you deploy updates to your systems in a controlled manner.

Windows Update is available through the Microsoft website, and it is used to provide the most current files for Windows operating systems. Examples of updates include security fixes, critical updates, updated help files, and updated drivers. You can access Windows Update by clicking the Windows Update icon in the system tray.

WSUS is used to leverage the features of Windows Update within a corporate environment by downloading Windows updates to a corporate server, which in turn provides the updates to the internal corporate clients. This allows administrators to test updates and have full control over what updates are deployed within the corporate environment.

Within an enterprise network that is using Active Directory, you would typically see automatic updates configured through Group Policy. Group policies are used to manage configuration and security settings via Active Directory. Group Policy is also used to specify what server a client will use for automatic updates.

If the WSUS client were part of an enterprise network that is using Active Directory, you would configure the client via a group policy.

Configuring Software Deployment Settings

In addition to the basic operations of assigning and publishing applications, you can use several other options to specify the details of how software is deployed. In the following sections, you will examine the various options that are available and their effects on the software installation process.

The Software Installation Properties Dialog Box

The most important software deployment settings are contained in the Software Installation Properties dialog box, which you can access by right-clicking the Software Installation item and selecting Properties from the context menu. The following sections describe the features contained on the various tabs of the dialog box.

MANAGING PACKAGE DEFAULTS

On the Deployment tab of the Software Installation Properties dialog box, you'll be able to specify some defaults for any packages that you create within this GPO. Figure 11.2 shows the Deployment options for managing software installation settings.

FIGURE 11.2
Deployment tab of the Software Installation Properties dialog box

The following options are used for managing software installation settings:

Default Package Location This setting specifies the default file system or network location for software installation packages. This is useful if you are already using a specific share on a file server for hosting the necessary installation files.

New Packages These settings specify the default type of package assignment that will be used when you add a new package to either the user or computer settings. If you'll be assigning or publishing multiple packages, you may find it useful to set a default here. Selecting the Advanced option enables Group Policy to display the package's Properties dialog box each time a new package is added (see Figure 11.3).

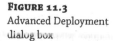

FIGURE 11.3
Advanced Deployment
dialog box

> **Advanced Deployment Options** ✕
>
> Advanced deployment options:
> ☐ Ignore language when deploying this package
>
> ☑ Make this 32-bit X86 application available to Win64 machines.
>
> ☐ Include OLE class and product information.
>
> Advanced diagnostic information:
>
> Product code: {5E076CF2-EFED-43A2-A623-13E0D62EC7E0}
>
> Deployment Count: 0
>
> Script name: \\StormWindAD.com\SysVol
>   \StormWindAD.com\Policies
>   \{087AB115-BF21-4A2D-89CE-67454BF7162A}
>   \User\Applications
>   \{C577BF4F-1F1D-4419-8614-53771FAA5C0F}.aas
>
>   OK   Cancel

Installation User Interface Options When installing an application, system administrators may or may not want end users to see all of the advanced installation options. If Basic is chosen, the user will be able to configure only the minimal settings (such as the installation location). If Maximum is chosen, all of the available installation options will be displayed. The specific installation options available will depend on the package itself.

Uninstall Applications When They Fall Out Of The Scope Of Management So far, you have seen how applications can be assigned and published to users or computers. But what happens when effective GPOs change? For example, suppose User A is currently located within the Sales OU. A GPO that assigns the Microsoft Office 2013 suite of applications is linked to the Sales OU. You decide to move User A to the Engineering OU, which has no software deployment settings. Should the application be uninstalled or should it remain?

If the Uninstall Applications When They Fall Out Of The Scope of Management option is checked, applications will be removed if they are not specifically assigned or published within GPOs. In this example, this means Office 2013 would be uninstalled for User A. If this box is left unchecked, however, the application will remain installed.

MANAGING FILE EXTENSION MAPPINGS

One of the potential problems associated with using many different file types is that it's difficult to keep track of which applications work with which files. For example, if you received a file with the filename extension .abc, you would have no idea which application you would need to view it.

Fortunately, through software deployment settings, system administrators can specify mappings for specific *filename extensions*. For example, you could specify that whenever users attempt to access a file with the extension .vsd, the operating system should attempt to open the file using Visio diagramming software. If Visio is not installed on the user's machine, the computer can automatically download and install it (assuming that the application has been properly advertised).

This method allows users to have applications automatically installed when they are needed. The following is an example of a sequence of events that might occur:

1. A user receives an email message that contains a PDF (.pdf) file attachment.

2. The computer realizes that the PDF file does not have the appropriate viewing application for this type of file installed. However, it also realizes that a filename extension mapping is available within the Active Directory software deployment settings.

3. The client computer automatically requests the PDF software package from the server, and it uses the Microsoft Windows Installer to install the application automatically.

4. The computer opens the attachment for the user.

Notice that all of these steps were carried out without any further interaction with the user.

You can manage filename extension mappings by right-clicking the Software Installation item, selecting Properties, and then clicking the File Extensions tab.

CREATING APPLICATION CATEGORIES

In many network environments, the list of supported applications can include hundreds of items. For users who are looking for only one specific program, searching through a list of all of these programs can be difficult and time-consuming.

Fortunately, methods for categorizing the applications are available on your network. You can easily manage the application categories for users and computers by right-clicking the Software Installation item, selecting Properties, and then clicking the Categories tab.

Figure 11.4 shows you the categories tab of the Software Installation package. When creating categories, it is a good idea to use category names that are meaningful to users because it will make it easier for them to find the programs they're seeking.

Once the software installation categories have been created, you can view them by clicking the Programs or Programs And Features icon in Control Panel. When you click Add New Programs, you'll see that several options appear in the Category drop-down list. Now when you select the properties for a package, you will be able to assign the application to one or more of the categories.

Removing Programs

As discussed in the beginning of the chapter, an important phase in the software management life cycle is the removal of applications. Fortunately, if you use the GPMC and the Windows Installer packages, the process is simple. To remove an application, you can right-click the package within the Group Policy settings and select All Tasks ➢ Remove. This brings up a removal text box (see Figure 11.5).

FIGURE 11.4
The Categories tab of
the Software Installation
Properties dialog box

FIGURE 11.5
Removing a software
package

When choosing to remove a software package from a GPO, you have two options,
shown here:

Immediately Uninstall The Software From Users And Computers   System administrators
can choose this option to ensure that an application is no longer available to users who are
affected by the GPO. When this option is selected, the program will be uninstalled

automatically from users and/or computers that have the package. This option might be useful, for example, if the license for a certain application has expired or if a program is no longer on the approved applications list.

Allow Users To Continue To Use The Software, But Prevent New Installations This option prevents users from making new installations of a package, but it does not remove the software if it has already been installed for users. This is a good option if the company has run out of additional licenses for the software but the existing licenses are still valid.

If you no longer require the ability to install or repair an application, you can delete it from your software distribution share point by deleting the appropriate Windows Installer package files. This will free up additional disk space for newer applications.

Microsoft Windows Installer Settings

Several options influence the behavior of the Windows Installer; you can set them within a GPO. You can access these options by navigating to User Configuration ➤ Administrative Templates ➤ Windows Components ➤ Windows Installer.

The options are as follows:

Always Install With Elevated Privileges This policy allows users to install applications that require elevated privileges. For example, if a user does not have the permissions necessary to modify the Registry but the installation program must make Registry changes, this policy will allow the process to succeed.

Prevent Removable Media Source For Any Install This option disallows the installation of software using removable media (such as a CD-ROM or DVD-ROM). It is useful for ensuring that users install only approved applications.

Prohibit Rollback When this option is enabled, the Windows Installer does not store the system state information that is required to roll back the installation of an application. System administrators may choose this option to reduce the amount of temporary disk space required during installation and to increase the performance of the installation operation. However, the drawback is that the system cannot roll back to its original state if the installation fails and the application needs to be removed.

Specify The Order In Which Windows Installer Searches This setting specifies the order in which the Windows Installer will search for installation files. The options include n (for network shares), m (for searching removal media), and u (for searching the Internet for installation files).

With these options, system administrators can control how the Windows Installer operates for specific users who are affected by the GPO.

Troubleshooting Group Policies

Because of the wide variety of configurations that are possible when you are establishing GPOs, you should be aware of some common troubleshooting methods. These methods will help isolate problems in policy settings or GPO links.

One possible problem with GPO configuration is that logons and system startups may take a long time. This occurs especially in large environments when the Group Policy settings must be transmitted over the network and, in many cases, slow WAN links. In general, the number of GPOs should be limited because of the processing overhead and network requirements during logon. By default, GPOs are processed in a synchronous manner. This means that the processing of one GPO must be completed before another one is applied (as opposed to asynchronous processing, where they can all execute at the same time).

When a group policy gets processed on a Windows-based operating system, client-side extensions are the mechanisms that interpret the stored policy and then make the appropriate changes to the operating system environment. When an administrator is troubleshooting a given extension's application of policy, the administrator can view the configuration parameters for that extension in the operating system's Registry. To view the extension in the Registry, you would view the following key:

```
HKEY_LOCAL_MACHINE\Software\Microsoft\Windows \CurrentVersion\Group Policy
```

The most common issue associated with Group Policy is the unexpected setting of Group Policy options. In Windows Server 2000, administrators spent countless hours analyzing inheritance hierarchy and individual settings to determine why a particular user or computer was having policy problems. For instance, say a user named wpanek complains that the Run option is missing from his Start menu. The wpanek user account is stored in the New Hampshire OU, and you've applied group policies at the OU, domain, and site levels. To determine the source of the problem, you would have to sift through each GPO manually to find the Start menu policy as well as to figure out the applicable inheritance settings.

Windows Server 2022 has a handy feature called *Resultant Set of Policy (RSoP)* that displays the exact settings that actually apply to individual users, computers, OUs, domains, and sites after inheritance and filtering have taken effect. In the example just described, you could run RSoP on the wpanek account and view a single set of Group Policy settings that represent the settings that apply to that account. In addition, each setting's Properties dialog box displays the GPO from which the setting is derived as well as the order of priority, the filter status, and other useful information, as you will see a bit later.

RSoP actually runs in two modes:

Logging Mode   *Logging mode* displays the actual settings that apply to users and computers, as shown in the example in the preceding paragraph.

Planning Mode   *Planning mode* can be applied to users, computers, OUs, domains, and sites, and you use it before you apply any settings. As its name implies, planning mode is used to plan GPOs.

Additionally, you can run the command-line utility gpresult.exe to get a quick snapshot of the Group Policy settings that apply to a user and/or computer. Let's take a closer look at the two modes and the gpresult.exe command.

RSoP in Logging Mode

RSoP in logging mode can query policy settings only for users and computers. The easiest way to access RSoP in logging mode is through the Active Directory Users and Computers tool, although you can run it as a stand-alone MMC snap-in if you want.

To analyze the policy settings for wpanek from the earlier example, you would right-click the user icon in Active Directory Users and Computers and select All Tasks ➤ Resultant Set of Policy (Logging). The Group Policy Results Wizard appears. The wizard walks you through the steps necessary to view the RSoP for wpanek.

The Computer Selection page, shown in Figure 11.6, requires you to select a computer for which to display settings. Remember that a GPO contains both user and computer settings, so you must choose a computer to which the user is logged on in order to continue with the wizard. If the user has never logged on to a computer, then you must run RSoP in planning mode because there is no logged policy information yet for that user.

FIGURE 11.6
The Computer Selection page of the Group Policy Results Wizard

The User Selection page, shown in Figure 11.7, requires you to select a user account to analyze. Because I selected a user from the Active Directory Users and Computers tool, the username is filled in automatically. This page is most useful if you are running RSoP in MMC mode and don't have the luxury of selecting a user contextually.

The Summary Of Selections page, shown in Figure 11.8, summarizes your choices and provides an option for gathering extended error information. If you need to make any changes before you begin to analyze the policy settings, you should click the Back button on the Summary screen. Otherwise, click Next.

After the wizard completes, you will see the window shown in Figure 11.9. This window displays only the policy settings that apply to the user and computer that you selected in the wizard. You can see these users and computers at the topmost level of the tree.

Any warnings or errors appear as a yellow triangle or red X over the applicable icon at the level where the warning or error occurred. To view more information about the warning or error, right-click the icon and select Properties.

FIGURE 11.9
The User Selection page
for the administrator on
computer WinSRV2016

You cannot make changes to any of the individual settings because RSoP is a diagnostic tool and not an editor, but you can get more information about settings by clicking a setting and selecting Properties from the context menu.

The Details tab of the user's Properties window, shown in Figure 11.10, displays the actual setting that applies to the user in question based on GPO inheritance.

FIGURE 11.10
The Details tab of the
object's Properties
window

RSoP in Planning Mode

Running RSoP in planning mode isn't much different from running RSoP in logging mode, but the RSoP Wizard asks for a bit more information than you saw earlier.

In the former example, wpanek couldn't see the Run option in the Start menu because his user account is affected by the New Hampshire GPO in the San Jose OU. As an administrator, you could plan to move his user account to the North America OU. Before doing so, you could verify his new policy settings by running RSoP in planning mode. Run the RSoP on the user wpanek under the scenario that you've already moved him from the San Jose OU to the North America OU. At this point, you haven't actually moved the user, but you can see what his settings would be if you did.

Using the *gpresult.exe* Command

The command-line utility gpresult.exe is included as part of the RSoP tool. Running the command by itself without any switches returns the following Group Policy information about the local user and computer:

◆ The name of the domain controller from which the local machine retrieved the policy information

◆ The date and time at which the policies were applied

◆ Which policies were applied

◆ Which policies were filtered out

◆ Group membership

You can use the switches shown in Table 11.1 to get information for remote users and computers and to enable other options.

NOTE   Table 11.1 is not a complete list. To see a complete list of the gpresult.exe command, visit Microsoft at www.microsoft.com.

TABLE 11.1:   gpresult switches

SWITCH	DESCRIPTION
/S *systemname*	Generates RSoP information for a remote computer name.
/USER *username*	Generates RSoP information for a remote username.
/x /h filename	Generates a report in either XML (/x) or HTML (/h) format. The filename and location is specified by the *filename* parameter.
/V	Specifies verbose mode, which displays more verbose information such as user rights information.
/Z	Specifies an even greater level of verbose information.

SWITCH	DESCRIPTION
/SCOPE MACHINE	Displays maximum information about the computer policies applied to this system.
/SCOPE USER	Displays maximum information about the user policies applied to this system.
>*textfile.txt*	Writes the output to a text file.

For example, to obtain information about user wpanek in a system called WILLPANEK, you would use the command gpresult/S WILLPANEK/USERwpanek.

Through the use of these techniques, you should be able to track down even the most elusive Group Policy problems. Remember, however, that good troubleshooting skills do not replace planning adequately and maintaining GPO settings!

Using the Group Policy Infrastructure Status Dashboard

In Windows Server 2022, the Group Policy Management MMC also allows you to see the Active Directory Domain Services Infrastructure status. To see the Group Policy Infrastructure Status Dashboard, open the Group Policy Management Console. Click on a GPO and then click the Status Tab. You would then click the Detect Now button to see the Infrastructure Dashboard (see Figure 11.11).

FIGURE 11.11
The Infrastructure Dashboard

The Bottom Line

Know how to use the Resultant Set of Policy (RSoP) tool to troubleshoot and plan Group Policy.   Windows Server 2022 includes the RSoP feature, which you can run in logging mode (Group Policy Results) or planning mode (Group Policy Modeling) to determine exactly which set of policies applies to users, computers, OUs, domains, and sites.

Master It You are the administrator of a large network. One user is complaining because they are not getting the company desktop. They are receiving a desktop with a dark black background. You need to figure out why this user is getting this background from a GPO.

Understand the difference between publishing and assigning applications. Some applications can be assigned to users and computers so that they are always available. Applications can be published to users so that the user may install the application with a minimal amount of effort when it is required.

Master It You are the administrator of a company that uses Azure and an onsite network. Most software gets deployed through the cloud. You have an application that needs to be installed to all onsite users through the domain.

Chapter 12

Understanding Cloud Concepts

So far, I have explained how to set up and build a Windows Server on an onsite domain. Now it's time for us to look at how to integrate your on-site domain to the cloud.

Before we actually connect the network to the cloud, it's important to understand how the cloud works and the different types of cloud setups that you can choose from.

In this chapter, I will explain the different types of cloud setups and the terminology that you will need to understand so that we can build our cloud network.

IN THIS CHAPTER YOU'LL LEARN

- ◆ Know how the cloud can help your network during high peak usage
- ◆ Understand the difference types of clouds

Understand Cloud Concepts

The cloud is one of the fastest growing areas of IT over the past few years. I want to make sure that you first understand what the cloud is. There is actually no such thing as the cloud; using the cloud means that you are loading your data or network on someone else's network.

This doesn't mean that the cloud is not a good thing. For many companies, the cloud allows them to use network components that they could never use in the past.

Cloud Advantages

The cloud can offer companies of any size a lot of benefits. Let's take a look at some of the benefits of the cloud.

High Availability (HA)   The capability of an application to remain running in a healthy state, without any substantial downtime, is known as HA. When an application is in a healthy state, it is responsive by allowing users to connect and interact with it.

Scalability   The increase or decrease of a services or resources at any particular time, regardless of the demand, is called scalability. Vertical scaling is adding additional resources to an existing server. This is also known as "scaling up."

Elasticity   This is a cloud service that automatically scales resources as needed. It is the ability to automatically increase or decrease computer processing, memory, and storage resources to meet the current demand. It is usually measured by system monitoring tools.

With cloud elasticity, a business can avoid for paying for resources that aren't being used and they don't have to worry about purchasing new equipment or maintaining current systems.

Cloud Agility   It is having the capability to quickly change your infrastructure that gives you the ability to adapt to changing business requirements. Cloud agility is all about giving corporations the ability to develop, test, and launch applications as needed and to do it quickly.

Fault Tolerance   Fault tolerance is a way to make sure that you are not too badly impacted if or when something unexpected happens. The cloud services architecture has redundancy built right in. With fault tolerance, if one component should fail, then another backup component will step up to the plate and take over.

Disaster Recovery   This is a blend of strategies and services that will back up data, applications and other resources to a public cloud or dedicated service providers. If or when a disaster occurs, the affected source can be restored and you can resume normal operations. Disaster recovery means that the cloud infrastructure can replicate application resources in an unaffected region so that the data is safe and the application availability isn't compromised.

Understanding CapEx vs. OpEx

When deciding if the cloud is a good fit for your company, you need to think about money. Obviously, money makes the IT world go around. When looking at building a network, you need to look at the money it would cost for you to build an on-site network or is it beneficial to use the cloud.

To make this decision, you must consider the cost of buying, building, and maintaining an on-site network versus using an online network. When making these decisions, you must understand the difference Capital Expenditures and Operational Expenditures.

CAPITAL EXPENDITURES (CapEx)

Capital Expenditures (CapEx) – is when a company spends money on their physical assets up front. This cost, over the life of the equipment, will depreciate. For example, if you pay in advance to acquire, upgrade, and/or support physical assets, then you can deduct these expenses from your tax bill. Some items that are considered CapEx include server costs, storage costs, network costs, backup and archive costs, Organization Continuity and Disaster Recovery Costs, Datacenter infrastructure costs, and technical personnel.

Server Costs

Server costs include the cost of supporting your servers as well as any hardware needed to support them. It's important to remember that when buying servers, you will want to incorporate fault tolerance and redundancy. These can include adding redundant and uninterruptible power supplies and server clustering, to name a few. If a server needs to be added or replaced, this becomes an upfront cost, which can affect the corporate cash flow.

Storage Costs

Storage costs include the costs that are associated with all storage hardware components and the support of those components. Depending on the level of redundancy and fault tolerance used, this can get costly. If you are part of a larger organization, you may want to create storage tiers where your most key applications utilize the fault tolerant storage devices while the lower priority data can utilize a storage device that is less expensive.

Network Costs

Networking costs include all of your on-site hardware components. These costs can include the routers, switches, access points, any cables, the wide area network (WAN), Internet connections, and more.

Backup and Archive Costs

Backup and archive costs are the costs associated with backing up your data. This also includes copying and archiving data. There may be upfront costs associated, such as the cost of purchasing hardware or backup tapes.

Organization Continuity and Disaster Recovery Costs

Organization continuity and disaster recovery costs are the costs associated on how you plan to recover from a disaster to make sure you can continue working without interruptions. This can include the creation of a disaster recovery site or the purchase of backup generators.

Datacenter Infrastructure Costs

Datacenter infrastructure costs are any costs associated with building and construction equipment. These costs may incur operational expenses. Some expenses can include, building maintenance; heating, ventilation, and air conditioning (HVAC), electricity, etc.

Technical Personnel

While not typically a capital expenditure, you need to take into account the costs associated with the personnel that are needed to maintain your on-premise datacenters as well as at the disaster recovery site.

OPERATIONAL EXPENDITURES (OpEx)

Operational Expenditures (OpEx) – are the costs of products and services that are being utilized at this moment. These expenses can be deducted from your tax bill within the same year. You are paying as you go. Some items that are considered OpEx include leasing software and customized features, scaling charges based on usage and demand, and billing at the user or organization level.

Leasing Software and Customized Features

Leasing software and customized features are considered a pay-per-use model. To ensure that your users do not misappropriate services or to ensure that provisioned accounts are being used properly, this requires that you actively manage your subscriptions. Billing will start as soon as you start utilizing those resources. If it's not used you will want to de-provision the resource in order to decrease costs.

Scaling Charges Based on Usage and Demand

Scaling charges are based on usage and demand. They can be billed in a number of different ways. Billing can be based on the number of users or the CPU usage times. They can also be based on the I/O operations per second (IOPS), allotted RAM, or the amount of storage used.

Billing at the User or Organization Level

Billing at the user or organizational level can be based on the pay-per-use model, this is also called your subscription. The subscription is the billing method. You will be billed for the services used. This is typically a recurring expense. You can scale your resources to meet your corporate needs.

Understanding Different Cloud Concepts

Many IT people don't know that when we are talking about the cloud, there are different types of cloud options. You need to understand the different types of cloud environments so that you can choose the best option for your organization.

PUBLIC CLOUD

Microsoft describes the public cloud as, "Computing services offered by third-party providers over the public Internet, making them available to anyone who wants to use or purchase them. They may be free or sold on-demand, allowing customers to pay only per usage for the CPU cycles, storage, or bandwidth they consume.". Public clouds are the most common way to deploy cloud resources. An example of a public cloud is Microsoft Azure. Public clouds can save you from the costs associated with having to buy, manage, and maintain on-site hardware and application resources. Public clouds have the following advantages:

High Reliability   To ensure against failures, there is a wide array of servers available.

Lower Costs   There is no need to purchase any hardware or software. You only have to pay for the services you use.

Near-unlimited scalability   To meet your corporate needs, on-demand resources are available.

No Maintenance   You will have no associated maintenance costs. Your service provider handles all the maintenance needed.

PRIVATE CLOUD

Microsoft describes the private cloud as, "computing services offered either over the Internet or a private internal network and only to select users instead of the general public.". A private cloud can also be called an internal or corporate cloud. A private cloud can either be located physically at your company's on-site datacenter, or it can be hosted by a third-party service provider.

Cloud services can be delivered in a private cloud in two models. One of these models is known as infrastructure as a service (IaaS). IaaS allows you to use infrastructure resources such as compute, network, and storage as a service. The other is platform as a service (PaaS), this let you deliver a wide array of applications. Private clouds can also be merged with public clouds to create what is known as a hybrid cloud. Private clouds have the following advantages:

Flexibility   You can customize the cloud environment to meet your corporate requirements.

High Scalability   Private clouds offer scalability and efficiency.

Improved Security   Since resources are not shared with others, private clouds provide a higher level of control and security.

HYBRID-BASED NETWORKS

A hybrid cloud combines both a private cloud with a public cloud. Having a hybrid cloud allows data and applications to be shared among them. This ability provides additional deployment options and more flexibility. Hybrid clouds have the following advantages:

Cost Effective   Hybrid clouds are on a pay-as-you-go model. You are renting the hardware and paying for the resources that you have used.

Current   The cloud providers maintain all the computer hardware and software.

Elasticity   Depending on demand or workload, you can add or remove resources automatically to meet your needs. You may notice that there are times when you utilize more resources, this will allow you to shift those resources depending on the demand.

Global   The cloud providers have datacenters located all over the world to implement performance, redundancy and compliance requirements.

Low Latency   Low latency is the capability of a computing system or network to provide responses with the least delay. A cloud service that assists users to quickly access an Internet Azure resource provides for faster and more reliable access.

Reliable   The cloud providers provide the backup, disaster recovery, and replication services.

Scalable   Depending on demand or workload, you can increase or decrease the resources and services used.

Secure   The cloud providers provide better security by implementing a broad set of policies, technologies, controls, and expert technical skills.

Understanding the Difference between IaaS, PaaS, and SaaS

Organizational networks are more than just building the physical network and adding servers. Networks are composed of many different components. Let's take a look at some of the different components and how you can use the cloud to use and support these different components.

Infrastructure as a Service

Infrastructure as a service (IaaS) is a cloud computing service that provides on-demand compute, storage, and networking resources on a pay-as-you-go basis over the Internet.

By utilizing an IaaS solution will help you reduce maintenance of your onsite datacenters and can help with the expense of hardware costs. It also allows you the flexibility to scale your resources depending on demand. You only pay for what you use.

IaaS ADVANTAGES

Using an IaaS comes with the following advantages:

Cost Reduction   An IaaS can eliminate capital expenses and reduce ongoing costs because you avoid the upfront expenses of setting up and managing an onsite datacenter.

Enhanced Security   With the appropriate SLA in place, your cloud service provider can provide better security for your applications and data than if you were to maintain them onsite.

Faster Access to New Apps   An IaaS can help you to innovate and get new apps to the users faster. Once you've launched a new product, the necessary computing infrastructure can be ready in a few minutes or hours rather than in days or weeks. This allows you to deliver your apps much faster.

Improved Business Continuity and Disaster Recovery   With the appropriate service level agreement (SLA) in place, IaaS can help reduce the cost of achieving high availability, business continuity, and disaster recovery.

Increased Scale and Performance of IT Workloads   IaaS allows you to scale globally and will adjust to changes in resource demand.

Increased Stability, Reliability, and Supportability   With IaaS, since the provider maintains all the hardware and software, there is no need for you to maintain and upgrade hardware or to troubleshoot any equipment issues. IaaS frees up your team to allow them to focus on your business rather than on IT infrastructure issues.

Reduced Capital Expenditures and Optimized Costs   IaaS gets rid of the costs associated with managing and configuring an onsite datacenter. When migrating to the cloud, this makes it extremely cost effective. IaaS providers use the pay-as-you-go subscription model.

Platform as a Service

According to Microsoft, "platform as a service (PaaS) is a complete development and deployment environment in the cloud, with resources that enable you to deliver everything from simple cloud-based apps to sophisticated, cloud-enabled enterprise applications."

You can purchase the required resources from a cloud service provider on a pay-as-you-go basis and then access those resources via a secure Internet connection.

PaaS includes infrastructure such as, servers, storage, and networking. It also consists of the middleware, development tools, business intelligence (BI) services, database management systems, and more.

PaaS allows you to avoid the costs of buying and managing software licenses. Basically, you manage the applications and services that they developed, and the cloud service provider manages all other aspects.

PaaS Advantages

PaaS has the following advantages:

Increased Development Capabilities   PaaS can provide your development team with new capabilities without the need to hire new staff.

Cut Coding Time   PaaS has development tools that can reduce the time it takes to code new applications by using pre-coded application components that are built into the platform. These include workflow, directory services, security features, search, and more.

Easy Development for Multiple Platforms   Service providers can offer you development options for multiple platforms. These can include computers, mobile devices, and browsers to make cross-platform applications easier to develop.

Efficient Management of the Application Life Cycle   PaaS provides all of the capabilities needed to support the complete web application life cycle. The life cycle includes building, testing, deploying, managing, and updating within the same integrated environment.

Support for Geographically Distributed Development Teams   Since the development environment is accessed over the Internet, it makes it easier for development teams to work together on projects, even when in remote locations.

Affordable Use of Sophisticated Tools   Since PaaS is a pay-as-you-go model, it makes it possible to use advanced development software and business intelligence (BI) tools as well as analytics tools that you typically could not afford to purchase.

Software as a Service

Over the Internet, software as a service (SaaS) allows users to connect to and use cloud-based applications. SaaS provides a software solution that is purchased on a pay-as-you-go basis from a cloud service provider. Basically, you are renting the use of an application and users connect to it over the Internet. Common examples are email, calendaring, and office tools (such as Microsoft Office 365).

All of the core infrastructure, middleware, application software, and application data are located in the service provider's datacenter. The service provider maintains all the hardware and software.

SaaS allows a company to get up and running quickly with little upfront costs. When employing a SaaS solution, you will be responsible for configuring it. Everything else is managed by the cloud provider.

SaaS Advantages

SaaS has the following advantages:

Access to App Data from Anywhere   Since the data is stored in the cloud, your users can access the information from any Internet-connected computer or mobile device. Since the application data is stored in the cloud, there will be no data lost if a user's computer or device fails.

Access to Sophisticated Applications   To provide SaaS applications to users, there is no need to purchase, install, update, or maintain any hardware, middleware, or software.

Easy Mobilization of Your Workforce   Users can access SaaS applications and data from any Internet-connected computer or mobile device. There is also no need to hire additional staff to maintain the applications.

Payment for Only What You Use   You will save money since the SaaS service will automatically scale up and down depending on your usage levels.

Free Client Software   Users can run most SaaS applications using their web browser without the need to download or install any software.

Compare and Contrast the Service Types

Table 12.1 shows you all of the different components and how IaaS, PaaS, and SaaS can be used in the cloud. Table 12.1 also shows the benefits of each of these components when deciding to use the cloud.

TABLE 12.1:   IaaS, PaaS, and SaaS Benefits and Features

FEATURE	IAAS	PAAS	SAAS
Upfront Costs	No upfront costs. Pay only for what is consumed.	No upfront costs. Pay only for what is consumed.	No upfront costs. Users pay for a subscription, usually on a monthly or annual basis.
User Ownership	User is responsible for the purchase, installation, configuration and management of their own software, operating systems, middleware, and applications.	User is responsible for the development of their own applications. But, they are not responsible for managing the server or infrastructure.	Users just use the application software. Users are not responsible for the maintenance or management of that software.
Cloud Provider Ownership	The cloud provider is responsible for making sure that the cloud infrastructure is available for the users. This includes the virtual machines, storage, and networking.	The cloud provider is responsible for the operating system management, network, and service configurations. Cloud providers deliver a complete managed platform on which to run the application.	The cloud provider is responsible for the provision, management, and maintenance of the application software.

The Bottom Line

Know how the cloud can help your network during high peak usage.   Microsoft Azure has many benefits that can help a company of any size. Understanding the different benefits can help you decide if moving to the cloud can be beneficial to your organization.

> **Master It**   You are the administrator of a large network. You have a financial application in Azure. You notice that every Thursday when the Finance department runs payroll reports, the usage of the financial server increases. What Azure component can help you with this issue?

Understand the different types of clouds.   Understanding the different types of clouds are important so that you can choose the right option for your organization. Knowing the differences between a Public cloud, Private cloud, and Hybrid cloud can help you decide which option is best for your network.

> **Master It**   You are the administrator of a large company that already has an on-site network. You are considering moving some of your server components to the cloud. You do not want to completely remove your on-site network.

Chapter 13

Configuring Azure

Now that you have seen the basics of using the cloud, it's time for us to start looking at Azure. In this chapter, I will show you some of the benefits of using Azure.

I will also show you how to configure the Azure dashboard and also how to customize that dashboard to make Azure an easier environment for you to move around and use.

Finally, you'll learn how to configure some basic Azure dashboard settings, including things like the administrator email and notifications.

IN THIS CHAPTER YOU'LL LEARN

◆ Understand the benefits of using Azure.

◆ Configure the Azure portal.

Understanding Azure Benefits

Before you decide to use Azure in your organization, you must determine if it's a good choice for your environment. Azure is a consumption-based model. This means that the more services you use in Azure, the more it will cost your organization.

This can be a benefit for your organization. You only pay for what you use. So, your organization can move the entire network to the cloud or only move certain components to help save money.

It's important that you understand the benefits and services you get from using Azure. That's where we will begin. Let's take a look at some of the Azure benefits.

Azure Benefits

Microsoft Azure offers an organization many benefits. Choosing the options that are right for your organization will depend on your organization's budget and circumstances. Microsoft Azure can offer your organization many advantages, but we will look at just some of the main ones.

APPLICATION DEVELOPMENT SPEED

When people think of the cloud and speed, they may think about how much lag they may encounter or how quickly they can access their information.

When Microsoft speaks of speed in the context of Azure, they are referring to how well Azure performs. Azure allows your teams to quickly produce, test, and deploy applications. Azure allows you to upgrade service plans or add new features quickly. You can rapidly recover data and utilize artificial intelligence (AI) and machine learning (ML) to process vast amounts of data, to analyze that data, and receive recommendations.

Microsoft Azure provides automated solutions to quickly speed up development of applications and also provides real-time solutions. Azure also provides templates and pre-built tools to build applications in minimal time. You don't have to create applications from scratch.

ENHANCED FLEXIBILITY

Another benefit of Microsoft Azure is enhanced flexibility. Azure has three features with enhanced flexibility: flexible service levels, flexible storage locations, and flexible coding language.

Flexible Service Levels Microsoft Azure provides flexible scalability services to its cloud storage so users can safely and easily access it. Companies only pay for what they use, so it makes it easier to change tiers to maximize your budget.

Flexible Storage Locations Microsoft has over 40 datacenters around the world for you to utilize. This allows you to back up your data in more than one location.

Flexible Coding Languages Azure utilizes many familiar coding tools, such as ASP, .NET, Visual Studio, Visual Basic, C, and C++. This allows you to develop applications in a language you are comfortable with.

INTEGRATED DELIVERY PIPELINE

Azure has a broad integrated delivery pipeline. This ranges from the development of an application to its deployment. It is an end-to-end solution. Azure ensures flexibility because all the tools are embedded in the same environment.

DISASTER RECOVERY

Azure covers all aspects of disaster recovery to quickly resolve issues, including backups and virtual systems testing.

Azure can help shield critical data and applications by offering an end-to-end backup and disaster recovery solution that can be integrated with your on-premises backup solutions.

Backups Azure provides a backup solution that can be used by enabling the data recovery option. You will be provided with the option to use Azure Backup either on-premises or on the cloud. You no longer need to have your own servers to keep your data safe, and accessing backups on the cloud takes much less time than using traditional methods of tapes and onsite servers.

Virtual Systems Testing Azure provides testing capabilities that allow you to test your application before launching it. You can run dev-test copies without disturbing users. This allows you to test new versions of applications using your existing live data to allow for a smooth transition. Azure provides a wide range of connections to increase the performance and usage by utilizing environments such as virtual private networks, delivery nodes, clear caches, and express route networks.

SECURITY

Security is extremely important. Azure can help safeguard your backup environment by using built-in security tools for hybrid and cloud environments and Azure also provides compliance using wide-range security and privacy regulations. Azure helps aid with security by using a single sign-on feature. This ability can be utilized by all users.

Microsoft utilizes a multitude of compliance certificates, including FERPA, GDPR, HIPAA, and IRS. You can also protect your data by using multifactor authentication, strict password requirements, and training.

Azure will send out notifications when you need to upgrade or enable a new protection feature. One feature included with Azure is the Key Vault feature. This feature will safeguard cryptographic keys and other secrets that are used by cloud applications and services.

With Microsoft's Defender for Cloud (previously called Azure Security Center) you can assess the security posture of your cloud resources and threat protection. You can even assess your security standings which will give you a secure score that rates you on your actions and provide tips to make your environment more secure.

Defender for Cloud fills three vital requirements when managing the security of your resources either in the cloud and on-premises:

◆ Continuous assessment: Allows you to understand your current security posture by providing a secure score. This score tells you your current security situation. The higher the score, the lower the risk level.

◆ Defend: Detects and resolves threats to your resources and services. This will provide security alerts. Defender for Cloud will detect threats to your resources and workloads. These alerts will appear in the Azure portal or can be emailed.

◆ Secure: Hardens all connected resources and services. This will offer security recommendations to improve your posture.

Understanding the Azure Dashboards

Microsoft Azure can support a number of dashboards in the Azure portal. Each dashboard will include tiles showing data from different Azure resources across different resource groups and subscriptions. You can also create different dashboards for different teams or clone an existing one.

In the Azure portal, dashboards provide a focused and organized view of your cloud resources. You can use dashboards as a workspace where you can monitor resources and launch tasks. The Azure portal provides a default dashboard as a starting point.

Using the Azure Dashboard

Dashboards provide a focused view of the resources in your subscription. When you first utilize Azure, you will be provided with a default dashboard. This dashboard can be customized to allow you to view only those resources that are most important to you. Changes that you make to the default view will affect your experience only. You can create other dashboards for your own use or publish customized dashboards to be shared with other users within your organization.

Each user can create up to 100 private dashboards. If you publish and share the dashboard, it will be implemented as an Azure resource in your subscription and will not count towards this limit.

Exercise 13.1 will show you how to create a new private dashboard using an assigned name. All dashboards are private when they are created; however, you can choose to publish and share the dashboard with other users.

EXERCISE 13.1   Create a New Dashboard:

1. Sign in to the Azure portal - `https://portal.azure.com`.

2. From the Azure portal menu, select Dashboard (see Figure 13.1). The default view may be already set.

FIGURE 13.1
Azure Dashboard

3. Select New Dashboard, then select Blank Dashboard (see Figure 13.2). This will open up the Tile Gallery. This is where you can select tiles and arrange those tiles onto an empty grid to design it how you'd like.

FIGURE 13.2
New Azure Dashboard

4. Select the My Dashboard text (see Figure 13.3) in the dashboard label and enter a name to identify the custom dashboard.

FIGURE 13.3
Naming New Azure
Dashboard

5. To save the dashboard as is, on the page header, select Done Customizing.

The dashboard view will now show your new dashboard. Select the arrow next to the dashboard name to see your available dashboards. The list might include dashboards that other users have created and shared.

Next, you can edit a dashboard. This will give you the ability to add, resize, and arrange the tiles to suit your needs. Exercise 13.2 will show you how to add tiles to a dashboard from the Tile Gallery.

EXERCISE 13.2 Add Tiles from the Tile Gallery:

1. Select Edit from the dashboard's page header (see Figure 13.4).

FIGURE 13.4
Edit Dashboard

2. Browse the Tile Gallery to find a certain tile or you can use the search field. Then, select the tile you want to be added to your dashboard.

FIGURE 13.5
Tile Gallery

Tile Gallery ✕

Drag and drop or select tile and click "Add". You can add other parts of the portal to the dashboard by pinning. Learn more ⧉

🔍 Filter tiles

All resources
An Azure resource is a manageable item that is available through Azure. Virtual machines, storage accounts,...

Clock
Display the time in the time zone of your choice.

3:46 PM

Markdown
Display custom, static content. For example, you can show basic instructions, an image, or a set of...

3. Select Add to add the tile to the dashboard with a default size and location or you can drag the tile to the grid and place it where you want.

4. If desired, resize or rearrange your tiles.

5. To save your changes, select Save in the page header (see Figure 13.6). You can also choose to preview the changes without saving by selecting the Preview button. This allows you to see how filters affect your tiles. From the preview screen, if you like the changes, you've made you can select Save to keep the changes. If you do not care for the changes, you can press Discard to remove them, or press Edit to go back to the editing options and make further changes.

FIGURE 13.6
Save Tile Gallery

| This dashboard has unsaved changes. | Preview | Save | Discard |

PIN CONTENT FROM A RESOURCE GROUP PAGE

Another way that you can add tiles to your dashboard is by adding them directly from a Resource Group page (see Figure 13.7). Many resource pages have a pin icon on the page header. This means that you can pin the tile to the source page. Here is what the pin looks like:

FIGURE 13.7
Resource Groups Page

Resource groups 📌 ···
Default Directory

If this icon is selected, you can then pin the tile to an existing private or shared dashboard (see Figure 13.8). By selecting Create New, an administrator will be able to create a new dashboard which will include the pin.

FIGURE 13.8
Pin to Dashboard

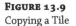

Pin to dashboard   ×

Existing   Create new

Type ⓘ
◉ Private
○ Shared

Dashboard
My Dashboard   ⌄

Copy a Tile to a New Dashboard

Administrators also have the ability to reuse a tile and use it on another dashboard. An administrator can copy it from one dashboard to another. To do this, select the context menu in the upper right corner and then select Copy as shown in Figure 13.9.

FIGURE 13.9
Copying a Tile

···   ✎ Customize

         ◯ Refresh

         ▢ Copy

         🗑 Remove from dashboard

Administrators can then select whether they want to copy the tile to an existing private or shared dashboard or create a copy of the tile within the dashboard you are currently working on. Administrators will also have the ability to create a new dashboard that will include a copy of the tile by selecting Create New.

Exercise 13.3 will show you the steps needed if you want to change the size of a tile or to rearrange the tiles on a dashboard.

EXERCISE 13.3   Resize or Rearrange Tiles

1. Select Edit from the page header.
2. Then, select the context menu in the upper right corner of a tile. The Configure Tile Size window will appear on the right hand side (see Figure 13.10). Tiles that support any size also include a "handle" in the lower right corner that lets you drag the tile to the size you want.

FIGURE 13.10
Configure Tile Size

3. To arrange your dashboard, select a tile and drag it to a new location on the grid.

SET AND OVERRIDE DASHBOARD FILTERS

Near the top of the dashboard, you will see several options where you can set the Auto Refresh and Time settings for the data displayed on the dashboard (see Figure 13.11). There are other options too to add additional filters.

FIGURE 13.11
Auto Refresh and Time
Settings

By default, the data will be refreshed hourly. To change this, select Auto Refresh and choose a new interval to refresh. Once you have made your selection, select Apply. The default time is set to UTC Time, showing the data for the Past 24 hours. To modify this, select the button and choose a new time range, time granularity, and/or time zone, then select Apply.

If you'd like to apply additional filters, then, select Add Filter. The options you see will vary depending on the tiles on your dashboard. Select the filter you'd like to use and the filter will then be applied to your data. If you'd like to remove the filter, select the X in its button.

Tiles that support filtering will have a filter icon in the top left corner as shown in Figure 13.12. If you set filters for a particular tile, the left corner of that tile displays a double filter icon, which indicates that the data has its own applied filters.

FIGURE 13.12
Filter Icon

MODIFY TILE SETTINGS

There may be times when a tile is not configured to show you exactly the information you want. You can configure them to show the required information. You can override the dashboard's default time settings and filters by customizing the tile data.

Data that is displayed on the dashboard shows current activity and based on the global filters that are set for that tile. But some tiles allow you to choose a different time span to display. To do this, follow the steps in Exercise 13.4.

EXERCISE 13.4   Customize the Time Span for a Tile

1. Select Customize tile data from the context menu in the right hand corner (as shown in Figure 13.13) or select the filter icon in the upper left corner of the tile.

   FIGURE 13.13
   Configure Tile Settings

2. Select the Override the Dashboard Time Settings (as shown in Figure 13.14) at the tile level checkbox.

   FIGURE 13.14
   Override the Dashboard
   Time Settings at the
   Tile Level

3. Next, choose the time span you'd like to display for the tile. You can select from the past 30 minutes to the past 30 days. You can also select a custom range.

4. Next, choose the time granularity that you'd like to display. You can select anywhere from one-minute intervals to one-month.

5. When done, select Apply.

CHANGE THE TITLE AND SUBTITLE OF A TILE

You may decide that you want to change the name of a tile, so, some tiles give you that ability. From the context menu, select Configure Tile Settings (as shown in Figure 13.15).

FIGURE 13.15
Configure Tile Settings

After you choose Configure Tile Settings, you can then make any changes that you want to make and then select Apply as shown in Figure 13.16.

FIGURE 13.16
Editing Tile Settings

DELETE A TILE

If you decide that you no longer want to have a tile on your dashboard, you can remove it (as shown in Figure 13.17). There are a couple different ways to remove a tile from the dashboard.

◆ In the upper right corner of the tile, select the context menu. Then choose Remove From Dashboard.

◆ Select the Edit icon to go into the customization mode. Then, hover the cursor over the upper right corner of the tile and then select the Delete icon.

FIGURE 13.17
Remove From
Dashboard Settings

CLONING A DASHBOARD

As an Administrator, you also have the ability to clone a dashboard. This allows an administrator to quickly enable a new dashboard. You are basically using an existing dashboard as a template.

In Exercise 13.5, I will show you the steps needed to clone a dashboard.

EXERCISE 13.5 Cloning a Dashboard

1. Ensure that the dashboard view you are viewing is the dashboard you want to clone.
2. Select the Clone icon in the page header.
3. A copy of the dashboard, which will be named "Clone Of [your dashboard name]," will open in edit mode. Then, continue to configure the dashboard how you'd like, rename it, and apply the changes.

PUBLISH, SHARING, AND DELETING A DASHBOARD

By default, whenever you create a dashboard, it will be private. The administrator who creates the dashboard will be the only person who can view that dashboard unless you publish and share it. If an administrator would like to share their dashboard with other users and allow that user to open it, the administrator needs to share the dashboard.

Exercise 13.6 will show you how to publish and share a dashboard with other administrators or users.

EXERCISE 13.6 Open a Shared Dashboard

1. Next to the dashboard name, you will want to select the arrow.
2. Then, select the dashboard from the list that is displayed. If the dashboard you want to open isn't listed:
   a. Select Browse All Dashboards (see Figure 13.18).

   FIGURE 13.18
   Browse All Dashboards

   b. In the Type field, select Shared Dashboards.
   c. You can then select one or more subscriptions. To filter dashboards by name, just enter text.
   d. Select a dashboard from the list of shared dashboards.

Administrators have the ability to delete a private or shared dashboard. Exercise 13.7 will show you how to delete a dashboard.

EXERCISE 13.7   Deleting a Dashboard

1. Select the dashboard you want to delete from the list.
2. From the page header, select the Delete icon.
3. For a private dashboard, select OK (as shown in Figure 13.19) on the confirmation box. For a shared dashboard, on the confirmation box, select the This Published Dashboard Will No Longer Be Viewable By Others checkbox. Then, select OK.

FIGURE 13.19
Delete the Dashboard

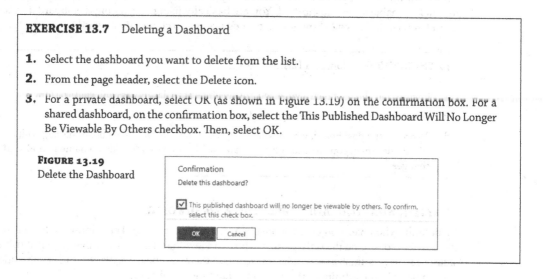

NOTE   Administrators can recover a deleted dashboard within 14 days of the delete as long as you are an Azure Global Administrators and you deleted the published dashboard in the Azure portal.

Configuring the Azure Portal Settings

Azure administrators also have the ability to modify the default settings of the Azure portal. Most of the settings that an administrator can change can be found in the Settings menu (shown as a spoke) which is at the top right side of the global pane header as shown in Figure 13.20.

FIGURE 13.20
Azure Portal Settings

There are several options that an Azure administrator will see. These settings include Directories + subscriptions, Appearance + Startup Views, Language + Region, My Information, and Signing Out + Notifications.

DIRECTORIES + SUBSCRIPTIONS

Azure administrators have the ability to manage their directories and set subscription filters by using the Directories + subscriptions pane. The Startup Directory will show you the default directory that you will see when you are signed into the Azure portal. If you want to choose a different startup directory, then an administrator will want to go to the Appearance + Startup Views page (this will be covered in the next section).

Select All Directories if you want to see a complete list of directories that you have access to. If you want to select a directory as a favorite, then, select the star icon to the left of the name. Any directory that has been marked as a favorite will be listed in the Favorites section.

If you want to switch to a different directory, then, select the directory that you want and then select the Switch button next to it as shown in Figure 13.21.

FIGURE 13.21
Switching Directories

You can also select the subscriptions that are filtered by default when you sign onto the Azure portal using the Directories + subscriptions page. Select Advanced Filters (as shown in Figure 13.22) if you wish to customize filters. You will see a confirmation pop up before continuing. Administrators can then create, modify, or delete subscription filters on the Advanced Filters page (as shown in Figure 13.23).

FIGURE 13.22
Enabling
Advanced Filters

FIGURE 13.23
Advanced
Filters Options

To create a new filter, Azure administrators will want to select the Create a Filter option (shown in Figure 13.24). Administrators can make up to 10 filters, each with a unique name that is between 8 and 50 characters long and contains only letters, numbers, and hyphens.

Once the Azure administrator has named the filter, the administrator will need to enter in at least one condition. In the Filter type field, select either Subscription Name, Subscription ID, or Subscription State and then select an operator and enter a value, as shown in Figure 13.25.

FIGURE 13.25
Operator Value Screen

Azure administrators can also create, modify, and delete filters. To create a filter, select Create. The filter will appear in the Active Filters list. If you want to modify or rename an existing filter, select the pencil icon next to the filter. Make your changes and then select Apply. To delete a filter, select the Delete icon (trash can) next to the filter. You cannot delete the default filter or any filter that is currently being used.

APPEARANCE + STARTUP VIEWS

The Appearance + Startup Views pane has two sections, the Appearance section and the Startup Views section (shown in Figure 13.26). The Appearance section allows an administrator to change menu behavior, the color theme, and if you'd like to use a high-contrast theme. The Startup Views section allows an administrator to set up the options for what you see when you first log into the Azure portal.

FIGURE 13.26
Appearance + Startup
Views Screen

The Menu behavior section allows an Azure administrator to change how the default Azure portal menu acts. Administrators can choose from a flyout or docked position.

◆ Flyout means that the menu will be hidden. To see the menu, you will need to select the menu icon in the upper left-hand corner. You will select this option to both open and close the menu.

◆ Docked means that the menu remains visible. You do have the option to collapse the menu if you'd like.

The theme an administrator selects will affect both the background and font colors when in the Azure portal. Administrators can choose one of the four preset color themes under the Theme section. To select a color theme, just choose the color thumbnail. The High contrast theme section allows you to choose a theme that can make the Azure portal easier to read. This can be helpful if a user has a visual impairment.

The Startup Views section allows an administrator to choose either to see the home page or the dashboard when you log into the Azure portal.

◆ The Home option will display the home page. The home page includes shortcuts to Azure services, recently used resources, and useful links to tools, documentation, and more.

◆ The Dashboard option will display your most recently used dashboard.

Azure administrators can also choose their startup directory views (as shown in Figure 13.27) when you log into the Azure portal. Administrators can either sign in to their last visited directory or they can select a directory.

LANGUAGE + REGION

The Language + Region pane (shown in Figure 13.28) has two sections that an administrator can configure: Language and Regional Format. These settings will affect how data such as currency will be displayed in the Azure portal.

FIGURE 13.27
Startup Views Screen

FIGURE 13.28
Language + Region Pane

To change the Language, the Azure administrator will use the drop-down list to choose from the list of available languages. To change the regional format, use the drop-down list to choose the regional format. When you are done, select Apply.

MY INFORMATION

The My Information pane allows administrators to update information such as their email address (see Figure 13.29). Near the top of the My Information pane, administrators will find options to export, restore, and delete settings.

FIGURE 13.29
My Information pane

Export allows administrators to export user settings, such as private dashboards, user settings such as favorite subscriptions or directories, and themes and other custom settings. To export portal settings, select Export settings. This creates a .json file that contains the user settings data.

To restore default settings, select Restore default settings. Administrators will be asked to confirm the action. Administrators also have the ability to delete user settings and dashboards by selecting Delete all settings and dashboards. Administrators will be asked to confirm this action if it is chosen.

SIGNING OUT + NOTIFICATIONS

The Signing Out + Notifications pane (shown in Figure 13.30) allows an Azure administrator to manage pop-up notifications and session time-outs.

FIGURE 13.30
Signing Out +
Notifications pane

The Signing Out section (shown in Figure 13.31) includes options to protect resources from unauthorized access. After a user has been idle for a given period of time, the user will be automatically signed out of the Azure portal. Azure administrators can change the duration by using the Hours and Minutes boxes and clicking Apply. Just note that an administrator in the Global Administrator role can override the idle time by enforcing a maximum idle time. This inactivity time-out setting will be applied at the directory level.

FIGURE 13.31
Inactive Signing Out
Settings

Notifications are system messages that relate to your current session. If pop-up notifications are turned on, the messages will display briefly in the top corner of the screen. To enable or disable pop-up notifications, select or clear the Enable Pop-Up Notifications check box.

The Bottom Line

Understand the Benefits of using Azure.   Microsoft Azure has many benefits that can help a company of any size. Understanding the different benefits can help you decide if moving to the cloud can be beneficial to your organization.

Master It   You are the administrator of a large network. You need to be able to quickly recover data in the event of data being deleted or in the event of a major disaster. What Azure component can help you with this issue?

Configure the Azure Portal.   Azure administrators also have the ability to modify the default settings of the Azure portal. Most of the settings that an administrator can change can be found in the Settings menu.

Master It   You are the administrator of a large company that has Azure users in multiple countries. You need to configure the language and region for these different users.

## Chapter 14

Understanding Azure Active Directory

In this chapter, it is time for us to start diving into the world of Azure Active Directory. Azure Active Directory is a cloud-based identity and access management service. The Azure environment is controlled by the Azure Resource Manager. It can be controlled by templates, PowerShell, the Azure portal, CLI, Cloud Shell, and APIs. Azure AD controls access to resources using RBAC and Conditional Access.

This is a very important topic because if you set up Azure Active Directory incorrectly, you may stop users from properly accessing the Azure environment, but even more important, you may give access to people that should not have access.

This chapter will introduce you to Azure Active Directory, but many of the topics in this chapter will be covered in greater detail throughout the rest of this book.

IN THIS CHAPTER YOU'LL LEARN

- Understand Azure AD integration.

- Configure Azure passwords.

Azure Active Directory

So now that you understand how to install Active Directory on your onsite network, it's time to see how to configure your Azure Active Directory. One big misconception is that Azure Active Directory is set up and configured the same way that your onsite Active Directory is set up. The advantage of Azure Active Directory is that there is no installation unless you decide to add another instance of Azure AD to your tenant. As soon as you set up your Azure subscription, Azure Active Directory is ready to go.

Understanding Azure AD

So, before we begin setting up your Azure Active Directory, let's take a look at some of the features that Azure Active Directory delivers. The following features are just some of the features available in Azure AD.

Simple Deployment   Administrators can easily set up Azure AD for their Azure AD directory. Managed users include cloud-only user accounts and user accounts synchronized from an on-premises directory.

Azure Devices   Administrators have the ability to easily join computers to the Azure network. Administrators can even set up Azure so that the Windows clients can automatically join to the Azure environment.

Setting Domain Names   Azure Administrators have the ability to create custom domain names (for example, WillPanek.com) that are either verified or unverified with the Azure AD Custom Domain Name Wizard. Administrators can also create domain names using the Microsoft suffix of onmicrosoft.com. If you want, you can create an Azure name of WillPanek.onmicrosoft.com. Administrators have a lot of flexibility when creating Azure names for your organization.

Group Policy Support   Azure Administrators have the ability to create and use built-in GPOs for both the user and computer containers. This gives administrators the ability to enforce company compliances for security policies. Administrators can create custom GPOs that can be assigned to Organizational Units (OUs) and this in turn will help administrators manage and enforce company policies.

For example, you can set a GPO up so that your users will use Folder Redirection. Folder Redirection allows a user to place a file in one folder but it gets redirected to another (this includes OneDrive).

To use a Group Policy to redirect OneDrive, you need the OneDrive sync to be at least build 18.111.0603.0004 or later. You can see the OneDrive build number in the About tab of the OneDrive settings.

NOTE   The Group Policy object for "OneDrive Known Folder Move" won't work if an administrator has already set up a Windows Folder Redirection policy to redirect a user's Documents, Pictures, or Desktop folders to a storage location other than OneDrive. If this has been done, the administrator must first remove the Redirection Group Policy Object that has already been created. The redirection for OneDrive doesn't affect the Music and Videos folders. So an administrator can keep them redirected with the Windows Group Policy object that is already created.

Azure AD Integration   One of the nice advantages of Azure is that Administrators do not need to manage or configure Azure AD replication. Azure user accounts, group membership, or even user hashes are automatically replicated between your onsite Active Directory and Azure AD. Azure AD tenant information is automatically replicated and synchronized to your onsite or Azure AD environments.

DNS Support   Administrators have the ability to set up, configure, and integrate DNS with your Azure network. DNS is a hostname resolution service and Azure allows administrators to easily configure DNS with many of the same DNS administration tools that you are currently familiar with.

High Availability   One of the most important requirements for any IT department is the ability to keep their network up and running. Some organizations require minimum downtime requirements. This means that your organization can only be down for a certain amount of time per year. Azure AD offers an organization the ability to set up high availability for your Azure environment.

This feature guarantees higher service resiliency and uptime. With built-in health monitoring, Azure offers automatic failure recovery by spinning up a new instance to take over for any failed instances. This feature provides automatic and continued services for your organization's Azure network.

Management Tools Support   Administrators have the ability to use the same tools that they are familiar with for managing their current domains. The Active Directory Administrative Center and Active Directory PowerShell utilities can be used when managing their Azure AD.

Azure AD Questions and Answers

The following section is questions and answers about features and functionality of Azure Active Directory. This section was taken directly from Microsoft's website (https://docs.microsoft .com/en-us/azure/active-directory-domain-services/faqs). I would recommend that you visit this page often for updates about features and Services.

Q.   Can I create multiple managed domains for a single Azure AD directory?

Answer: No. You can only create a single managed domain serviced by Azure AD Domain Services for a single Azure AD directory.

Q.   Can I enable Azure AD Domain Services in an Azure Resource Manager virtual network?

Answer: Yes. Azure AD Domain Services can be enabled in an Azure Resource Manager virtual network. Classic Azure virtual networks are no longer supported for creating new managed domains.

Q.   Can I migrate my existing managed domain from a classic virtual network to a Resource Manager virtual network?

Answer: Not currently. Microsoft will deliver a mechanism to migrate your existing managed domain from a classic virtual network to a Resource Manager virtual network in the future.

Q.   Can I enable Azure AD Domain Services in an Azure CSP (Cloud Solution Provider) subscription?

Answer: Yes.

Q.   Can I enable Azure AD Domain Services in a federated Azure AD directory? I do not synchronize password hashes to Azure AD. Can I enable Azure AD Domain Services for this directory?

Answer: No. Azure AD Domain Services needs access to the password hashes of user accounts, to authenticate users via NTLM or Kerberos. In a federated directory, password hashes are not stored in the Azure AD directory. Therefore, Azure AD Domain Services does not work with such Azure AD directories.

Q.   Can I make Azure AD Domain Services available in multiple virtual networks within my subscription?

Answer: The service itself does not directly support this scenario. Your managed domain is available in only one virtual network at a time. However, you may configure connectivity between multiple virtual networks to expose Azure AD Domain Services to other virtual networks.

Q.   Can I enable Azure AD Domain Services using PowerShell?

Answer: Yes.

Q.   Can I enable Azure AD Domain Services using a Resource Manager Template?

Answer: No, it is not currently possible to enable Azure AD Domain Services using a template. Instead use PowerShell.

Q.   Can I add domain controllers to an Azure AD Domain Services managed domain?

Answer: No. The domain provided by Azure AD Domain Services is a managed domain. You do not need to provision, configure, or otherwise manage domain controllers for this domain. These management activities are provided as a service by Microsoft. Therefore, you cannot add additional domain controllers (read-write or read-only) for the managed domain.

Q.   Can guest users invited to my directory use Azure AD Domain Services?

Answer: No. Guest users invited to your Azure AD directory using the Azure AD B2B invite process are synchronized into your Azure AD Domain Services managed domain. However, passwords for these users are not stored in your Azure AD directory.

Q.   Can I connect to the domain controller for my managed domain using Remote Desktop?

Answer: No. You do not have permissions to connect to domain controllers for the managed domain via Remote Desktop. Members of the 'AAD DC Administrators' group can administer the managed domain using AD administration tools such as the Active Directory Administration Center (ADAC) or AD PowerShell. These tools are installed using the 'Remote Server Administration Tools' feature on a Windows server joined to the managed domain.

Q.   I've enabled Azure AD Domain Services. What user account do I use to domain join machines to this domain?

Answer: Members of the administrative group 'AAD DC Administrators' can domain-join machines. Additionally, members of this group are granted remote desktop access to machines that have been joined to the domain.

Q.   Do I have domain administrator privileges for the managed domain provided by Azure AD Domain Services?

Answer: No. You are not granted administrative privileges on the managed domain. Both 'Domain Administrator' and 'Enterprise Administrator' privileges are not available for you to use within the domain. Members of the domain administrator or enterprise administrator groups in your on-premises Active Directory are also not granted domain/enterprise administrator privileges on the managed domain.

Q.   Can I modify group memberships using LDAP or other AD administrative tools on managed domains?

Answer: No. Group memberships cannot be modified on domains serviced by Azure AD Domain Services. The same applies for user attributes. You may however change group memberships or user attributes either in Azure AD or on your on-premises domain. Such changes are automatically synchronized to Azure AD Domain Services.

Q. How long does it take for changes I make to my Azure AD directory to be visible in my managed domain?

Answer: Changes made in your Azure AD directory using either the Azure AD UI or PowerShell are synchronized to your managed domain. This synchronization process runs in the background. Once initial synchronization is complete, it typically takes about 20 minutes for changes made in Azure AD to be reflected in your managed domain.

Q. Can I extend the schema of the managed domain provided by Azure AD Domain Services?

Answer: No. The schema is administered by Microsoft for the managed domain. Schema extensions are not supported by Azure AD Domain Services.

Q. Can I modify or add DNS records in my managed domain?

Answer: Yes. Members of the 'AAD DC Administrators' group are granted 'DNS Administrator' privileges, to modify DNS records in the managed domain. They can use the DNS Manager console on a machine running Windows Server joined to the managed domain, to manage DNS. To use the DNS Manager console, install 'DNS Server Tools', which is part of the 'Remote Server Administration Tools' optional feature on the server. More information on utilities for administering, monitoring and troubleshooting DNS is available on TechNet.

Q. What is the password lifetime policy on a managed domain?

Answer: The default password lifetime on an Azure AD Domain Services managed domain is 90 days. This password lifetime is not synchronized with the password lifetime configured in Azure AD. Therefore, you may have a situation where users' passwords expire in your managed domain, but are still valid in Azure AD. In such scenarios, users need to change their password in Azure AD and the new password will synchronize to your managed domain. Additionally, the 'password-does-not-expire' and 'user-must-change-password-at-next-logon' attributes for user accounts are not synchronized to your managed domain.

Q. Does Azure AD Domain Services provide AD account lockout protection?

Answer: Yes. Five invalid password attempts within 2 minutes on the managed domain cause a user account to be locked out for 30 minutes. After 30 minutes, the user account is automatically unlocked. Invalid password attempts on the managed domain do not lock out the user account in Azure AD. The user account is locked out only within your Azure AD Domain Services managed domain.

Q. Can I failover Azure AD Domain Services to another region for a DR event?

Answer: No. Azure AD Domain Services does not currently provide a geo-redundant deployment model. It is limited to a single virtual network in an Azure region. If you want to utilize multiple Azure regions, you need to run your Active Directory Domain Controllers on Azure IaaS VMs.

Q. Can I get Azure AD Domain Services as part of Enterprise Mobility Suite (EMS)? Do I need Azure AD Premium to use Azure AD Domain Services?

Answer: No. Azure AD Domain Services is a pay-as-you-go Azure service and is not part of EMS. Azure AD Domain Services can be used with all editions of Azure AD (Free, Basic, and, Premium). You are billed on an hourly basis, depending on usage.

MANAGING AZURE AD

So now that we have looked at some of the features of Azure AD along with the common questions and answers about Azure AD, it's time to go through the Azure AD Dashboard. Figure 14.1 shows you the Azure AD Dashboard (you get to the Azure AD dashboard by clicking on Azure AD on the left side menu of the main dashboard). Let's take a look at some of the different options on the left side starting with Overview.

FIGURE 14.1
Viewing Azure AD Dashboard

Overview

The Overview section of the Azure AD Dashboard is the figure you are looking at in Figure 14.1. The first thing you will notice in the center of the screen is the default Azure AD directory and the number of users on Azure.

On the left-hand side, you can add Users, Groups, External Identities, Roles and Administrators, Administrative Units, Enterprise Applications, Devices, App Registrations, Identity Governance, Application Proxy, Licenses, Azure AD Connect, and other Azure AD options.

Users

The Users section (under Manage) on the left side allows you to view all of your current Azure AD user accounts (see Figure 14.2). Under the Users section, an administrator can also create New Users, New Guest Users, Reset Passwords, Delete Users, Multi-Factor Authentication, Refresh your Screen, or set up your Columns.

FIGURE 14.2
Viewing User Section

FIGURE 14.2
Viewing User Section

Another task that can be created in the User's section is the ability to manipulate the user's settings. The User Settings link allows you to setup how the user can launch and view applications, how the user can register applications, and if the user can access the Azure AD administration portal. Administrators can also manage External user and access panel control from the settings section.

The User section also allows administrators to see how often the user is logging into Azure (this allows you to perform an access review) and administrators can also get audit information about the user account. Finally, in the User section, you can also troubleshoot user issues and also open a support ticket with Microsoft for additional help.

Groups

The Groups section allows an administrator to create and manage groups (see Figure 14.3). In the Groups section, you can create new groups, manage group settings for all groups, manage group membership, and delete groups. Administrators can also do auditing on groups along with troubleshooting group issues or opening a support ticket with Microsoft for additional help.

FIGURE 14.3
Viewing Group Section

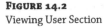

External Identities

The External Identities section allows you to work with user accounts from other organizations. The Organizational Relationship section also allows you to invite users who already own an Azure Active Directory account or a Microsoft Account. If they have one of these account types already setup, they can automatically sign in without any further configuration from an Administrator.

In the Settings section of External Identities (see Figure 14.4), Administrators can setup what guest accounts can do regarding Azure. For example, an Administrator can decide if guest user access is limited or if users can invite other users to use your organization's Azure network. Finally, you can setup Collaboration restrictions (which domains you can invite users from) for your guest user accounts.

FIGURE 14.4
Viewing the Settings
Section of External
Identities

The Lifecycle Management section of External Identities also allows an Administrator to setup Terms of use agreements while also allowing Administrators to have auditing of their guest users. Finally, Administrators can troubleshoot issues or opening a support ticket with Microsoft for additional help.

Roles and Administrators

The Roles and Administrators section (shown in Figure 14.5) allows you to see just some of the available Azure AD roles and what each role does.

FIGURE 14.5
Roles and
Administrators Section

In Table 14.1, I will show you just some of the different roles that are available and what each role does in Azure AD. This table was taken directly from Microsoft's website.

NOTE   **Azure AD Roles**   When you are in the Azure AD Roles and Administrators section, you can click on any of these roles to see who currently has this role in your organization.

TABLE 14.1:   Azure Roles

ROLE	DESCRIPTION
Application Administrator	Can create and manage all aspects of app registrations and enterprise apps.
Application Developer	Can create application registrations independent of the 'Users can register applications' setting.
Attack Payload Author	Can create attack payloads that an administrator can initiate later.
Attack Simulation Administrator	Can create and manage all aspects of attack simulation campaigns.
Authentication Administrator	Can access to view, set, and reset authentication method information for any non-admin user.
Authentication Policy Administrator	Can create and manage the authentication methods policy, tenant-wide MFA settings, password protection policy, and verifiable credentials.
Azure AD Joined Device Local Administrator	Users assigned to this role are added to the local administrators group on Azure AD-joined devices.
Azure DevOps Administrator	Can manage Azure DevOps organization policy and settings.
Azure Information Protection Administrator	Can manage all aspects of the Azure Information Protection product.
B2C IEF Keyset Administrator	Can manage secrets for federation and encryption in the Identity Experience Framework (IEF).
B2C IEF Policy Administrator	Can create and manage trust framework policies in the Identity Experience Framework (IEF).
Billing Administrator	Can perform common billing related tasks like updating payment information.
Cloud App Security Administrator	Can manage all aspects of the Cloud App Security product.
Cloud Application Administrator	Can create and manage all aspects of app registrations and enterprise apps except App Proxy.
Cloud Device Administrator	Limited access to manage devices in Azure AD.

TABLE 14.1: Azure Roles *(CONTINUED)*

ROLE	DESCRIPTION
Compliance Administrator	Can read and manage compliance configuration and reports in Azure AD and Microsoft 365.
Compliance Data Administrator	Creates and manages compliance content.
Conditional Access Administrator	Can manage Conditional Access capabilities.
Customer LockBox Access Approver	Can approve Microsoft support requests to access customer organizational data.
Desktop Analytics Administrator	Can access and manage Desktop management tools and services.
Directory Readers	Can read basic directory information. Commonly used to grant directory read access to applications and guests.
Directory Synchronization Accounts	Only used by Azure AD Connect service.
Directory Writers	Can read and write basic directory information. For granting access to applications, not intended for users.
Domain Name Administrator	Can manage domain names in cloud and on-premises.
Dynamics 365 Administrator	Can manage all aspects of the Dynamics 365 product.
Edge Administrator	Manage all aspects of Microsoft Edge.
Exchange Administrator	Can manage all aspects of the Exchange product.
Exchange Recipient Administrator	Can create or update Exchange Online recipients within the Exchange Online organization.
External ID User Flow Administrator	Can create and manage all aspects of user flows.
External ID User Flow Attribute Administrator	Can create and manage the attribute schema available to all user flows.
External Identity Provider Administrator	Can configure identity providers for use in direct federation.

ROLE	DESCRIPTION
Global Administrator	Can manage all aspects of Azure AD and Microsoft services that use Azure AD identities.
Global Reader	Can read everything that a Global Administrator can, but not update anything.
Groups Administrator	Members of this role can create/manage groups, create/manage groups settings like naming and expiration policies, and view groups activity and audit reports.
Guest Inviter	Can invite guest users independent of the 'members can invite guests' setting.
Helpdesk Administrator	Can reset passwords for non-administrators and Helpdesk Administrators.
Hybrid Identity Administrator	Can manage AD to Azure AD cloud provisioning, Azure AD Connect, and federation settings.
Identity Governance Administrator	Manage access using Azure AD for identity governance scenarios.
Insights Administrator	Has administrative access in the Microsoft 365 Insights app.
Insights Business Leader	Can view and share dashboards and insights via the Microsoft 365 Insights app.
Intune Administrator	Can manage all aspects of the Intune product.
Kaizala Administrator	Can manage settings for Microsoft Kaizala.
Knowledge Administrator	Can configure knowledge, learning, and other intelligent features.
Knowledge Manager	Can organize, create, manage, and promote topics and knowledge.
License Administrator	Can manage product licenses on users and groups.
Message Center Privacy Reader	Can read security messages and updates in Office 365 Message Center only.
Message Center Reader	Can read messages and updates for their organization in Office 365 Message Center only.
Modern Commerce User	Can manage commercial purchases for a company, department, or team.
Network Administrator	Can manage network locations and review enterprise network design insights for Microsoft 365 Software as a Service applications.
Office Apps Administrator	Can manage Office apps cloud services, including policy and settings management, and manage the ability to select, unselect, and publish 'what's new' feature content to end-user's devices.

TABLE 14.1:   Azure Roles (*CONTINUED*)

ROLE	DESCRIPTION
Partner Tier1 Support	Do not use - not intended for general use.
Partner Tier2 Support	Do not use - not intended for general use.
Password Administrator	Can reset passwords for non-administrators and Password Administrators.
Power BI Administrator	Can manage all aspects of the Power BI product.
Power Platform Administrator	Can create and manage all aspects of Microsoft Dynamics 365, Power Apps, and Power Automate.
Printer Administrator	Can manage all aspects of printers and printer connectors.
Printer Technician	Can register and unregister printers and update printer status.
Privileged Authentication Administrator	Can access to view, set, and reset authentication method information for any user (admin or non-admin).
Privileged Role Administrator	Can manage role assignments in Azure AD, and all aspects of Privileged Identity Management.
Reports Reader	Can read sign-in and audit reports.
Search Administrator	Can create and manage all aspects of Microsoft Search settings.
Search Editor	Can create and manage the editorial content such as bookmarks, Q and As, locations, and floor plan.
Security Administrator	Can read security information and reports, and manage configuration in Azure AD and Office 365.
Security Operator	Creates and manages security events.
Security Reader	Can read security information and reports in Azure AD and Office 365.
Service Support Administrator	Can read service health information and manage support tickets.
SharePoint Administrator	Can manage all aspects of the SharePoint service.
Skype for Business Administrator	Can manage all aspects of the Skype for Business product.
Teams Administrator	Can manage the Microsoft Teams service.
Teams Communications Administrator	Can manage calling and meetings features within the Microsoft Teams service.

ROLE	DESCRIPTION
Teams Communications Support Engineer	Can troubleshoot communications issues within Teams using advanced tools.
Teams Communications Support Specialist	Can troubleshoot communications issues within Teams using basic tools.
Teams Devices Administrator	Can perform management related tasks on Teams certified devices.
Usage Summary Reports Reader	Can see only tenant level aggregates in Microsoft 365 Usage Analytics and Productivity Score.
User Administrator	Can manage all aspects of users and groups, including resetting passwords for limited admins.
Windows 365 Administrator	Can provision and manage all aspects of Cloud PCs.
Windows Update Deployment Administrator	Create and manage all aspects of Windows Update deployments through the Windows Update for Business deployment service.

Enterprise Applications

The Enterprise applications section allows an Administrator to view, setup, and configure your organization's Enterprise applications. Administrators can also setup an Application proxy within the Enterprise application section. An application proxy allows an Administrator to provide single sign-on (SSO) and secure remote access for web applications hosted on your on-premises network.

The Enterprise applications section also allows an Administrator to setup user settings for your Enterprise applications. These settings include users giving consent to applications accessing data on their company networks, users adding applications to their Access panel, and if users can only see Microsoft 365 in the M365 portal.

The Enterprise Applications section allows an Administrator to also setup Conditional access (setting up application policies), seeing who has logged into the applications, and auditing. Administrators can also troubleshoot application issues or opening a support ticket with Microsoft for additional help.

Devices

The Devices section allows an Azure AD Administrator to setup which devices can access Azure AD. Administrators can also setup device settings and device roaming settings (Enterprise State Roaming). Administrators can do auditing and troubleshooting from the Device section.

In the Device section, you also have the ability to setup BitLocker keys. Administrators can view and copy BitLocker keys so that users have the ability to recover encrypted drives. BitLocker keys are only available for Windows devices that have been encrypted using BitLocker and those keys are stored in Azure AD.

Administrators can find these BitLocker keys when they view a device's details by selecting Show Recovery Key. By selecting Show Recovery Key, this will generate an audit log. Administrators can find the BitLocker keys in the KeyManagement category of the audit log.

Licenses

The Licenses section allows you to view purchased licensing for additional Azure AD components. If you purchase additional Azure AD components (for example: Azure Active Directory Premium P2 or Enterprise Mobility + Security E5), those additional components will show up in this Licenses section. You can also see if there are any licensing issues in this section.

The Licenses section also allows you to view additional components that are available and what those components do.

Azure AD Connect

Azure AD Connect (see Figure 14.6) allows an Administrator to integrate their Azure AD with your Windows Server AD or another directory on your network. One of the nice advantages of the Azure AD Connect section is that it allows an Administrator to download and install Azure AD Connect by using Azure Active Directory Connect Download link. As you can see in Figure 14.6, Azure AD and my domain have already been connected by using Seamless single sign-on.

FIGURE 14.6
Viewing the Azure AD
Connect Section

Azure AD Connect helps you integrate your on-premises Active Directory with Azure AD. This allows your users to be more productive by giving those users access to both cloud and on-premises resources by using a common user account for accessing both networks. By using Azure AD Connect, users and organizations can take advantage of the following features:

◆ Users can have a common hybrid identity that allows them to access on-site or cloud-based services that use both Windows Server Active Directory and Azure Active Directory.

◆ Administrators have the ability to provide conditional access based on their device and user identity, network location, application resource, and multifactor authentication.

◆ Users can use this common identity in Azure AD, Office 365, Intune, SaaS apps and third-party applications.

◆ Developers can create applications that use the common identity model thus integrating applications into on-site Active Directory or cloud based Azure applications.

To use Azure AD Connect, your on-site network must be using Windows Server 2008 or higher.

The Azure AD Connect section allows you to setup how your users will seamlessly pass through between both networks. Administrators can setup seamless connections by using a Federation server (including AD Federation Server), Seamless single sign-on, or Pass-through authentication.

Custom Domain Names

The Custom Domain Names section allows you to add and verify new domain names (see Figure 14.7). When you first build your Azure subscription, your new Azure AD tenant comes with an initial domain name (for example, `willpanek.onmicrosoft.com`).

FIGURE 14.7
Viewing the Custom Domain Names section

Administrators can't change or delete the initial domain name that is created, but Administrators do have the ability to add your organization's domain names to the list of supported names. Adding custom domain names allows an Administrator to create usernames that are familiar to your users, such as `wpanek@willpanek.com`.

After you register your custom domain name, you can make sure it's valid in Azure AD. As you can see in Figure 14.7, `JohnDoe.com` has not been verified. You can verify a custom domain name by clicking on the domain name. This will take you to a screen where you can verify the custom domain name.

After creating a DNS TXT or MX record, you can click on the Verify button to have Azure verify the custom domain name. These DNS records must be created either on your web server's

DNS server (ISP or hosting company) or your on-site DNS server if you are hosting your own website. This step ensures that your company owns the custom name that you are trying to register.

Mobility (MDM and MAM)

One feature that many organizations have started to implement is the ability for their employees to bring in their own devices (Bring Your Own Device - BYOD) to work.

Also, many organizations have started issuing device like tablets to their employees and many companies do not mind if you use those devices for personal use. These are reasons why Microsoft has implemented Mobility into their Azure AD networks.

Devices (either personal or corporate) have the ability to be connected to a corporate Azure AD network by using the Device Settings link.

Once these devices are connected to Azure, an administrator can control these devices by using Microsoft Intune and Microsoft Intune Enrollment utilities (as shown in Figure 14.8). At the time this book was written, Microsoft has starting using Microsoft Endpoint Manager for Intune. But as you can see, Intune is still being shown as the utilities.

FIGURE 14.8
Mobility (MDM and MAM) screen

NOTE **Mobile Devices** When a user connects their personal device to a corporate network, the user should understand that corporate policies may affect their devices and settings.

Password Reset

The Password Reset section allows an Administrator to determine if they want to enable Self-service password resets (SSPR). If an organization decides to enable this feature, users will be able to reset their own passwords or unlock their accounts.

An Administrator can allow all accounts to use the SSPR (see Figure 14.9) or they can just choose certain groups that will have the ability to do SSPR.

FIGURE 14.9
Setting the Self-Service
Password Reset

In the Password Reset section, Administrators can also choose to use Authentication methods. Authentication methods allow an organization to verify that the user is who they say they are. Methods for this include verification by mobile app notification, mobile app code, email, mobile phone, office phone, or security question. Administrators can choose between a single verification or by using multiple verifications.

Administrators can also require registrations when a user logs into Azure AD and admins can also setup password resets so that the user is notified if their password changes. Administrators can also be notified when Administrator passwords are reset. Also, in the Password reset section, admins can choose to enable a custom helpdesk link (under the Customization link) for users.

Administrators can configure password changes to be replicated back (password writeback) to an Active Directory network by configuring On-premises integration. Password writeback, when enabled in Azure AD Connect and SSPR, allows users who change or reset their password in Azure to have those passwords also be updated back to the on-premises Active Directory Domain environment as well.

Administrators can do auditing and troubleshooting from the Password reset section.

Company branding

The Company branding section allows an organization to setup custom text and graphics that your users will see when they sign into Azure Active Directory.

This allows your organization to setup their logo and custom color schemes. Organizations can provide a consistent look and feel for their users when they sign into their Azure Active Directory pages.

Properties

The Properties section allows an Azure AD Administrator to change settings that include the Tenant name, Notification language, Tenant ID, Technical contact email, Global privacy contact, Privacy statement URL, and Access management person for Azure.

Security

The Security section allows an administrator to view an Overview of your security policies and security issues. Security is a big part of Azure AD because unlike an On-site network, the Azure AD network can be accessed from anywhere in the world. So, making sure your Azure AD security is strong, is a very important task for any Azure Administrator.

Azure Active Directory offers a range of security features to protect your organization. Some of these features include:

- Azure AD Conditional Access

- Azure AD Identity Protection

- Microsoft Defender for Cloud

- Identity Secure Score

- Named locations

- Authentication methods

- Multi Factor Authentication (MFA)

NOTE All of the Azure Security settings will be covered in greater detail throughout the rest of this book.

Conditional Access The Conditional Access section (see Figure 14.10) allows an Azure AD Administrator to set security policies. When it comes to Azure, one of the biggest concerns for organizations is cloud-based security. Azure allows users to access their networks from anywhere in the world and from almost any device. Because of this, just securing resource access is not enough. This is where Conditional Access Policies comes in to play.

FIGURE 14.10
Conditional Access
Policies section

Conditional Access policies allow an organization to set how resources are accessed using access control decisions (who have access to resources) through Azure AD. Setting up Conditional Access policies allows an organization to have automated access control decisions based on the policies that your organization sets. Some of the situations that Conditional Access policies can help with are sign-in risk, network location risk, device management, and client applications.

Identity Secure Score The Identity Secure Score section allows an Administrator to view their Azure AD Identity Security Score. The Identity Secure Score is an indicator for how aligned

Azure AD is with Microsoft's best practices recommendations for your organization's security setup.

The Identity Secure Score is an integer number and the higher the number, the better your security settings align with Microsoft's recommendations. The score helps an organization objectively measure their identity security position, plan for identity security improvements, and review the successful implementation of your organization's improvements.

On this Identity Secure Score dashboard, an organization will be able to view your organization's score, comparison graph, trend graph, and a list of identity security best practices.

So, the way this works is that Azure views your security configuration every 48 hours. Its then takes what it sees and compares your organization's settings against Microsoft's best practices. Based on that evaluation, your organization's security score is calculated. Based on that security score, an administrator can adjust their security settings and policies to make improvements.

CONFIGURING OBJECTS

Now that we have looked at some of the different sections within Azure AD, let's look at how to create objects like users and groups.

User accounts allow employees to log into the Azure network. In Exercise 14.1, I will show you how to create a user account in Azure AD.

EXERCISE 14.1   Creating an Azure AD User Account

1. Log into the Azure dashboard.

2. Click on the Azure Active Directory link.

3. Under Manage, click the Users link.

4. Click on the link +New user.

5. Type in the name of your user's name and a username. For this lab, I used George Washington as my user's name and GWashington@wpanek.onmicrosoft.com as the username.

6. Click on Profile and put in the user's name and job information. Click the OK button when done filling in the profile information.

7. We are not going to add this user to a group yet. Make sure the Directory role is set to User.

8. You can click on the Show Password box to see the temporary password assigned. Then click the Create button.

9. You should now see your user account . If you would like to change any user information, double click on the user account and make changes. Be sure to save any changes that are made.

In Exercise 14.2, I will show you how to create a group in Azure AD.

EXERCISE 14.2 Creating an Azure AD Group Account

1. Log into the Azure dashboard.

2. Click on the Azure Active Directory link.

3. Under Manage, click the Groups link.

4. Click on the link +New group.

5. Under the Group type pull down, choose Security. Security groups are the group type you use when you want the group to be assigned to resources. Office 365 groups allow users to collaboration with other users by giving them access to a shared mailbox, calendar, files, SharePoint site, and more.

6. In the Group name box, type in the name of your group. I used Marketing for my group name.

7. In the Group description field, type in a description for your group.

8. In the Membership type pull down, choose Assigned. Assigned groups allow an administrator to add specific users to be members of the group and to have unique permissions. Dynamic user groups allow an administrator to use dynamic group rules to automatically add and remove members. Dynamic device groups allow an administrator to use dynamic group rules to automatically add and remove devices.

9. Click the Create button.

Self-Service Password Reset

As stated before, the Password Reset section allows an Administrator to determine if they want to enable Self-service password resets (SSPR). If an organization decides to enable this feature, users will be able to reset their own passwords or unlock their accounts.

An Administrator can choose from three SSPR options. Administrators can choose None, Selected, and All Users. If an administrator chooses None, then no one can reset their own passwords. Administrators can also set up the option of Selected to choose which users can reset their password or they can choose All Users. This will allow all users to reset their passwords. To setup SSPR, the following Prerequisites must be met;

◆ An Azure AD tenant subscription with the minimum of at least one trial license enabled.

◆ Global Administrator account that can be used to enable SSPR.

◆ A non-administrator test account with a password that you know.

◆ A pilot group account to test with the non-administrator test account (the user account needs to be a member of this group).

In Exercise 14.3, I will show you how to setup the Self-Service Password Reset option in Azure Active Directory. To complete this exercise, you must have created a user and group in exercises 14.1 and 14.2.

EXERCISE 14.3   Setting Up Self-Service Password Reset

1. From your existing Azure AD tenant, click on the Azure Active Directory.

2. Select Password Reset.

3. From the Properties page, under the option Self Service Password Reset Enabled, choose the Selected option.

4. From Select group, choose your pilot group.

5. Click Save.

6. From the Authentication methods page, make the following choices and then click Save:

   Number of methods required to reset: 1

   Methods available to users:

   Mobile phone

   Office phone

7. From the Registration page, make the following choices:

   Require users to register when they sign in: Yes

   Set the number of days before users are asked to

   reconfirm their authentication information: 365

In Exercise 14.4, I will show you how to test the Self-Service Password Reset option. For this exercise to be completed, you must have completed the previous exercise (Exercise 14.3). This test must be done with a normal user account. You can't run this test using an administrator account.

EXERCISE 14.4   Testing the Self-Service Password Reset

1. Open a new browser window in InPrivate or incognito mode, and browse to `https://aka.ms/ssprsetup`.

2. Sign in with a non-administrator test user and register your authentication phone.

3. Once complete, click the button marked looks good and close the browser window.

4. Open a new browser window in InPrivate or incognito mode and browse to `https://aka.ms/sspr`.

5. Enter your non-administrator test users' User ID, the characters from the CAPTCHA, and then click Next.

6. Follow the verification steps to reset your password.

The Bottom Line

Understand Azure AD Integration.   Microsoft Azure has many benefits that can help a company of any size connect their on-site domain with their Azure Active Directory network.

Master It   You are the administrator of a large network. You need to quickly connect your on-site domain to your Azure network.

Configure Azure Passwords.   Azure administrators have multiple ways to allow users to reset or change their own passwords.

Master It   You are the administrator of a large company that has Azure users in multiple areas. You need to allow users to reset or change their own passwords.

Chapter 15

Creating a Hybrid Network

Once you have decided to add your on-site domain to Azure, the next step is to connect the two networks together. Microsoft has multiple ways that allow you to connect the two networks together.

In this chapter, I will show you how to connect your on-site domain to Azure using Azure AD Connect. I will also show you how to setup and manage this connection.

I will show you how to setup Authentication Methods, Multi-Factor Authentication, and resetting passwords.

IN THIS CHAPTER YOU'LL LEARN

- ◆ Understand Azure AD Connect
- ◆ Configure Azure Recovery

Creating a Hybrid Network

One nice feature of using both an on-site and Azure network is that Microsoft has many different tools to help you connect both networks. Connecting both networks is important so that users can seamlessly move between the two networks.

Microsoft's identity solutions extend your organization's on-site network with the Azure network features. These solutions create a common user identity for authentication and authorization to all resources. The advantage is that the users can access these resources no matter where they reside. This is what Microsoft refers to as *hybrid identity*.

To properly setup your hybrid identity, one of the following authentication methods can be used. Which one you decide to use is all depended on your environment scenario. There are three available methods are:

- ◆ Password hash synchronization (PHS)
- ◆ Pass-through authentication (PTA)
- ◆ Federation

So, what is the real advantage of setting up both networks using one of these methods? When you choose one of the authentication methods, you provide your users with *Single Sign-On (SSO)* capabilities. Single sign-on allows your users to sign in once but have access to resources on both networks. This is what gives your users seamless access to all resources. So, let's take a look at some of the available Identity solutions.

Password Hash Synchronization with Azure AD

One of the hybrid identity sign-in methods that you can use is called *Password hash synchronization*. Azure AD and your on-site Active Directory synchronize with each other by using a hash value. The hash value is created based on the user's password. This way the two systems can stay in sync with each other. Azure AD Connect is also required for this setup to function properly.

Password hash synchronization is a feature that is part of the Azure AD Connect sync and it allows you to log into Azure AD applications like O365. The advantage is that your users log into their account using their on-site username and password. This helps users because it reduces the number of username and passwords that they need to know.

Another advantage to your organization is that they can use password hash synchronization as a backup sign-on method if your organization decides to use Federation services with Active Directory Federation Services (AD FS). To setup password hash synchronization, your environment needs to implement the following;

♦ Azure AD Connect.

♦ Directory synchronization between your on-site Active Directory and your Azure AD instance.

♦ Have password hash synchronization enabled

Azure Active Directory Pass-Through Authentication

Another option for allowing your users to sign into both on-site and cloud-based applications using the same passwords is *Azure AD Pass-Through Authentication*. Organizations can use Azure AD Pass-Through Authentication instead of using Azure AD Password Hash Synchronization. The organizational benefits for using Azure AD Pass-Through Authentication is the ability to enforce on-site Active Directory security and password policies.

This will help your organization with costs because your IT support desk will not be inundated by user's calls trying to remember their different passwords. This will help lower your IT department budget for total cost of ownership (TCO). Less calls to support means less support people needed. Some of the key benefits to using Azure AD Pass-Through Authentication are as follows;

♦ Better User Experience

   ♦ Users can use the same account password to sign into both your Azure AD and On-Site AD networks.

   ♦ Users don't need to talk to IT as often to reset passwords for multiple accounts.

   ♦ Azure AD allows your users to do their own password management using the Self-Service Password Management tools.

♦ Easy Deployment

   ♦ There is no need to deploy a large infrastructure on-site. Azure AD network can handle most of your networking services.

   ♦ Less budgeting needed for on-site IT departments. Since your Azure AD and your on-site AD can easily integrate with each other, there is no need for large IT departments on-site.

- Security
    - One nice advantage is that on-site passwords will never be stored in the Azure cloud.
    - Users's accounts are protected using Azure AD Conditional Access policies. These policies include Multi-Factor Authentication (MFA), filtering for brute force password attacks, and stopping legacy authentication.
    - The Azure agent will only allow outbound connections from within your network. The advantage of this means that you are not required to load an agent on your perimeter network.
    - With the use of certificate-based authentication, organizations get secure connections between the Azure agent and Azure AD.
- Highly Available
    - By installing additional Azure agents onto on-site servers, you can get high availability of Azure sign-in requests.

Federation with Azure AD

To understand what Federation can do for your organization, you must first understand Trusts. *Federation* (including Active Directory Federation Services (AD FS)) are just Trusts on steroids. Understanding what a Trust can do for your organization will help you understand why we use Federation.

UNDERSTANDING TRUSTS

Trust relationships make it easier to share security information and network resources between domains. As was already mentioned, standard transitive two-way trusts are automatically created between the domains in a tree and between each of the trees in a forest. When configuring trusts, you need to consider two main characteristics:

Transitive Trusts   By default, Active Directory trusts are *transitive trusts*. The simplest way to understand transitive relationships is through this example: If Domain A trusts Domain B and Domain B trusts Domain C, then Domain A implicitly trusts Domain C. If you need to apply a tighter level of security, trusts can be configured as intransitive.

One-Way vs. Two-Way   Trusts can be configured as one-way or two-way relationships. The default operation is to create *two-way trusts* or *bidirectional trusts*. This makes it easier to manage trust relationships by reducing the trusts you must create. In some cases, however, you might decide against two-way trusts. In one-way relationships, the trusting domain allows resources to be shared with the trusted domain but not the other way around.

When domains are added together to form trees and forests, an automatic transitive two-way trust is created between them. Although the default trust relationships work well for most organizations, there are some reasons you might want to manage trusts manually:

- You may want to remove trusts between domains if you are absolutely sure you do not want resources to be shared between domains.
- Because of security concerns, you may need to keep resources isolated.

In addition to the default trust types, you can configure the following types of special trusts:

External Trusts   You use *external trusts* to provide access to resources that cannot use a forest trust. In some cases, external trusts could be your only option. External trusts are always nontransitive, but they can be established in a one-way or two-way configuration.

Default SID Filtering on External Trusts   When you set up an external trust, remember that it is possible for hackers to compromise a domain controller in a trusted domain. If this trust is compromised, a hacker can use the security identifier (SID) history attribute to associate SIDs with new user accounts, granting themselves unauthorized rights (this is called an *elevation-of-privileges attack*). To help prevent this type of attack, Windows Server 2022 automatically enables SID filter quarantining on all external trusts. SID filtering allows the domain controllers in the trusting domain (the domain with the resources) to remove all SID history attributes that are not members of the trusted domain.

Realm Trusts   *Realm trusts* are similar to external trusts. You use them to connect to a non-Windows domain that uses Kerberos authentication. Realm trusts can be transitive or nontransitive, one-way or two-way.

Cross-Forest Trusts   *Cross-forest trusts* are used to share resources between forests. They have been used since Windows Server 2000 domains and cannot be nontransitive, but you can establish them in a one-way or a two-way configuration. Authentication requests in either forest can reach the other forest in a two-way cross-forest trust. If you want one forest to trust another forest, you must set it (at a minimum) to at least the forest function level of Windows Server 2003.

Selective Authentication vs. Forest-Wide Authentication   Forest-wide authentication on a forest trust means that users of the trusted forest can access all of the resources of the trusting forest as long as they have the appropriate permissions. Selective authentication means that users cannot authenticate to a domain controller or resource server in the trusting forest unless they are explicitly allowed to do so.

Shortcut Trusts   In some cases, you may actually want to create direct trusts between two domains that implicitly trust each other. Such a trust is sometimes referred to as a *shortcut trust*, and it can improve the speed at which resources are accessed across many different domains. Let's say you have a forest, as shown in Figure 15.1.

Users in the NY.US.WillPanek.com domain can access resources in the London. UK.WillPanek.com domain, but the users must authenticate using the parent domains to gain access (NY.US.WillPanek.com to US.WillPanek.com to WillPanek.com to UK.WillPanek. com to finally reach London.UK.WillPanek.com). This process can be slow. An administrator can set up a one-way trust from London.UK.WillPanek.com (trusting domain) to NY. US.WillPanek.com (trusted domain) so that the users can access the resources directly.

TIP   Perhaps the most important aspect to remember regarding trusts is that creating them only *allows* you to share resources between domains. The trust does not grant any permissions between domains by itself. Once a trust has been established, however, system administrators can easily assign the necessary permissions.

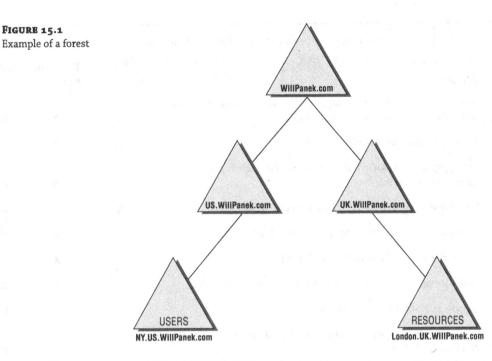

FIGURE 15.1
Example of a forest

UNDERSTANDING FEDERATION

So now that you understand trusts, it's easier to understand Federation because Federation is just a group of domains that have an established trust. These domains can be between sites or between separate organizations.

Remember, even though it's your company on Azure, Azure is owned by Microsoft. So, you are technically setting up a trust between your company and Microsoft's network (onmicrosoft.com).

When setting up Federation, the trust level can be set to whatever the organization needs for their users. You do not need to just give open access to everyone. Also, Federation is just the mechanism to allow access across the trust. You still need to setup user's permissions to your resources.

When you setup authentication and authorization, using Federation, between your on-site network and Azure AD, all user authentications happen on-site. This allows an organization to have better levels of access control.

Common Identity Scenarios

Table 15.1 was taken directly from Microsoft's website and it shows some of the common hybrid identity and access management scenarios along with their recommendations as to which hybrid identity option would be suitable for each.

NOTE   **Understanding the Identity Table**   In the following table, the three headers are abbreviated. Column 2, PHS and SSO, stands for Password hash synchronization with single sign-on. Column 3, PTA and SSO, stands for Pass-through authentication and single sign-on. Finally, Column 4 stands for Federated single sign-on using Active Directory Federation Services.

TABLE 15.1: Common Identity Scenarios and Recommendations

Scenario	PHS AND SSO	PTA AND SSO	AD FS
Sync new user, contact, and group accounts created in my on-premises Active Directory to the cloud automatically.	X	X	X
Set up my tenant for Office 365 hybrid scenarios	X	X	X
Enable my users to sign in and access cloud services using their on-premises password	X	X	X
Implement single sign-on using corporate credentials	X	X	X
Ensure no password hashes are stored in the cloud		X	X
Enable cloud multi-factor authentication solutions		X	X
Enable on-premises multi-factor authentication solutions			X
Support smartcard authentication for my users			X
Display password expiry notifications in the Office Portal and on the Windows 10 desktop			X

Azure AD Connect

Once you decide that you want your on-site network to be integrated with Azure AD, you need to install a component that allows both versions of Active Directory to work together. This component is called Azure AD Connect.

Azure AD Connect is a Microsoft utility that allows you to setup a hybrid design between Azure AD and your on-site AD. It provides some of the following features:

- Password hash synchronization
- Pass-through authentication
- Federation integration
- Synchronization
- Health Monitoring

AZURE AD CONNECT HEALTH MONITORING

Azure AD Connect Health Monitoring is a way that an administrator can monitor their on-site identity infrastructure and maintain a constant connection to all of your Azure services.

To access the Azure AD Connect Health information, an administrator would need to connect to the Azure AD Connect Health portal. The portal can be used to view alerts, usage information, performance monitoring, and other key information. The Azure AD Connect Health portal gives you a one stop shop for all of your Azure AD Connect monitoring.

Creating and Verifying a Custom Domain Name

Once you have decided to create a Hybrid network between your on-site domain and Azure, you need to add your domain name to Azure. Once you add the Custom Domain Name in Azure, you need to create either a DNS .TXT record or an MX record.

Once you open the Azure Portal, you click on Azure Active Directory. On the left side menu, click on Custom Domain Name. Click the Add button and enter the name of your domain. Once you do this, Azure will show you the settings for creating either creatin a TXT or MX record. Open your domain DNS and create the TXT file. It's preferred that you create a TXT record in DNS. Use an MX record only if your DNS server does not allow TXT records.

After you open your domain DNS server, create a new TXT record. Copy the information from Azure into your new TXT record. After the TXT record is created on your DNS server, in Azure, click Verify to verify the Custom Domain Name. Once the verification process happens, you can continue with Azure AD Connect.

Be aware that the verification process can take 24-48 hours. So, make sure this is done well before you connect the two networks together.

Installing Azure AD Connect

Before you can install Azure AD Connect, you need to make sure that your infrastructure and your Azure network have some prerequisites setup. The following is a list of requirements for installing Azure AD Connect:

- Azure AD
- On-site Active Directory
- Azure AD Connect server
- If you plan to use the feature password writeback, the domain controllers must be on Windows Server 2016 or later.
- SQL Server database used by Azure AD Connect
- Azure AD Global Administrator account
- Enterprise Administrator account
- Connectivity between networks
- PowerShell and .Net 4.6.2 or higher Framework setup
- Enabled TLS 1.2 for Azure AD Connect.

In Exercise 15.1, I will show you how to download and install Azure AD Connect. To complete this exercise, you must have an onsite version of AD that can be connected to Azure.

EXERCISE 15.1   Downloading and Installing Azure AD Connect

1. Go to the Azure AD Connect download page at www.microsoft.com/en-us/download/details.aspx?id=47594.

2. Click the Download button.

3. When the download box appears, choose to download the AzureADConnect.msi file to a network location. Once the download is complete, close the download box.

4. Log into the server (where you wish to install Azure AD Connect) as the local administrator.

5. Navigate to the AzureADConnect.msi file and double-click on the file to start the install.

6. On the Welcome screen, select the box to agree to the license terms and then click Continue.

7. On the Express settings page, click Use Express Settings.

8. On the Connect to Azure AD page, enter the Azure global administrator's username and password and then click Next.

9. The Connect to AD DS page will appear, enter the username and password for an on-site enterprise admin and then click Next.

10. The Azure AD sign-in configuration page will appear. Review every domain marked Not Added and Not Verified. Make sure domains are verified in Azure AD. Once the domains are verified in Azure, click the Refresh symbol. If you need to verify your domains, go into Azure Active Directory, and then select Custom domain names. Enter the domain names for your on-site domain.

11. On the Ready to configure page, click Install.

12. When the installation completes, click Exit.

13. After the installation has completed, you will need to sign off and sign in again before you can use or setup any other services.

AZURE VPN GATEWAY

As I have stated throughout this book, most (if not all) companies will have both an on-site network and an Azure network. Because of this, you will need to know how to connect both networks together. This is where you would use a Site-to-Site VPN gateway connection.

Site-to-Site VPN gateway connections allow you to connect both networks together over a secure IPsec/IKE VPN tunnel. To make this type of connection between networks, you need to have a VPN device located on-site. This VPN device will require a public IP address on the external side (the side facing the internet) of the device.

To use a Site-to-Site VPN connection, you must meet the following requirements:

◆ Compatible VPN device with an administrator who can configure the device.

◆ An external public IP address for that VPN device.

◆ Knowledge of your on-site IP configuration and subnetting. None of your on-site IP subnets can overlap your Azure virtual network subnets.

Example Values for Site-to-Site VPN Connection

To help IT people better understand and configure Site-to-Site VPN connections, Microsoft released example values on their website. These example values can be used to setup a test environment or they can be used to help you better understand what values are needed to setup a Site-to-Site VPN connection.

NOTE **Site-to-Site VPN Connection Examples** The following examples were taken directly from Microsoft's website, `https://docs.microsoft.com/en-us/azure/vpn-gateway/ vpn-gateway-howto-site-to-site-resource-manager-portal`.

- ◆ VNet Name: TestVNet1
- ◆ Address Space: 10.1.0.0/16
- ◆ Subscription: The subscription you want to use
- ◆ Resource Group: TestRG1
- ◆ Location: East US
- ◆ Subnet: FrontEnd: 10.1.0.0/24, BackEnd: 10.1.1.0/24 (optional for this exercise)
- ◆ Gateway Subnet name: GatewaySubnet (this will auto-fill in the portal)
- ◆ Gateway Subnet address range: 10.1.255.0/27
- ◆ DNS Server: 8.8.8.8 - Optional. The IP address of your DNS server.
- ◆ Virtual Network Gateway Name: VNet1GW
- ◆ Public IP: VNet1GWIP
- ◆ VPN Type: Route-based
- ◆ Connection Type: Site-to-Site (IPsec)
- ◆ Gateway Type: VPN
- ◆ Local Network Gateway Name: Site1
- ◆ Connection Name: VNet1toSite1
- ◆ Shared key: For this example, we use abc123. But, you can use whatever is compatible with your VPN hardware. The important thing is that the values match on both sides of the connection.

Creating the VPN Gateway

Now that you have an understanding of why you would need a VPN gateway, let's look at what it takes to create a VPN gateway. Since every VPN device is different, I will show you how to create the actual Site-to-Site VPN connection in Exercise 15.2. You need to have someone create the connection on the VPN device.

EXERCISE 15.2   Creating the Site-to-Site VPN Connection

1. Log into the Azure dashboard.
2. On the left side of the portal page, click the + Create a resource and then type '**Virtual Network Gateway**' in the search box. In the Results section, click Virtual Network Gateway.
3. In the 'Virtual Network Gateway' page, click the Create button.
4. On the Create Virtual Network Gateway page, enter the values for your virtual network gateway settings.
   - **Name**: This is the name of your gateway object.
   - **Gateway type**: Select VPN. VPN gateways use the VPN type.
   - **VPN type**: Choose the VPN type that fits your configuration. Route based VPNs are the most common type.
   - **SKU**: Select your gateway SKU. This will depend on the VPN type you select.
   - **Enable active-active mode**: If you are creating an active-active gateway configuration, choose this checkbox. If you are not creating an active-active gateway configuration, leave this checkbox unselected.
   - **Location**: Choose your appropriate geographical location.
   - **Virtual network**: Choose the virtual network you want for this gateway. You can choose the virtual network we created earlier in this book.
   - **Gateway subnet address range**: This setting will only be seen if you did not already create a gateway subnet for your virtual network. If you did create a valid gateway subnet, this setting will not appear.
   - **Public IP address**: This setting specifies the public IP address that gets associated to the VPN gateway. Make sure Create new is the selected radio button and type a Name for your public IP address.
   - Unless your configuration specifically requires BGP ASN, leave this configuration's checkbox unchecked. If BGP ASN is required, the default setting for ASN is 65515. You can change this if needed.
5. Click Create. The settings will be validated and you'll see the "Deploying Virtual Network Gateway" message on the dashboard. This can take up to 45 minutes. Refresh your portal page to see the current status.

Creating the Local Network Gateway

The next step that we must complete is creating the local network gateway. The local network gateway refers to your on-site network. What you need to do is give your on-site network a name that Azure can use to access that network.

After you name the on-site network on Azure, you then need to tell Azure what IP address that it needs to use to access the on-site VPN device. You also need to specify the IP address prefix (that is located on your on-site location) that will be used to route traffic through the VPN gateway and to the VPN device.

In exercise 15.3, I will show you how to setup the local network gateway. To complete this exercise, you need to know the IP address information for your on-site test or live network.

EXERCISE 15.3   Creating the Local Network Gateway

1. Log into the Azure dashboard.

2. On the left side of the portal page, click the + Create a resource and then type **Local network gateway** in the search box. In the Results section, click Virtual Network Gateway.

3. In the Local Network Gateway page, click the Create button.

4. On the Create Local Network Gateway page, enter the values for your virtual network gateway settings.

   ◆ **Name**: Specify the name of your local network gateway.

   ◆ **IP address**: This is the public IP address of the VPN device.

   ◆ **Address Space**: This is the IP address ranges for the local network.

   ◆ **Configure BGP settings**: Use this setting when configuring BGP. Otherwise, don't check this checkbox.

   ◆ **Subscription**: Verify your current Azure subscription is showing.

   ◆ **Resource Group**: You can create a new resource group or choose one that you have already created.

   ◆ **Location**: Choose your appropriate geographical location.

5. Click the Create button.

Once you have finished creating the VPN connection, you will need to configure the companies VPN device. As stated above, Site-to-Site connections require a VPN device. Once the VPN device is configured properly, your site-to-site communications are completed.

UNDERSTANDING ExpressRoute

ExpressRoute allows you to setup another way to connect your two networks. ExpressRoute allows you to connect your internal network to your external network using a private connection provided by your connection provider. Using ExpressRoute allows you to connect your internal network with any or all of the different Microsoft networks including Azure, Microsoft 365, and Dynamics 365.

Since the connection is through your connection provider and not the Internet, ExpressRoute is a much faster, more reliable, better security, and lower latencies connection over the Internet.

Implement Active Directory Federation Services

As I stated in the beginning of this chapter, there are many different types of Federation products on the market. If you decide to purchase or use a third-party Federation product, most will work when connecting your Hybrid networks. But since Microsoft has its own version of Federation Services, that's the one we will focus on.

Active Directory Federation Services (AD FS) demands a great deal of preparation and planning to ensure a successful implementation. The type of certificate authority used to sign the AD FS server's certificate must be planned. The SSL encryption level must be negotiated with the partnering organization. For instance, how much Active Directory information should be shared with the partnering organization? What should the DNS structure look like to support federation communications? You must explore all of these questions before implementing AD FS. In the following sections, I will discuss how to deploy AD FS and the configurations used to set up a federated partnership between your on-site network and Azure AD.

What Is a Claim?

A *claim* is an identifiable element (email address, username, password, and so on) that a trusted source asserts about an identity, such as, for example, the SID of a user or computer. An identity can contain more than one claim, and any combination of those claims can be used to authorize access to resources.

Windows Server 2022 extends the authorization identity beyond using the SID for identity and enables administrators to configure authorization based on claims published in Active Directory.

Today, the claims-based identity model brings us to cloud-based authentication. One analogy to the claims-based model is the old airport check-in procedure.

1. You first check in at the ticket counter.

2. You present a suitable form of ID (driver's license, passport, credit card, and so on). After verifying that your picture ID matches your face (authentication), the agent pulls up your flight information and verifies that you've paid for a ticket (authorization).

3. You receive a boarding pass (token). The boarding pass lets the gate agents know your name and frequent flyer number (authentication and personalization), your flight number and seating priority (authorization), and more. The boarding pass has bar-code information (certificate) with a boarding serial number proving that the boarding pass was issued by the airline and is not a (self-signed) forgery.

Active Directory Federation Service is Microsoft's claims-based identity solution providing browser-based clients (internal or external to your network) with transparent access to one or more protected Internet-facing applications.

When an application is hosted in a different network than the user accounts, users are occasionally prompted for secondary credentials when they attempt to access the application. These secondary credentials represent the identity of the users in the domain where the application is hosted. The web server hosting the application usually requires these credentials to make the most proper authorization decision.

AD FS makes secondary accounts and their credentials unnecessary by providing trust relationships that send a user's digital identity and access rights to trusted partners. In a federated environment, each organization continues to manage its own identities, but each organization can also securely send and accept identities from other organizations. This seamless process is referred to as *single sign-on (SSO)*.

Windows Server 2022 AD FS federation servers can extract Windows authorization claims from a user's authorization token that is created when the user authenticates to the AD FS federation server. AD FS inserts these claims into its claim pipeline for processing. You can configure Windows authorization claims to pass through the pipeline as is, or you can configure AD FS to transform Windows authorization claims into a different or well-known claim type.

CLAIMS PROVIDER

A *claims provider* is a federation server that processes trusted identity claims requests. A federation server processes requests to issue, manage, and validate security tokens. Security tokens consist of a collection of identity claims, such as a user's name or role or an anonymous identifier. A federation server can issue tokens in several formats. In addition, a federation server can protect the contents of security tokens in transmission with an X.509 certificate.

For example, when a StormWind user needs access to Fabrikam's web application, the StormWind user must request claims from the StormWind AD FS server claim provider. The claim is transformed into an encrypted security token, which is then sent to Fabrikam's AD FS server.

RELYING PARTY

A *relying party* is a federation server that receives security tokens from a trusted federation partner claims provider. In turn, the relying party issues new security tokens that a local relying party application consumes. In the prior example, Fabrikam is the relying party that relies on the StormWind's claims provider to validate the user's claim. By using a relying party federation server in conjunction with a claims provider, organizations can offer web single sign-on to users from partner organizations. In this scenario, each organization manages its own identity stores.

ENDPOINTS

Endpoints provide access to the federation server functionality of AD FS, such as token issuance, information card issuance, and the publishing of federation metadata. Based on the type of endpoint, you can enable or disable the endpoint or control whether the endpoint is published to AD FS proxies.

Table 15.2 describes the property fields that distinguish the various built-in endpoints that AD FS exposes. The table includes the types of endpoints and their methods of client authentication. Table 15.3 describes the AD FS security modes.

TABLE 15.2:   AD FS Endpoints

NAME	DESCRIPTION
WS-Trust 1.3	An endpoint built on a standard Simple Object Access Protocol (SOAP)–based protocol for issuing security tokens.
WS-Trust 2005	An endpoint built on a prestandard, SOAP-based protocol for issuing security tokens.
WS-Federation Passive/SAML Web SSO	An endpoint published to support protocols that redirect web browser clients to issue security tokens.
Federation Metadata	A standard-formatted endpoint for exchanging metadata about a claims provider or a relying party.

TABLE 15.2: AD FS Endpoints *(CONTINUED)*

NAME	DESCRIPTION
SAML Artifact Resolution	An endpoint built on a subset of the Security Assertion Markup Language (SAML) version 2.0 protocol that describes how a relying party can access a token directly from a claims provider.
WS-Trust WSDL	An endpoint that publishes WS-Trust Web Services Definition Language (WSDL) containing the metadata that the federation service must be able to accept from other federation servers.
SAML Token (Asymmetric)	The client accepts a SAML token with an asymmetric key.

TABLE 15.3: AD FS Security Modes

NAME	DESCRIPTION
Transport	The client credentials are included at the Transport layer. Confidentiality is preserved at the Transport layer (Secure Sockets Layer [SSL]).
Mixed	The client credentials are included in the header of a SOAP message. Confidentiality is preserved at the Transport layer (SSL).
Message	The client credentials are included in the header of a SOAP message. Confidentiality is preserved by encryption inside the SOAP message.

CLAIM DESCRIPTIONS

Claim descriptions are claim types based on an entity's or user's attribute, like a user's email address, common name, or UPN. AD FS publishes these claim types in the federation metadata and most common claim descriptions are preconfigured in the AD FS Management snap-in.

The claim descriptions are published to federation metadata, which is stored in the AD FS configuration database. The claim descriptions include a claim type URI, name, publishing state, and description.

CLAIM RULES

Claim rules define how AD FS processes a claim. The most common rule is using a user's email address as a valid claim. The email address claim is validated through the partner's Active Directory email attribute for the user's account. If there is a match, the claim is accepted as valid.

Claim rules can quickly evolve into more complex rules with more attributes such as a user's employee ID or department. The key goal of claim rules is to process the claim in a manner that validates the user's claim and to assemble a user's profile information based on a sufficient number of attributes to place the user into a role or group.

THE ATTRIBUTE STORE

Attribute stores are the repositories containing claim values. AD FS natively supports Active Directory by default as an attribute store. SQL Server, AD LDS, and custom attribute stores are also supported.

AD FS ROLE SERVICES

The AD FS server role includes federation, proxy, and web agent services. These services enable the following:

◆ Web SSO

◆ Federated web-based resources

◆ Customizing the access experience

◆ Managing authorization to access applications

Based on your organization's requirements, you can deploy servers running any one of the following AD FS role services:

Active Directory Federation Service Microsoft federation solution for accepting and issuing claims-based token for users to experience a single sign-on to a partnered web application.

Federation Service Proxy The Federation Service Proxy forwards user claims over the Internet or DMZ using WS-Federation Passive Requestor Profile (WS-F PRP) protocols to the internal ADFS farm. Only the user credential data is forwarded to the Federation Service. All other datagram packets are dropped.

Claims-Aware Agent The claims-aware agent resides on a web server with a claims-aware application to enable the Microsoft ASP.NET application to accept AD FS security token claims.

Windows Token-Based Agent The Windows token-based agent resides on a web server with a Windows NT token-based application to translate an AD FS security token to an impersonation-level Windows NT token-based authentication.

AD FS in Windows Server 2022

The Active Directory Federation Services role in Windows Server 2022 includes the first introduced the following features:

◆ HTTP.SYS

◆ Server Manager integration

◆ AD FS deployment cmdlets in the AD FS module for Windows PowerShell

◆ Interoperability with Windows authorization claims

◆ Web proxy service

HTTP.SYS

Prior AD FS versions relied on IIS components for the AD FS claim functions. Microsoft has improved the overall claims handling performance and SSO customization by building the AD FS 3.0 code on top of the standard kernel mode driver—HTTP.SYS. This approach also avoids the huge security "no-no" of hosting IIS on a domain controller.

The classic `netsh` HTTP command can be entered to query and configure HTTP.SYS. AD FS proxy server introduces interesting deployment nuisances and "gotchas" with HTTP.SYS, which I will discuss in the upcoming section "Web Proxy Service."

IMPROVED INSTALLATION EXPERIENCE

The installation experience for Active Directory Federation Services 3.0 was cumbersome, requiring multiple hotfixes, as well as .NET Framework 3.5, Windows PowerShell, and the Windows Identity Foundation SDK. Windows Server 2022's AD FS role includes all of the software you need to run AD FS for an improved installation experience.

WEB PROXY SERVICE

The kernel mode (HTTP.SYS) in Windows Server 2022 includes server name indication (SNI) support configuration. I strongly recommend verifying that your current load balancer/reverse proxy firmware supports SNI. This prerequisite is a sore spot for most AD FS 3.0 upgrade projects in the field. Therefore, it's worthwhile checking the following:

- Your preferred load balancer/device needs to support SNI.

- Clients and user agents need to support SNI and should not become locked out of authentication.

- All SSL termination endpoints vulnerable to the recent heartbleed bug (`http://heartbleed.com`) need to be patched, exposing OpenSSL libraries and certificates.

AD FS DEPENDENCY CHANGES IN WINDOWS SERVER

Active Directory Federation Services was built on a claims-based identity framework called *Windows Identity Foundation (WIF)*. Prior to Windows Server 2022, WIF was distributed in a software development kit and the .NET runtime. WIF is currently integrated into version 4.5 of the .NET Framework, which ships with Windows Server 2016 or higher.

WINDOWS IDENTITY FOUNDATION

WIF is a set of .NET Framework classes; it is a framework for implementing claims-based identity for applications. Any web application or web service that uses .NET Framework version 4.5 or newer can run WIF.

NEW CLAIMS MODEL AND PRINCIPAL OBJECT

Claims are at the core of .NET Framework 4.5. The base claim classes (`Claim`, `ClaimsIdentity`, `ClaimsPrincipal`, `ClaimTypes`, and `ClaimValueTypes`) all live directly in `mscorlib`. Interfaces are no longer necessary to plug claims in the .NET identity system. `WindowsPrincipal`,

GenericPrincipal, and RolePrincipal now inherit from ClaimsPrincipal, WindowsIdentity, and GenericIdentity, and FormsIdentity now inherits from ClaimsIdentity. In short, every principal class will now serve claims. The integration classes and interfaces (WindowsClaimsIdentity, WindowsClaimsPrincipal, IClaimsPrincipal, and IClaimsIdentity) have thus been removed. The ClaimsIdentity object model also contains various improvements, which makes it easier to query the identity's claims collection.

As you climb further up "Mount Federation," you will realize that not all vendor SAML flavors are compatible, and configuration challenges can bring even the most seasoned system integrators to their knees. SAML deserves an entire book, so to avoid this chapter reaching encyclopedia size, I will touch on just a few pointers.

AD FS negotiates SAML authentication in order of security strength from the weakest to the strongest, as shown in Table 15.4. The default mode, Kerberos, is considered the strongest method. The authentication precedence can be tuned by executing the PowerShell command Set-AD FSProperties -AuthenticationContextOrder to select an order to meet your organization's security requirements.

TABLE 15.4:   SAML-Supported Authentication Methods

AUTHENTICATION METHOD	AUTHENTICATION CONTEXT CLASS URI
Username/password	urn:oasis:names:tc:SAML:3.0:ac:classes:Password
Password-protected transport	urn:oasis:names:tc:SAML:3.0:ac:classes:Password ProtectedTransport
Transport Layer Security (TLS) client	urn:oasis:names:tc:SAML:3.0:ac:classes:TLSClient
X.509 certificate	urn:oasis:names:tc:SAML:3.0:ac:classes:X509
Integrated Windows authentication	urn:federation:authentication:windows
Kerberos	urn:oasis:names:tc:SAML:3.0:classes:Kerberos

Configuring a Web Application Proxy

One of the advantages of using the Remote Access role service in Windows Server 2022 is the Web Application Proxy. Normally, your users access applications on the Internet from your corporate network. The *Web Application Proxy* reverses this feature, and it allows your corporate users to access applications from any device outside the network.

Administrators can choose which applications to provide reverse proxy features, and this allows administrators the ability to give access selectively to corporate users for the desired application that you want to set up for the Web Application Proxy service.

The Web Application Proxy feature allows applications running on servers inside the corporate network to be accessed by any device outside the corporate network. The process of allowing an application to be available to users outside of the corporate network is known as *publishing*.

Web Application Proxies works different than a normal VPN solution because when an administrator publishes applications through Web Application Proxy, end users get access only to applications that the administrator published. Administrators have the ability to deploy the Web Application Proxy alongside a VPN as part of your Remote Access deployment for your organization.

Web Application Proxy can function as an AD FS proxy and it also preauthenticates access to web applications using Active Directory Federation Services (AD FS).

PUBLISHING APPLICATIONS

One disadvantage to corporate networks are that the machines that access the network are normally devices issued by the organization. That's where Web Application Proxy publishing can help.

Web Application Proxy allows an administrator to publish an organization's applications, thus allowing corporate end users the ability to access the applications from their own devices. This is becoming a big trend in the computer industry; it's called *bring your own device (BYOD)*.

In today's technology world, users are buying and using many of their own devices, even for business work. Because of this, users are comfortable with their own devices. Web Application Proxy allows an organization to set up applications and enable their corporate users to use these applications with the devices the users already own, including computers, tablets, and smartphones.

The client side is easy to use as long as the end user has a standard browser or Office client. End users can also use apps from the Microsoft Windows Store that allow the client system to connect to the Web Application Proxy.

CONFIGURING PASS-THROUGH AUTHENTICATION

Now when setting up the Web Application Proxy so that your users can access applications, you must have some kind of security or everyone with a device would be able to access and use your applications.

Therefore, Active Directory Federation Services (AD FS) must always be deployed with Web Application Proxy. AD FS gives you features such as single sign-on (SSO). *Single sign-on* allows you to log in one time with a set of credentials and use that set of credentials to access the applications over and over. To use a Web Application Proxy, you should set your firewall to allow for ports 443 and 49443.

When an administrator publishes an application using the Web Application Proxy, the method that users and devices use for authentication is known as preauthentication. The Web Application Proxy allows for two forms of preauthentication:

AD FS Preauthentication   AD FS preauthentication requires the user to authenticate directly with the AD FS server. After the AD FS authentication happens, the Web Application Proxy then redirects the user to the published web application. This guarantees that traffic to your published web applications is authenticated before a user can access it.

Pass-Through Preauthentication   When using Pass-through Preauthentication, a user is not required to enter credentials before they are allowed to connect to published web applications.

Pass-through authentication is truly a great benefit for your end users. Think of having a network where a user has to log in every time that user wants to access an application. The more times you make your end users log into an application, the more chances there are that the end user will encounter possible issues. Pass-through authentication works in the following way:

1. The client enters a URL address on their device, and the client system attempts to access the published web application.

2. The Web Application Proxy sends the request to the proxy server.

3. If the backend server needs the user to authenticate, the end user needs to enter their credentials only once.

4. After the server authenticates the credentials, the client has access to the published web application.

To access applications easily that are published by the Web Application Proxy and use the AD FS preauthentication, end users need to use one of the following types of clients:

◆ Any HTTP client that supports redirection (web browsers). When Web Application Proxy receives an incoming message, the Web Application Proxy redirects the user to an authentication server and then back to the original web address authenticated.

◆ Rich clients that use HTTP basic.

◆ Clients that uses MSOFBA.

◆ Clients that use the Web Authentication Broker for authentication like Windows Store apps and RESTful applications.

Active Directory Federation Services Installation

The following sections describe how to install and deploy Active Directory Federation Services roles on computers running Windows Server 2022 (see Exercise 15.4). You will learn about the following:

◆ Deploying AD FS role services using Windows PowerShell

◆ Supporting upgrade scenarios for AD FS

EXERCISE 15.4 Installing the AD FS Role on a Computer Using Server Manager

1. Start Server Manager.

2. Click Manage and click Add Roles And Features. Click Next.

3. The Add Roles And Features Wizard shows the Before You Begin screen. Click Next.

4. Click Role-Based Or Feature-Based Installation on the Select Installation Type screen. Click Next.

5. Click the server on which you want to install Active Directory Federation Services from the Server Pool list on the Select Destination Server screen. Click Next.

6. Select the Active Directory Federation Services check box on the Select Server Roles screen. Server Manager will prompt you to add other features associated with this role, such as management tools. Leave the default selections. Click Add Features to close the dialog.

7. Click Next on the Select Server Roles screen.

8. Click Next on the Select Features screen.

9. Server Manager shows the Active Directory Federation Services screen. This screen displays simple role introduction and important AD FS configuration information. Click Next.

10. From the Select Server Roles screen, select the check box next to the AD FS role services to install on the computer. Click Next.

11. Server Manager prompts you to add other features associated with this role, such as management tools. Leave the default selections. Click Add Features to close the dialog.

12. Read the Confirm Installation Selections screen. This screen provides a list of roles, role services, and features that the current installation prepares on the computer. Click Install to begin the installation.

ROLE INSTALLATION USING WINDOWS PowerShell

To view the installation state of AD FS using Windows PowerShell, open an elevated Windows PowerShell console, type the following command, and press Enter:

```
Get-WindowsFeature "adfs*","*fed*"
```

UPGRADING TO WINDOWS AD FS 2022

Windows Server 2022 AD FS role supports upgrading version 3.0 of Active Directory Federation Services. You cannot upgrade versions of AD FS prior to version 3.0 using Windows Server 2022.

Table 15.5 represents the support upgrade matrix for the AD FS role in Windows Server 2022.

TABLE 15.5:   Support Upgrade Matrix for the AD FS Role in Windows Server 2022

AD FS AND OPERATING SYSTEM VERSION	WINDOWS SERVER 2022 UPGRADE SUPPORTED
AD FS 3.0 running on Windows Server 2008	No
AD FS 3.0 running on Windows Server 2008 R2	No
AD FS 3.0 Proxy running on Windows Server 2008	No
AD FS 3.0 Proxy running on Windows Server 2008 R2	No
AD FS 1.1 running on Windows Server 2008	No
AD FS 1.1 running on Windows Server 2008 R2	No
AD FS 1.1 Proxy running on Windows Server 2008	No
AD FS 1.1 Proxy running on Windows Server 2008 R2	No
AD FS 1.1 Web Agents on Windows Server 2008 or Windows Server 2008 R2	No

CONFIGURING ACTIVE DIRECTORY FEDERATION SERVICES

Windows Server 2022 delineates role installation and role deployment. Role installations make staged role services and features available for deployment. Role deployment enables you to configure the role service, which enables the role service in your environment. AD FS in Windows Server 2022 uses the same deployment tools as AD FS 3.0. However, an entry point to start these tools is included in Server Manager. Server Manager indicates that one or more role services are eligible for deployment by showing an exclamation point inside a yellow triangle on the Action Flag notification.

AD FS Graphical Deployment

The Run The AD FS Management snap-in link in Windows Server 2022 Server Manager is how you perform the initial configuration for the AD FS roles using the graphical interface. Alternatively, you can start the AD FS management console using the AD FS Management tile on the Start screen. The Start screen tile points to the `Microsoft.IdentityServer.msc` file located in the `c:\windows\adfs` folder.

To configure AD FS, select Start ➤ Run and type **FsConfigWizard.exe**; alternatively, click the `FsConfigWizard.exe` file located in the `c:\windows\adfs` folder.

Exercise 15.5 uses the AD FS Federation Server Configuration Wizard. To complete this exercise, you'll need an active SSL certificate assigned to the server and a managed service account for AD FS service.

EXERCISE 15.5 Configuring the AD FS Role on the Computer Using Server Manager

1. Select Create The First Federation Server In The Federation Server Farm.
2. Select the administrative account with permissions to configure the AD FS server and click Next.
3. Select the server certificate from the SSL certificate drop-down list.
4. Select the AD FS service name from the drop-down list.
5. Type **ADFS-Test** in the federation service's Display Name field and click Next.
6. Select Create A Database On This Server Using Windows Internal Database and click Next.
7. Click Next on the Review Options screen.
8. If the prerequisites check is successful, click Configure on the Prerequisite Check screen.
9. If the Result screen displays "This Server was successfully configured," you can click Close.

Deployment Using Windows PowerShell

Windows Server 2022 includes the Active Directory Federation Services module for Windows PowerShell when you install the AD FS role using Server Manager. The AD FS module for Windows PowerShell includes five new cmdlets to deploy the AD FS role:

- `Add-AdfsProxy`
- `Add-AdfsFarmNode`
- `Export-AdfsDeploymentSQLScript`
- `Install-AdfsStand-alone`
- `Install-AdfsFarm`

NOTE These AD FS cmdlets provide the same functionality as the command-line version of the AD FS Federation Server Configuration Wizard, `fsconfig.exe`. The AD FS role in Windows Server 2022 includes `fsconfig.exe` to remain compatible with previously authored deployment scripts. New deployments should take advantage of the deployment cmdlets included in the AD FS module for Windows PowerShell .

Add-AdfsProxy Configures a server as a federation server proxy.

FederationServiceName Specifies the name of the federation service for which a server proxies requests.

FederationServiceTrustCredentials Specifies the credentials of the Active Directory identity that is authorized to register new federation server proxies. By default, this is the account under which the federation service runs or an account that is a member of the Administrators group on the federation server.

ForwardProxy Specifies the DNS name and port of an HTTP proxy that this federation server proxy uses to obtain access to the federation service.

Add-AdfsFarmNode Adds this computer to an existing federation server farm.

CertificateThumbprint Specifies the value of the certificate thumbprint of the certificate that should be used in the SSL binding of the default website in IIS. This value should match the thumbprint of a valid certificate in the Local Computer certificate store.

OverwriteConfiguration Must be used to remove an existing AD FS configuration database and overwrite it with a new database.

SQLConnectionString Specifies the SQL Server database that will store the AD FS configuration settings. If a database is not specified, AD FS uses Windows Internal Database to store configuration settings.

ServiceAccountCredential Specifies the Active Directory account under which the AD FS service runs. All nodes in the farm must have the same service account.

PrimaryComputerName Specifies the name of the primary federation server in the farm that this computer will join.

PrimaryComputerPort Specifies the value of the HTTP port that this computer uses to connect with the primary computer in order to synchronize configuration settings. Specify a value for this parameter only if the HTTP port on the primary computer is not 80.

ACTIVE DIRECTORY FEDERATION SERVICES CERTIFICATES

There are three types of certificates used by an AD FS implementation:

◆ Service communications

◆ Token decrypting

◆ Token signing

The service communications certificate is required for communication with web clients over SSL and with web application proxy services using Windows Communication Foundation (WCF) components. This certificate is specified at configuration time for AD FS.

The token decrypting certificate is required to decrypt claims and tokens received by the federation service. The public key for the decrypting certificate is usually shared with relying parties and others to encrypt the claims and tokens using the certificate.

The token signing certificate is required to sign all claims and tokens created by the server. You can have multiple token encrypting and signing certificates for an implementation, and new ones can be added within the AD FS management tool.

RELYING PARTY TRUST

The federation service name originates from the SSL certificate used for AD FS. The SSL certificate can be template based and needs to be enrolled and used by IIS.

The next step in setting up AD FS is to configure a relying party trust. A relying party trust can be configured with a URL acquired from the relying party. The URL contains the federation metadata used to complete the federation trust configuration. The federation metadata may also be exported to a file that can then be imported into the relying-party trust. There is also a manual option for configuring a relying-party trust.

See Table 15.6 for the Federation Metadata fields.

TABLE 15.6:   Federation Metadata Fields

FIELD	DESCRIPTION
Display Name	This is the friendly display name given to this relying party trust.
Profile	Select AD FS Profile for the standard Windows Server 2012 AD FS, or select AD FS 1.0 And 1.1 Profile for AD FS configurations that need to work with older versions of AD FS.
Certificate	This is the optional certificate file from the relying party for token encryption.
URL	This is the URL for the relying party. WS-Federation Passive Protocol URL or SAML 2.0 WebSSO protocols are supported.
Identifiers	This is the unique identifier used for this trust.
Authorization Rules	Selecting this permits all users to access the relying party or denies all users access to the relying party, depending on the needs of this trust.

CONFIGURING CLAIMS PROVIDER AND TRANSFORM CLAIMS RULES

Claims provider trust rules are configured within the AD FS management console and are configured on a per-trust basis. Planning claims rules involves determining what claims are needed by the relying party to complete the authentication and authorization process and which users will need access to the relying party trust. The relying party determines what claims need to be received and trusted from the claims provider.

Trust rules start with templates as the basis for the rule. There are different types of claims templates depending on the type of rule being used. The claims rule templates for transforms are described in Table 15.7.

TABLE 15.7:   Transform Claims Rule Templates

TEMPLATE	DESCRIPTION
Send LDAP Attributes as Claims	Attributes found in an LDAP directory (such as Active Directory) can be used as part of the claim.
Send Group Membership as Claim	The group memberships of the logged-in user are sent as part of the claim.
Transform an Incoming Claim	This is used for configuring a rule to change an incoming claim. Changes include both the type and the value of an incoming claim.
Pass Through or Filter an Incoming Claim	This performs an action such as pass-through or filter on an incoming claim based on certain criteria, as defined in the rule.
Send Claims Using a Custom Rule	This creates a rule that's not covered by a predefined template, such as an LDAP attribute generated with a custom LDAP filter.

DEFINING WINDOWS AUTHORIZATION CLAIMS IN AD FS

Windows Server 2022 stores information that describes Windows authorization claims in the configuration partition of Active Directory. Windows refers to this information as *claim types*; however, Active Directory Federation Services typically refers to this information as claim descriptions. There are more than 40 claim descriptions available in the AD FS Windows Server 2022 release.

The Active Directory Federation Services role included in Windows Server 2022 lets you configure AD FS to include Windows authorization claims in the AD FS claim pipeline. To simplify this configuration, you can create *claim descriptions* in AD FS. Claim types in Windows authorization claims are analogous to claim descriptions in AD FS. The Windows authorization claim ID maps to the AD FS claim description's claim identifier.

To simplify AD FS configuration using Windows authorization claims, create a claim description in AD FS for each Windows authorization claim you intend to deploy in AD FS.

CREATE CLAIM PASS-THROUGH AND TRANSFORMATION RULES

You need to configure a claim rule with the Active Directory Claims Provider Trusts Wizard to insert Windows authorization claims into the AD FS claims pipeline.

Creating a claim description makes it easier to select the incoming claim type. Alternatively, you can type the claim type ID directly in the Incoming Claim Type list. A *pass-through claim rule* enables the Windows authorization claim to enter the AD FS claim pipeline. A pass-through claim leaves the claim type ID intact. Therefore, the pass-through claim ID begins with ad://ext, whereas most claim description URIs begin with http://. In addition, you can create a claim transformation claim rule on the Active Directory Claim Provider Trust Wizard to transform a Windows authorization claim into a well-known claim description.

Creating a claim provider trust claim rule enables the Windows authorization claim to enter the AD FS claim pipeline. However, this does not ensure that AD FS sends the Windows authorization claim. AD FS claim processing begins with the claim provider. This allows the claim to enter the pipeline. Claim processing continues for the targeted relying party—first with the issuance authorization rules and then with the issuance transform rules.

You can configure Windows authorization claims in claims rules configured on a relying party. By default, a relying party does not have any issuance transform rules. Therefore, AD FS drops all claims in the pipeline destined for a relying party when the relying party does not have any rules that pass incoming claims. Additionally, issuance authorization rules determine whether a user can receive claims for a relying party and, therefore, access the relying party.

Choose the claims types from the list of inbound rules created in the Active Directory claim provider trust that you want to send to the designated relying party. Then create rules that continue to pass the selected claim types through the pipeline to the relying party. Alternatively, you can create a rule that passes all the inbound claims to the relying party.

NOTE   The AD FS role in Windows Server 2022 cannot provide claim information when the incoming authentication is not Kerberos. Clients must authenticate to AD FS using Kerberos authentication. If Windows authorization claims are not entering the AD FS claim pipeline, then make sure the client authenticates to AD FS using Kerberos and the correct service principal name is registered on the computer/service account.

ENABLING AD FS TO USE COMPOUND AUTHENTICATION FOR DEVICE CLAIMS: COMPOUND AUTHENTICATION

Windows Server 2022 enhances Kerberos authentication by introducing compound authentication. Compound authentication enables a Kerberos TGS request to include two identities: the identity of the user and the identity of the user's device. Windows accomplishes compound authentication by extending Kerberos Flexible Authentication Secure Tunneling (FAST) or Kerberos armoring.

During normal Kerberos authentication, the Kerberos client requesting authentication for a service sends the ticket-granting service (TGS) a request for that service. Using Kerberos armoring, the TGS exchange is armored using the user's ticket-granting ticket (TGT). Prior to sending the ticket-granting service reply (TGS-REP) to the client, the KDC checks the 0x00020000 bit in the value of the msDS-SupportedEncryptionTypes attribute of the security principal's object running the service. An enabled bit means that the service can accept compound authentication. The KDC sends the TGS-REP, which includes the service's ability to support compound authentication.

The Kerberos client receives the ticket-granting service TGS-REP that includes compound authentication information. The Kerberos client then sends another ticket-granting service request (TGS-REQ), with the difference being that this TGS-REQ is armored with the device's TGT rather than the user. This allows the KDC to retrieve authentication information about the principal and the device.

The Active Directory Federation Services role included in Windows Server 2022 automatically enables compound authentication when creating an AD FS web farm. During the creation of the first node in the farm, the AD FS configuration wizard enables the compound authentication bit on the msDS-SupportedEncryptionTypes attribute on the account that you designate to run the

AD FS service. If you change the service account, then you must manually enable compound authentication by running the `Set-ADUser -compoundIdentitySupported:$true` Windows PowerShell cmdlet.

VERIFY MULTIFACTOR ACCESS CONTROL MECHANISM

In this phase, you will verify the multifactor access control policy that you set up in the previous phase. You can use the following procedure to verify that a test AD user can access your sample application because the test account belongs to the Finance group. Conversely, you will use the procedure to verify that AD users who do not belong to the Finance group cannot access the sample application.

1. On your client computer, open a browser window and navigate to your sample application: `https://webserv1.contoso.com/claimapp`. This action automatically redirects the request to the federation server, and you are prompted to sign in with a username and password.

2. Type in the credentials of a test AD account to be granted access to the application.

3. Type in the credentials of another test AD account that does not belong to the Finance group.

AD FS and AD Connect

Now that we have looked at Azure AD Connect and AD FS, let's take a look at how they can be set up together. When you decide to setup AD FS and AD Connect, there are different ways that you can accomplish this. The first way, and the easiest way, is to connect both services together is to do an Express Settings setup. When you do an Express Settings setup (see Figure 15.2), you just make a few choices and then AD FS and AD Connect can work together.

FIGURE 15.2
Azure AD
Connect Express

The second way that you can set up AD FS and AD Connect is to do a Custom setup. When you choose to do a Custom setup, the administrator can choose how AD FS and AD Connect will work together. The following are User sign-in options (see Figure 15.3) that you can setup in Azure AD Connect. Besides Azure AD Connect working with AD FS, you can setup Azure AD Connect to work with other sign in option:

FIGURE 15.3
Azure AD Connect user
Sign-in options

Password Hash Sync (PHS)   Users will be able to log into Microsoft cloud-based services using their on-site username and password. The user's passwords will be automatically synchronized to Azure AD as a password hash and the actual user authentication will occur in the cloud. Password Hash Sync also help protect against security issues. These include:

Smart Lockout   Smart Lockout assists in stopping brute force passwords attacks against a user's account.

IP Lockout   IP Lockout allows Azure to find IP addresses that are acting inappropriately on your network., For example, if you have an IP address that is trying to hit multiple user accounts, these IP addresses will be blocked. But your users will still be able to access their accounts by logging in properly to Azure.

Leaked Credentials   Leaked Credentials notifies an administrator if a username and password has been exposed or leaked due to phishing, malware, and password reuse on third-party websites that have been breached.

Pass-Through Authentication   Users will be able to sign into Microsoft cloud-based services using the same username and password that they use in their on-site network. The user's password is passed onto the on-site Active Directory domain controller to be validated.

Federation with AD FS   Users will be able to sign into Microsoft cloud services using the same password that they use for their on-site network. The user will be redirected to their on-site AD FS to sign in and authentication will occur through the on-site network.

Federation with PingFederate   Users will be able to sign into Microsoft cloud services using the same password that they use for their on-site network. The user will be redirected to their on-site PingFederate service to sign in and authentication will occur through the on-site network.

Do Not Configure   This option is chosen if no user sign-in feature is installed. Administrators would choose this option if they have a third-party federation server or other solution already set up.

Enable Single Sign-On   If you are using AD FS, this option is not available. AD FS has its own version of Single Sign-on (SSO) making this choice unavailable.

NOTE   When it comes to setting up Azure AD Connect, there are many other settings that you can choose to use. Settings like Exchange, Azure AD App settings, and others. To see how to set up all of the different Azure AD Connect settings, please visit Microsoft's website at `https://docs.microsoft.com/en-us/azure/active-directory/hybrid/how-to-connect-install-custom`.

Planning Azure AD Authentication Options

Azure AD is a centralized identity provider in the cloud and authentication is the process of verifying that you are who you say you are. It helps protect a user's identity and also simplifies the log-in experience. The Microsoft identity platform makes it easier to authorize and authenticate by providing identity as a service.

In Azure AD, authentication entails more than just verifying a username and password. Azure AD authentication includes the components that will be used to increase security and reduce the need for to contact the help desk for assistance. These components include:

◆ Azure AD Multi-Factor Authentication

◆ Hybrid integration to enforce password protection policies for an on-premises environment

◆ Hybrid integration to write password changes back to on-premises environment

◆ Passwordless authentication

◆ Self-service password reset

Azure AD Multi-Factor Authentication

Azure AD Multi-Factor Authentication allows you to choose a variety of different authentication methods during sign-in, such as receiving a phone call or receiving a verification code, or a text message (as seen in Figure 15.4).

FIGURE 15.4
Multi-Factor
Authentication Methods

By requiring a second form of authentication, you will be increasing your security. If you only use passwords to authenticate a user, this can potentially open doors for an attacker.

Azure AD Multi-Factor Authentication works by requiring two or more of the following:

◆ Something you know, such as a password.

◆ Something you have, such as a trusted device, like a phone or hardware key, which cannot be easily duplicated.

◆ Something you are, such as biometrics like a fingerprint or face scan.

PASSWORD PROTECTION

By default, Azure AD blocks weak passwords. An example of a weak password is Password1. Weak and known passwords are added to a global banned password list that is enforced and updated automatically so, if a user tries to use one of the passwords on the list, they will get a notification that they need to create a password that is more secure.

To boost your security, you can also define a custom password protection policy that will use filters to block different variations of passwords such as those containing names or locations.

You can also incorporate Azure AD password protection with an on-premises AD environment to create hybrid security. An on-premise component will get the global banned password list and the custom password protection policy and then the domain controllers will use both to process password change events. This will make sure that strong passwords will be enforced regardless of how a user changes their passwords.

PASSWORDLESS AUTHENTICATION

Passwordless Authentication is an authentication method that will allow your users to obtain access without answering any security questions or entering a password. This eliminates the requirement of a user to create and remember passwords.

To strengthen security, expand on the users experience, and to help reduce operation expenses, Passwordless Authentication can be used with Multi-Factor Authentication (MFA) and Single Sign-On (SSO) solutions.

When signing in using the passwordless authentication method, the credentials are provided by using approaches such as a fingerprint using biometrics with Windows Hello for Business, or a FIDO2 security key. An attacker cannot easily duplicate these forms of authentication.

SELF-SERVICE PASSWORD RESET (SSPR)

Self-service password reset allows a user to change or reset their password without any assistance from help desk or the administrator. If a user gets locked out of their account or cannot remember their password, they can simply follow prompts to get themselves back into the system. This ability reduces the number of help desk service calls and prevents loss of employee productivity.

SSPR allows users to:

◆ Change their password - this is used when the user knows their password and wants to change it.

◆ Reset their password - this is used when the user cannot sign in, because they forgot password, and want to reset it.

◆ Unlock their account—this is used when the user cannot sign in because the account is now locked and they want to unlock it.

TO ENABLE SELF-SERVICE PASSWORD RESET

Azure AD allows you to enable SSPR to either None, Selected, or All users (see Figure 15.5). Using the Azure portal, you can only enable one Azure AD group for SSPR.

1. Using an account with global administrator permissions, sign in to the Azure portal.

2. Search for and select Azure Active Directory, then select Password Reset from the menu on the left side.

3. From the Properties page, under the option Self-Service Password Reset Enabled, choose Selected.

4. If your group isn't visible, choose No Groups Selected, browse for and select your Azure AD group, and then choose Select.

5. To enable SSPR for the select users, click Save.

FIGURE 15.5
Enable Self-Service
Password Reset

FIGURE 15.5
Enable Self-Service
Password Reset

Azure AD Connect Sync—Understand and Customize Synchronization

Objects and credentials from an on-premises AD DS domain can be synchronized to Azure AD using Azure AD Connect in a hybrid environment. Once those objects are synchronized to Azure AD, the automatic background sync makes the objects and credentials available to applications using the managed domain.

A main component of Azure AD Connect is the Azure Active Directory Connect synchronization services (Azure AD Connect sync).

Azure AD Connect Sync handles all of the operations that pertain to synchronizing identity data between your on-premises environment and Azure AD. Azure AD Connect sync replaces DirSync, Azure AD Sync, and Forefront Identity Manager.

The Azure AD Connect sync service consists of two components:

◆ The on-premises Azure AD Connect sync component, also called the sync engine.

◆ The service side in Azure AD, called Azure AD Connect sync service.

These settings are configured by the Azure AD Module for Windows PowerShell. To see the configuration in your Azure AD directory, run Get-MsolDirSyncFeatures (as shown in Figure 15.6).

FIGURE 15.6
Get-MsolDirSync
Features Screen

```
PS C:\> Connect-MsolService
PS C:\> Get-MsolDirSyncFeatures

ExtensionData                          DirSyncFeature                      Enabled
------------                          --------------                      -------
System.Runtime.Serialization.Extensi... DeviceWriteback                    False
System.Runtime.Serialization.Extensi... DirectoryExtensions                True
System.Runtime.Serialization.Extensi... DuplicateProxyAddressResiliency    True
System.Runtime.Serialization.Extensi... DuplicateUPNResiliency             True
System.Runtime.Serialization.Extensi... EnableSoftMatchOnUpn               False
System.Runtime.Serialization.Extensi... PasswordSync                       True
System.Runtime.Serialization.Extensi... SynchronizeUpnForManagedUsers      False
System.Runtime.Serialization.Extensi... UnifiedGroupWriteback              True
System.Runtime.Serialization.Extensi... UserWriteback                      True
```

Many of these settings can only be changed by Azure AD Connect. The following settings can be configured by Set-MsolDirSyncFeature.

◆ EnableSoftMatchOnUpn - this allows objects to join on userPrincipalName in addition to primary SMTP address.

◆ SynchronizeUpnForManagedUsers - this allows the sync engine to update the userPrincipalName attribute for managed/licensed (non-federated) users.

Once you have enabled a feature, it cannot be disabled again. Table 15.8 shows you the settings configured by Azure AD Connect and cannot be modified by `Set-MsolDirSyncFeature`.

TABLE 15.8: Settings Configured by Azure AD Connect

DirSyncFeature	Note
DeviceWriteback	Azure AD Connect: Enables device writeback
DirectoryExtensions	Azure AD Connect sync: Directory extensions
DuplicateProxyAddressResiliency DuplicateUPNResiliency	Allows an attribute to be quarantined when it is a duplicate of another object rather than failing the entire object during export.
Password Hash Sync	Implement password hash synchronization with Azure AD Connect sync
Pass-Through Authentication	User sign-in with Azure Active Directory Pass-Through Authentication
UnifiedGroupWriteback	Group writeback
UserWriteback	Not currently supported.

Creating an Azure Recovery Policy

For the purpose of failover, a recovery plan groups machines into recovery groups. It works by creating smaller units that can be used for failover. These units usually represent apps. Recovery plans can do the following:

◆ Be customized by adding an order, instructions, and/or other tasks.

◆ Be used for failover to and failback from Azure.

◆ Define how machines will fail over and in what order they will start.

◆ Have a machine that is listed in several recovery plans.

◆ Have up to 100 instances added to one recovery plan.

◆ Run a failover once the plan has been defined.

You should use recovery plans to pattern an app around your needs. To help reduce the recovery time objective (RTO), you can automate the recovery tasks. By using a recovery plan, you ensure that you are prepared for migration or for disaster recovery, if needed. You can run test failovers of the recovery plans as well make sure everything is working as you have planned.

Model Apps

To capture app-specific properties, you will want to plan and create a recovery group. You generally customize a recovery plan so that the machines in each tier will start in the appropriate order after a failover event.

For example, consider a three-tier application with a web front end, middleware, and a SQL server backend.

◆ The SQL backend should start first, then the middleware, followed by the web front end.

◆ This order makes sure that the app is working when the last machine starts.

◆ This order also makes sure that when the middleware starts and attempts to connect to the SQL Server tier, the tier is already up and running.

◆ This order also ensures that the front-end server starts last so that the user won't connect to the web front-end until all other components are running and ready to accept requests.

You will want to add groups to the recovery group, and then add the machines into the groups in order to order to create this.

◆ Sequencing is used where order is specified. To improve application recovery RTO, actions run in parallel.

◆ Machines in a single group fail over in parallel.

◆ Machines in different groups fail over in group order. So, Group 2 machines start their failover only after all the machines in Group 1 have failed over and started.

Here is what takes place when you run a failover on the recovery plan that has this customization in action:

1. A shutdown step attempts to turn off the on-premises machines. The exception is if you are running a test failover. If you are running a test failover, the primary site continues to run.

2. The shutdown will trigger a parallel failover of all the machines that are in the recovery plan.

3. The failover prepares virtual machine disks using replicated data.

4. The startup groups run in order and will start the machines in each group: first, Group 1, then Group 2, and finally, Group 3. If there are more than one machine in any group, then all the machines start in parallel.

Automate Tasks in Recovery Plans

Administrators can use a recovery plan to enforce order and to automate the actions needed by using Azure Automation runbooks for failover to Azure, or they can use scripts since recovering large applications can be very complex.

You can insert pauses for manual actions into recovery plans for tasks that cannot be automated. There are several types of tasks you can configure:

◆ Azure VM after failover tasks. When you are failing over to Azure, you may need to perform actions so that you can connect to the VM after failover. Example:

    ◆ On the Azure VM, create a public IP address.

    ◆ On the Azure VM, assign a network security group to the network adapter.

    ◆ Add a load balancer to an availability set.

◆ Tasks inside VM after failover. These may include reconfiguring the app that is running on the machine so that it works correctly in the new environment. Example:

◆ Modifying the database connection string inside the machine

◆ Changing the web server rules or configurations

Run a Test Failover on Recovery Plans

Administrators can use a recovery plan to trigger a test failover. Here are some best practices that can be used:

◆ Before running a full failover, you should always complete a test failover on an app. This will help to ensure whether the app continues to work properly on the recovery site.

◆ If something is missing, you can trigger a clean-up and then run the test failover again.

◆ Until you are sure that the application recovers fully, you can run the test failover a number of times.

◆ You may need to build customized recovery plans for each application and run a test failover on each because each application is different.

◆ You should run test failovers quarterly since applications and their dependencies change often.

Create a Recovery Plan

To create a recovery plan, follow these steps:

1. Select Recovery Plans (Site Recovery) ➤ +Recovery Plan in the Recovery Services vault.

2. Specify a name for the plan in Create Recovery Plan.

3. Then, select a source and target depending on the machines in the plan, and select Resource Manager for the deployment model (see Table 15.9). The source location must have machines that are enabled for failover and recovery.

TABLE 15.9: Selecting a Source and Target Machine

FAILOVER	SOURCE	TARGET
Azure to Azure	Select the Azure region.	Select the Azure region.
VMware to Azure	Select the configuration server.	Select Azure.
Physical machines to Azure	Select the configuration server.	Select Azure.
Hyper-V to Azure	Select the Hyper-V site name.	Select Azure.
Hyper-V (managed by VMM) to Azure	Select the VMM server.	Select Azure.

Administrators should note some of the following:

- You can use a recovery plan for both of these options:
    - Failover to Azure
    - Failback from Azure

- You must have machines that are enabled for failover and recovery in the source location.

- A recovery plan can contain machines with the same source and target.

- The same plan can include VMware VMs and Hyper-V VMs managed by VMM.

- The same plan can include VMware VMs and physical servers.

- All VMs in a recovery plan must replicate into a single subscription. If an administrator wants to replicate different VMs to different subscriptions, then you will want to use more than one recovery plan. One or more for each target subscription.

4. In **Select Items Virtual Machines**, select the machines (or replication group) to be added to the plan. Then click OK.

    - Machines are added to the default group in the plan. All machines in this group start at the same time after failover.

    - An administrator can only select machines in the source and target locations that are specified.

5. Click OK to finish creating the plan.

ADD A GROUP TO A PLAN

In order to identify different behaviors on a group-by-group basis, you can create additional groups and add machines to different groups. An administrator can indicate when machines in a group should start after failover or specify customized actions per group. A machine or replication group can only belong to one group in a recovery plan.

1. In Recovery Plans, right-click the plan and choose Customize. By default, all the added machines are located in default Group 1.

2. Click +Group. New groups are numbered in the order in which they were added. You can add up to seven groups.

3. Select the machine you want to move to the new group, click Change Group, and select the new group. You can also right-click the group name and choose Protected Item and then add machines to the group.

ADD A SCRIPT OR MANUAL ACTION

By adding a script or manual action, you can customize a recovery plan. If you are replicating to Azure, you can integrate Azure automation runbooks into your recovery plan. If you are replicating Hyper-V VMs that are managed by System Center VMM, you can create a script on the on-premises VMM server and include it in the recovery plan. When you add a script to your recovery plan, it will add a new set of actions for the group. If you add a manual action, then as soon as the recovery plan runs, it will stop where you placed the manual action. This will bring up a dialog box that will prompt you to indicate when the manual action is complete.

Scripts can also be applied during failover to the secondary site and during failback from the secondary site to the primary. Support will depend upon the replication scenario. Table 15.10 shows some of the different scenarios.

TABLE 15.10:   Selecting a Source and Target Machine

SCENARIO	FAILOVER	FAILBACK
Azure to Azure	Runbook	Runbook
Hyper-V site to Azure	Runbook	N/A
Hyper-V with VMM to Azure	Runbook	Script
VMware to Azure	Runbook	N/A
VMM to secondary VMM	Script	Script

How to Add a Script or Manual Action

If an administrator wants to create a custom script or manual action, they would use the following steps:

1. In the recovery plan, you will want to click on the step where the action is to be added and then specify the action:

   a. If you want the action to take place before the machines in the group are started after failover, then select Add Pre-Action.

   b. If you want the action to take place after the machines in the group start after failover, then select Add Post Action. To move the position of the action, you can select the Move Up or Move Down button.

2. Select either the Script or Manual action in Insert Action.

3. To add a manual action, perform the following:

   a. Type in a name for the action and then type in action instructions.

   b. Specify if you want to add the manual action for all types of failover: Test, Failover, Planned Failover (if relevant). Then click **OK**.

4. To add a script, perform the following:

   a. If adding a VMM script, select **Failover** To VMM, script and in the **Script Path** type the relative path to the share.

   b. If you're adding an Azure automation run book, then specify the **Azure Automation Account** where the runbook is located and select the appropriate **Azure Runbook Script**.

5. Make sure the script runs as expected by running a test failover of the recovery plan.

The Bottom Line

Understand Azure AD Connect. Microsoft Azure allows a company of any size to connect their on-site domain with their Azure Active Directory network.

Master It You are the administrator of a large network. You need to quickly connect your on-site domain to your Azure network.

Configure Azure Recovery. Azure administrators have the ability to setup Azure Recovery to protect their apps and data.

Master It You are the administrator of a large company that has Azure users in multiple areas. You need to make sure that you setup Azure recovery.

Chapter 16

Understanding Microsoft Endpoint

In this chapter, I will cover the benefits of using Microsoft Endpoint and the tools and applications that will help IT administrators manage their software and applications.

I will also talk about Autopilot and how you can use Autopilot to deploy operating systems to new or repurposed machines. It is truly a zero-touch installation.

IN THIS CHAPTER YOU'LL LEARN

- ◆ Understand MDM
- ◆ Using AutoPilot

Using Microsoft Endpoint Manager

Microsoft Endpoint Manager is used for maintaining, monitoring, and protecting your end users and endpoints. Whether you are using the cloud or an on-premises networks, Microsoft Endpoint Manager will help keep your data safe and secure. It consists of the tools and services that you can use to monitor and maintain your endpoints. Endpoints include the following items:

- ◆ Apps
- ◆ Desktop computers
- ◆ Embedded devices
- ◆ Mobile devices
- ◆ Servers
- ◆ Shared devices
- ◆ Virtual machines

Microsoft Endpoint Manager includes a variety of services:

- ◆ Azure Active Directory (Azure AD)
- ◆ Co-management
- ◆ Configuration Manager
- ◆ Desktop Analytics

- Endpoint Manager Admin Center

- Microsoft Intune

- Windows Autopilot

Endpoint Manager uses Azure Active Directory (Azure AD) to identity devices, groups, multifactor authentication (MFA), and users.

Co-management is used to join an already existing on-premises Configuration Manager asset to the cloud by using either Intune or another Microsoft 365 cloud service. An administrator will determine which service will be the management authority.

Desktop Analytics is a cloud-based service that works in conjunction with Configuration Manager. It helps an administrator to make important decisions regarding the update readiness of a Windows client. Desktop Analytics looks at the data from your company along with data collected from millions of other devices that are connected to the Microsoft cloud to help provide information on apps, security updates, and more. Desktop Analytics is used to keep Windows 10 devices current.

The Endpoint Manager Admin Center is used as a comprehensive website that is used to manage devices and create policies. It is where you can locate the Microsoft Intune service as well as other settings related to device management.

Microsoft Intune is a cloud-based mobile device management (MDM) and mobile application management (MAM) provider that you use for apps and devices. Using the cloud, Intune can be used to create and check for compliance, deploy apps, and change device features and settings on a variety of devices.

Windows Autopilot is used to streamline the way devices get deployed, reset, and repurposed, by using a deployment method that requires no interaction from the IT department. Autopilot is used to preconfigure devices and to automatically enroll devices into Intune. Your users simply unbox the device and turn it on and Windows Autopilot will configure it from the cloud using just a few steps.

What deployment method should you use? This is a question that is often asked. There really is no right or wrong answer. Use what works best for you or your organization and consider what you wish to accomplish. You can start with Windows Autopilot if you are continually provisioning new devices or you can use Intune if you add rules and control settings for your apps, devices, and users.

Endpoint Manager can be thought of in three separate parts: the cloud, on-premises, and cloud + on-premises.

Cloud   All your data is stored in Azure. This method provides you with the benefits of mobility in the cloud as well as the security advantages that are provided by Azure.

On-Premises   If you aren't ready to use the cloud, then you can keep your existing systems in house. All hardware and software applications are hosted onsite.

Cloud + On-Premises   This is also referred to as a hybrid. These environments use a combination of both cloud and on-premises solutions.

There are a number of benefits of using Microsoft Endpoint Manager. These benefits are used to manage and protect your endpoints. They allow you to do the following:

- Confirm that user devices are configured and protected according to corporate policies.

- Confirm that your corporate security rules are in place.

- Ensure that corporate services are available to your end users and on all of their devices.

- Ensure that your company is utilizing correct credentials in order to access and share corporate information.

- Protect the apps and devices that access your resources.

- Protect the data that your users are accessing.

NOTE   If you have Microsoft Endpoint Configuration Manager or Microsoft Intune then you already have Microsoft Endpoint Manager. These are all now one management system.

Using Mobile Device Management

Mobile Device Management (MDM) is basically a way in which administrators can manage mobile devices. It refers to a set of functions and features that regulate the use of mobile devices to make sure they are compliant with corporate policies.

MDM allows an administrator to maintain, secure, and enforce mobile endpoint policies. MDM allows administrators to set up Windows 10/11 policies that can incorporate a wide variety of scenarios, such as the ability to control a user's access to the Windows Store or the ability to access the corporate VPN.

To help administrators manage corporate security policies and business applications, Windows 10 and Windows 11 provide an enterprise management solution that consists of two parts:

- The enrollment client, which enrolls and configures the device to communicate with the enterprise management server

- The management client, which synchronizes with the management server to check for updates and apply policies

MDM administers mobile devices without joining them to an on-premises Active Directory Domain Services (AD DS). In order to manage a device using MDM, MDM is implemented by using an MDM authority and MDM clients. Microsoft offers two MDM authority solutions:

- Basic Mobility and Security (Microsoft 365)

- Microsoft Intune

Once the device is enrolled, administrators can still implement policies and profiles to manage the device. Each of these solutions use Microsoft 365 Endpoint Manager for administering the MDM solutions. They each manage enrolled devices, but they provide distinct capabilities.

MDM client functionality is included with the Windows 10/11 operating system. MDM includes the delivery of applications, settings, and data to devices that are enrolled to MDM. Windows 10/11 devices can be enrolled to MDM by any of these methods by:

- Being enrolled into Azure AD (if Azure AD and MDM are configured)
- Using Group Policies in a hybrid environment
- Using a provisioning package
- Using the Settings app
- Manually configuring

MDM authority, such as Intune, can provide these capabilities:

- Application Management
- Configuring devices
- Device enrollment
- Monitoring and reporting
- Selectively delete data

Application Management   Administrators can install apps and manage settings by using both MDM and Mobile Application Management (MAM).

Configuring Devices   Administrators can utilize profiles and policies to configure devices, to control what users can access, and to set device settings to comply with corporate policies.

Device Enrollment   MDM can manage only supported devices that have been enrolled. In order to manage a device, the device can either include the MDM client functionality, such as Windows 10, or you must install a Company Portal app (for example, on Android or iOS devices).

Monitoring and Reporting   The MDM management tool, you can get a notification if a device is having an issue or if a policy was not properly applied. Enrolled devices can also be added to groups. You can also configure Windows Autopilot device deployment by using Intune.

Selectively Delete Data   Should a device ever get lost or stolen, or if a user leaves your company, you can wipe the corporate data is that is on the device. A wipe is basically just erasing the data from the hard disk on the device. You have to option to either wipe all the data on the device or perform a selective wipe, which will leave the user's personal data on the device intact.

Even if a device isn't a member of the domain, the device can be managed by MDM. If a device is a Windows 10/11 device that is a member of the domain, then it can be managed by Group Policy and MDM simultaneously. With Windows 10 version 1803 and newer, administrators can regulate whether a Group Policy setting or an MDM policy setting will take precedence if there is a conflict.

You can manage the following Windows 10/11 configuration areas by using MDM:

- Application management
- Device configuration and security
- Enrollment
- Inventory
- Remote assistance
- Unenrollment

Application management has the following benefits:

- Custom Windows Store
- Business Store Portal (BSP) app deployments; license reclaim
- Enterprise app management
- Line-of-business (LOB) app management
- Win32 (MSI) app management
- App inventory (LOB/Store apps)
- App allow/deny lists using AppLocker
- Windows Information Protection (WIP)

Device configuration and security includes the following benefits:

- Device update control
- Email provisioning
- Enterprise Wi-Fi
- Extended set of policies for client certificate management
- Kiosk, Start screen, Start menu configuration, and control
- MDM push
- VPN management

Enrollment benefits are as follows:

- Azure AD integration
- Bulk enrollment
- Converged protocol
- Provisioning
- Simple bootstrap

Inventory as the following benefit:

♦ Additional device inventory

Remote Assistance benefits are as follows:

♦ Enhanced inventory for compliance decisions

♦ Full device wipe

♦ Remote lock, PIN reset, ring and find

Unenrollment benefits are as follows:

♦ Removal of enterprise configuration (apps, certs, profiles, policies) and enterprise-encrypted data (with EDP)

♦ Unenrollment with alerts

Introduction and Overview of Policy Settings Using Basic Mobility and Security (Microsoft 365)

Within Microsoft 365, the Basic Mobility and Security service provides a built-in MDM solution that provides the core device management features.

NOTE The Basic Mobility and Security service is hosted by the Intune service and contains a subset of Intune services. Even though it has some of the features used by Intune, according to Microsoft, it's not an "Intune-lite" solution.

Administrators can use Basic Mobility and Security to manage many types of mobile devices. To manage the mobile devices, each person must have an applicable Microsoft 365 license, and their device must be enrolled in Basic Mobility and Security. Once it's set up and the devices are enrolled, administrators can manage the devices, block access to the device, and even wipe the device.

When creating policies or profiles, they can only be deployed by assigning them to groups of users. Administrators can't directly assign a policy to a specific user or to an individual device. The user will receive an enrollment message on their device and once they have completed the device enrollment, then their device will be constrained by the policies that the administrator sets. Then, using the MDM management tool, administrators can monitor the policy deployment.

Using Basic Mobility and Security, administrators can manage these mobile devices settings:

Organization-Wide Device Access Settings Administrators can specify whether they want to allow or deny access to Exchange mail for devices that are not supported by Basic Mobility and Security and which groups should be excluded from access control.

Device Security Policies Administrators can use these policies to protect devices from unauthorized access. These policies include password settings, encryption settings, managing email profile settings, and settings that control the use of device features, such as Bluetooth and videoconferencing.

Many MDM solutions help protect organizational data by making sure users and devices meet specific requirements. These are known as compliance policies and act as the rules and settings that users and devices must meet in order to be compliant.

When paired with Conditional Access requirements, administrators can deny users and devices that do not meet your rules. Administrators can use some of these policies to help affect the entire Microsoft 365 experience.

Compliance Microsoft uses the default compliance rules that are built into Configuration Manager settings for mobile devices, but, then made new configuration items (CIs) and then added built-in compliance rules whose values are based on Microsoft's digital security requirements. Microsoft then created a configuration baseline for those CIs and targeted the configuration baseline to the collection of mobile devices.

Messaging The default policies for Exchange align policy settings between Exchange ActiveSync (EAS) and MDM.

Security The default policies enforce Microsoft corporate compliance settings on mobile devices, such as password policy and encryption settings.

Introduction and Overview of Policy Settings Using Microsoft Intune

Microsoft Intune is a cloud-based service that focuses on Mobile Device Management (MDM) and Mobile Application Management (MAM). With Intune, administrators can control how their mobile devices are used. It also allows you to configure specific policies which control applications using application management.

Intune allows administrators to control how mobile devices are utilized whether it's a corporate owned or personal device. On personal devices, Intune can help ensure that corporate data is protected, and it can also isolate the corporate data from personal data.

Intune allows administrators to manage multiple devices per person and the regardless of the different platforms that are run on the different devices.

NOTE Administrators cannot start using Basic Mobility & Security if they are already using Microsoft Intune.

In Intune, users will see a dialog box that tells them about the policies and then they can select to allow the policies or they can cancel device enrollment.

Administrators can manage the same settings in Microsoft Intune as in Basic Mobility and Security. But there are also other settings that allow Intune administrators to manage. Some of these include:

- Application deployment, configuration policies, and protection policies

- Conditional Access

- Device compliance policies

- Device configuration policies

- Device enrollment and restrictions

- Software updates, which include Windows 10/11 update rings and update policies for iOS

While Basic Mobility & Security is part of the Microsoft 365 plans, and Microsoft Intune is a standalone product included with certain Microsoft 365 plans. Table 16.1 identifies which plans provide each MDM solution.

TABLE 16.1: Microsoft 365 Plans

PLAN	BASIC MOBILITY & SECURITY	MICROSOFT INTUNE
Microsoft 365 Apps	Yes	No
Microsoft 365 Business Basic	Yes	No
Microsoft 365 Business Standard	Yes	No
Office 365 E1	Yes	No
Office 365 E3	Yes	No
Office 365 E5	Yes	No
Microsoft 365 Business Premium	Yes	Yes
Microsoft 365 Firstline 3	Yes	Yes
Microsoft 365 Enterprise E3	Yes	Yes
Microsoft 365 Enterprise E5	Yes	Yes
Microsoft 365 Education A1	Yes	Yes
Microsoft 365 Education A3	Yes	Yes
Microsoft 365 Education A5	Yes	Yes
Microsoft Intune	No	Yes
Enterprise Mobility & Security E3	No	Yes
Enterprise Mobility& Security E5	No	Yes

Understanding AutoPilot

Windows Autopilot is a set of programs that helps simplify and streamline bulk deployment, setup, and configuration of devices. Autopilot allows an administrator to truly have a zero-touch installation of the Windows client operating system.

Administrators can use Autopilot to reset, repurpose, and recover devices. By using Autopilot, you can reduce the time spent on deploying, managing, and retiring devices.

Autopilot allows an administrator to:

◆ Auto-enroll devices into MDM services.

◆ Automatically join devices to Azure Active Directory (Azure AD) or Active Directory (via Hybrid Azure AD Join).

◆ Create and auto-assign devices to configuration groups based on a device's profile.

◆ Customize out-of-box-experience (OOBE) content specific to the organization.

Autopilot allows administrators to set up and preconfigure new Windows devices for their organization, right out of the box, without the need of building an image or infrastructure to manage. Users go through the process by themselves, without making any decisions and without the need to involve an IT administrator.

By using Autopilot Reset, existing devices can be quickly prepared for a new user. The Reset capability can also be used if a device needs to be fixed in order to bring the device back to a working state.

Administrators can provide new devices to their end users without the need to build, maintain, and apply custom operating system images to the devices by using Microsoft Intune and Autopilot. Once deployed, Windows devices can be managed by tools such as Microsoft Intune, Windows Update for Business, Configuration Manager, and other similar tools.

Autopilot allows an administrator to get a list of device IDs from a manufacturer. The device IDs get entered into your Azure environment. The IT administrator assigns a device profile to that machine and that's it. Once the user logs into the internet, the machine automatically recognizes that it is part of your organization and the installation is completed. Without any IT intervention.

Autopilot Benefits

Administrators would have to spend hours upon hours building and customizing images that would be used to later deploy devices. But, with Autopilot, you do not need to reimage or manually set up new devices before giving them to your end users.

Devices can be shipped to your users directly from the vendor. It only takes a few simple actions to make the device ready to use. The end user just connects to the network and verifies their credentials. Beyond that, everything else is automated by Autopilot. Some of the key Autopilot benefits include:

Easy Device Setup   Users connect their devices to the Internet, answer some quick setup questions, and Autopilot installs all preconfigured user, device, and app policies.

Increased Employee Satisfaction   Devices configured with Autopilot provide users with an easy login experience that reduces the need for tech support.

Saves Time and Resources   Instead of spending hours setting up devices, you can create a customized OOBE of preconfigured apps and settings and then deploy them to the users device using the cloud.

Ability to Use It Anywhere   Devices configured using Autopilot can be shipped anywhere and set up wherever. The user only needs an Internet connection.

Autopilot Prerequisites

Autopilot relies on specific capabilities that are available in Windows 10/11, Azure Active Directory (Azure AD), and MDM services. Let's take a look at the requirements for Autopilot.

SOFTWARE REQUIREMENTS

In order to use Autopilot, a supported version of Windows 11 or Windows 10 semi-annual channel is required.

NETWORKING REQUIREMENTS

The network requirements depend on various Internet-based services. Access to these services must be provided for Autopilot to function properly.

- Ensure DNS name resolution for Internet DNS names.

- Allow access to all hosts through ports 80 (HTTP), 443 (HTTPS), and 123 (UDP/NTP).

LICENSING REQUIREMENTS

Autopilot depends on specific capabilities available in Windows 10/11 and Azure AD and an MDM service such as Microsoft Intune. One of the following subscriptions is required:

- Microsoft 365 Business Premium subscription

- Microsoft 365 F1 or F3 subscription

- Microsoft 365 Academic A1, A3, or A5 subscription

- Microsoft 365 Enterprise E3 or E5 subscription, which include all Windows 10, Microsoft 365, and EM+S features (Azure AD and Intune)

- Enterprise Mobility + Security E3 or E5 subscription.

- Intune for Education subscription

- Azure Active Directory Premium P1 or P2 and Microsoft Intune subscription (or an alternative MDM service)

According to Microsoft, the following subscriptions are also recommended, but not required:

- Microsoft 365 Apps for Enterprise (formerly Office 365 Pro Plus)

- Windows Subscription Activation, to automatically upgrade devices from Windows 10 Pro to Windows 10 Enterprise

CONFIGURATION REQUIREMENTS

Before Autopilot can be used to support common Autopilot scenarios, the following configuration tasks must be done:

- Configure Azure AD automatic enrollment.

- Configure Azure AD custom branding.

- Enable Windows Subscription Activation.

Some scenarios have other requirements. There are typically two tasks that should be performed:

- Device registration—Devices must be added to Autopilot to support most Autopilot scenarios.

- Profile configuration—Once devices have been added to Autopilot, a profile of settings must be applied to each device.

AUTOPILOT PROFILES

Autopilot profiles control how Windows is installed on user devices. The profiles contain settings that are automatically set and optional settings that you can set up manually. Automatically set options include:

◆ Skip Cortana, OneDrive, and OEM registration - this option will skip the installation of apps such as Cortana and OneDrive.

◆ Sign in experience with your company brand - if you have an "Add your company branding to Microsoft 365 Sign In page," then the device will get that experience when signing in.

◆ MDM auto-enrollment with configured AAD accounts - The user identity will be managed by Azure AD. The user will log in using their Microsoft 365 Business Premium credentials.

Manually set options include:

◆ Skip privacy settings (Off by default) - if this is set to On, the user will not see the license agreement for the device and Windows when they first sign in.

◆ Don't allow the user to become the local admin - if this is set to On, the user will not be able to install any personal apps.

Deployment Scenarios

Administrators have several different ways that they can deploy Autopilot. Some of these include:

◆ User-driven mode

◆ Self-deploying mode

◆ Windows Autopilot Reset

◆ Pre-Provisioning

◆ Support for existing devices

USER-DRIVEN MODE

Autopilot user-driven mode allows you to configure new Windows devices to automatically transform them from their factory state to a ready-to-use state. This process doesn't require that the administrator even touch the device. The devices can be shipped or distributed to the end user directly with the following instructions:

1. Unbox the device, plug it in, and turn it on.

2. Choose a language, locale, and keyboard.

3. Connect it to a wireless or wired network with Internet access.

4. Specify your corporate email address and password.

The rest of the process is automated and the device will automatically do the following:

1. Join the organization.

2. Enroll in Intune (or another MDM service).

3. Get configured as defined by the company.

SELF-DEPLOYING MODE

Self-deployment mode is very similar to user-driven mode. This mode allows you to deploy a device with little to no user interaction. For devices with an Ethernet connection, no user interaction is required, however, for devices connected using Wi-Fi, the user must only:

◆ Choose the language, locale, and keyboard.

◆ Make a network connection.

Self-deploying mode provides the following:

◆ Joins the device to Azure Active Directory.

◆ Enrolls the device in Intune (or another MDM service) using Azure AD for automatic MDM enrollment.

◆ Makes sure that all policies, applications, certificates, and networking profiles are provisioned on the device.

◆ Uses the Enrollment Status Page to prevent access until the device is fully provisioned.

Self-deploying mode does not support Active Directory Join or Hybrid Azure AD Join. All devices will be joined to Azure AD.

WINDOWS AUTOPILOT RESET

Takes the device back to a business-ready state by:

◆ Removing personal files, apps, and settings.

◆ Reapplying a device's original settings.

◆ Setting the region, language, and keyboard to the original values.

◆ Maintaining the device's identity connection to Azure AD.

◆ Maintaining the device's management connection to Intune.

The Autopilot Reset process automatically keeps information from the existing device:

◆ Wi-Fi connection details.

◆ Provisioning packages previously applied.

◆ A provisioning package present on a USB drive when the reset process is started.

◆ Azure AD device membership and MDM enrollment information.

When Autopilot reset is used on a device, the device's primary user will be removed and the next person who signs in after the reset will become the new primary user.

It's important to note that the Autopilot Reset does not support Hybrid Azure AD joined devices; a full device wipe will be required. Once a hybrid device goes through a full device reset, it may take up to 24 hours for it to be ready to be deployed.

PRE-PROVISIONING

This was once referred to as the Autopilot white glove feature, but, it has been renamed to Windows Autopilot for Pre-provisioned deployment. With Autopilot for pre-provisioned deployment, the provisioning process is split with the time-consuming portions being done by the IT administrators, partners, or OEMs (this is called the technician flow) and the end user just needs to perform a few necessary settings and policies and then they can begin using their device (this is called the user flow). Autopilot for pre-provisioned deployment supports two distinct scenarios. They are:

- User-driven deployments with Azure AD Join - The device will be joined to an Azure AD tenant.

- User-driven deployments with Hybrid Azure AD Join - The device will be joined to an on-premises Active Directory domain, and separately registered with Azure AD.

Each scenario consists of two parts, a technician flow and a user flow.

SUPPORT FOR EXISTING DEVICES

Autopilot for existing devices only supports user-driven Azure AD and Hybrid Azure AD profiles. Self-deploying and pre-provisioning profiles are not supported.

Windows Autopilot Devices

Devices that have been registered with the Autopilot service are displayed in the Admin Center. As seen in Figure 16.1, in the Admin Center under Devices ➤ Enroll devices | Windows enrollment ➤ Windows Autopilot Deployment Program ➤ Devices.

FIGURE 16.1
Autopilot Deployment

Devices that are listed in Intune under Devices ➤ Windows | Windows devices are not the same as Windows Autopilot devices (Devices ➤ Enroll devices | Windows enrollment ➤ Windows Autopilot Deployment Program | Devices).

Windows Autopilot devices are added to the list of Windows devices when both of the following are complete:

◆ The Autopilot registration process is successful.

◆ A licensed user has signed in on the device.

Planning for Secure Applications Data on Devices

One issue that every IT admin must decide upon is how to deploy applications safely and securely to their organization's users and computers. There are dozens of utilities that allow you to deploy and manage applications. Azure includes its own set of tools for managing and maintaining applications.

Configuring Managed Apps for Mobile Application Management (MAM)

Sometimes the assumption is made that Mobile Device Management (MDM) is the same as Mobile Application Management (MAM). However, that is not necessarily the case. In layman's terms, MDM is more about controlling devices where MAM is concerned with your company applications and data.

MAM is software that protects and enables you to control company applications on your end users' devices. It allows you to apply and enforce policies on apps and limit the sharing of corporate data. It also allows you to separate corporate from personal data on these devices.

MOBILE APPLICATION MANAGEMENT (MAM) BASICS

Intune MAM refers to the suite of Intune management features that allow you to publish, push, configure, secure, monitor, and update mobile apps to your users. It allows you to manage and protect your company data within an application. Intune MAM supports two configurations:

Intune MDM + MAM   Administrators can manage apps using MAM on devices that are enrolled with Intune mobile device management (MDM). To manage apps using MDM + MAM, users should use Intune in the Microsoft Endpoint Manager admin center.

Unenrolled Devices with MAM Managed Applications   Administrators can manage corporate data and accounts in apps using MAM on unenrolled devices or devices enrolled with third-party EMM providers. To manage apps using MAM, users should use Intune in the Microsoft Endpoint Manager admin center.

Most app-related information can be found in the Apps workload. You can find this by following these steps:

1. Sign into the Microsoft Endpoint Manager admin center.

2. Select Apps.

The apps workload provides links to access common app information and functionality. The top of the App workload navigation menu provides commonly used app details:

◆ Overview: Allows you to view the tenant name, MDM authority, tenant location, account status, app installation status, and app protection policy status.

◆ All apps: Displays a list of all available apps and see their statuses.

◆ Monitor apps: There are a few options under this section:

  ◆ App licenses: Can view, assign, and monitor volume-purchased apps from the app stores.

  ◆ Discovered apps: Can view apps that were assigned by Intune or installed on a device.

  ◆ App install status: Can view the status of an app assignment that you created.

  ◆ App protection status: Can view the status of an app protection policy for a selected user.

◆ By Platform: Can select these platforms to view the available apps by platform:

  ◆ Windows

  ◆ iOS

  ◆ MacOS

  ◆ Android

◆ Policy: There are a few options under this section:

  ◆ App protection policies: Choose this option to associate settings with an app and help protect the company data it uses.

  ◆ App configuration policies: Choose this option to supply settings that might be required when a user runs an app.

  ◆ iOS app provisioning profiles: iOS apps include a provisioning profile and code that is signed by a certificate. When the certificate expires, the app can no longer be run. Intune provides you with the tools to assign a new provisioning profile policy to devices that have apps that are nearing expiration.

  ◆ S mode supplemental policies: Choose this option to authorize additional applications to run on your managed S mode devices.

  ◆ Policies for Office apps: Choose this option to create mobile app management policies for Office mobile apps that connect to Microsoft 365 services.

  ◆ Policy sets: Choose this option to create an assignable collection of apps, policies, and other management objects that you have built.

- Other: There are a few options under this section:

  - App selective wipe: Choose this option to remove only corporate data from a selected user's device.

  - App categories: Can add, pin, and delete app category names.

  - E-books: Some app stores give you the ability to purchase multiple licenses for an app or books that you want to use in your company.

- Help and support. Choose this to troubleshoot, request support, or view Intune status.

Add an App Using Intune

This is an example of how to use Intune to add and assign an app for your corporate users. You will first want to sign into the Microsoft Endpoint Manager admin center as a Global administrator or an Intune Service administrator.

Perform these steps to add an app to Intune:

1. Sign into Microsoft Endpoint Manager admin center and select Apps ➤ All Apps ➤ Add.

2. In the App type drop-down box, select Windows 10.

3. Click Select. The Add app steps are displayed.

4. Confirm the default details in the App suite information step and click Next.

5. Confirm the default settings in the App settings step and click Next.

6. Select the group assignments for the app.

7. Click Next to display the Review + Create page. Review the values and settings you entered for the app.

8. When you are done, click Create to add the app to Intune.

Assign the App to a Group

Once you have added an app using Microsoft Intune, you can assign the app to additional groups of users or devices.

Perform these steps to assign an app to a group:

1. In Intune, select Apps ➤ All Apps.

2. Select the app that you want to assign.

3. Click Properties. Next to Assignments, click Edit.

4. Click Add Group under the Required section. The Select Group pane is displayed.

5. Find the group that you want to add and click Select at the bottom of the pane.

6. Click Review + Save ➤ Save to assign the group.

You now have assigned the app to an additional group.

Install the App on the Enrolled Device

Your end users must install and use the Company Portal app to install an app that is available in Intune.

1. Log in to the enrolled Windows 10 Desktop device. The device must be enrolled with Intune and must be signed in using an account contained in the group that was assigned to the app.

2. From the Start menu, open the Microsoft Store. Then, find the Company Portal app and install it.

3. Launch the Company Portal app.

4. Click the app that you added using Intune.

5. Click Install.

Protecting Enterprise Data using Windows Information Protection (WIP)

Information protection in today's cybersecurity settings consist of four different parts. These parts consist of:

♦ Device Protection - protect system and data when a device is lost or stolen.

♦ Data Separation - Containment and data separation.

♦ Leak Protection - Prevent unauthorized users and apps from accessing and leaking data.

♦ Sharing Protection - Protect data when shared with others, or shared outside of corporate devices and control.

Windows Information Protection (WIP) helps protect corporate data in a world that is increasingly becoming a Bring Your Own Device (BYOD) environment. Since many organizations are allowing employees to connect their own devices to their network, the possibility of corporate data being compromised because of non-corporate programs running on these personnel devices is increasing. WIP helps protect information by separating corporate applications and corporate data from being disclosed by personal devices and personal applications.

WIP was previously known as Enterprise Data Protection (EDP). WIP is a built-in Windows 10 and Windows 11 feature that allows an administrator to maintain and monitor company data separate from any personal data that is on a user's device.

WIP aids in protecting against possible data leaks and protects enterprise apps and data on both enterprise-owned and personal devices without interfering with the user's experience while on the corporate network. Users do not need to open any special apps or enter into any specific modes in order for WIP to work. Users just use apps that they are used to and WIP will provide the data protection.

Besides separating corporate and personal data, WIP can also determine which users and apps have access to particular data and can determine what users are allowed to do with that corporate data. For example, an administrator has the ability to stop a user from copying corporate data from an approved app and pasting that data into another unapproved app.

The WIP Intune policy maintains a list of protected apps, corporate network locations, the levels of protection granted, and the encryption settings. WIP provides the following:

♦ Allows an administrator to track issues and find corrective actions by using audit reports.

♦ Integrates with existing management systems to deploy, configure and manage WIPs. Management systems can include Microsoft Intune, System Center Configuration Manager (SCCM), or an MDM.

♦ Provides added protection for present line-of-business apps without needing to update any apps.

♦ Provides the capability to remove corporate data from Intune MDM enrolled devices while, at the same time, not touching the personal data on a device.

♦ Separates personal data from corporate data, without the need for the user to change apps or settings.

An administrator can set a WIP policy with a different level of protection and management modes. There are four protection and management modes. They are as follows (see Figure 16.2):

♦ Block: Prevents users from engaging in unauthorized actions, such as copying and pasting corporate data. WIP searches for unacceptable data sharing and will stop the user from performing any further.

♦ Override: Alerts users whenever they try to execute an unauthorized action. The user can ignore the warning and proceed with the unauthorized action; however, WIP will log the event in its audit log where an administrator can review it later.

♦ Silent: Will run in the background, tracking the user's actions with no indicator of an unauthorized action and logging any inappropriate data sharing. However, if an action is blocked, the action will be prevented as usual.

♦ Off: WIP is disabled and provides no protection or auditing.

NOTE It's not recommended, but an administrator can turn off WIP. This can be done without data loss to the devices that were managed by WIP. WIP can be turned back on, but the previously applied decryption and policy information will not be automatically reapplied.

WIP uses System Center Configuration Manager (SCCM) to design and implement WIP policies. Once an administrator has set up SCCM they must create a configuration item for WIP; this is the WIP policy.

CREATING A CONFIGURATION ITEM FOR WIP

To create a configuration item for WIP, follow the following steps:

1. Open the SCCM console, click the Assets And Compliance node, expand the Overview node, expand the Compliance Settings node, and then expand the Configuration Items node (see Figure 16.3).

2. Click the Create Configuration Item button. The Create Configuration Item Wizard will start (see Figure 16.4).

FIGURE 16.2
Configure Windows
Information Protection
Settings

FIGURE 16.3
System Center
Configuration
Manager console

FIGURE 16.4
Create Configuration
Item Wizard

3. On the General Information screen, type a name (required) and a description (optional) for the policy into the Name and Description boxes.

4. In the Specify The Type Of Configuration Item That You Want To Create area, pick the option that represents whether you'd like to use SCCM for device management, and then click Next. The options are as follows:

◆ Settings For Devices Managed With The Configuration Manager Client: Windows 10

◆ Settings For Devices Managed Without The Configuration Manager Client: Windows 8.1 And Windows 10

5. On the Supported Platforms screen (see Figure 16.5), click the Windows 10 box, and then click Next.

6. On the Device Settings screen (see Figure 16.6), select Windows Information Protection, and then click Next.

The Configure Windows Information Protection settings page appears, where an administrator can configure a policy for the company.

When an administrator creates a process in SCCM, they can choose the apps that will be granted access to corporate data via WIP. Apps on the list can protect and restrict data from being copied or moved to unapproved apps.

FIGURE 16.5
Create Configuration
Item Wizard - Supported
Platforms

FIGURE 16.6
Create Configuration
Item Wizard - Device
Settings

The steps to add app rules are based on the type of rule template that is being applied. An administrator can add the following:

◆ Store app (known as a Universal Windows Platform (UWP) app

◆ Signed Windows desktop app

◆ AppLocker policy file

In the follow sections, we will be adding Microsoft OneNote, which is a store app, to the App Rules list.

ADDING A MICROSOFT STORE APPLICATION

There may be times when you need to add a Microsoft Store application to the App Rules list. The following steps will show you how to complete this task:

1. From the App Rules area (see Figure 16.7), click Add. The Add App Rule box appears.

2. In the Title box, add a name for the app. In this example, it's Microsoft OneNote.

3. In the Windows Information Protection Mode drop-down list, click Allow. Clicking Allow turns WIP on to help protect that app's company data.

4. Pick Store App from the Rule Template drop-down list. The box will change to show the store app rule options.

5. Type the name of the app and the name of its publisher, and then click OK. For this UWP app example, the Publisher is CN=Microsoft Corporation, O=Microsoft Corporation, L=Redmond, S=Washington, C=US and the Product name is Microsoft .Office.OneNote.

After configuring the policy, an administrator can review all of the settings by looking at the Summary screen. Click on Summary to review the policy choices and then click Next to finish and save the policy.

WIP FILE BEHAVIOR

Files and apps can be categorized as either work or personal. Where you get the file and where you save new files determines whether files are protected by WIP.

When working with existing files:

◆ If you get a file from a corporate location, it will automatically be WIP-protected.

◆ If you get it from a personal location, it will not be WIP-protected.

When saving new files:

◆ If you save it to a corporate location, it will be WIP-protected.

◆ If you save it to a personal location, it will not be WIP-protected.

Enlightened apps also provide the option when saving a file to choose if it's corporate-related or personal. However, if you store a work file to a personal location, WIP gives you the option of saving it as a personal file or saving it at a different location.

FIGURE 16.7
Create Configuration
Item Wizard - Add
App Rule

FIGURE 16.7
Create Configuration
Item Wizard - Add
App Rule

Determine the Enterprise Context of an App

You can check the context of an app on your machine by using Windows Task Manager. But you must first activate the Enterprise Context column. To activate the column, perform the following:

1. Open Task Manager and, if you aren't already in the detail view, select More details.

2. Select the Details tab.

3. Right-click in the column heading area and then choose Select columns.

4. Scroll down, check the Enterprise Context option, and then select OK to close the box.

5. The Enterprise Context column will now be visible in Task Manager.

The Enterprise Context column displays what each app can do with your corporate data:

◆ Domain - If your domain is displayed the app is running in corporate-related mode and protects the content the app is currently accessing.

◆ Personal - If Personal is displayed, the app is running in personal mode and can't touch any work data or resources.

◆ Exempt - If Exempt is displayed, the app is running in trusted mode and WIP policies are bypassed.

Monitor WIP Events

A device protected by WIP will generate different events that are saved to the event log on the local machine. WIP will create audit events in the following situations:

◆ A user changes the File ownership for a file from corporate to personal data.

◆ Data is marked as corporate data but shared to a personal app or webpage. Can be through copy and paste, drag and drop, sharing a contact, uploading to a personal webpage, or if the user grants a personal app temporary access to a protected file.

◆ An app has custom audit events.

You can use Windows Event Forwarding to collect the WIP audit events and then view those events using Event Viewer.

Changing File Ownership

It is possible to change the file ownership using Windows Explorer, you simply just check the File ownership and change it from Personal to Work, or vice versa. When you perform this operation, it will be saved to the event log.

CONFIGURE INTUNE APPLICATION PROTECTION POLICIES FOR DEVICES

App protection policies (APP) are a set of rules that make sure a company's data remains safe or contained in a managed app. A policy can be a rule that is enforced if a user tries to access or move the data, or is a set of actions that are monitored when a user is using the app. A managed app is an app that has app protection policies applied to it, and can be managed by Intune. App protection policies can apply to apps running on devices that may or may not be managed by Intune.

You can use Intune APP separate of any MDM solution. This allows you to protect corporate data with or without enrolling devices in a device management solution. You can restrict access to corporate resources by applying app-level policies.

APPs can be configured for apps that run on devices that are:

◆ Enrolled in Microsoft Intune - these devices are typically corporate owned.

◆ Enrolled in a third-party MDM solution - these devices are typically corporate owned.

◆ Not enrolled in any MDM solution - these devices are typically owned by the user and the devices are not managed or enrolled in Intune or other MDM solutions.

There are a number of benefits when using APP. Some of the benefits include:

◆ Protecting corporate data at the app level - Since MAM does not require device management, you can protect corporate data on both managed and unmanaged devices.

◆ End-user productivity is not affected and policies do not apply when using the app in a personal context - the policies are applied only in a work context, which gives you the ability to protect corporate data without touching personal data.

◆ App protection policies makes sure that the app-layer protections are in place - so, you can:

◆ Require a PIN to open an app in a work context

◆ Control the sharing of data between apps

◆ Prevent the saving of company app data to a personal storage location

◆ MDM, in addition to MAM, makes sure that the device is protected - so, you can require a PIN to access the device, or you can deploy managed apps to the device.

The choices available in APP allow you to customize the protection to meet your specific needs. To help you prioritize mobile client endpoint hardening, Microsoft has introduced taxonomy for its APP data protection framework for iOS and Android mobile app management.

The APP data protection framework is organized into three different configuration levels, with each level building off the previous level:

◆ Enterprise basic data protection (Level 1) - ensures that apps are protected with a PIN and encrypted and performs selective wipe operations.

◆ Enterprise enhanced data protection (Level 2) - introduces APP data leakage prevention mechanisms and minimum OS requirements. This is the configuration that is applicable to most mobile users accessing work or school data.

◆ Enterprise high data protection (Level 3) - introduces advanced data protection mechanisms, enhanced PIN configuration, and APP Mobile Threat Defense. This configuration is desirable for users that are accessing high risk data.

Create an App Protection Policy

The following steps will walk you through the process of creating an App Protection Policy:

1. In Intune, select Apps ➤ App protection policies ➤ Create Policy ➤ Windows 10.

2. Enter the following details:

◆ Name: The name of this app protection policy.

◆ Description [Optional] - The description of this app protection policy.

◆ Enrollment state - This will show if the device is enrolled or not.

3. Under Protected apps, click Add. The Add apps pane is displayed.

4. Choose the apps that must adhere to this policy and click OK.

5. Click Next to display the Required settings.

6. Click Allow Overrides to set the Windows Information Protection mode. Selecting this option will block enterprise data from leaving the protected app.

7. Click Next to display the Advanced settings.

8. Click Next to display the Assignments.

9. Click Select groups to include, click the group, and click Select.

10. Click Next to display the Review + create step.

11. Click Create to create your policy.

Change Existing Policies

You can also edit an existing policy and apply it to the targeted users. But you need to be aware that when you make changes to an existing policy, any user who is already signed in to the apps will not see the changes for an eight-hour period. In order to see the effects of changes immediately, the end user must sign out of the app and then sign back in.

Change Policy Settings

1. In the App protection policies pane, select the policy you wish to modify.

2. In the Intune App Protection pane, select Properties.

3. Next to the section corresponding to the settings you want to change, select Edit. Then change the settings to new values.

4. Click Review + Create to review the updated settings for this policy.

5. Select Save to save your changes. Repeat the process to select a settings area and modify and then save your changes until all your changes are complete. You can then close the Intune App Protection - Properties pane.

The Bottom Line

Understand MDM. Microsoft Device Management allows an administrator to manage and configure Windows devices.

> **Master It** You are the administrator of a large network. One of your employees just informed you that their laptop was stolen. The Device was enrolled into Microsoft Device Management.

Using Autopilot. Autopilot allows an organization to quickly and easily install operating systems onto new or repurposed machines without any IT personnel building each machine.

> **Master It** Your organization is going to be purchasing 50 new devices from the same vendor. You need to setup all 50 devices without using images or IT Intervention.

## Chapter 17

Configuring Security

In this chapter, I am also going to talk about defending your Windows systems by using the built-in security features called Windows Defender Security Center. I will show you the different ways that you can protect your system using the Defender Security Center options.

I will show you how to protect your Windows client and server devices by using the Windows Firewall. The Windows Firewall can help protect your client systems from being illegally breached, but when you're building a network, your Windows Firewall should NOT be your only firewall. Your network connection to the Internet should also be protected by some type of firewall, but that is an entirely different course (depending on your firewall type).

I am also going to dive into protecting Windows and also using Azure to help protect your network. Windows offers protection like Windows Firewall and Azure offers organizations multiple ways to protect devices and data by using Azure tools like Windows Defender Application Guard, Windows Defender Advanced Threat Protection, and Windows Defender Antivirus.

So, let's get started by looking at protecting your Windows devices by using Windows Firewall.

IN THIS CHAPTER YOU'LL LEARN

- ◆ Understand how to configure Windows Firewall
- ◆ Use Windows Defender Application Control

Managing Windows Security

Without showing my age, I have been in the computer industry for over 30 years. When I first got into networking, security basically was just protecting files from unauthorized access from people in your own organization. Today, that is completely changed. We still have to make sure that our servers and data is protected from unauthorized employee access, but we also have to spend much of our time protecting our networks from outside threats.

Unfortunately, there is no magic pill or solution to stop these external threats. Even if you decide that you want to completely disconnect your network from the Internet, your organization can still be attacked. One of the main reasons is because of our end-users. In today's technology world, most of our users have devices that they use at home and also on their corporate network.

So, when we talk about network security, it's not just a single thing that we can do to protect our network. To truly protect our networks, we need to use multiple layers of security. This not only includes tools and devices that we can put on our physical network like hardware based firewalls and Intrusion Detection Systems, but also tools that we can add to our devices to help keep them secure.

Microsoft Windows devices (client- and server based) includes built-in Windows Security (see Figure 17.1) including antivirus protection. Windows devices are automatically protected from the very moment that your users start using Windows. Windows Security is always scanning the system for viruses, malware (malicious software), and security dangers.

Not only does Windows provide real-time protection, but Microsoft also continually does operating system updates to make sure that your corporate devices stay safe and that the devices are protected from any new threats.

FIGURE 17.1
Windows Security
dialog box

Windows Defender Security Center

Windows includes the Windows Defender Security Center (see Figure 17.2). The Windows Defender Security Center is a built-in Windows application that protects your system from viruses and spyware. It is included free with the operating system, and once you turn your operating system on, Windows Defender starts automatically protecting your system.

The Windows Defender Security Center has multiple options that you can set to help protect your system. So, let's take a look at some of these options.

I am going to show the options that are available on a Windows 10/11 Client system. Windows Server 2022 only has the following options: Virus and Threat Protection, Firewall and Network Protection, App & Browser Control, and Device Security. The reason that I am covering the client-side options is because it is important to configure both the Server Firewall protection and the Client Firewall protection to ensure that your network has multiple layers of security.

FIGURE 17.2
Windows Defender
Security Center

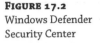

Virus & Threat Protection   Windows will automatically monitor for threats that can impact your device, run scans on your system, and get updates to help protect against any new threats. Windows has an antivirus program built in and it will get automatic updates when your Windows systems get updated.

Account Protection   Administrators can configure the user's sign-in options and account settings. These settings are included while using Windows 10/11.

Firewall & Network Protection   Windows includes a Windows Firewall and the Windows Firewall allows administrators to help prevent unauthorized users or malicious software from accessing your computer.

App & Browser Control   Administrators can configure update settings for Windows Defender SmartScreen and this helps protect your Windows devices against potentially dangerous applications, downloads, files, and web sites. This gives administrators the ability to control exploit protection and customize settings that will help protect your Windows devices.

Device Security   Windows Device Security allows administrators to use built-in security options to defend their organization's Windows devices from malicious software attacks.

Device Performance & Health   Windows allows administrators to view the status information about a device's performance health. This helps administrators keep their organization's devices clean and up-to-date with the latest version of Windows. These settings are included while using Windows 10/11.

Family Options   The Family Options feature in Windows Security is not a feature that most administrators will configure in a corporate environment. These options provide tools to help manage children's computer access. Parents can use Family Options to help keep their children's devices clean and up-to-date with the latest version of Windows and to protect their children when they are on the Internet. These settings are included while using Windows 10/11.

EXERCISE 17.1   Running an Advanced Scan

1. Click Start ➢ Settings ➢ Update & Security ➢ Windows Security and then choose Virus & Threat Protection.

2. Choose the link Run A New Advanced Scan (see Figure 17.3).

FIGURE 17.3
Run A New Advanced Scan link

Windows Defender Security Center

- Home
- Virus & threat protection
- Account protection
- Firewall & network protection
- App & browser control
- Device security
- Device performance & health
- Family options

○ Virus & threat protection

View threat history, scan for viruses and other threats, specify protection settings, and get protection updates.

Threat history
Last scan: 9/28/2019 (quick scan)

0   22152
Threats found   Files scanned

Scan now

Run a new advanced scan

Virus & threat protection settings
Cloud-delivered protection is off. Your device may be vulnerable.

Virus & threat protection updates
Last update: 12:36 PM Friday, October 04, 2019

3. Make sure the radio button is on Full Scan and choose the Scan Now button (see Figure 17.4).

FIGURE 17.4
Advanced Scans options

← Windows Defender Security Center

- Home
- Virus & threat protection
- Account protection
- Firewall & network protection
- App & browser control
- Device security
- Device performance & health
- Family options

Advanced scans

Run full, custom, or Windows Defender Offline scan.

⦿ Full scan
Checks all files and running programs on your hard disk. This scan could take longer than one hour.

○ Custom scan
Choose which files and locations you want to check.

○ Windows Defender Offline scan
Some malicious software can be particularly difficult to remove from your device. Windows Defender Offline can help find and remove them using up-to-date threat definitions. This will restart your device and will take about 15 minutes.

Scan now

4. The scan will take a while. After the scan finishes, close the Defender Security Center.

In Exercise 17.1, I will show you how to run an advanced virus and threat scan on your Windows device.

Now that you understand how to work with the Windows Security Center, let's take a closer look at how to configure your Windows Firewall within that Security Center.

Configuring Windows Firewall

Windows Firewall, which is included with Windows, helps prevent unauthorized users or malicious software from accessing your computer. Windows Firewall does not allow unsolicited traffic, which is traffic that was not sent in response to a request, to pass through the firewall.

Understanding Windows Firewall Basics

You configure Windows Firewall by clicking Start ➢ Settings ➢ Update & Security ➢ Windows Security and then choosing Firewall & Network Protection. You can then decide what firewall options you want to set (as shown in Figure 17.5), like changing firewall notifications, turning Windows Firewall on or off, restoring defaults, configuring advanced settings, and troubleshooting.

FIGURE 17.5
Windows Firewall
settings dialog box

The Windows Firewall settings dialog box allows you to turn Windows Firewall on or off for both private and public networks. The On setting will block incoming sources, and the Turn Off Windows Firewall setting will allow incoming sources to connect.

There is also a check box for Block All Incoming Connections. This feature allows you to connect to networks that are not secure. When Block All Incoming Connections is enabled, all incoming connections (even ones allowed in the allowed apps list) will be blocked by Windows Firewall.

Windows Firewall with Advanced Security

You can configure more-advanced settings by configuring Windows Firewall with Advanced Security (WFAS). To do so, click Start ➢ Settings ➢ Update & Security ➢ Windows Security ➢ Firewall & Network Protection ➢ Advanced Settings. The Windows Firewall With Advanced Security dialog box appears, as shown in Figure 17.6.

FIGURE 17.6
Windows Firewall With
Advanced Security
settings

The scope pane to the left shows that you can set up specific inbound and outbound rules, connection security rules, and monitoring rules. The central area shows an overview of the firewall's status when no rule is selected in the left pane. When a rule is selected, the central area shows the rule's settings. The right pane shows the same actions as the Actions menu on the top. These are just shortcuts to the different actions that can be performed in Windows Firewall. Let's take a more detailed look at some of the elements in Windows Firewall.

INBOUND AND OUTBOUND RULES

Inbound and outbound rules consist of many preconfigured rules that can be enabled or disabled. Obviously, inbound rules (see Figure 17.7) monitor inbound traffic, and outbound rules monitor outbound traffic. By default, many are disabled. Double-clicking a rule will bring up its Properties dialog box (Figure 17.8).

You can filter the rules to make them easier to view. Filtering can be based on the profile the rule affects, on whether the rule is enabled or disabled, or on the rule group. You can filter a rule by clicking which filter type you want to use in the right pane or by clicking the Actions menu on the top of the screen.

FIGURE 17.7
Inbound rules

FIGURE 17.8
An inbound rule's
Properties dialog box

If you can't find a rule that is appropriate for your needs, you can create a new rule by right-clicking Inbound Rules or Outbound Rules in the scope pane and then selecting New Rule. The New Inbound (or Outbound) Rule Wizard will launch, and you will be asked whether you want to create a rule based on a particular program, protocol or port, predefined category, or custom settings.

As you are setting up the firewall rules, you have the ability to configure authenticated exceptions. No matter how well your system security is set up, there are almost always times when computers on your network can't use IPsec. This is when you set up authenticated exceptions. It's important to understand that when you set up these authenticated exceptions, you are reducing the security of the network because it allows computers to send unprotected IPsec network traffic. So make sure that the computers that are added to the authenticated exceptions list are managed and trusted computers only. Table 17.1 shows you some of the most common port numbers and what those port numbers are used for.

TABLE 17.1:   Common Port Numbers

PORT NUMBER	ASSOCIATED APPLICATION OR SERVICE
20	FTP Data
21	FTP Control
22	Secure Shell (SSH)
23	Telnet
25	SMTP
53	DNS
67/68	DHCP/BOOTP
80	HTTP
102	Microsoft Exchange Server
110	POP3
443	HTTPS (HTTP with SSL)

Complete Exercise 17.2 to create a new inbound rule that will allow only encrypted TCP traffic.

EXERCISE 17.2 Creating a New Inbound Rule

1. Click Start ➤ Settings ➤ Update & Security ➤ Windows Security ➤ Firewall & Network Protection.

2. Click the Advanced Settings link.

3. Right-click Inbound Rules and select New Rule.

4. Choose a rule type. For this exercise, choose Custom so you can see all the options available to you. Then click Next.

5. At the Program screen, choose All Programs. Then click Next.

6. Choose the protocol type as well as the local and remote port numbers that are affected by this rule. For this exercise, choose TCP, and ensure that All Ports is selected for both Local Port and Remote Port. Click Next to continue.

7. At the Scope screen, choose Any IP Address for both local and remote. Then click Next.

8. At the Action screen, choose Allow The Connection Only If It Is Secure. Click Next.

9. At the Users screen, you can experiment with these options if you want by entering users to both sections. Once you click one of the check boxes, the Add and Remove buttons become available. Click Next to continue.

10. At the Computers screen, you can choose what computers you will authorize or allow through this rule (exceptions). Again, you can experiment with these options if you want. Click Next to continue.

11. At the Profiles screen, choose which profiles will be affected by this rule. Select one or more profiles and click Next.

12. Give your profile a name and description, and then click Finish. Your custom rule will appear in the list of inbound rules, and the rule will be enabled.

13. Double-click your newly created rule. Notice that you can change the options that you previously configured.

14. Delete the rule by right-clicking the new rule and choosing Delete. A dialog box will appear asking you if you are sure. Click Yes.

15. Close Windows Firewall.

CONNECTION SECURITY RULES

Connection security rules are used to configure how and when authentication occurs. These rules do not specifically allow connections; that's the job of inbound and outbound rules. You can configure the following connection security rules:

◆ Isolation: To restrict a connection based on authentication criteria

◆ Authentication Exemption: To specify computers that are exempt from authentication requirements

- Server-to-Server: To authenticate connections between computers
- Tunnel: To authenticate connections between gateway computers
- Custom

Monitoring

The Monitoring section shows detailed information about the firewall configurations for the Domain Profile, Private Profile, and Public Profile settings. These network location profiles determine what settings are enforced for private networks, public networks, and networks connected to a domain.

🌐 Real World Scenario

Use More Than Just Windows Firewall

When doing consulting, it always makes me laugh when I see small to midsize companies using Microsoft Windows Firewall and no other protection. Microsoft Windows Firewall should be your *last* line of defense. You need to make sure that you have good hardware firewalls that separate your network from the world.

Also watch Windows Firewall when it comes to printing. I have run into many situations where a printer that needs to communicate with the operating system has issues when Windows Firewall is enabled. If this happens, make sure that the printer is allowed in the Allowed Programs section of the Windows Firewall.

Datacenter Firewall

Firewalls allow an administrator to setup policies on who or what can be allowed past the firewall. For example, if you want to allow DNS traffic to pass through the firewall, you would enable port 53. If you want the traffic to leave the firewall, you would configure port 53 outbound. If you want to have the traffic enter into the company, you would configure inbound.

Datacenter Firewalls are included with Windows Server 2022 network layer, Stateful, multi-tenant firewalls. Network administrators that work with virtual network tenants can install and then configure firewall policies. These firewall policies can help protect their virtual networks from unwanted traffic from Internet and intranet networks.

The Datacenter Firewall allows you to setup granular access control lists (ACLs) and this allows you to apply firewall policies at the VM interface level or at the subnet level. To create ACLs on the Datacenter Firewall, an administrator can use Windows PowerShell.

The following is an example of the PowerShell command that is used to assign the ACL to the AccessControlList property of the network interface.

```
$nic.properties.ipconfigurations[0].properties.AccessControlList = $acl
```

Windows Server 2022 Datacenter Firewalls give you the following tenant benefits.

- Administrators have the ability to define firewall rules that help protect Internet-facing workloads on virtual networks.

- Administrators have the ability to define firewall rules to protect data between virtual machines on the same layer 2 or different layer 2 virtual subnets.

- Administrators have the ability to define firewall rules to protect and isolate network traffic between tenants on a virtual network from a service provider.

So now that we have taken a look at Windows Firewall, let's look at protecting your Windows devices by using Azure.

Managing Security

Another way that you can help defend your corporate devices is by using Microsoft Azure. Azure has many different tools that allow an administrator to control and protect a company's Windows devices.

Earlier in the chapter, I talked about using the Windows Defender Security Center. Now we are going to look at using Windows Defender in Azure.

Implementing Azure Windows Defender Advanced Threat Protection

When talking about Windows Defender, it can be a little confusing to people. The reason for this is that Windows has come with Windows Defender and Azure also now comes with Windows Defender. So when IT people are discussing Defender, it's important that they specify which version they are talking about. I am going to talk about Azure's version of Windows Defender and the benefits that it provides to organizations.

Your organization's IT department can have even better threat protection when they combine Azure Windows Defender Advanced Threat Protection (Windows Defender ATP) with Azure Advanced Threat Protection (Azure ATP) as shown in Figure 17.9. Figure 17.9 was taken directly from Microsoft's website and it shows all of the different ways Azure ATP and Windows Defender ATP can work together.

Azure ATP allows organizations to monitor domain controller traffic while Windows Defender ATP allows organizations to monitor endpoints (for example, user's devices). Organizations can use both of these defenses together for the best possible protection and both of can be managed by using a single Azure interface.

When deciding to integrate Azure ATP and Windows Defender ATP together, you get the benefits of both systems working together. Some of these benefits include:

Endpoint Behavioral Sensors   Endpoint behavioral sensors are sensors that are built into the Windows operating system and these sensors gather and process behavioral data for things like the registry, files, processors, and communications. This data is then sent to the Windows Defender ATP.

Azure ATP Sensors and Stand-Alone Sensors   These sensors can be placed directly onto your domain controllers or they can be set up to port mirror directly from your domain controller to Azure ATP. These sensors have the ability to collect and parse traffic for multiple protocols that work with authentication, authorization, or just for informational gathering.

Threat Intelligence   Threat intelligence comprises multiple Microsoft tools, security groups, and third-party threat defending partners. Threat intelligence allows Windows Defender ATP to properly recognize tools and activities that hackers use and then report alerts when those tools or activities are observed.

FIGURE 17.9
Inbound rules

Cloud Security Analytics   Cloud security analytics uses multiple detection signals and Microsoft insights to detect and recommend protection against advanced threats.

Azure ATP uses multiple technologies to detect suspicious behavior during all phases of a cyber based attack. These phases include:

The Investigation Phase (Reconnaissance)   This is the phase where hackers gather information on a target organization. This phase can include information gathering by using Internet investigation, dumpster diving, etc.

Scanning Phase   This phase is when an attacker tries to scan for vulnerabilities. These can be port scanners (looking for open ports to access), vulnerability scanning (looking for known vulnerabilities), and network scanning (looking at network components like routers and firewalls).

Access Phase   This is the phase when hackers try to gain access to your network based off of the investigation phase and scanning phase.

Maintaining Access Phase   This is the phase when hackers try to put back doors or software in place so that the hackers can continue to gain access to your network.

Clearing Their Tracks Phase   Hackers that are any good will try to clear their tracks so that no one knows that they were there. This is when hackers will try to delete logs and any evidence that the hack even took place.

Windows Defender ATP uses Microsoft technologies and expertise to help detect and stop the different phases of a hacker. By using their experience, Microsoft has put in advanced methods to detect hacking before the hacks take place.

Understanding Windows Defender Application Guard

One of the biggest issues that we have in IT is the Internet. It's a world game changer and a company game changer. But that also means it's an IT game changer. We in IT, have to rethink how we protect our networks, and that's because of the Internet.

Years ago, hackers had to use phone lines and that helped prevent a lot of hacker wannabes. Phone lines were easy to track and it could be expensive for a young hacker to spend a lot of money on phone calls, especially if they were unsuccessful with their hacks.

Today, anyone can hack from anywhere because of the World Wide Web, and they pay only a monthly fee for Internet access. So we must rethink how we protect our data and our companies. This is where Application Guard can help us.

Application Guard was specifically designed for Windows and Microsoft Internet browsers (Edge and Internet Explorer [IE]). Application Guard works with Windows Edge to isolate untrusted websites, thus protecting your organization's network and data while users are working on the Internet.

As an Enterprise Administrator, you can pick and choose which websites are defined as trusted sites. These sites can be internal websites, external websites, company websites, and cloud-based organizations. If a site is not on the trusted list, it is considered untrusted and automatically isolated when a user visits.

When a user accesses a website (using Edge or IE) that is not on the trusted list, Microsoft Edge will be automatically opened in an isolated Hyper-V enabled container. This container will be a separate environment from the host operating system, and this will help protect untrusted websites from causing damage to the Windows system. Also, since the website will be isolated, any type of attack will not affect the corporate network or its data.

Windows Defender Application Guard is disabled by default. Windows Defender Application Guard works in two modes: Standalone or Enterprise. Standalone mode allows a non-corporate user to use Windows Defender Application Guard without any administrator-configured policies. Enterprise mode is used in an enterprise environment and can be configured automatically by the Enterprise Administrator.

WINDOWS DEFENDER APPLICATION GUARD STANDALONE MODE

If a user wants to use Standalone mode on Windows 10/11 or Windows Server, they need to be using either Windows 10 Enterprise edition (version 1709 or higher) or Windows 10 Pro edition (version 1803 or higher). The user must install Application Guard manually on their Windows device and then they need to manually start Microsoft Edge in Application Guard while they are browsing untrusted sites.

Exercise 17.3 will show you how to install Windows Defender Application Guard using the Windows Control Panel.

EXERCISE 17.3 Installing Windows Defender Application Guard

1. Right-click Start ➤ Control Panel ➤ Large Icon View ➤ Programs And Features.
2. Click the link Turn Windows Features On Or Off.
3. Scroll down and check the box for Windows Defender Application Guard (shown in Figure 17.10) and then click the OK button.

FIGURE 17.10
Installing Windows Defender Application Guard

Windows Features — □ ×

Turn Windows features on or off

To turn a feature on, select its check box. To turn a feature off, clear its check box. A filled box means that only part of the feature is turned on.

- ☐ RIP Listener
- ⊞ ☐ Services for NFS
- ⊞ ☐ Simple Network Management Protocol (SNMP)
- ☐ Simple TCPIP services (i.e. echo, daytime etc)
- ⊞ ☑ SMB 1.0/CIFS File Sharing Support
- ☐ SMB Direct
- ☐ Telnet Client
- ☐ TFTP Client
- ☐ Windows Defender Application Guard
- ☐ Windows Hypervisor Platform
- ☐ Windows Identity Foundation 3.5
- ⊞ ☑ Windows PowerShell 2.0
- ⊞ ☑ Windows Process Activation Service
- ☐ Windows Projected File System (Beta)
- ☐ Windows Subsystem for Linux
- ☐ Windows TIFF IFilter
- ☑ Work Folders Client

[OK] [Cancel]

4. After Windows Defender Application Guard installs, close Control Panel.

Users can also install Windows Defender Application Guard by using PowerShell. To do this, you need to right click on PowerShell and choose the top option of Run as Administrator (see Figure 17.11).

FIGURE 17.11
Opening PowerShell as an administrator

Tasks

- Run as Administrator
- Run ISE as Administrator
- Windows PowerShell ISE

- Windows PowerShell
- Unpin from taskbar

Once you are in the PowerShell window, you want to run the following PowerShell command and then you need to restart the Windows device:

Enable-WindowsOptionalFeature -online -FeatureName Windows-Defender-ApplicationGuard

In Exercise 17.4, I will show you how to use Windows Defender Application Guard in Standalone mode. I will be using Windows and Microsoft Edge for this exercise. To complete this exercise, you must complete Exercise 17.3 and install Windows Defender Application Guard on your Windows device.

EXERCISE 17.4   Using Windows Defender Application Guard

1. Open Microsoft Edge.

2. From the options menu, choose New Application Guard Window (see Figure 17.12).

FIGURE 17.12
New Application Guard
Window option

3. You will need to wait for Application Guard to set up the isolated environment (see Figure 17.13). This may take a few moments.

FIGURE 17.13
Application Guard
Starting Screen

4. As you can see in Figure 17.14, I opened Microsoft's website in Application Guard mode and you can see that in the upper left hand corner of the window. Close Edge.

FIGURE 17.14
Microsoft's website in
Application Guard mode

WINDOWS DEFENDER APPLICATION GUARD ENTERPRISE MODE

Windows Defender Application Guard in the enterprise environment is not much different for the user as in Standalone mode. The main difference is that the Enterprise Administrator configures the Windows Defender Application Guard application. The Enterprise Administrator sets up and configures the application. When a user accesses an untrusted website, Windows Defender Application Guard automatically starts.

So, let's take a look at some of the enterprise based systems will benefit from Windows Defender Application Guard:

Enterprise Desktops and Laptops   Enterprise desktops are machines that are joined to your domain and they are managed by your company's administrators. Enterprise Administrators can configure Windows Defender Application Guard through System Center Configuration Manager or Microsoft Intune.

Bring Your Own Device (BYOD) Laptops   Normally organizations that allow users to use their own devices for company business need to follow company rules. So these devices are normally managed by the Enterprise Administrators through Microsoft Intune. If a user wants to use a personal device but they don't want to follow corporate rules, most companies won't allow the use of the personal device.

In Exercise 17.5, I will show you how to use Windows Defender Application Guard in Enterprise mode. Before your organization can use Application Guard in Enterprise mode, administrators must install Windows Enterprise edition (version 1709 or higher) on their corporate network or the needed functionality will not work.

EXERCISE 17.5   Windows Defender Application Guard Enterprise

1. Install Application Guard using either a Group Policy object, System Center, or MDM.

2. In a Group Policy, set the Network Isolation settings that you want followed (see Figure 17.15). To set this option, in your GPO editor go to Administrative Templates\Network\Network Isolation\Enterprise Resource Domains Hosted In The Cloud.

FIGURE 17.15
Network Isolation GPO

3. Next go to Administrative Templates\Network\Network Isolation\Domains categorized as both work and personal setting. Enter in the websites that you trust.

4. Next go to Computer Configuration\Administrative Templates\Windows Components\ Windows Defender Application Guard\Turn On Windows Defender Application Guard In Enterprise Mode.

5. Select the Enabled radio button, choose Option 1 (see Figure 17.16), and click OK.

FIGURE 17.16
Turn On Windows
Defender Application
Guard In Enterprise
Mode setting

6. Close the GPO editor.

Understanding Windows Defender Credential Guard

Windows Server 2022 and Windows Enterprise uses a security measure called Windows Defender Credential Guard. Windows Defender Credential Guard is a virtualization-based security to help isolate critical files so that only system software that is privileged can access those critical files.

Once enabled, a Windows machine that is part of Active Directory or Azure Active Directory will have the systems credentials protected by Windows Defender Credential Guard.

After an administrator enables Windows Defender Credential Guard, the Local Security Authority (LSA) process in the operating system works with a new component named the isolated LSA. The isolated process stores and protects the system's critical data.

Once data is stored by the isolated LSA process, the system then uses the virtualization-based security to protect the data and that data is no longer accessible to the rest of the operating system.

To enable Windows Defender Credentials Guard, the following requirements should be met:

◆ Machine must support Virtualization based security (required)

◆ Secure boot (required)

◆ TPM 1.2 or 2.0, either discrete or firmware (preferred - provides binding to hardware)

◆ UEFI lock (preferred - prevents attacker from disabling with a simple registry key change)

The Virtualization-based security requires:

- 64-bit CPU

- CPU virtualization extensions plus extended page tables

- Windows hypervisor (does not require Hyper-V Windows Feature to be installed)

If an administrator wants to use Windows Defender Credential Guard in a Hyper-V virtual machine, the following requirements need to be met:

- The Windows 10 (version 1607 or higher) or Windows Server 2016 (or higher) system must have Hyper-V with Input Output Memory Management Unit (IOMMU).

- The Hyper-V virtual machine must be set as Generation 2 and virtual TPM needs to be enabled.

Once administrators have met the minimum requirements for setting up Windows Defender Credential Guard, they can enable it by either using the Windows Defender Device Guard hardware readiness tool, Group Policy Objects, or directly in the registry.

In Exercise 17.6, I will show you how to enable Windows Defender Credential Guard using a Group Policy Object.

EXERCISE 17.6 Windows Defender Credential Guard

1. Open the Group Policy Management Console on Windows Server 2022.

2. Create a new GPO and click the GPO and choose Edit.

3. Go to Computer Configuration ➤ Administrative Templates ➤ System ➤ Device Guard.

4. Double click the option Turn On Virtualization Based Security and then choose the Enabled option (see Figure 17.17).

FIGURE 17.17
Turn On Virtualization Based Security setting

5. In the Turn On Virtualization Based Security option, select Platform Security Level box, choose either Secure Boot or Secure Boot and DMA Protection.

6. In the Credential Guard Configuration box, click Enabled with UEFI lock, and then click the OK button.

7. Close the Group Policy Management Console.

Implementing and Managing Windows Defender Exploit Guard

Another way that Microsoft has started protecting systems is by using Windows Defender Exploit Guard. Windows Defender Exploit Guard helps protect your Windows system against malware, ransomware, and other types of attacks. It does this by reducing the attack surface of a device.

So does it mean when someone says that they are reducing the attack surface of a system. The way I always explain it is in this way. I am a huge hockey fan. When I lived in New Jersey, I used to go to dozens of hockey games.

Now think of a hockey net (or soccer net) as the Windows system. During one of the hockey intermissions (when the players get a break), they would bring out a piece of plexiglass, and on the bottom of the plexiglass, there was an opening just a bit bigger than a hockey puck. Then they would give someone a stick and a puck and allow them to shoot at the net from the center of the ice. If the puck went in, they would win a car or money or whatever the prize was that night.

Now think of the open net as Windows. You can have a great goaltender (your firewall), but if someone is good enough, they can still get the puck by the goaltender. Now think of the plexiglass. The only way that someone can score is by getting the puck in that tiny little opening. This is an example of a reduced attack surface. The goaltender doesn't need to protect the entire net. They just need to protect that tiny opening.

Windows Defender Exploit Guard is your plexiglass on the Windows operating system. When you protect common ways that hackers exploit the system, the hackers now have to get into the system by using that tiny little opening.

Windows Defender Exploit Guard helps protect your system from common malware hacks that use executable files and scripts that attack applications like Microsoft Office (for example, Outlook). Windows Defender Exploit Guard also looks for suspicious scripts or behavior that is not normal on the Windows system.

One of the common hacks today is ransomware. This is when a hacker takes over your system and requests a ransom to release your files. During this time, the hackers are holding your documents hostage until you pay. Once Windows Defender Exploit Guard is enabled, folders and files are assessed to determine if they are safe from or vulnerable to ransomware threats.

There are multiple ways to turn on Windows Defender Exploit Guard. Administrators can enable the Windows Defender Credential Guard by using the Windows Defender Security Center, a Group Policy Object, Microsoft Endpoint Configuration Manager, or Mobile Device Management (MDM) using Microsoft Intune.

In Exercise 17.7, I will show you how to enable Windows Defender Exploit Guard using the Windows Defender Security Center.

EXERCISE 17.7 Windows Defender Exploit Guard

1. Open the Settings center by clicking on the Start button and clicking on the Settings (the spoke) icon.

2. Choose Update And Security.

3. Click on Windows Security and choose Virus & Threat Protection.

4. Choose Ransomware Protection and make sure the setting is turned on (see Figure 17.18).

FIGURE 17.18
Turn On
Ransomware setting

5. Click Protected Folders (see Figure 17.19) to see what folders are currently protected. You can click + Add A Protected Folder to add additional folders.

FIGURE 17.19
Protected Folders screen

6. If you would like an application to have access, you can click on the link Allow An App Through Controlled Folder Access. Once you click the link, you can add an application that will be allowed access (see Figure 17.20).

FIGURE 17.20
Allow An App Through
Controlled Folder
Access screen

7. Close the Security Center (reboot if you made any changes).

Once Windows Defender Exploit Guard is enabled, when the Windows system suspects that a file is a danger, the Windows system will display a Virus and Threat Warning screen (see Figure 17.21). This protection is completed in real time as the Windows system is operating.

FIGURE 17.21
Virus and Threat
Warning screen

Another part of controlling application exploitation is when users try to get applications from the Web and Microsoft Store. Administrators have the ability to set up and use Microsoft Windows Defender SmartScreen (see Figure 17.22).

Windows Defender SmartScreen helps administrators protect their employees when they try to visit websites that have previously been reported as phishing or malware websites. Windows Defender SmartScreen also helps Windows if an employee tries to download potentially malicious files.

SmartScreen allows Windows to determine if a downloaded application or an application installer may be potentially malicious. It does this by doing the following:

◆ Looking at downloaded files and seeing if those files are on a list of known malicious software sites or if programs that are to be downloaded are known to be unsafe. If any file or program is on these lists, SmartScreen will prompt the user with a warning to let that user know that the data or site might be malicious.

◆ When a user downloads a file or program that isn't on the list, SmartScreen will show the user a warning prompt to just advise caution.

FIGURE 17.22
Windows Defender
SmartScreen

Another way your organization can help protect their users against downloading applications that are possibly harmful is using Windows Defender Application Control.

Using Windows Defender Application Control

So now that we have discussed how to protect the system and system files, let's talk about protecting applications. When an application runs, it has the ability to access data with the same access to data that a user has. Because of this, Microsoft has created Windows Defender Application Control (WDAC) to help stop attacks of data through the use of applications.

For many years, if a user had local admin rights and they wanted to install an application onto a corporate machine, they just did it. Users just assume that applications that they buy or download is just trustworthy.

Administrators can now use Windows Defender Application Control to ensure that only applications that you explicitly allow can run on the Windows computers.

Windows Defender Application Control allows an administrator to control applications and this is a big advantage over just using antivirus software. By stopping applications from running unless an administrator explicitly allows the application is just another layer of protection that organizations can utilize in their war against data theft.

For many years, top level security analysts have stated that application control is one of the best ways for addressing the many threats that executable based malware is used against companies. Now, administrators can add another layer of security by listing what applications can specifically run on their own Windows corporate systems.

If an administrator wants to create policies for use with Windows Defender Application Control, they need to meet the following system requirements:

◆ Windows 10/11 Enterprise

◆ Windows Server 2022

◆ Windows Server 2019

◆ Windows Server 2016

Administrators can configure Windows Defender Application Control through the use of a Group Policy Object or by using Mobile Device Management (MDM) and Microsoft Intune. After Windows Defender Application Control is setup, administrators can create and configure policies by using GPOs or Intune.

The Bottom Line

Understand how to configure Windows Firewall.   Using the Windows Firewall with Advanced Security can help you stop incoming or outgoing traffic.

> **Master It**   You are the administrator of a large network. One of your employee laptops has FTP ports 20/21 enabled. Your organization does not allow employees to use FTP servers.

Use Windows Defender Application Control.   Windows Defender Application Control allows an administrator to control which applications are allowed on a Windows system.

> **Master It**   Your organization is concerned about hacker using applications to steal or use unauthorized data. They have asked you to come up with a solution to protect data from applications.

Chapter 18

Creating Azure Policies

In this chapter, I will discuss how to set up and configure Azure policies. Setting up Azure policies will allow administrators to set rules on how users and devices connect to their Azure network.

Policies can be set for multiple areas of Azure, from Azure logins to Microsoft Endpoint Manager. Microsoft Endpoint Manager allows administrators to deploy Windows operating systems and software and also control devices that are connected to Endpoint Manager and Azure.

Having the options to set rules by using different policies gives an administrator and an organization flexibility and protection for users and devices that are trying to connect to their Azure environment.

IN THIS CHAPTER YOU'LL LEARN

- ◆ Understand how to configure Compliance Policies
- ◆ Understand how to configure Configuration Profiles

Azure Devices and Policies

The Devices section in Azure allows an Azure AD Administrator to setup which devices can access Azure AD. Administrators can also setup device settings and device roaming settings (Enterprise State Roaming). Azure AD Administrators can do auditing and troubleshooting from the Device section.

But to make sure that your users and devices can access Azure, you need to make sure that you purchase Azure licenses. The Licenses section in Azure AD allows you to view purchased licensing for additional Azure AD components. If you purchase additional Azure AD components (for example: Azure Active Directory Premium P2 or Enterprise Mobility + Security E5), those additional components will show up in this Licenses section. You can also see if there are any licensing issues in this section.

The Licenses section also allows you to view additional components that are available and what those components do. Azure AD Administrators can also view auditing and get trouble-shooting from this section.

So, after you purchase your licenses and you are ready to go, you can then configure Azure AD with Compliance Policies. These policies allow you to setup and configure how Windows client devices will work within the Azure network.

Before we dive into policies and profiles for your devices, let's take a look at Microsoft Endpoint Manager and Microsoft Intune. The Microsoft Endpoint Manager admin center is where you can find the Microsoft Intune services along with other mobile device software. It's important to understand a little about Microsoft Endpoint Manager because even though these policies and profiles are added to devices and users, you create them in Microsoft Endpoint Manager.

Microsoft Endpoint Manager is a device management system. Microsoft Endpoint Manager allows administrators to manage mobile devices, mobile applications, and PC management capabilities all from the cloud.

Administrators using Intune can provide their users with access to corporate applications, data, and resources from almost anywhere and on almost any device while also keeping your corporate information secure.

Microsoft Intune also helps you save money because Intune allows you to license users instead of licensing devices. So, if you have a user that works from multiple devices (laptop, tablet and Windows phone) you only pay once for the user license instead of multiple times for all of the user's devices.

Administrators can use Microsoft Endpoint Manager and Intune to support and manage Windows devices. Administrators can use them on a Windows device for:

◆ Enrollment

◆ Organization resource access

◆ Application management

◆ Policies

◆ Inventory

◆ Reporting

Remote wipe Microsoft Intune provides mobile device management, mobile application management, and PC management capabilities from the cloud. Using Intune, organizations can provide their employees with access to corporate applications, data, and resources from virtually anywhere on almost any device, while helping to keep corporate information secure.

Microsoft Endpoint Manager is an add-on to your Azure subscription but if you want to deploy software using the cloud or setup rules for how your devices and users will function, Microsoft Endpoint Manager is a subscription that you should add to your cloud-based utilities. Let's now look at how you can setup policies and profiles for your devices and users.

Compliance Policies

One of the advantages to using Azure is the ability to protect the corporate data by ensuring that users and devices meet certain requirements. When using Intune, this is referred to as compliance policies. Compliance policies are rules and settings that your users and their devices must follow in order to connect and access Microsoft Endpoint Manager.

Compliance polices, along with Conditional Access, ensures that administrators can stop users and devices that don't follow the rules that your organization has determined as necessary for access. For example, the Intune administrator can require some of the following:

◆ Corporate users must enter a password on their mobile devices to access data.

◆ Administrators can ensure that the device hasn't been cracked, rooted, or jail broken and that devices are under a minimum threat level.

◆ Administrators can ensure that devices have a minimum operating system along with updates.

Azure Active Directory, along with Conditional Access, allows Microsoft Endpoint Manager and Intune to enforce the compliance policies that your organization wants to use. When devices enroll into Microsoft Endpoint Manager, the registration begins with Azure AD and the device information gets placed into Azure AD. Part of this registration process is the device's compliance status. The device compliance status is then used by the policies in Conditional Access, and based on that, corporate resources are either blocked or allowed.

One advantage that you get using compliance policies is that an administrator can assign the policy to either a user (using a user group) or a device (using a device group). If a policy is assigned to a user, all the user's devices are also checked for policy compliance.

NOTE Microsoft recommends that if you are using Windows 10 version 1803 or higher, the policy should be deployed to the device group if the user doesn't enroll the device. By using device groups, Azure administrators can use compliancy reporting to ensure that the devices meet complexity.

CONDITIONAL ACCESS

The Conditional Access section (see Figure 18.1) allows an Azure AD Administrator to set security policies. When it comes to Azure, one of the biggest concerns for organizations is cloud-based security. Azure allows users to access their networks from anywhere in the world and from almost any device. Because of this, just securing resource access is not enough. This is where Conditional Access Policies comes in to play.

FIGURE 18.1
Conditional Access
Policies section

Conditional Access policies allow an organization to set how resources are accessed using access control decisions (who have access to resources) through Azure AD. Setting up Conditional Access policies allows an organization to have automated access control decisions based on the policies that your organization sets. Some of the situations that Conditional Access policies can help with are sign-in risk, network location risk, device management, and client applications.

With Conditional Access

If a device complies to the policy rules that you have configured, that device can get access to data, email, and other company resources. If the device does not meet the minimum policies that you have setup, then that device will not have access to any of the company's resources. This is how conditional access works when it is setup and enabled.

Without Conditional Access

If you decide that you do not want to use conditional access, you can still use compliance policies. If you decide to use compliance policies without conditional access, you can access reports showing the device compliance status. Administrators can evaluate this information and decide if conditional access is then needed or if you can continue to use Azure without any Conditional Access policies.

Creating a Compliance Policy

To create a compliance policy, the Azure administrator needs to ensure that a few requirements and steps are completed before creating the policies. The following requirements are needed to setup compliance policies:

- Intune
- If you use Conditional Access, then you need Azure Active Directory (AD) Premium edition. Intune compliance doesn't require Azure AD.
- Use a supported platform:
    - Android device administrator
    - Android AOSP (preview)
    - Android Enterprise
    - iOS
    - MacOS
    - Windows 10/11
    - Windows 8.1
- Enroll devices in Intune (required to see the compliance status).
- Enroll devices to one user, or enroll without a primary user. Single devices cannot be enrolled to multiple users.

The administrator must also enroll devices in Microsoft Endpoint Manager. It is also necessary to enroll a device to one user or enroll the device without a primary user assigned. Enrolling devices to multiple users is not supported.

Once you have logged in to Azure Active Directory, you can see which devices don't meet Device Compliance Policies. In Azure AD, click Devices. The Devices Overview page will show you if you have any devices that are not compliant (as seen in Figure 18.2).

FIGURE 18.2
Devices Overview page

Once you have ensured that your organization has met the minimum requirements to set up compliance policies, the next step is to actually create a policy. The following steps will walk you through the process of creating a policy:

1. Sign into the Microsoft Endpoint Manager portal.

2. Select Devices and then select Compliance Policies. Administrators can choose from the following options:

   ◆ **Overview**: This will show you a summary of devices along with the number of devices that are compliant or not evaluated. This screen will also show the list of policies and individual settings in those policies.

   ◆ **Manage**: This screen allows an administrator to create new device policies and send notifications to noncompliant devices, and it will also allow an administrator to enable network fencing. Network fencing allows an administrator to create a compliance policy based on a network location.

   ◆ **Monitor**: This section allows an administrator to check the compliance status of their devices along with checking the status at the setting and policy levels.

   ◆ **Setup**: This option allows an administrator to use built-in compliance policies, use Jamf Pro software to manage your end users' Macs, add a mobile threat defense connector, and enable Microsoft Defender advanced threat protection (ATP).

3. Select Policies ➢ Create Policy. To create a policy, the administrator needs to fill in the following properties:

   ◆ **Name**: Administrators need to enter a name for the new policy.

- **Description**: Administrators should enter a description for the policy so that the policy is easy to recognize and maintain in the future. This setting is optional, but highly recommended.

- **Platform**: Here is where the administrator can choose the platform of their devices. Administrators have the following options to choose from:

  - Android

  - Android enterprise

  - iOS

  - MacOS

  - Windows 8.1 and later

  - Windows 10 and later

- **Settings**: This section allows the administrator to choose which policy settings that they want to implement.

4. Once you are completed filling in all the sections, click OK and then choose Create to save your changes.

The policy is now created and the policy will now show up in the policy list. The next step is to assign the policy to your user groups. To assign user groups to your policy, complete the following steps:

1. Choose the policy that you want to assign to a user group. Policies are shown in Device Compliance ➤ Policies.

2. Select the policy and then choose Assignments. Administrators have the ability to include or exclude Azure Active Directory (AD) security groups.

3. To see your Azure AD security groups, choose the Selected Groups option. Select the user groups that you want this policy to apply to and then choose Save to deploy the policy to the users.

MIGRATING POLICIES TO MDM

Once an organization decides to move to Microsoft Azure, one of the tasks that an administrator will need to consider is moving on-site Group Policy Object (GPOs) settings to MDM. The first thing that the administrator needs to do before migrating their GPOs to MDM is to analyze their current GPOs and figure out what needs to be moved to the MDM management tool in Azure.

Microsoft understands that GPO analysis needs to be done and that's why they developed the MDM Migration Analysis Tool (MMAT) to help administrators complete this task.

MMAT looks at your organization's GPOs and see which ones have been created for a user or computer. MMAT then generates a report that an administrator can use to see which equivalent MDM policies will need to be set. The report that MMAT will generate can be in both XML and HTML formats.

If your Azure administrator decides that they want to use the MMAT, they will need to complete the following steps:

1. Install the Remote Server Administration Tools (RSAT).

2. Install the zipped folder for MMAT to your computer and unzip the folder.

3. Open Windows PowerShell as an administrator.

4. In PowerShell, change the directory location to where you installed the MMAT files (these files include PowerShell scripts).

5. Run the following PowerShell script:

```
Set-ExecutionPolicy -ExecutionPolicy Unrestricted -Scope Process
$VerbosePreference="Continue" ./Invoke-MdmMigrationAnalysisTool.ps1
-collectGPOReports -runAnalysisTool
```

After the `Invoke-MdmMigrationAnalysisTool.ps1` script is completed, the Azure administrator will be able to look at three reports:

MDMMigrationAnalysis.xml   This file is the XML version of the MMAT report and it contains information about the policies that are set for the targeted user and computer. It will also show you how these policies map to MDM.

MDMMigrationAnalysis.html   This file is the HTML version of the XML report.

MdmMigrationAnalysisTool.log   This file is a log file that will give Azure administrators more information about how the MMAT tool ran.

Device Configuration Profiles

Another way to set up Intune rules as an Administrator is a Device Configuration Profile. Profiles work like policies since they are also another way to put rules onto your Microsoft Endpoint Manager devices.

Microsoft Endpoint Manager, along with device configuration profiles, allows an administrator to configure settings and features that can be enabled or disabled on the different devices that your users will connect with.

DEVICE CONFIGURATION PROFILE OPTIONS

Device configuration profile settings and features are added to your configuration profiles. Administrators can build these profiles for devices and platforms, including iOS, Android, and Windows. After these profiles are built, an Intune administrator can apply or assign them to their devices. The device configuration setting and features can include some of the following:

Administrative Templates   Administrative templates have hundreds of Windows 10 (and above) settings that an administrator can set for programs and features including Internet Explorer, OneDrive, Office, and other programs. These settings are very similar to setting up GPOs, but they are all cloud-based settings.

Certificates   Certificate settings allow an Intune administrator to configure certificates for applications like Wi-Fi, VPN, and email profiles. These settings can be configured for many different devices, including Android and Android Enterprise, iOS and MacOS, Windows 8.1, and Windows 10 and later.

Custom Profile   Custom profile settings allow an Intune Administrator to configure options that are not automatically included with Intune. For example, an administrator can set a custom profile that allows you to create ADMX-backed policy or even enable self-service password resets. Custom profile allows you to set options for Android and Android Enterprise, and iOS and macOS devices.

Delivery Optimization   Delivery optimization allows Intune administrators to set up and configure updates to Windows 10 (and above) devices that connect to the cloud.

Device Features   Device features make it easy for administrators to configure iOS and macOS devices. These settings allow you to configure things like AirPrint, notifications, and lock screen messages. Administrators can set these configurations on iOS and macOS devices.

Device Restrictions   Device restrictions allow an Intune administrator to configure settings for things like hardware, data, and security settings on your devices. Device restrictions can be created to prevent iOS device users from using their device's camera. Device restrictions can be used on Android and Android Enterprise, iOS and macOS, Windows 10 Team, and Windows 10 and later devices.

Edition Upgrade   Edition upgrade allows you to upgrade Windows 10 (and later) devices to a newer version of Windows.

Email   Email options allow you to create, monitor, and assign Email Exchange ActiveSync email settings for your devices. For example, email profiles allow your users to have access to your organization's email while using their own personal devices. Email options can be set for Android and Android Enterprise, iOS, and Windows 10 and later devices.

Endpoint Protection   Endpoint protection allows you to set Windows 10 (and above) options for BitLocker and Windows Defender settings. For example, you can set Windows Defender for a threat score setting. If a user with a High threat score rating attempts to access cloud-based resources, you can stop this device from accessing your resources.

Identity Protection   Identity protection allows an Intune administrator to control the Windows Hello for Business experience on Windows 10 and Windows 10 Mobile devices. Identity protection settings allow you to configure options for devices such as PINs and gestures for Windows Hello for Business.

Kiosk   Kiosk settings allow an administrator to configure a Windows 10 (and later) device to run a single application or run many applications. Kiosk systems are normally designed in a location where many people can use the same device and that device will only run limited applications. Administrators have the ability to also customize other features including a start menu and a web browser. Kiosk settings are also available for Android and Android Enterprise and iOS devices but you need to configure these devices as device restrictions. So it can still function as a Kiosk device but it's configured differently.

Shared Multi-User Device   Shared multi-user devices are devices where multiple users will use the device to do day to day activities. This is different than a Kiosk based machine. Kiosk based machines are machines used by many users but they run limited programs. Shared multi-user devices are devices that users use to do their job while at work, but other users will use the same device. These devices normally run all of the organization's software so people can do their jobs. For example, if you are in an environment where you have shift workers. You may have multiple shifts and different people will use a machine when they are working during their shift.

Shared multi-user device settings allow an administrator to control many of the device features and manage these shared devices through Intune.

BUILDING DEVICE CONFIGURATION PROFILES

One nice advantage that you will notice is that building device configuration profiles work a lot like building device compliances. Many of the same settings are available as you build the device configuration profile. To build a device configuration profile, you would complete the following steps:

1. Sign in to the Microsoft Endpoint Manager portal.

2. Select **Devices** and then select **Compliance Policies**. Administrators can choose from the following options:

   ♦ **Overview**: This will show you the status of your profiles and it also provides additional details on the different profiles that you have assigned to your users and devices.

   ♦ **Manage**: This screen allows an administrator to create device profiles, upload PowerShell scripts that can run within the profile, and add data plans to eSIM devices.

   ♦ **Monitor**: This section allows an administrator to view the status of a device configuration profile and see if that profile was a success or failure. This screen also allows you to view logs about your profiles.

   ♦ **Setup**: This option allows an administrator to add a certificate authority or enable Telecom Expense Management in the profile.

3. Select **Profiles ➤ Create Profile** to create a profile. The Intune administrator needs to fill in the following properties:

   ♦ **Name**: Administrators need to enter a name for the new profile.

   ♦ **Description**: Administrators should enter a description for the profile so that the profile is easy to recognize and maintain in the future. This setting is optional, but highly recommended.

   ♦ **Platform**: Here is where the administrator can choose the platform of their devices. Administrators have the following options to choose from:

     ♦ Android

     ♦ Android Enterprise

     ♦ iOS

- ◆ MacOS
- ◆ Windows 8.1 and later
- ◆ Windows 10 and later

◆ **Profile Type:** Select the type of settings you want to create. The list that will be shown will depend on the platform you choose.

◆ **Settings:** This section allows the administrator to choose which profile settings that they want to implement.

4. Once you are completed filling in all the sections, select **OK** and then choose **Create** to save your changes.

Once you are completed building the device configuration profile, the next step would be to add a scope tag to the profile. Scope tags allow an administrator to assign and filter policies to a specific group (for example HR or Sales) of employees. To add a scope tag, complete the following steps.

1. Select **Scope (Tags)**.

2. Select **Add** to create a new scope tag. Or, select an existing scope tag from the list.

3. Click OK to save your changes.

PowerShell Commands

In the following table (Table 18.1), I will show you some of the PowerShell commands available for Azure Active Directory settings and Azure Policies. You must be using a newer version of PowerShell on your on-site servers or client machines. If you run into any issues trying to run these commands, please check out a newer version of Microsoft PowerShell on Microsoft's website.

TABLE 18.1:   PowerShell Commands for Azure Active Directory

COMMAND	DESCRIPTION
Add-AzureADAdministrativeUnitMember	This command allows an Azure Admin to add an administrative unit member.
Add-AzureADApplicationPolicy	Administrators can use this command to add an application policy.
Add-AzureADScopedRoleMembership	This command allows an Azure Admin to add a scoped role membership to an administrative unit.
Add-AzureADServicePrincipalPolicy	Administrators can use this command to add a service principal policy.

COMMAND	DESCRIPTION
`Get-AzureADAdministrativeUnit`	This command allows an Azure admin to view an administrative unit.
`Get-AzureADAdministrativeUnitMember`	Administrators can use this command to view a member of an administrative unit.
`Get-AzureADApplicationPolicy`	This command allows an Azure admin to view an application policy.
`Get-AzureADDirectorySetting`	Administrators can use this command to view a directory setting.
`Get-AzureADDirectorySettingTemplate`	This command allows an Azure admin to view a directory setting template.
`Get-AzureADObjectSetting`	Administrators can use this command to view an object setting.
`Get-AzureADPolicy`	This command allows an Azure admin to view a policy.
`Get-AzureADPolicyAppliedObject`	Administrators can use this command to view the objects to which a policy is applied.
`Get-AzureADScopedRoleMembership`	This command allows an Azure admin to view a scoped role membership from an administrative unit.
`Get-AzureADServicePrincipalPolicy`	Administrators can use this command to view the service principal policy.
`New-AzureADAdministrativeUnit`	This command allows an Azure admin to create an administrative unit.
`New-AzureADDirectorySetting`	Administrators can use this command to create a directory settings object.
`New-AzureADObjectSetting`	This command allows an Azure admin to create a settings object.
`New-AzureADPolicy`	Administrators can use this command to create a policy.
`Remove-AzureADAdministrativeUnit`	This command allows an Azure admin to remove an administrative unit.
`Remove-AzureADAdministrativeUnitMember`	Administrators can use this command to remove an administrative unit member.

TABLE 18.1: PowerShell Commands for Azure Active Directory *(CONTINUED)*

COMMAND	DESCRIPTION
Remove-AzureADDirectorySetting	This command allows an Azure admin to delete a directory setting in Azure Active Directory.
Remove-AzureADObjectSetting	Administrators can use this command to delete settings in Azure Active Directory.
Remove-AzureADPolicy	This command allows an Azure admin to delete a policy.
Remove-AzureADScopedRoleMembership	Administrators can use this command to remove a scoped role membership.
Set-AzureADDirectorySetting	This command updates a directory setting in Azure Active Directory.
Set-AzureADObjectSetting	This command allows an Azure admin to update object settings.
Set-AzureADPolicy	Administrators can use this command to update a policy.
sGet-AzureADApplicationProxyConnectorGroup Members	Retrieve the members of an Application Proxy connector group

The Bottom Line

Understand how to configure Compliance Policies. Using Compliance Policies allows your administrators to set up Azure rules that need to be followed by all users and/or devices.

Master It You are the administrator of a large network. Your organization uses a hybrid network setup between your on-site network and Azure. You have been informed that you need to setup a policy to make sure all users and devices are following the proper compliancy rules.

Understand how to configure Configuration Profiles. Configuration profiles allow an administrator to configure settings and features that can be enable or disable on the different devices that your users will use to access Azure and Microsoft Endpoint Manager.

Master It Your organization has a hybrid network setup. Your organization uses both Microsoft and Apple iOS devices. You have been asked to setup access for the iOS Apple devices.

The Bottom Line

Each of The Bottom Line sections in the chapters suggest exercises to deepen skills and understanding. Sometimes there is only one possible solution, but often you are encouraged to use your skills and creativity to create something that builds on what you know and lets you explore one of many possible solutions.

Chapter 1: Understanding Windows Server 2022

Understand the roles and features in Windows Server 2022. Choosing the right server operating system depends on the roles and features that you need for your organizational needs. The proper operating system depends on the job functions and requirements that are needed to set your network up properly.

Master It You are an administrator that needs to set up a Windows Server that needs easy access for connecting to the cloud. You are not worried about physical security since the server will be locked in a secure server room.

Solution Windows Server 2022 is the best way to go. If your organization does not need cloud access, the Windows Server 2016 may be as high as you need to go. Since the server is going to be in a locked server room, you can choose a version of Windows Server 2022 with the Desktop Experience.

Understand the different versions of Windows Server 2022. When choosing how to set up Windows Server 2022, there are different ways that you can set up how the system functions. You can choose between using the GUI version of Windows Server 2022 or a non-GUI version.

Master It One of the important things that you need to know is how the server needs to be setup. You are an administrator that needs to setup Windows Server 2022. The server will not be in a secure server room. You need to choose a version of Windows Server 2022 installation that addresses these security concerns.

Solution When choosing a version and type of Windows Server 2022 installation, your choice should be based on security needs and functionality. Understanding that the GUI version is the easiest way to set up and configure Windows Server 2022, but if security is the main concern for your needs, then using a non-GUI version of Windows Server 2022, like Server Core, may be the better way to go.

Know the features and roles that have been removed. Understanding what features and roles have been removed or are no longer being developed is an important task.

Master It You are the administrator for your organization and you need to choose a server version that allows for Active Directory, DNS, DHCP, and other features.

Solution   Administrators need to understand what Roles or Features that they need for their organization. Administrators do not want to purchase an operating system if the Role or Feature that you need is being removed.

Chapter 2: Understanding Virtualization

Understand server virtualization.   Choosing the right type of virtualization can help an organization access the applications that you need to run properly on your network.

Master It   You are an administrator that needs to setup a network that will need multiple servers running. Your organization can't afford to buy servers for each server that is needed.

Solution   Windows Server 2022 is the best way to go. If your organization wants to run multiple operating systems on the same host, Windows Hyper-V is an excellent way to setup your infrastructure.

Understand the Hyper-V features.   Knowing the advantages of Hyper-V is important so that you can create and configure Hyper-V virtualization properly. There are different virtualization vendors. By knowing the features of Hyper-V, you can determine if it's the right virtual server for your organization.

Master It   You are an IT admin for a mid-size company. Your company is thinking about using Hyper-V for both Windows and Linux operating systems.

Solution   As an administrator, you should have a good understanding of the Hyper-V features. Understanding the Hyper-V features allows you to decide if Hyper-V can handle your organizations virtual needs. Hyper-V guests can handle different operating systems like Windows Server, Linux, and FreeBSD Image Deployments.

Chapter 3: Installing and Configuring Hyper-V

Know the virtualization requirements.   Understanding server requirements that are needed to install and configure Hyper-V.

Master It   You are an administrator that needs to setup Hyper-V virtualization. You are not sure what features of Hyper-V will need to be configured based on the systems requirements.

Solution   As an administrator that needs to setup Hyper-V virtualization, you must know the resources required on Windows Server 2022 to install and configure Hyper-V. Knowing proper installation and configuration settings of Hyper-V and it's various basic aspects of configuring the virtualization environment is important to properly setting up Hyper-V Virtual Machines.

Know how to build virtual machines.   Understanding how to build and configure virtual machines is one of the most important tasks when building a virtual network. Understanding how the Hyper-V role works on Windows Server 2022 is important so that when you setup and configure Hyper-V, you understand what is happening within the virtual machines.

Master It You are an administrator for a mid-size company. Your company has asked you to build and configure new virtual machines using Hyper-V.

Solution As an administrator, you should understand how to properly configure the virtual machines. Virtual machines are the servers that are running on the Hyper-V server. Configuring these virtual machines properly will guarantees that your network will operate without issues or errors.

Chapter 4: Installing Windows Server 2022

Know which Server 2022 version to install Understanding which version of Windows Server 2022 that is proper for your organization.

Master It You are an administrator that needs to setup a server in a secure locked environment. You want to have a server desktop for easy management of the server.

Solution Install Windows Server 2022 with the Desktop Experience. The Desktop Environment allows administrators to easily use wizards and desktop tools to manage and configure your server.

Master It You are an administrator that needs to setup a server in a non-secure environment. You are worried about security and want to make sure that it is more difficult for any to make changes on the server.

Solution Install Windows Server 2022 Server Core. Server Core does not have a Desktop Environment. All configuration and management needs to be done using the Command Prompt or PowerShell commands. This is an excellent option for an environment that may be less secure.

Understand how to deploy updates It is important to understand the different ways that you can deploy updates to your servers and client operating systems. You can allow your servers and users to connect to Microsoft and all get the same updates or you can control the updates using WSUS.

Master It You are an administrator that needs to setup a server that allows all of your servers and end-users to get company approved updates for their operating systems and Microsoft applications.

Solution Install WSUS onto a Windows Server 2022 server. Windows Server Update Services is one way to have your end users receive important updates from Microsoft. WSUS gives administrators the ability to download, test, and approve updates before they get released onto the network.

Chapter 5: Understanding IP

Understand subnetting and when to use it. If an organization is large and has many computers or if its computers are geographically dispersed, it's sensible to divide its large network into smaller ones connected by routers. These smaller networks are called subnets.

Master It You are an administrator of a large network. All computers are on the same network and the network only has a single router (connecting the network to the Internet). You notice that there is a lot of broadcast traffic on the network. You want to reduce some of the broadcast traffic.

Solution You decide that you want to install multiple routers and subnet your network. Broadcast traffic does not go through the router. There is one type of broadcast traffic that will pass through a router. DHCP Discovery Broadcasts will be passed through a router if that option is configured.

Understand subnet masks. For the subnet address scheme to work, every machine on the network must know which part of the host address will be used as the subnet address. The network administrator creates a 32-bit subnet mask consisting of 1s and 0s. The 1s in the subnet mask represent the positions that refer to the network or subnet addresses. The 0s represent the positions that refer to the host portion of the address.

Master It You are the administrator of an organization that has multiple subnets. You think that one of the computers is set with an IP address from a different subnet.

Solution Every subnet on a network has its own range of IP addresses that can be on that subnet. Looking at the computer's IP information, the computer address, the subnet mask, and the default gateway should all be on the same subnet.

Chapter 6: Implementing DNS

Understand DNS. DNS was designed to be a robust, scalable, and high-performance system for resolving friendly names to TCP/IP host addresses. Microsoft's DNS is based on a widely accepted set of industry standards. Because of this, Microsoft's DNS can work with both Windows- and non-Windows-based networks.

Master It You are an administrator of a large network. All computers are on the same network. You need to configure a Windows service that allows you to turn hostnames into IP addresses.

Solution DNS is a standard set of protocols that defines a mechanism for querying and updating address information in the database, a mechanism for replicating the information in the database among servers, and a schema of the database. DNs allows you to resolve hostnames into IP addresses.

Understand DNS records. Understanding which DNS records to use for each server, computer, host, and service is one of the most important ways to best set up your network. Setting up the proper DNS records will ensure that your connection to Azure will work seamlessly.

Master It You are the administrator of an organization that has decided to use cloud-based services. You need to be sure that your DNS records are set properly and that you use the proper record for each component.

Solution The SOA record defines the general parameters for the DNS zone, including who is the authoritative server. NS records list the name servers for a domain; they allow other name servers to look up names in your domain. A host record (also called an address record or an A record) statically associates a host's name with its IP addresses. Pointer records (PTRs) map an IP address to a hostname, making it possible to do reverse lookups. Alias records allow you to use more than one name to point to a single host. The MX record tells you which servers can accept mail bound for a domain. SRV records tie together the location of a service (like a domain controller) with information about how to contact the service.

Understand Dynamic Updates.   As an IT administrator, you have the ability to configure all of the DNS records manually or you can use Dynamic Updates. Configuring DNS records manually will work for an organization where IP addresses are manually assigned to hosts. But if your network automatically assigns IP addresses to host, this can be a very difficult task because IP addresses can change daily.

> **Master It**   You are the administrator of an organization that has 1,000 hosts on the network. You need to set up the DNS server and clients to update the DNS database automatically.
>
> **Solution**   Configuring DNS Dynamic Updates allows your clients to automatically add their IP addresses to DNS. Be aware that not all hosts, like printers, may be able to dynamically update. So you may still need to manually add a few records.

Chapter 7: Understanding Active Directory

Know the prerequisites for promoting a server to a domain controller.   You should understand the tasks that you must complete before you attempt to upgrade a server to a domain controller. Also, you should have a good idea of the information you need in order to complete the domain controller promotion process.

> **Master It**   You are an administrator of a large network. You need to install Windows Server 2022 Active Directory on your network.
>
> **Solution**   Windows Server 2022 Active Directory has specific requirements for both the computer and the services installed. For example, DNS is an Active Directory requirement. An administrator can install DNS before the Active Directory installation or during the Active Directory installation.

Understand domains, Trees, and Forests.   Understanding which way to setup Active Directory is one of the most important tasks that you will undertake. If you choose the wrong option, you may need to manually build connections between your networks instead of Active Directory doing it for you.

> **Master It**   You are the administrator of an organization that has decided to buy out a company called Sybex.com. You want Sybex.com to be part of your current Active Directory structure. But it is important that Sybex.com keeps its own naming structure.
>
> **Solution**   During the Active Directory installation process, you will choose to create a new Tree in an existing Forest. This will allow you to create a separate naming structure for Sybex.com but it will be part of your Active Directory Forest.

Chapter 8: Administering Active Directory

Understand the Purpose of OUs.   You should understand that OUs are used to create a hierarchical, logical organization for objects within an Active Directory domain. They are like storage containers for objects, but you can put rules on those containers.

Master It   You are an administrator of a large network. You need to set up your Active Directory users by geographic location.

Solution   Windows Server 2022 Active Directory allows you to build OUs. When creating OUs, you can create OUs based on departments, geographic location, etc. Remember, this is your organization's Active Directory structure, just set it up so that it has logic behind why you did what you did.

Know Groups and Group Strategies.   You can build and use three groups: domain local, global, and universal. Understand the group strategies and when they apply. Understand when to us Security groups vs. Distributed groups.

Master It   You are the administrator of an organization that has decided to buy out a company called Sybex.com. You need to create groups that stay in their tree only.

Solution   When creating groups, you can setup three main group: domain locals, global, and universal groups. Domain local groups have to stay in the domain that the group is created. Global groups can access any domain in the same tree. Universal groups can access any domain in the forest. So in this situation, global groups would be the best option.

Chapter 9: Configuring DHCP

Understand DHCP.   You should understand why you need to install and configure DHCP. DHCP may not always be the best option for small companies, but with large companies, DHCP will help reduce IP configuration errors.

Master It   You are an administrator of a large network with 2,000 hosts. You need to easily set up all 2,000 hosts using IPv4.

Solution   Windows Server 2022 DHCP helps administrators set up all of your hosts using IP while cutting down on administrator errors. By having DHCP handle all IP host configuration, it helps ensure that hosts get proper IP addresses no matter what subnet they belong too.

Know how to verify authorization of a DHCP server.   Once you have installed the DHCP role onto a server, you need to verify that the server is authorized in the Active Directory network. This helps ensure that only authorized DHCP servers issue IP address information to your domain users.

Master It   You are the administrator of an organization that has decided to install the DHCP role. After you install the DHCP role, what do you need to do next to ensure users only get authorized IP address information?

Solution   You authorize the DHCP server using the DHCP snap-in. When you authorize a server, you're actually adding its IP address to the Active Directory object that contains a list of the IP addresses of all authorized DHCP servers.

Chapter 10: Building Group Policies

Understand the purpose of GPOs.   System administrators use Group Policy to enforce granular permissions for users in an Active Directory environment.

Master It   You are an administrator of a large network with 3,500 hosts. You need to easily set up a policy to run a script when users log into the domain.

Solution   Windows Server 2022 GPOs help administrators to easily execute Startup and Shutdown scripts. An administrator can create scripts, like PowerShell scripts, and have those scripts execute when a user logs onto the domain or logs off the domain.

Understand user and computer settings.   Certain Group Policy settings may apply to users, computers, or both. Computer settings affect all users that access the machines to which the policy applies. User settings affect users, regardless of which machines they log on to.

Master It   You are the administrator of an organization that has decided to implement a new domain password policy. This policy will apply to all users on the domain.

Solution   Password policies are created in the Security settings of the Computer section of the GPOs. When you install Active Directory, a default password policy is created for you. It's created in the Domain Default Policy GPO. You can alter this GPO to set up the settings that your organization wants to implement.

It is a general rule that we do not use the Default Domain Policy to create new policies, but you may need to alter it to fit your needs. If you need a new policy, it's best to create it. This way, if the policy becomes invalid or is just set up incorrectly, you are not changing the Default Domain Policy.

Know the interactions between Group Policy objects and Active Directory.   GPOs can be linked to Active Directory objects. This link determines to which objects the policies apply. GPOs can be applied to sites, domains, or OUs. You can set up local policies on Windows systems, but domain-based policies are set on sites, domains, and OUs.

Master It   You are the administrator of an organization that has decided to implement a new policy for a specific set of users.

Solution   If you have a group of users that need the same policies because they do the same job, you can create an OU for those users, like a Sales OU, and then create a policy for that OU. This way the GPO will apply to just the users in that OU.

Chapter 11: Advanced Group Policy Options

Know how to use the Resultant Set of Policy (RSoP) tool to troubleshoot and plan Group Policy.   Windows Server 2022 includes the RSoP feature, which you can run in logging mode (Group Policy Results) or planning mode (Group Policy Modeling) to determine exactly which set of policies applies to users, computers, OUs, domains, and sites.

Master It You are the administrator of a large network. One user is complaining because they are not getting the company desktop. They are receiving a desktop with a dark black background. You need to figure out why this user is getting this background from a GPO.

Solution Windows Server 2022 RSoP allows you to select a user and see what GPOs are affecting that user account. You need to open the Group Policy Management MMC and choose Group Policy Results. Run a report showing all of the GPOs affecting the user. Find which GPO is changing their desktop and fix or delete the GPO so that they get the company GPO desktop settings.

Understand the difference between publishing and assigning applications. Some applications can be assigned to users and computers so that they are always available. Applications can be published to users so that the user may install the application with a minimal amount of effort when it is required.

Master It You are the administrator of a company that uses Azure and an onsite network. Most software gets deployed through the cloud. You have an application that needs to be installed to all onsite users through the domain.

Solution You can create a GPO to assign the software to the user or the computer. If you assign it to the user, it will appear on the Start menu but it is not installed until the user initiates the installation. If you assign the software to the computer, it will automatically be installed to all users on that system.

Chapter 12: Understanding Cloud Concepts

Know how the cloud can help your network during high peak usage. Microsoft Azure has many benefits that can help a company of any size. Understanding the different benefits can help you decide if moving to the cloud can be beneficial to your organization.

Master It You are the administrator of a large network. You have a financial application in Azure. You notice that every Thursday when the Finance department runs payroll reports, the usage of the financial server increases. What Azure component can help you with this issue?

Solution Elasticity is a cloud service that automatically scales resources as needed. It is the ability to automatically increase or decrease computer processing, memory, and storage resources to meet the current demand. It is usually measured by system monitoring tools. With cloud elasticity, a business can avoid for paying for resources that aren't being used and they don't have to worry about purchasing new equipment or maintaining current systems.

Understand the different types of clouds. Understanding the different types of clouds are important so that you can choose the right option for your organization. Knowing the differences between a Public cloud, Private cloud, and Hybrid cloud can help you decide which option is best for your network.

Master It   You are the administrator of a large company that already has an on-site network. You are considering moving some of your server components to the cloud. You do not want to completely remove your on-site network.

Solution   A hybrid cloud combines both a private cloud with a public cloud. Having a hybrid cloud allows data and applications to be shared amongst them. This ability provides additional deployment options and more flexibility.

Chapter 13: Configuring Azure

Understand the Benefits of using Azure.   Microsoft Azure has many benefits that can help a company of any size. Understanding the different benefits can help you decide if moving to the cloud can be beneficial to your organization.

Master It   You are the administrator of a large network. You need to be able to quickly recover data in the event of data being deleted or in the event of a major disaster. What Azure component can help you with this issue?

Solution   Azure can help shield critical data and applications by offering an end-to-end backup and disaster recovery solution that can be integrated with your on-premise backup solutions.

Configure the Azure Portal.   Azure administrators also have the ability to modify the default settings of the Azure portal. Most of the settings that an administrator can change can be found in the Settings menu.

Master It   You are the administrator of a large company that has Azure users in multiple countries. You need to configure the language and region for these different users.

Solution   The Language + region pane has two sections that an administrator can configure: Language and Regional format. This will affect how the data such as currency will be displayed in the Azure portal. To change the Language, the Azure administrator will use the drop-down list to choose from the list of available languages.

Chapter 14: Understanding Azure Active Directory

Understand Azure AD Integration.   Microsoft Azure has many benefits that can help a company of any size connect their on-site domain with their Azure Active Directory network.

Master It   You are the administrator of a large network. You need to quickly connect your on-site domain to your Azure network.

Solution   Setup and configure Azure AD Integration using the Azure AD Connect tool. One of the nice advantages of Azure is that Administrator do not need to manage or configure Azure AD replication. Azure user accounts and group membership are automatically replicated between Azure AD and AD Domain services.

Configure Azure Passwords. Azure administrators have multiple ways to allow users to reset or change their own passwords.

Master It You are the administrator of a large company that has Azure users in multiple areas. You need to allow users to reset or change their own passwords.

Solution Password Reset section allows an Administrator to determine if they want to enable Self-service password resets (SSPR). If an organization decides to enable this feature, some or all users will be able to reset their own passwords or unlock their accounts.

Chapter 15: Creating a Hybrid Network

Understand Azure AD Connect. Microsoft Azure allows a company of any size to connect their on-site domain with their Azure Active Directory network.

Master It You are the administrator of a large network. You need to quickly connect your on-site domain to your Azure network.

Solution Setup and configure Azure AD Integration by using Azure AD Connect. Azure AD Connect is a Microsoft utility that allows you to setup a hybrid design between Azure AD and your on-site AD. Azure AD Connect allows you to setup the connection by using either Password hash synchronization, Pass-through authentication, or Federation integration.

Configure Azure Recovery. Azure administrators have the ability to setup Azure Recovery to protect their apps and data.

Master It You are the administrator of a large company that has Azure users in multiple areas. You need to make sure that you setup Azure recovery.

Solution For the purpose of failover, a recovery plan groups machines into recovery groups. It works by creating smaller units that can be used for failover. These units usually represent apps.

Chapter 16: Understanding Microsoft Endpoint

Understand MDM. Microsoft Device Management allows an administrator to manage and configure Windows devices.

Master It You are the administrator of a large network. One of your employees just informed you that their laptop was stolen. The Device was enrolled into Microsoft Device Management.

Solution Should a device ever get lost or stolen, or if a user leaves your company, you can wipe the corporate data is that is on the device. A wipe is basically just erasing the data from the hard disk on the device. You have to option to either wipe all the data on the device or perform a selective wipe, which will leave the users personal data on the device intact.

Using Autopilot. Autopilot allows an organization to quickly and easily install operating systems onto new or repurposed machines without any IT personnel building each machine.

> **Master It** Your organization is going to be purchasing 50 new devices from the same vendor. You need to setup all 50 devices without using images or IT Intervention.

> **Solution** Autopilot allows an administrator to get a list of device IDs from a manufacturer. The device IDs get entered into your Azure environment. The IT administrator assigns a device profile to that machine and that's it. Once the user logs into the internet, the machine automatically recognizes that it is part of your organization and the installation is completed. Without any IT intervention.

Chapter 17: Configuring Security

Understand how to configure Windows Firewall. Using the Windows Firewall with Advanced Security can help you stop incoming or outgoing traffic.

> **Master It** You are the administrator of a large network. One of your employee laptops has FTP ports 20/21 enabled. Your organization does not allow employees to use FTP servers.

> **Solution** Using the Windows Firewall with Advanced Security, create a new rule that disables Ports 20/21 for all incoming and outgoing traffic.

Use Windows Defender Application Control. Windows Defender Application Control allows an administrator to control which applications are allowed on a Windows system.

> **Master It** Your organization is concerned about hacker using applications to steal or use unauthorized data. They have asked you to come up with a solution to protect data from applications.

> **Solution** When an application runs, it has the ability to access data with the same access to data that a user has. Because of this, Microsoft has created Windows Defender Application Control (WDAC) to help stop attacks of data through the use of applications.

Chapter 18: Creating Azure Policies

Understand how to configure Compliance Policies. Using Compliance Policies allows your administrators to set up Azure rules that need to be followed by all users and/or devices.

> **Master It** You are the administrator of a large network. Your organization uses a hybrid network setup between your on-site network and Azure. You have been informed that you need to setup a policy to make sure all users and devices are following the proper compliancy rules.

> **Solution** Make sure you understand how compliance polices, along with Conditional Access, ensures that administrators can stop users and devices that don't follow the rules that your organization has determined as necessary for access.

Understand how to configure Configuration Profiles. Configuration profiles allow an administrator to configure settings and features that can be enable or disable on the different devices that your users will use to access Azure and Microsoft Endpoint Manager.

Master It Your organization has a hybrid network setup. Your organization uses both Microsoft and Apple iOS devices. You have been asked to setup access for the iOS Apple devices.

Solution Another way to setup Intune rules as an Administrator is a Device Configuration Profile. Profiles work like policies since they are also another way to put rules onto your Microsoft Endpoint Manager devices. Microsoft Endpoint Manager, along with device configuration profiles, allows an administrator to configure settings and features that can be enabled or disabled on the different devices that your users will connect with.

Index